D0428349

Discover
Switzerland

Experience the best of Switzerland

This edition written and researched by

Nicola Williams, Kerry Christiani,
Gregor Clark, Sally O'Brien

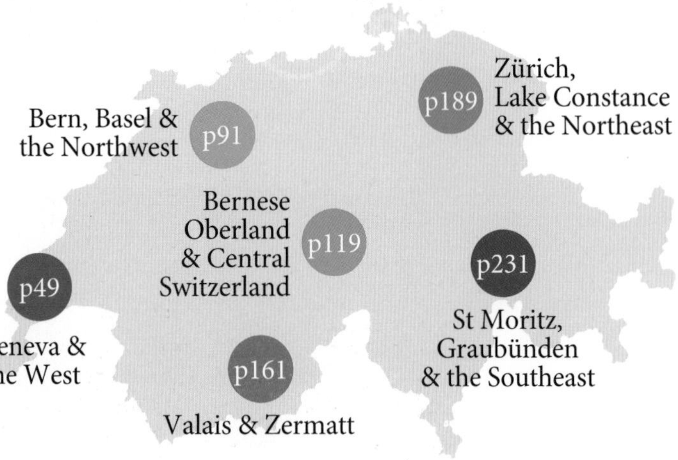

Bern, Basel &
the Northwest **p91**

p189 Zürich,
Lake Constance
& the Northeast

Bernese
Oberland
& Central **p119**
Switzerland

p49

Geneva &
the West

p231

St Moritz,
Graubünden
& the Southeast

p161

Valais & Zermatt

Contents

Contents

On the Road

In Focus

Survival Guide

This Is Switzerland

No one has a hard time conjuring images of Switzerland: Alps, chocolate, cows with bells, cable cars, mountain meadow hikes, tidy old villages, yodelling, lake steamers, cheese (lots of tasty cheese!) and much more. And the reality lives up to the iconography. This orderly nation – where a train is officially late if it's three minutes off – is a splendid place to explore winter or summer, whether you're cliché-hunting or ready for a surprising adventure.

What giddy romance Zermatt, St Moritz and other legendary names evoke.

From the intoxicating chink of Verbier glitterati hobnobbing over champagne in ice-carved flutes to the reassuring bell jangle of cows coming home in Kandersteg, Switzerland is a harmonious tableau of beautiful images. This small, land-locked country is so darn easy to step into and experience.

Switzerland begs outdoor escapades with its larger-than-life canvas of hallucinatory landscapes.

Skiing and snowboarding in the winter wonderlands of Graubünden, Bernese Oberland and Central Switzerland are obvious choices. Or you can hop on an engineering marvel of a train and travel to the crevassed ice on Jungfraujoch (3454m), at what seems like the top of the world.

The perfect antidote to this rich Alpine land is a surprise set of cities.

There's the capital Bern, with its Old Town and world-class modern art; Germanic Basel and its bold architecture; shopping-chic Geneva astraddle Europe's largest lake; and ubercool Zürich with its rooftop bars and atypical Swiss street grit.

Smaller but equally beguiling are Lucerne, St Gallen, Chur and Lausanne.

Here medieval wooden structures complement ancient stones, and old towns beg exploration. You may be charmed by a castle or simply a scrumptious slice of cake. Either way, Switzerland never fails to reward.

> **This small, landlocked country is so darn easy to step into and experience**

Twilight over Zermatt and the Matterhorn (p178)

DANITA DELIMONT / GETTY IMAGES ©

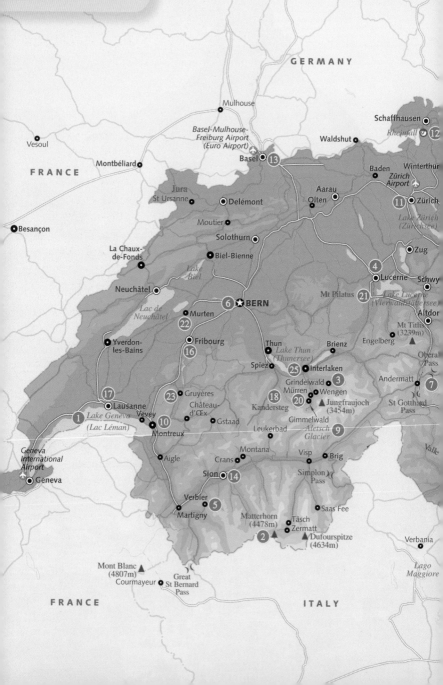

25 Switzerland's Top Highlights

Lake Geneva

The emerald vines marching uphill in perfect unison from the shores of Lake Geneva in Lavaux (p83) are staggering. But the urban viewpoint from which to admire Europe's largest lake is Geneva (p58), French-speaking Switzerland's most cosmopolitan city, where canary-yellow *mouettes* (seagulls) ferry locals across the water and Mont Blanc peeps in on the action. Strolling Old Town streets, savouring a vibrant cafe society and making the odd dash beneath its iconic pencil fountain is what life's about for the 180 nationalities living here. Below: Lavaux vineyards alongside Lake Geneva

MONTICO LIONEL / HEMISPICTURE.COM / GETTY IMAGES ©

2

Matterhorn

This charismatic peak has more pulling power than most; a precocious beauty who demands to be admired, ogled and repeatedly photographed at sunset, sunrise, in different seasons and from every last angle. There is no finer place to base yourself to explore the Matterhorn than Zermatt (p178), one of Europe's most-desirable Alpine resorts, in fashion with the skiing, climbing, hiking and hip hobnobbing set since the 19th century. Darling, you'll love it.

Grindelwald's Jungfrau Region

No trio is more immortalised in mountaineering legend than Switzerland's 'big three' – Eiger (Ogre), Mönch (Monk) and Jungfrau (Virgin) – peaks that soar to the sky above the gorgeous, traditional 19th-century resort of Grindelwald (p135). And whether you choose to schuss around on skis, shoot down Europe's longest toboggan run on the back of an old-fashioned sledge, bungee jump in the Gletscherschlucht or ride the train up to Europe's highest station at 3454m, your pulse will race. James Bond, eat your heart out. *Below: A hiker takes in Eigre and Jungfrau*

The Best...
Mountain Vistas

EIGER, JUNGFRAU & MÖNCH

Hike from Grindelwald/ Wengen or ride the cable car or train to Kleine Scheidegg for dramatic close-ups of Switzerland's big trio. (p134)

ALETSCH GLACIER

A shimmering 23km-long glacier, best seen from Bettmerhorn. (p186)

SCHILTHORN

This 360-degree vista takes in 200 peaks stretching from Mt Titlis to Mont Blanc in France. (p145)

JUNGFRAUJOCH

An uplifting lookout to 4000m peaks, the Aletsch Glacier and as far as the Black Forest beyond. (p140)

The Best...
Serious Ski Runs

VERBIER
Almost vertical and pummelled with moguls; off-piste, some of Switzerland's best powder. (p172)

JUNGFRAU REGION
It just doesn't get better than Inferno, a 16km black run. (p134)

LAAX
Snowboarding mecca with Europe's smallest and largest half-pipes. (p248)

WENGEN
Aptly named black run 'Oh God' and legendary off-piste White Hare at the foot of the Eiger north face. (p143)

ST MORITZ
Spectacular and jaw-dropping glacier descents at 3000m. (p240)

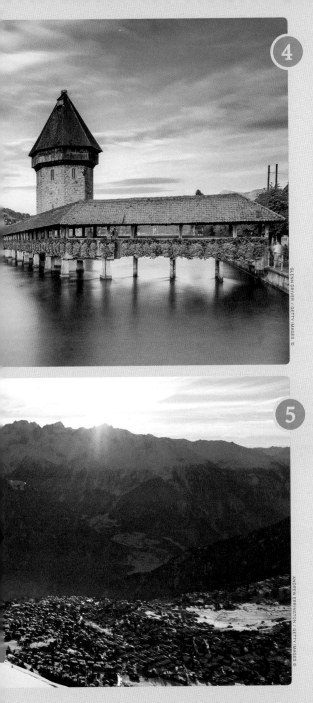

4 Lakeside Lucerne

Medieval bridge strolling is the principal charm of this irresistible Romeo in Central Switzerland. Throw sparkling lake vistas, an alfresco cafe life, candy-coloured architecture and Victorian curiosities into the cooking pot and lakeside Lucerne (p151) could well be the start of a very beautiful love affair. The town under your belt, step back to savour the ensemble from a wider perspective: views across the lake of green hills, meadows and hidden lake resorts from atop Mt Pilatus (p158) or Mt Rigi (p159). Left: Kapellbrücke, Lucerne

GLENN DRIVER / GETTY IMAGES ©

5 Skiing Verbier

Switzerland never looks better than on a crisp winter's day, when the Alpine heights and forests are blanketed in snow. Nowhere else in Europe has higher peaks or better views. Shaking up this snow-globe scene are the skiers, snowboarders, sledders, skaters, and snowshoers. There are plenty of ski resorts to choose from but Verbier (p172) combines the best of all: legendary powder, glitz, great nightlife and activities for every taste and budget.

ANDREW ERRINGTON / GETTY IMAGES ©

Bern

Medieval cobbled streets, arcaded boutiques, a dancing clock and 16th-century folk figures frolicking in fountains: Switzerland's capital, Bern (p100), does not fit the quintessential 'capital city' image. Indeed, few realise this small town *is* the capital, situated as it is in the flat, unassuming middle bit of the country. Yet its unexpectedness, cemented by the new millennium 'hills' of Renzo Piano's Zentrum Paul Klee (p100), is precisely its charm.

Glacier Express to St Moritz

It's one of the world's most-mythical train rides, linking two of Switzerland's glitziest Alpine resorts. Hop aboard the iconic red train with floor-to-ceiling windows in Zermatt, and sit back and savour shot after cinematic shot of green peaks, glistening Alpine lakes, glacial ravines and other hallucinatory landscapes. Pulled by steam engine when it first puffed out of the station in 1930, the Glacier Express (p256) traverses 91 tunnels and 291 bridges on its journey to St Moritz (p240). The icing on the cake: lunch in the vintage restaurant car.

Hiking in the Swiss National Park

No country in Europe is more synonymous with magnificent and mighty hiking than Switzerland, and its high-altitude national park (p245), with eagle-dotted skies, is the place to do it. Follow trails through flower-strewn meadows to piercing blue lakes, knife-edge ravines, rocky outcrops and Alpine huts where shepherds make summertime cheese with cows' milk, fresh that morning from the bell-clad herd. Nature gone wild and on the rampage, this park provides a rare and privileged glimpse of Switzerland before the dawn of tourism.

8

The Best...
Hikes

GLACIER HIKE
Be blown away by the frosty landscape surrounding the Aletsch Glacier. (p186)

CASTLE HIKE
Follow the Chemin Fleuri (Flower Path) 4km from Montreux to lakeside Château de Chillon. (p88)

VINEYARD WALK
The Bisse de Clavau walk through the vine-strewn Rhône Valley is especially beautiful on a golden September day. (p175)

ALPS CLOSE-UPS
Walk downhill from Kleine Scheidegg to Wengen. (p137)

17

Aletsch Glacier

One of the world's natural marvels, this mesmerising glacier (p186) of gargantuan proportions in the Upper Valais is like a 23km-long, five-lane highway powering between mountain peaks at altitude. Its ice is glacial-blue and 900m thick at its deepest point. The view of Aletsch from Jungfraujoch will make your heart sing, but for the hardcore adrenalin surge, nothing beats getting up close: hike between crevasses with a mountain guide from Riederalp, or ski above it on snowy pistes in Bettmeralp.

The Best...
Castles & Abbeys

CHILLON
Follow the Flower Path from Montreux to this huge stone castle on Lake Geneva's shore. (p88)

THUN
No *schloss* (castle) in Germanic Switzerland is as fairy tale as Thun's red-turreted beauty. (p147)

ST GALLEN
This grand abbey safeguards an extraordinary rococo library. (p223)

BELLINZONA
Unesco-listed trio of medieval castles in Italianate Ticino. (p254)

SION
Bewitching pair of 13th-century châteaux on rocky outcrops above vines. (p175)

Romance in Montreux

As if one of the world's most-legendary jazz festivals (p43) with open-air concerts on the shore of Lake Geneva is not enough, Montreux has a castle to add to the French-style romance. From the well-known lakeside town with a climate so mild that palm trees grow, a flower-framed footpath follows the water south to Château de Chillon (p88). Historic, sumptuous and among Switzerland's oldest, this magnificent stone château built by the Savoys in the 13th century is everything a castle should be.
Left: Crowds at the Montreux Jazz Festival

Zürich Lifestyle

One of Europe's most liveable cities, Zürich (p198), in German-speaking Switzerland, is an ode to urban renovation. It's also hip (yes, this is where Google employees shoot down a slide to lunch). With enough of a rough edge to resemble Berlin at times, Zürich is all about drinking in waterfront bars, dancing until dawn in Züri-West (p209), shopping for recycled fashion accessories in Kreis 5 and boogying with the best of them at Europe's largest street party, the city's wild and wacky, larger-than-life Street Parade (p43) in August. Right: Patrons at a bar in Zürich's Niederdorf quarter

TRAVELSTOCK44 / LOOK-FOTO / GETTY IMAGES ©

Splash of the Rheinfall

So moved were Goethe and Lord Byron by the wispy waterfalls of Staubbach Falls, fairytale threads of spray ensnaring the cliffside in Lauterbrunnen, that they composed poems exalting their ethereal beauty. Yet it is the theatrical, crash-bang-wallop splash of the thunderous Rheinfall (p217), guarded by a twin set of medieval castles, in northeastern Switzerland that really takes your breath away.

Art & Architecture in Basel

Contemporary architecture is Basel's golden ticket – seven winners of the Pritzker Prize have a living design in or around this city, which sits plump on the Rhine. Kick off with a hop across the German border to the Vitra Design Museum, designed by architect Frank Gehry; and devote the rest of the day to Switzerland's best private collection of modern art in a long, light-flooded building by Renzo Piano – the dream fusion of art and architecture at Fondation Beyeler (p106). Left: Vitra Design Museum

DANIEL SCHOENEN / LOOK-FOTO / GETTY IMAGES ©

Sion & Valaisian Wine

Swiss vintages aren't plentiful outside Switzerland, making their tasting and discovery a joyous experience. Gentle walking trails tread through steeply terraced vineyards in Valais, producer of the country's best wines, and many *vignerons* (winegrowers) open their doors for tasting and buying. Pair a vineyard walk near Sion (p175) with the region's autumnal *brisolée*, the traditional feast built around local chestnuts, cheese, cold meats and *vin nouveau*. Below: Valais vineyard

The Best...
Art Museums

KUNSTHAUS
As you'd expect, Zürich's main art gallery has a vast collection of masterpieces. (p202)

SAMMLUNG OSKAR REINHART AM RÖMERHOLZ
Combines a grand collection of old masters with big modern names in Winterthur. (p212)

FONDATION PIERRE GIANADDA
The star of Martigny has Picasso, Cézanne et al. (p170)

FONDATION BEYELER
Switzerland's best collection of contemporary art is in Basel. (p106)

ZENTRUM PAUL KLEE
Bern's answer to the Guggenheim. (p100)

FONDATION PIERRE ARNAUD
Dazzling art in a dazzling mirrored piece of contemporary architecture. (p176)

The Best...
Lakes

LAKE GENEVA
This vast body of water has boats linking oodles of cute towns and cities. (p49)

LAKE LUCERNE
The medieval city's front yard is this stunning lake surrounded by green hillsides. (p158)

LAKE ZÜRICH
Beautiful Lake Zürich saves the city from being a big sprawl. (p199)

LAGO DI LUGANO
A sinuous lake in the sun-drenched south. (p261)

LAKE THUN
Along with Lake Brienz, this startlingly turquoise lake provides a dramatic entrance to Interlaken. (p145)

⑮

Lago di Lugano

An intrinsic part of Switzerland's unique charm is its mixed bag of languages and cultures. And no spot on Swiss earth exalts the country's Italianate soul with such gusto as Lago di Lugano (p261) in Ticino, a shimmering Alpine lake fringed with palm-tree promenades and pretty-girl villages of delicate pastel hues. Lugano (p257), the biggest town on the lake and the country's third-largest affluent banking centre to boot, is vivacious and busy with porticoed alleys, cafe-packed piazzas and boats yo-yoing to other places on the lake. Left: Santuario della Madonna del Sasso alongside Lago di Lugano; Above: Ticino town centre

LEFT: THOMAS STANKIEWICZ / LOOK-FOTO / GETTY IMAGES ©; ABOVE: WALTER BIBIKOW / GETTY IMAGES ©

Fribourg Café Life

There is no finer spot in Switzerland to sit back and lap up the country's magnificent language divide than on a café pavement terrace in Fribourg (p111). Lounge over *un café* on the west bank of this buzzy student town in the Jura, then hop across the river for a German-chatter fuelled kaffee. Cafes range from historic to cutting-edge contemporary, and key streets include pedestrian rue de Lausanne, Grand-Rue in the 12th-century Old Town and place des Ormeaux.

RICHARD I'ANSON / GETTY IMAGES ©

Lausanne

To this day the night watch scales the bell tower inside the Gothic cathedral in Lausanne (p73) to call out the hour. This hilly place in the heart of the Lake Geneva wine country has an Old Town dominated by a great cathedral. Narrow lanes meander up and down the hills and where bridges cross over streets, summertime bars let you imbibe under massive stone arches. Down on the waterfront is one of Lake Geneva's prettiest promenades. Visit via train or lake steamer.

Vie Ferrate in Kandersteg

Anyone who fancies mountaineering but with the security of being attached to the rock face should clip onto a *via ferrata* (Klettersteig in German). Though safer and easier for beginners than climbing, these vertigo-inducing fixed-cable traverses involving ladders, zip-lines and tightrope-style bridges aren't for the faint-hearted. This hiking and climbing hybrid is all the rage in Switzerland and you can try it at resorts throughout the Alps, but for real knuckle-whitening stuff, clamp on to the one in Kandersteg (p149).

Below: Climbing in Kandersteg

The Best...
Hotels

HÔTEL BEL'ESPERANCE
A rooftop terrace only adds to the charms of this simple gem. (p66)

HÔTEL BEAU-RIVAGE PALACE
Easily the most stunningly located hotel in Lausanne, this luxury lakeside address is suitably sumptuous. (p67)

HOTEL SCHWEIZERHOF
A top five-star option in Bern. (p103)

GLETSCHERGARTEN
A rustic timber chalet in beautiful Grindelwald. (p138)

GASTHAUS BARGIS
Quaint dark-wood chalet in Klosters dating to the 18th century. (p251)

The Best...
Family Travel

VERKEHRSHAUS
Fly a plane or travel to the moon at Lucerne's Transport Museum. (p153)

ZENTRUM PAUL KLEE
Interactive art exhibits and workshops in Bern. (p100)

ALIMENTARIUM
Fun cookery workshops at Nestlé's Vevey home. (p85)

GSTAAD
Loop-the-loop Alpine Coaster, husky rides and guided llama and goat hikes. (p149)

GRINDELWALD
Summer scooter trail, gentle walks and ski pistes for every age and ability. (p135)

St Gallen

What a feast: St Gallen (p221) has an extraordinary rococo library that is a top Unesco site, a zany red square to chill in and taverns in half-timbered houses – all rooted in a deeply Germanic, rural world. As a bonus it has a fine Alps setting that gives you a panoply of peaks from which to choose, either for mere gazing or surmounting, or some sort of hike in between. At night you can get cosy in a traditional Swiss restaurant and let the cheese work its magic.

Right: Stiftsbibliothek (p222)

STUART DEE / GETTY IMAGES ©

Mürren & Gimmelwald

20

Heidi may be fictional, but her Alpine village lifestyle isn't. Switzerland will meet all your storybook fantasies: the hilltop hamlets in the Bernese Oberland offer cowbells as your wake-up call, and when it turns crisp at night, you can snuggle by a crackling fire. Sound idyllic? You bet. Mürren (p143) has scenery, skiing and hiking to make your heart sing. Pick a log chalet for dress-circle views of the Eiger, Mönch and Jungfrau. To be at one with nature, tiptoe away from the crowds to cute-as-a-button Gimmelwald (p144) nearby.

Left: Hikers near Mürren

BOB POOL / GETTY IMAGES ©

Mt Pilatus Circle

This is one of Switzerland's great day trips. At 2132m, Mt Pilatus (p158) not only has good views but it lets you enjoy almost every form of transport the country offers. Leave Lucerne by steamer and glide across the namesake lake to the village of Alpnachstad. Here you catch a cog railway to the summit. Catch sweeping views through the trees as the train's gears grind away pulling you up the steepest railway of its kind in the world. Heading back, take a cable car and a bus. Fun!

Murten

Once upon a time villages across Europe were encircled by walls to keep out marauding bands looking to loot, pillage and worse. Almost every town tore down its walls by the 19th century with very few exceptions. An easy day trip from Bern, Murten (p114) is just such a town. Its medieval walls still encircle its handful of streets and you can romp from one tower to the next, imagining the night watch on guard for invaders. It's the perfect castle fantasy.

Fondue in Gruyères

Why not enjoy one of Switzerland's favourite meals right at the source of its main ingredient, Gruyère cheese? The village of Gruyères (p114; it carries an 's', the cheese doesn't) is an appealing place in its own right, with houses hundreds of years old tumbling down the side of a mountain to a classic cobblestoned heart. You can visit local cheese dairies to enjoy tastes of the savoury, nutty cheese and then choose the perfect spot for a classic pot of oozing, luxurious fondue.

The Best...
Swiss Restaurants

MICHEL'S STALLBEIZLI
Dining doesn't get more back-to-nature than at this converted barn in luxe Gstaad. (p150)

WIRTSHAUS GALLIKER
An old-style tavern dating to 1856. (p155)

LE NAMASTÉ
This cosy mountain cabin is always packed. (p174)

CHEZ VRONY
Super-chic Zermatt restaurant with organic cuisine and Matterhorn view. (p181)

BÄUMLI
Timeless eatery that showcases all the typical specialities. (p224)

Lake Constance

Serving as a liquid nexus between Switzerland, Germany and Austria, Central Europe's third largest lake, Lake Constance (p219), is an ideal way to connect all three of these closely linked cultures. A network of boats criss-cross its usually smooth waters. You can hop from one town – and country – to the next (and there's a lot of good ones to hop to) or you can settle back up on deck and enjoy sweeping Alpine views reflected on the cool, blue waters. Best perhaps is some combination of the two.

24

The Best...
Chocolate

ST GALLEN
Hot chocolate, pralines and truffles to die for at Chocolaterie. (p221)

LUGANO
A spin through the history of chocolate and tastings at the Museo del Ciocco-lato Alprose. (p257)

BROC
Watch Swiss chocolate being made at the Cailler chocolate factory. (p117)

FRIBOURG
Villars chocolate at factory prices and creamy hot chocolate with chocolate shavings. (p111)

ZÜRICH
Café Sprüngli, epicentre of sweet Switzerland, in business since 1836. (p198)

(25)

Interlaken Adventures

With the heart of the Alps a beckoning vista and two lakes serving as watery bookends, Interlaken (p128) may be the sportiest place in a very sporty country. Adventure guides and outfitters seem as common as majestic vistas. Pulse-stirring options include white-water rafting, canyoning, paragliding, ice climbing, mountain climbing, hikes of every theme and difficulty, skiing, snowboarding – and the list just goes on. Chances are someone has thought of an adventure for you that you haven't thought of yet. Above: Skydiving over Interlaken

Switzerland's
Top Itineraries

Zürich to Lucerne
Classic Switzerland

5 DAYS

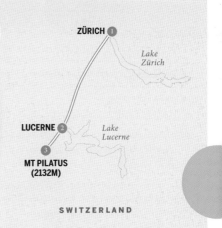

ZÜRICH ①
Lake Zürich

LUCERNE ② Lake Lucerne
③
MT PILATUS
(2132M)

SWITZERLAND

Short on time? Spend two days exploring Switzerland's main city and then two in beautiful Lucerne, many people's favourite Swiss city. That saves you time for a return day trip from Lucerne, which includes fun boat and train trips and a taste of the Alps.

① Zürich (p198)

Start with the city's must-see sights. The 13th-century **Fraumünster** is a Zürich landmark with a modern touch: stained-glass windows by Marc Chagall. Wander the heart of the **old town**, noticing the stolid Swiss banks hiding their secrets, and amble along the **lakefront**, with distant mountains hinting at things to come. On day two stop into the **Kunsthaus**, which has an unsurpassed collection of masterpieces; bone up on a little bit of the nation's fascinating history at the **Schweizerisches Landesmuseum**. Along the way, enjoy fine coffee at **cafes** and hearty Swiss fare in any of many **restaurants**.

ZÜRICH ⬤ LUCERNE

🚆 **One scenic hour** From Zürich's Hauptbahnhof to Lucerne's Hauptbahnhof. 🚗 **One hour** Depending on traffic on the A4 and A14.

② Lucerne (p151)

A swan gliding past the **Kapellbrücke**, Lucerne's iconic wooden bridge, is likely to be one of your first impressions of this beautiful city, which sits right on its namesake lake. As you walk though the old town, you'll find a good mix of urban buzz and historic charm. Pause for a glimpse of the **Lion Monument**, which moved 19th-century visitors including Mark Twain. On your second day, stroll the lakefront with its posh cafes and sweeping views. After an easy 3km you'll find the **Verkehrshaus**, the most popular museum in Switzerland. Thrill to learn all the ways the Swiss have cleverly knitted their Alp-covered country with trains, cable cars, boats and more.

LUCERNE ⬤ MT PILATUS

This is a circular day trip that combines many forms of transport; see p126 for details.

③ Mt Pilatus (p158)

A lake boat, the world's steepest cog railway and a cable car are all part of this day trip that takes you from Lucerne to the 2132m peak of **Mt Pilatus** and back again in one fun circular route. From the summit, you'll see the Alps and Lake Lucerne spread out around and below you. There are many good well-marked short hikes from the top.

Kapellbrücke, Lucerne (p151)
IZZET KERIBAR / GETTY IMAGES ©

5 DAYS

Zermatt to St Moritz
The Glacier Express

This mythical 290km train journey has been a traveller-must ever since the birth of winter tourism in the Alps. Do it any time of year – in one glorious 7½-hour stretch or as several sweet nuggets interspersed with overnights in Switzerland's most glamorous Alpine mountain resorts.

1 Zermatt (p178)

The looming Matterhorn almost seems to wave farewell as you head off on your great railway adventure from **Zermatt**, the ski and holiday town at its base. From here, the narrow-gauge railway winds north down the valley to **Visp** and **Brig**. Both are important crossroads and have been for centuries.

From here, the train swings northeast along the pretty eastern stretch of the Rhône Valley through attractive villages such as **Betten** and **Fiesch**.

2 Bettmeralp (p187)

Hop off in Betten and catch a cable car up to car-free village **Bettmeralp**, where you can spend the night and enjoy a beguiling Alpine town that has activities for visitors winter and summer. From here you can go onwards up to **Bettmerhorn** or **Eggishorn** via cable cars for a look at the Unesco-listed **Aletsch Glacier**. This ribbon of ice stretches all the way back 23km to the Jungfrau region.

Back in the valley on the Glacier Express, the train trundles towards the **Furka Pass** (which it circumvents by tunnel) and descends on the new mega ski resort of **Andermatt**. In winter you can stop here and hit the slopes with their ultra-modern facilities.

3 Chur (p246)

Heading towards Chur, the stretch of tracks that climbs up and through the **Oberalp Pass** (2033m) is the literal high point of the Glacier Express journey. Expect everybody to be snapping pics like mad. From here it meanders alongside the Vorderrhein River, through Disentis/Mustér to **Chur**, where the train splits for its dual end points (St Moritz and Davos). Chur has a charmer of an old town – Switzerland's oldest – and is a good overnight stop to wander around, have a fine meal and possibly go for an Alpine meadow hike the next day.

4 St Moritz (p240) or Davos (p251)

The glamour of Switzerland's original ski resort is a suitable finish for such a famous journey. In winter you can join the famous on the **St Moritz** powder. In summer you can hike the surrounding Alps. The alternative end point for the Glacier Express, **Davos** is a modern and vibrant resort town.

ZERMATT ⟳ ST MORITZ/DAVOS

🚌 In one go, the Glacier Express takes 7½ hours from Zermatt to St Moritz or Davos (the train splits), but you can do it in little nibbles and easily take five days by overnighting at some of the great little towns on the way.

Glacier Express (p241)
BRUCE YUANYUE BI / GETTY IMAGES ©

10 DAYS

Basel to Wengen
Reaching Ever Higher

Start at Basel, the nexus for France, Germany and Switzerland. From the banks of the Rhine, travel through rolling hills to Bern, then cut across to lovely Lucerne, heading ever more upwards. Finally make the big climb to Grindewald and eye- and ear-popping Wengen.

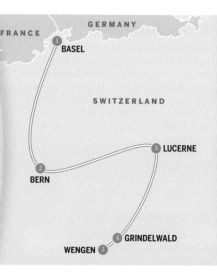

1 Basel (p105)

Basel mixes ancient architecture with cutting-edge design. It has a commanding position on the banks of the Rhine and its train station is linked by fast trains to Paris, Frankfurt and beyond. You can spend a full day here wandering. If you drive to Bern, stop at **Augusta Raurica**, an ancient Roman town.

BASEL ◗ BERN

🚃 **70 minutes** From Basel's main station to Bern's main station. 🚗 **Two hours** On the A1.

2 Bern (p100)

Albert Einstein worked as a bureaucrat here at the dawn of the 20th century, but he was obviously bored as his mind turned to solving the mysteries of the universe. While you may not find the same sort of inspiration in **Bern**, you'll likely yourself lingering for at least a day in ancient **arcades** and fine **museums**.

BERN ◗ LUCERNE

🚃 **One hour** From Bern's main station to Lucerne's main station. 🚗 **1¾ hours** On the scenic Route 10.

3 Lucerne (p151)

Often topping polls ranking Switzerland's favourite cities, **Lucerne** combines its too-beautiful-for-words lakeside location with some urban charms. Museums include the wildly popular **Verkehrshaus**, which explores all the ways the Swiss have knitted their country together, the Alps notwithstanding. The old town has fine restaurants or you can pick from the many **lakeside cafes**.

LUCERNE ◗ GRINDELWALD

🚃 **2½ hours** From Lucerne's main station to Grindelwald. 🚗 **1½ hours** On the A8.

4 Grindelwald (p135)

Grindelwald is the kind of place where you can just let your feet choose a direction in the morning and it's bound to end well. Cable cars, trains and footpaths take you right up into the Alps where the **walking** is simply superb. You can let a couple of days drift by in a blur of beautiful scenery. When you move on to Wengen, the train goes via **Kleine Scheidegg**, where you can veer off for the fabled **Jungfraujoch** day trip.

GRINDELWALD ◗ WENGEN

🚃 **One hour** From Grindelwald to Wengen via Kleine Scheidegg.

5 Wengen (p143)

Perfectly perched on a mountainside, **Wengen** has sweeping views across to Jungfrau and its siblings. Opportunities for **skiing** and **hiking** abound (depending on the season) but perhaps its greatest allure is sitting and soaking up one of the world's great views.

Basel's Rathaus (town hall; p109)
DAVE PORTER PETERBOROUGH UK / GETTY IMAGES ©

10 DAYS

Montreux to Klosters
French and Italian Switzerland

Although much of Switzerland speaks German (64%), the French (19%) and Italian (8%) minorities are sizeable and have influence across the country. This tour takes in wine-growing regions, the Matterhorn, sunny Lugano and famous ski resorts.

GERMANY

FRANCE

AUSTRIA

LIECHTENSTEIN

SWITZERLAND

KLOSTERS 6

1 MONTREUX

2 SION

4 BELLINZONA

3 ZERMATT
MATTERHORN
(4478M)

5 LUGANO

ITALY

① Montreux (p87)

Genteel **Montreux** brims with posh lakeside cafes where you can sample wines that come from the surrounding hillside vineyards. Go for a lakeside stroll to one of Switzerland's best castles, **Château de Chillon**. It's everything a kid of any age could hope for in the cool-fortification department. Get lost amidst the towers and courtyards, and learn its history.

MONTREUX ➡ SION

🚃 **45 minutes** From Montreux's main station to Sion's main station. 🚗 **One hour** Via the A9.

② Sion (p175)

French Switzerland continues through this riverside town, which is surrounded by yet more **vineyards**. Take a day to go hiking among the grapes and indulge in some delicious tastings.

SION ➡ ZERMATT

🚃 **1½ hours** From Sion's main station to Visp (30 minutes), then change trains for Zermatt (one hour). 🚗 **1½ hours** Via the A9 to Visp (30 minutes), then transfer to the train for car-free Zermatt (one hour).

③ Zermatt (p178)

Even Walt Disney couldn't ignore the **Matterhorn**. And once you're in this quaint mountain resort, your gaze will be pulled ever-upwards to its sheer granite sides. There's plenty of winter skiing, but summer hikes past flower-strewn meadows and looming glaciers are tops. Back in **Zermatt**, enjoy nightlife more lively than your typical mountain hamlet.

ZERMATT ➡ BELLINZONA

🚃 Return by train to Visp. **3¾ hours** From Visp to Bellinzona. 🚗 **Two hours** Via Route 19 and the A2.

④ Bellinzona (p254)

What could be more evocative than **three medieval stone castles** guarding this ancient city? Bellinzona has always been a gateway to Italy from the north, and even the squares are called piazzas thanks to the Italian heritage.

BELLINZONA ➡ LUGANO

🚃 **20 minutes** From Bellinzona main station to Lugano main station. 🚗 **30 minutes** Via the A2.

⑤ Lugano (p257)

Lugano is filled with surprises, especially on market days when food browsing is like going on a treasure hunt. But don't waste too much time ashore: head out onto **Lago di Lugano** for gentle boat trips amid beautiful mountain vistas.

LUGANO ➡ KLOSTERS

🚃 **Four hours** From Lugano main station to Klosters. 🚗 **2½ hours** Via the A13.

⑥ Klosters (p250)

One of the first Swiss winter resorts, **Klosters** has always held on to traditions that have hints of a Victorian past. Here you'll find yourself in German-speaking Switzerland. The skiing (here and at neighbouring **Davos**) is fab, and in summer those famed Swiss hiking paths spread out in all directions.

A lakeside view of Château de Chillon (p88)
MICHELE FALZONE / GETTY IMAGES ©

2 WEEKS

Geneva to St Gallen
Switzerland's Top Sights

Switzerland may be small but seeing the best it has to offer is truly a grand tour. Geneva, Bern, the heart of the Alps, fabulous Lucerne and Zürich are just some of the stops, and there are many options for day trips.

1 Geneva (p58)

The international city of **Geneva** is a fine introduction to all that is genteel about Switzerland. Its old town beguiles and it has great dining thanks to all the diplomats stationed here. Head out for a lake cruise and gaze up France's **Mont Blanc**.

GENEVA ⊃ LAUSANNE

🚃 **40 minutes** From Geneva's main station to Lausanne's main station. 🚗 **One hour** On the A1.

2 Lausanne (p73)

From its beautiful lakeside location – you can get here by boat – **Lausanne** climbs the hills up to the main train station and beyond. Lanes wander hither and yon and **cafes** shelter under soaring arched stone bridges. Enjoy the famous **vineyard views**.

LAUSANNE ⊃ BERN

🚃 **65 minutes** From Lausanne's main station to Bern's main station. 🚗 **1¼ hours** On the A1.

3 Bern (p100)

The Swiss capital harks back to the middle ages with old buildings spilling down to the river. **Museums** vie with a historic riverside park where bears roam. There are good day trips from here, including ancient walled **Murten** and the home of Switzerland's best cheese: **Gruyères**.

BERN ⊃ INTERLAKEN

🚃 **One hour** From Bern's main station to Interlaken Ost station. 🚗 **One hour** On the A6.

4 Interlaken (p128)

The adventure capital of Switzerland, **Interlaken** is beautifully surrounded by lakes. But it's easy to quickly be drawn to towns and villages that dot the sides of the **magnificent Alps** stretching out before you. Names like **Grindelwald**, **Wengen** and **Mürren** are the stuff of summer and winter legends.

INTERLAKEN ⊃ JUNGFRAUJOCH

🚃 **2¼ hours** From Interlaken Ost station to the top of Jungfraujoch. The return takes the same amount of time.

Stunning views over the French border to Mont Blanc
MENNO BOERMANS / GETTY IMAGES ©

6 Lucerne (p151)

Old medieval **wooden bridges** link the old town of this fabled city of cuteness. Wander the lakefront for lovely views and take in plenty of attractions along the way. If you have time there are more Alpine day trips here (such as **Mt Pilatus** and **Mt Titlis**).

LUCERNE ➡ ZÜRICH

🚆 **One hour** From Lucerne's main station to Zürich's main station. 🚗 **One hour** Depending on traffic on the A4 and A14.

7 Zürich (p198)

Another place that makes full use of its namesake lake, the largest city in Switzerland combines conservative tradition with cutting-edge fun. In summer, swim in the lake from one of many **lakeside cafes** and **clubs** or head to trendy districts and watch movies outside. At any time you can get lost in the city's excellent **museums**.

ZÜRICH ➡ ST GALLEN

🚆 **One hour** From Zürich's main station to St Gallen's main station. 🚗 **One hour** On the A1.

5 Jungfraujoch (p140)

One of the world's great journeys takes three trains from Interlaken, each surmounting tracks more precipitous than the last. You start in a beautiful river valley to **Lauterbrunnen** and then change trains for a ride filled with views to the Alpine outpost of **Kleine Scheidegg**. A final switch and you are on a train that bores up through the mountain to the summit of **Jungfraujoch**. Once at the top, you won't be able to get enough of the **Alpine wonderland views** (although you'll need to return to Interlaken before the last trains.)

INTERLAKEN ➡ LUCERNE

🚆 **Two hours** From Interlaken Ost station to Lucerne's main station. 🚗 **One hour** On the A8 and Route 4.

8 St Gallen (p221)

Step back to the past at this town set among the Alps, which boasts the remarkable and Unesco-recognised **Stiftsbibliothek**.

Switzerland Month by Month

Top Events

⭐ **Lucerne Festival,** April

⭐ **Montreux Jazz,** July

✳️ **Swiss National Day,** 1 August

✳️ **Zürich Street Parade,** August

🍴 **L'Escalade,** 11 December

January

🏇 **Cartier Polo World Cup**
Upper-crust St Moritz is the chic venue for this four-day event that sees world-class polo players saddle up and battle it out on a frozen lake. Buy tickets online (www.polomoritz.com), dress up and don't forget your shades.

✳️ **Harder Potschete**
What a devilish day it is on 2 January in Interlaken when warty ogre-like *Potschen* run around town causing folkloric mischief. The party ends on a high with cockle-warming drinks, upbeat folk music and fiendish merrymaking.

✳️ **Vogel Gryff**
Another old folkloric celebration, this street party sees a larger-than-life savage, griffin and lion chase away winter in Basel with a drum dance on a city bridge.

February

✳️ **Carnival**
Never dare call the Swiss goody two-shoes again: pre-Lenten parades, costumes, music and all the fun of the fair sweep through Catholic cantons during *Fasnacht* (carnival). Catch the party – stark raving bonkers – in Lucerne or Basel.

March

🏃 **Engadine Ski Marathon**
Watching 11,000 cross-country skiers warming up to the rousing sound of *Chariots of Fire* is unforgettable – as is, no doubt, the iconic 42km cross-country ski marathon for the athletes who ski across frozen lakes and through

February: *Fasnacht* celebrations, Basel (p110)
WALTER BIBIKOW / GETTY IMAGES ©

pine forests and picture-perfect snow scenes in the Engadine.

April

Sechseläuten
Winter's end is celebrated in Zürich on the third Monday of the month with costumed street parades and the burning of a firework-filled 'snowman', aka the terrifying *Böögg*. Be prepared to be scared.

Lucerne Festival
Easter ushers in this world-class music festival with chamber orchestras, pianists and other musicians from all corners of the globe performing in Lucerne. True devotees of the festival can return in summer and November.

June

St Galler Festspiele
It's apt that Switzerland's 'writing room of Europe', aka St Gallen, should play host to this wonderful two-week opera season. The curtain rises in late June with performances spilling into July.

July

Montreux Jazz
A fortnight of jazz, pop and rock in early July is reason enough to slot elegant Montreux into your itinerary. Some concerts are free, some ticketed, and dozens are staged alfresco with lake views from heaven.

Paléo Festival
Another Lake Geneva goodie, this six-day open-air world-music extravaganza – a 1970s child – is billed as the king of summer music fests. Nyon in late July is the date to put in the diary.

August

Swiss National Day
Fireworks light up lakes, mountains, towns and cities countrywide on this national holiday celebrating Switzerland's very creation.

Sertig Schwinget
This high-entertainment festival in Davos sees thickset men with invariably large tummies battle it out in sawdust for the title of *Schwingen* (Swiss Alpine wrestling) champion.

Zürich Street Parade
Mid-August brings with it Europe's largest street party in the form of Zürich's famous Street Parade, established in 1992.

October

Foire du Valais
Cows battle for the title of bovine queen on the last day of the cow-fighting season at this 10-day regional fair in Martigny in the lower Valais. Everyone rocks up for it, a great excuse to drink and feast.

December

L'Escalade
Torch-lit processions in the Old Town, fires, a run around town for kids and adults alike and some serious chocolate-cauldron smashing and scoffing make Geneva's biggest festival on 11 December a riot of fun.

What's New

For this new edition of Discover Switzerland, *our authors hunted down the fresh, the transformed, the hot and the happening. Here are a few of our favourites. For up-to-the-minute recommendations, see lonelyplanet.com/switzerland.*

1 **BOND WORLD 007**
Embark on a thrilling interactive romp through the world of a secret agent – helicopter simulator, bob sled et al – at the heady height of 2970m atop Schilthorn. (p145)

2 **CLASSY SLEEPS**
Swiss accommodation is naturally classy as luxurious newcomers W Hotel (p174) in Verbier, B2 Boutique Hotel & Spa (p205) in a renovated Zürich brewery, Hotel Lavaux (p84), between Unesco-protected vines, and fairytale Château Gütsch (p155) more than prove.

3 **L'AMARR@GE**
The last word in sustainable design, Geneva's bright-red swimming pool afloat its namesake lake is shaped like the Swiss flag and heated by a neighbouring hotel's air-conditioning rejects. (p65)

4 **FONDATION PIERRE ARNAUD**
Switzerland's contemporary art collection is outstanding and this dazzling lakeside gallery near Crans-Montana, mountain peaks looming large on its brilliant mirrored facade, makes it even better. (p176)

5 **OLYMPIC MUSEUM**
Suisse Romande's most visited *musée*, on the shore of Lake Geneva in Lausanne, has been reborn as an even bigger, brighter and more beautiful champ of a museum. (p76)

6 **VITRA SLIDE TOWER**
What's not like about the whimsical, 38m-long corkscrew slide designed by Carsten Höller in the grounds of the Vitra Design Museum, Weil am Rhein? (p107)

7 **WELLNESSHOSTEL 4000**
Not one to sit on its laurels, the Swiss Hostelling Association has opened a groundbreaking hostel in Saas Fee – with designer spa, pool and wellness centre. (p185)

8 **SWISS CHOCOLATE EXPERIENCE**
Twirl through the history of Swiss chocolate with this zany, multimedia 'funfair' ride at Lucerne's Transport Museum. (p153)

Get Inspired

Books

Slow Train to Switzerland (Diccon Bewes) Beautiful evocation of the original Swiss tour, from London to Lucerne, as it was 1863 and as it is today.

Films

Heidi The 1937 version with Shirley Temple is considered the definitive cliché, although there are versions from 1954 (also a favourite), 1968, 1993 and 2005.

James Bond Several 007 movies have been filmed at least partially in Switzerland. *Goldfinger* (1964) is an early example, followed a short time later by *On Her Majesty's Secret Service* (1969), which memorably uses Schilthorn in the Jungfrau region.

Music

Monday's Ghost (2008) and **1983** (2010) are popular folk ballads featuring the fragile voice of Bern-born singer Sophie Hunger (www.sophiehunger.com) who flips between English, German and Swiss German.

Alpenhorn This pastoral wind instrument, used to herd cattle in the mountains, is 2m to 4m long with a curved base and a cup-shaped mouthpiece. The shorter the horn, the harder it is to play. Catch a symphony of a hundred-odd alpenhorn players blowing in unison on the 'stage' – usually alfresco and invariably lakeside between mountain peaks – and you'll be won over forever.

Stress Switzerland's hottest hip-hop artist, known for his occasional political and controversial lyrics.

Websites

SBB CFF FFS (www.sbb.ch) The Swiss railways official site.

Switzerland Travel Centre (www.swisstravelsystems.ch) Transport info, including travel passes.

Swiss Info (www.swissinfo.ch) Swiss news and current affairs.

Swiss World (www.swissworld.org) People, culture, lifestyle and the environment.

Lonely Planet (www.lonelyplanet.com/switzerland) Information, hotel bookings, traveller forum.

Short on time?

This list will give you an instant insight into the country.

Read *Heidi* by Johanna Spyri. The most-famous Swiss novel is about an orphan living with her grandfather in the Swiss Alps who is ripped away to the city.

Listen Traditional Swiss yodelling has never been so hot. Catch yodel rock Sonalp in concert or tune in at www.sonalp.com to understand why.

Watch Sister (2012) Ursula Meier's award-winning film about the complicated dynamics between poor siblings at a Swiss ski resort.

Log on www.myswitzerland.com is the main website for Swiss tourism.

A bovine resident poses in front of the Eiger

Need to Know

Currency
Swiss franc (in this book Sfr)

Languages
German, French, Italian, Romansch

Money
Visa, MasterCard and Amex widely accepted.

ATMs
ATMs at every airport, most train stations and every second street corner.

Visas
Not needed with passports from the EU, Iceland, Norway, USA, Canada, Australia or New Zealand.

Mobile Phones
European and Australian phones work. Use a Swiss SIM card for cheaper calls.

Wi-Fi
Wi-Fi is widely available at most accommodation, train stations and cafes.

Internet Access
Smartphones and wi-fi have closed many internet cafes.

Tipping
At sit-down restaurants round up your bill by 5% to 10%.

For more information, see Survival Guide (p297).

When to Go

Basel
GO Jul & Aug, Dec.

Zürich
GO Apr–Aug

Bern
GO Jul, Aug & Nov

Swiss Alps
GO late Dec–early Apr, May–Aug

Geneva
GO Anytime, Jun–Sep

- Warm to hot summers, mild winters
- Warm to hot summers, cold winters
- Mild summers, cold winters
- Cold climate
- Polar climate, below zero year round

High Season
(Jul & Aug, Dec–Apr)
- In July and August, walkers and cyclists hit high-altitude trails.
- Christmas and New Year see lots of ski activity.
- Late December to early April is high season in ski resorts.

Shoulder
(Apr–Jun & Sep)
- Look for deals in ski resorts and traveller hotspots.
- Spring is idyllic with warm temperatures, flowers and local produce.
- Watch the grape harvest in autumn.

Low Season
(Oct–Mar)
- Mountain resorts go into snooze mode from mid-October to early December.
- Prices are up to 50% less than in high season.
- Sights and restaurants are open fewer days and shorter hours.

Advance Planning

- **Six months before** Reserve ski-resort accommodation if you're visiting during holidays.
- **Three months before** Reserve your accommodation in popular summer destinations such as Lucerne and the Jungfrau region.
- **One month before** For summer travel, reserve your seats on the Glacier Express.
- **One week before** Ponder the weather, whether walking in summer or skiing in winter.

Daily Costs

Budget less than Sfr200

o Dorm bed: Sfr30–60

o Free admission to some museums first Saturday or Sunday of every month

o Lunch out (Sfr20–30) and self-cater after dark

Midrange Sfr200–300

o Double room in two- or three-star hotel: Sfr200–350

o Dish of the day (tagesteller, plat du jour, piatto del giorno) or fixed two-course menu: Sfr40–70

Top End more than Sfr300

o Double room in four- or five-star hotel: from Sfr350

o Lower rates Friday to Sunday in city business hotels

o Three-course dinner in an upmarket restaurant: from Sfr100

Exchange Rates

Australia	A$1	Sfr0.76
Canada	C$1	Sfr0.78
Europe	€1	Sfr1.05
Japan	¥100	Sfr0.81
New Zealand	NZ$1	Sfr0.74
UK	UK£1	Sfr1.45
US	US$1	Sfr0.97

For current exchange rates see www. xe.com.

Important Numbers

Swiss telephone numbers start with an area code that must be dialled every time, even when making local calls.

o **Switzerland country code** 📞41
o **International access code** 📞00
o **Ambulance** 📞144
o **Police** 📞117
o **Swiss Mountain Rescue** 📞1414

What to Bring

o **Sunglasses and hat** Needed year-round; all that snow makes for sharp glare.

o **Sturdy walking shoes** Should be comfortable, broken in and at least water-resistant.

o **Warm socks** Needed for summer Alpine hikes.

o **Jacket** Even in summer, glaciers are cold.

o **Sweet tooth** A love of cheese helps too.

Arriving in Switzerland

o Zürich Airport

SBB trains – Up to nine hourly to Hauptbahnhof from 6am to midnight.

Taxis – Around Sfr60 to the centre.

Coaches – During winter ski season, to Davos and other key resorts.

o Geneva Airport

SBB trains – At least every 10 minutes to Gare de Cornavin.

Taxis – Sfr30–50 to the centre.

Coaches & minibuses – In winter to Verbier, Saas Fee, Crans-Montana and French ski resorts.

Getting Around

o **Trains** You can use Switzerland's fast, efficient and integrated railway for your entire trip.

o **Boats** Use scenic boats to link your journey, especially on Lakes Geneva, Lucerne and Zürich.

o **Bus** The postal-bus system goes where trains don't, is efficient and integrated with the railways.

o **Car** More hindrance than pleasure. Hard to park in cities, and many resorts such as Zermatt and Wengen are car-free.

Sleeping

o **Hotels** Everywhere and in all price ranges. Top-end properties are often legendary.

o **Rental Accommodation** Common at winter resorts; with a kitchen, one or more private bedrooms and a common room. Great for groups.

Be Forewarned

It's a safe and healthy place to travel. Enjoy!

Geneva & the West

Lake Geneva, Western Europe's biggest lake, stretches like a giant liquid mirror between the French-speaking Swiss canton of Vaud (north) and France (south). Its west end is Geneva, Europe's most urbane city. Museums, cafes and famous international agencies cluster around the lakeside, with its exclamation point of a fountain.

Further east Lake Geneva is lined by the elegant student city of Lausanne and a phalanx of pretty smaller towns, and the Swiss side of the lake presents the marvellous emerald spectacle of tightly ranked vineyards spreading in terraces up the steep hillsides of the Lavaux area – the source of some very fine tipples.

Down by the water, the lake is lined by fairy-tale châteaux, luxurious manor houses and modest beaches, often backed by peaceful woodland. In the mild climate around Montreux, palm trees grow.

Château de Chillon (p88), Montreux
ANGELO CAVALLI / GETTY IMAGES ©

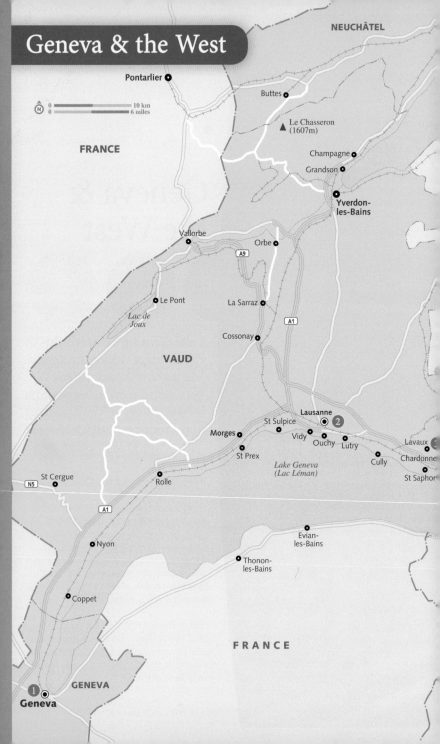

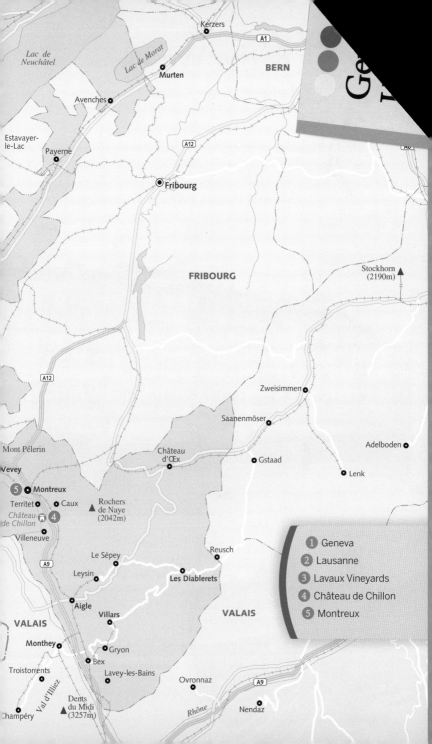

Geneva & the West's Highlights

Geneva

Switzerland's most international city (p58) has a fabulous location on its namesake lake. Organisations like the Red Cross and UN fill streets with people speaking seemingly every language under the Genevois sun and enjoying every luxury, watch museums and chocolate shops included. Cafe life is naturally vibrant, museums are fine, and Geneva's bijou old town is an elegant hop and skip from that signature pencil of a sky-high fountain everyone knows

Lausanne

Lac Léman, as French-speaking Swiss know Lake Geneva, might be flat and mirror-smooth but the lakeside student town of Lausanne (p73), Switzerland's fourth-largest city, is hilly. Vast stone bridges soar over narrow chasms of buildings, funky cafes sit snug inside bridge arches, and a cathedral-pierced Old Town begs random wanton exploration. A bevy of brilliant art museums and the family-friendly Olympic Museum are the icing on the stylish cake.

CARLOS WUNDERLIN / GETTY IMAGES ©

Lavaux Vineyards

East of Lausanne, bright, pea-green vineyards stagger dramatically up steeply terraced slopes from the lakeshore to form the utterly breath-taking and fabulous Lavaux wine region (p83) – deservedly a Unesco World Heritage site and a pilgrim-age no gourmet should miss. Walking between vines, tasting with local *vignerons* (wine makers), and devoting hours on end to the serious business of lunching between vines is what Lavaux is all about.

Château de Chillon

One of Switzerland's sweetest walks is possibly along the Chemin Fleuri (Flower Path), a footpath which meanders 4km southeast from Montreux, along the water to the magnificent Château de Chillon (p88). Up there with the country's finest castles, the oval-shaped 13th-century fortress is a maze of courtyards, towers, halls and dungeons.

Montreux

Arriving by belle époque paddle steamer is the most romantic way of arriving in this celebrity town (p87) on the Swiss Riviera, a genteel place where palm trees stud silky-smooth lake promenades and market stalls spill across the waterfront each Friday. Eng-lish literati luxuriated in the good life here in the 19th century, the Montreux Jazz Festival struck gold in 1967 and a decade on, rock band Queen rocked into town. How glam!

Geneva & the West's Best…

Ancient Places

○ **Cathédrale St-Pierre**
Scale the towers of Geneva's mainly Gothic, 11th-century cathedral. (p59)

○ **Place de la Palud**
Lausanne's medieval market square. (p74)

○ **Cathédrale de Notre Dame** Switzerland's finest Gothic cathedral in Lausanne Old Town. (p73)

○ **Coppet** Lakeside medieval village. (p81)

○ **Château de Morges** A 13th-century beauty built by a Savoy duke. (p81)

○ **Nyon** Roman town with fairytale castle. (p82)

Lake Life

○ **CGN** Sail aboard a belle époque steamer. (p72)

○ **Quai du Mont-Blanc**
Flowers, statues, art and Mont Blanc views. (p63)

○ **Jet d'Eau** Dash beneath a 140m-tall, pencil fountain in the lake. (p64)

○ **Hôtel-Restaurant de la Plage** Lake Geneva's best *filets de perche* (perch fillets). (p83)

○ **Vevey** Bijou, boutique-studded lake town.

Museums

○ **Musée International de la Réforme** Historical exhibits bring to life all things Reformation. (p59)

○ **Musée Olympique** Sport-buff must: the Olympic story from inception to present. (p76)

○ **Alimentarium** Dedicated to all things edible. (p85)

○ **Musée de l'Art Brut**
Remarkable art created by society's disadvantaged. (p75)

○ **Patek Phillipe Museum**
The fine art of luxurious Swiss watches. (p63)

Need to Know

Winetasting

○ **Aigle** Capital of the Chablais wine-producing region with a castle and wine museum. (p86)

○ **Lavaux Vinorama** State-of-the-art wine tasting and discovery centre in Unesco-protected vineyards. (p85)

○ **Lavaux Express** Tractor-pulled tourist train through Lavaux' vineyards and villages. (p84)

○ **Caveau des Vignerons** Wine cellar in Nyon's 12th-century castle. (p82)

○ **Chardonne** Easy walking trails through pea-green vines. (p85)

ADVANCE PLANNING

○ **Two months before** Book hotels in Geneva and Lausanne, always popular. Research Swiss rail passes.

○ **One month before** Start plotting how you'll bounce around the region – when you'll take the train, float along on a boat or set off on foot.

RESOURCES

○ **Geneva Tourism** (www.geneve-tourisme.ch) Where to start for the region's premier city.

○ **Vaud: Lake Geneva Region Tourist Office** (www.lake-geneva-region.ch) Covers the region.

○ **Spotted by Locals** (www.spottedbylocals.com/geneva) Geneva tips by locals.

○ **Lonely Planet** (www.lonelyplanet.com/switzerland/geneva)

GETTING AROUND

○ **Ferry** Sail scenically between Lake Geneva cities, including Geneva and Lausanne. The best way to get around the region.

○ **Train** Fast and frequent trains link every important city and town in the region. No reservations necessary.

○ **Car** Not needed unless you want to putter about the tiny villages of the wine region around Aigle.

○ **Walk** Spectacular shoreline promenades abound, linking towns and sights on the lake.

BE FOREWARNED

○ **Winter** When the rest of Switzerland is revelling in winter sports, things get very quiet on the shores of Lake Geneva. Lake boats and tours are sharply curtailed or don't sail at all. The walks on the waterfront, and those among the wineries, can be bitterly cold.

○ **Weather** Even in August, cold winds can wash down from glacier-clad mountains, so be prepared for anything nature dishes out.

○ **Festivals** Hugely popular events like Montreux Jazz can soak up every spare room in the region.

t: Musée Olympique (p76), Lausanne; **Above:** Geneva's Jet d'Eau

(LEFT) GARY CRALLE / GETTY IMAGES ©; (ABOVE) SYLVAIN SONNET / GETTY IMAGES ©

55

Geneva & the West Itineraries

Lake Geneva is the focus of the region and these itineraries show you the best places to stop along its shores.

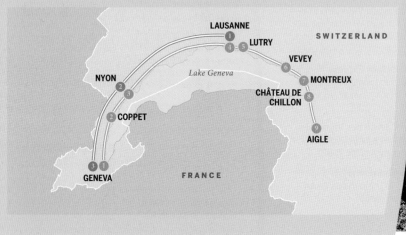

BEST OF LAKE GENEVA

LAUSANNE TO GENEVA

3 DAYS

❶**Lausanne** (p73) is a lakeside favourite, with an evocative medieval centre. Start at Place de la Palud (p74), the beautiful main square near the Gothic Cathédrale de Notre Dame (p73). Vault or hurdle over to the Musée Olympique (p76); the city is home to the International Olympic Committee. Stroll the lakefront and enjoy some creative modern European fare for dinner.

On day two, catch a boat to Roman ❷**Nyon** (p82) and visit its hilltop castle. Board a lake boat for Geneva and settle back to enjoy the sensational views of the

French Alps. On China-blue-sky days you can see Mont Blanc.

Once ashore in beguiling, smart and stylish ❸**Geneva** (p58), wander the lakefront along Quai du Mont-Blanc (p63) then hop abaord a yellow 'seagull' shuttle boat to cross the lake. On dry land the other side, ponder the Jet d'Eau (p64) from every angle. Walk the streets of the Old Town and peek into the Cathédrale St-Pierre (p59). When night falls, take your pick of cuisines and dine at one of the world-class cafes or restaurants Geneva is renowned for.

LAKE GENEVA RAMBLE
GENEVA TO AIGLE

Synchronise your watch in ① **Geneva** (p58) at the flower clock in Jardin Anglais (p59). Then train it to ② **Coppet** (p81), a medieval town on Lake Geneva's shores. From here sail, train or walk to ③ **Nyon** (p82), another ancient town that tumbles down the hillside to the lake.

A quick train ride and you're in ④ **Lausanne** (p73). Wander the hilly streets, pause for a drink at a bar built into a bridge and revel in the wild creativity of the Musée de l'Art Brut (p75). In the morning, sail to ⑤ **Lutry** (p84) in the

Lavaux wine region (p83), and later to ⑥ **Vevey** (p85), with its giant fork sticking out the lake and engaging lakeside museum run by local big shot Nestlé.

It's a quick train to ⑦ **Montreux** (p87) where you can visit the studio rock band Queen recorded several albums in. Next day walk the Chemin Fleuri (Flower Path) to ⑧ **Château de Chillon** (p88). Spend another night in Montreux and then train it to ⑨ **Aigle** (p86) for wine and castles, and a final overnight stay.

Aigle's fairy-tale château (p86)
YVES MARCOUX / DESIGN PICS / GETTY IMAGES ©

Discover Geneva & the West

At a Glance

○ **Geneva** The region's premier city, packed with museums and restaurants.

○ **Lausanne** (p73) Medieval splendour amid hillside charms.

○ **La Côte** (p81) Luxuriant 'wine country' lakeshore between Geneva and Lausanne.

○ **Lavaux Wine Region** (p83) Fabled, Unesco-protected vineyards.

○ **Swiss Riviera** (p85) Glittering lakeside stretch with jazzy Montreux at its helm.

GENEVA

POP 189,000 / ELEV 375M

Sleek, slick and cosmopolitan, Geneva is a rare breed of a city: it's one of Europe's priciest, its people chatter in every language under the sun and it's constantly perceived as the Swiss capital (it isn't). Superbly strung around the shores of Europe's largest Alpine lake, this is only Switzerland's third-largest city.

Yet the whole world is here: 200-odd governmental and nongovernmental international organisations fill the city's plush hotels, feast on its incredible choice of international cuisine, and help prop up Geneva's famed overload of banks, luxury jewellers and chocolate shops.

But where's the urban grit? Not in the lakeside's silky-smooth promenades and iconic fountain of record-breaking heights, nor in its pedestrian Old Town. To find the rough cut of the diamond, dig into the Pâquis quarter or walk along the Rhône's industrial shores where local neighbourhood bars hum with attitude. This is the Geneva of the Genevois...or as close as you'll get.

◎ Sights

Geneva's major sights are split by the Rhône, which flows through the city to create its greatest attraction – the lake – and several distinct neighbourhoods. On the left bank (*rive gauche*), mainstream shopping districts Rive and Eaux-Vives climb uphill from the water to Plainpalais and Vieille Ville (Old Town), while the right bank (*rive droite*) holds grungy bar- and club-hot Pâquis, the train station area and the international quarter that houses most world organisations.

Cathédrale St-Pierre, Geneva
MANFRED GOTTSCHALK / GETTY IMAGES ©

OLD TOWN

Geneva's **Vieille Ville** (Old Town) is a short walk south from the lakeside.

Jardin Anglais
Gardens

(Quai du Général-Guisan) Before tramping up the hill, join the crowds getting snapped in front of the flower clock in Geneva's flowery waterfront garden, which was landscaped in 1854 on the site of an old lumber-handling port and merchant yard. The **Horloge Fleurie** (Flower Clock; **Quai du Général-Guisan**), Geneva's most photographed clock, is crafted from 6500 plants and has ticked since 1955 in the garden. Its second hand, 2.5m long, claims to be the world's longest.

Cathédrale St-Pierre
Cathedral

(www.espace-saint-pierre.ch; Cour St-Pierre; admission free, towers adult/child Sfr5/2; ☺9.30am-6.30pm Mon-Sat, noon-6.30pm Sun Jun-Sep, 10am-5.30pm Oct-May) **FREE** Begun in the 11th century, Geneva's cathedral is predominantly Gothic with an 18th-century neoclassical facade. Between 1536 and 1564 Protestant John Calvin preached here; see his seat in the north aisle. Inside the cathedral 77 steps spiral up to the attic – a fascinating glimpse at its architectural construction – from where another 40 lead to the top of the panoramic **northern** and **southern towers**.

In summer, free carillon (5pm) and organ (6pm) concerts fill the cathedral and its surrounding square with soul.

Site Archéologique de la Cathédrale St-Pierre
Archaeological Site

(☏022 310 29 29; www.site-archeologique.ch; Cour St-Pierre; adult/child Sfr8/4; ☺10am-5pm Tue-Sun) The highlights of this small archaeological site in the basement of Geneva's cathedral are fine 4th-century mosaics and the tomb of an Allobrogian chieftain.

Musée International de la Réforme
Museum

(☏022 310 24 31; www.musee-reforme.ch; Rue du Cloître 4; adult/child Sfr10/5; ☺10am-5pm Tue-Sun) This modern museum in an 18th-century mansion zooms in on the Reformation. State-of-the-art exhibits

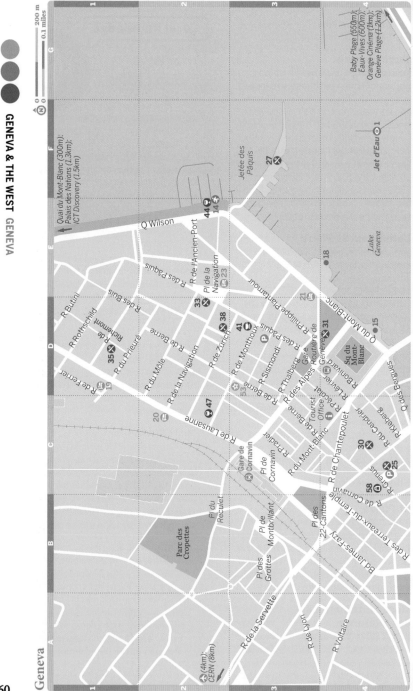

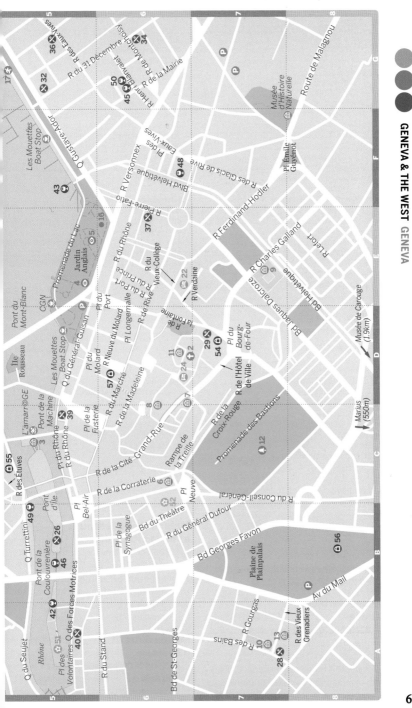

61

Geneva

and audiovisuals bring to life everything from the earliest printed bibles to the emergence of Geneva as 'Protestant Rome' in the 16th century, and from John Calvin all the way to Protestantism in the 21st century. A combined ticket covering museum, cathedral and archaeological site is Sfr18/10 per adult/child.

Musée Barbier-Mueller
Art Museum

(☎022 312 02 70; www.barbier-mueller.ch; Rue Jean Calvin 10; adult/child Sfr8/5; ☉11am-5pm) Protestant John Calvin lived in the house opposite this refined gallery space, filled with objects from so-called primitive societies – think pre-Columbian South Ameri-

can art treasures, Pacific Island statues, and shields and weapons from Africa.

Maison de Rousseau et de la Literature
Museum

(☎022 310 10 28; www.m-r-l.ch; Grand-Rue 40; adult/child Sfr5/3; ☉11am-5.30pm Tue-Sun) A 25-minute audiovisual display traces the troubled life of Geneva's greatest thinker, Jean-Jacques Rousseau. He was born in this house in 1712.

Musée d'Art et d'Histoire
Art Museum

(☎022 418 26 00; www.ville-ge.ch/mah; Rue Charles Galland 2; ☉11am-6pm Tue-Sun) FREE Built between 1903 and 1910, this elegant museum is set to get even better. World-class architect Jean Nouvel is working on a Sfr127 million renovation of the building, which holds masterpieces such as Konrad Witz' *La pêche miraculeuse* (c 1440–44), portraying Christ walking on water on Lake Geneva, in its treasure chest. There are excellent temporary exhibitions (adult/child Sfr15/free).

The museum will close in 2016 for builders to move in, and will not open again until 2022.

PLAINPALAIS

Between the Rhône and Arve rivers, this district is home to a bevy of museums.

Musée d'Art Moderne et Contemporain Art Museum
(MAMCO; ☑022 320 61 22; www.mamco.ch; Rue des Vieux-Grenadiers 10; adult/child Sfr8/free; ☉noon-6pm Tue-Fri, 11am-6pm Sat & Sun; 🚊Musée d'Art Moderne) Set in an industrial 1950s factory, the Modern and Contemporary Art Museum plays cutting-edge host to young, international and cross-media exhibitions. It's free the first Sunday of the month and between 6pm and 9pm the first Wednesday of every month.

Parc des Bastions Park
It's all statues – not to mention a giant chess board – in this green city park where a laidback stroll uncovers Red Cross cofounder Henri Dufour (who drew the first map of Switzerland in 1865) and the 4.5m-tall figures of Bèze, Calvin, Farel and Knox (in their nightgowns ready for bed). Depending on what's on, end with an art-driven exhibition across the square at **Le Rath** (☑022 418 33 40; Place Neuve; price varies).

RIGHT BANK

Cross the water aboard a seagull, using Geneva's only road-traffic bridge Pont du Mont-Blanc (notorious for traffic jams) or on foot across pedestrian footbridge Pont de la Machine.

Quai du Mont-Blanc Waterfront
Flowers, statues, outdoor art exhibitions and views of Mont Blanc (on clear days

If You Like...
Watches

If seeing ads and shops everywhere for Switzerland's famous watches has whet your appetite, consider these timely attractions:

1 PATEK PHILLIPE MUSEUM
(☑022 807 09 10; www.patekmuseum.com; Rue des Vieux-Grenadiers 7; adult/child Sfr10/free; ☉2-6pm Tue-Fri, 10am-6pm Sat) This elegant museum by one of Switzerland's leading luxury watchmakers displays exquisite timepieces and enamels from the 16th century to the present.

2 CITÉ DU TEMPS
(www.citedutemps.com; Pont de la Machine 1; ☉9am-6pm) This 19th-century industrial building straddling Lake Geneva was constructed in the 1840s to provide the city's public fountains with water. Today it hosts temporary art exhibitions on its 1st floor and **La Collection Swatch** – the world's largest collection of the funky Swiss watches dating from 1983 to 2006 – on its 2nd.

only) abound on this picturesque northern lakeshore promenade, which leads past the **Bains des Pâquis**, where Genevans have frolicked in the sun since 1872, to **Parc de la Perle du Lac**, a city park where Romans built ornate thermal baths. Further north, the peacock-studded lawns of **Parc de l'Ariana** ensnare the UN and Geneva's pretty **Jardin Botanique** (Botanic Garden).

Palais des Nations Historic Building
(☑022 907 48 96; www.unog.ch; Av de la Paix 14; adult/child Sfr12/7; ☉10am-4pm Mon-Sat Jul & Aug, 10am-noon & 2-4pm Mon-Sat Sep-Jun) Home to the UN since 1966, the Palais des Nations was built between 1929 and 1936 to house the now-defunct League of Nations. Visits are by guided tour (reserve in advance online; bring ID card or passport) and include entry to the surrounding 46-hectare park, generously peppered with century-old trees and peacocks. Spot the grey monument coated with heat-

SYLVAIN SONNET / GETTY IMAGES ©

⭐ Don't Miss
Jet d'Eau

When landing by plane, this lakeside fountain is the first dramatic glimpse you get of Geneva. The 140m-tall structure shoots up water with incredible force – 200km/h, 1360 horsepower – to create the sky-high plume, kissed by a rainbow on sunny days. At any one time, 7 tonnes of water is in the air, much of which sprays spectators on the pier beneath. Two or three times a year it is illuminated pink, blue or another colour to mark a humanitarian occasion.

The Jet d'Eau is Geneva's third pencil fountain. The first shot water into the sky for 15 minutes each Sunday between 1886 and 1890, to release pressure at the city's water station, and the second spurted 90m high from the Jetée des Eaux-Vives on Sundays and public holidays from 1891 onwards. The current one was born in 1951.

NEED TO KNOW
Quai Gustave-Ador

resistant titanium, donated by the USSR to commemorate the conquest of space.

Musée International de la Croix- Rouge et du Croissant-Rouge   Museum
(www.micr.org; Av de la Paix 17; adult/child Sfr15/7; ⏰10am-6pm Wed-Mon Apr-Oct, 10am-5pm Nov-Mar) Compelling multimedia exhibits at Geneva's fascinating International Red Cross and Red Crescent Museum trawl through atrocities perpetuated by humanity. The litany of war, documented in films, photos, sculptures and soundtracks, is set against the aims of the organisation created by Geneva businessmen and philanthropists Henri Dunant and Henri Dufour in 1864. Temporary exhibitions command an additional entrance fee. Take bus 8 from Gare de Cornavin to the Appia stop.

CERN
Laboratory

(☎ 022 767 84 84; www.cern.ch; Meyrin; ⏰ guided tour 11am Mon-Sat, 1pm Mon, Tue, Thu & Fri) FREE Founded in 1954, the European Organisation for Nuclear Research, 8km west of Geneva, is a laboratory for research into particle physics. It accelerates protons down a 27km circular tube (the Large Hadron Collider, the world's biggest machine) and the resulting collisions create new matter. Two exhibitions shed light on its work and two-hour guided tours in English delve deeper; reserve online 15 days ahead and bring your ID or passport. From the train station take tram 18 to CERN (Sfr3, 40 minutes).

ICT Discovery
Museum

(☎ 022 730 61 55; www.ictdiscovery.org; Rue de Varembé 2; ⏰ 10am-1pm & 2-5pm Mon-Fri) FREE The evolution of information technology, from primitive times through to the future, is explored in this fascinating exhibition peppered with hands-on gadgets and devices to fiddle with and a games room (test your reaction to a volcanic explosion or a cyber attack). Kids love the tablet with excellent multimedia guide that's provided on arrival. Bring ID or your passport to enter the building, home to the ITU (the UN's information and communication technologies agency).

🖐 Tours

The one-stop shop for boat, bus and electric-train tours is **Ticket Point** (☎ 022 781 04 06; www.ticket-point.ch; Quai du Mont-Blanc), which has all the schedules and sells tickets at its waterfront kiosk on Quai du Mont-Blanc.

CGN
Boat

(☎ 084 881 18 48; www.cgn.ch; Quai du Mont-Blanc) Lake cruises, some aboard beautiful belle époque steamers, by Lake Geneva's main boat operator.

Swissboat
Boat

(www.swissboat.com; Quai du Mont-Blanc 4; ⏰ May-Oct) Thematic cruises – castles, nature and so on – around the lake and along the Rhône River.

Trains & Trolleys Tours
Electric Train

(☎ 022 781 04 04; www.trains-tours.ch; Place du Rhône) 🚋 Short city tours by electric train along the lake (adult/child Sfr8.90/5.90, 45 minutes) past fabulous parks and residences, departing from Rotonde Mont Blanc; or into the Old Town (adult/child Sfr10.90/6.90, 45 minutes) with departures from Place du Rhône.

Les Corsaires
Train

(☎ 022 735 43 00; www.lescorsaires.ch; Jardin Anglais; adult/child Sfr8/5; ⏰ 10.15am-10.15pm Mar-Oct) At least hourly departures year-round along the left bank to Parc des Eaux-Vives and back again aboard

Geneva for Children

Predictably, the lake is an endless source of family entertainment: feed the ducks and swans; rent a pedalo, speedboat or sleek sailing boat from **Les Corsaires** (☎ 022 735 43 00; www.lescorsaires.ch; Quai Gustave-Ador 33; ⏰ 10.30am-8.30pm Apr-Oct); try stand-up paddleboarding at the **Centre Nautique de Pâquis** (Marti Marine; ☎ 022 732 88 21; www.martimarine.ch; Quai du Mont-Blanc 31); fly down the water slide at 1930s lakeside swimming pool complex **Genève Plage** (☎ 022 736 24 82; www.geneve-plage.ch; Port Noir; adult/child Sfr7/3.50; ⏰ 10am-8pm mid-May–mid-Sep); or dive head-first into the swimming pool at L'amarr@GE.

Other amusing options include an electric train tour, the Tarzan-inspired tree park with rubber tyre swings at lakeside **Baby Plage** (Quai Gustave-Ador), and the well-equipped playgrounds for toddlers in lakeside **Parc de la Perle du Lac.** Younger kids adore the stuffed animals at the Musée d'Histoire Naturelle, while CERN and ICT Discovery are just the ticket for teens.

Detour: Carouge

Bohemia strikes in Carouge where the lack of any real sights – bar fashionable 18th-century houses overlooking courtyard gardens and tiny **Musée de Carouge** (Place de la Sardaigne 2; ⊘2-6pm Tue-Sun) FREE displaying 19th-century ceramics – is part of the charm.

Carouge was refashioned by Vittorio Amedeo III, king of Sardinia and duke of Savoy, in the 18th century in a bid to rival Geneva as a centre of commerce. In 1816 the Treaty of Turin handed it to Geneva and today its narrow streets are filled with bars, boutiques and artists' workshops.

Trams 12 and 13 link central Geneva with Carouge's plane-tree-studded central square, **Place du Marché**, abuzz with market stalls Wednesday and Saturday morning. Horses trot along the streets during April's **Fête du Cheval**, and horse-drawn carriages line up on Place de l'Octroi in December to take Christmas shoppers for a ride.

a solar-powered red train; count on 45 minutes' journey time.

🛏 Sleeping

Plug into the complete list at www.geneva -hotel.ch. Rates in Geneva's predominantly business, midrange and top-end hotels are substantially higher Monday to Thursday.

When checking in, be sure to get your free Public Transport Card, which offers unlimited bus travel for the duration of your stay.

Hôtel Bel'Esperance — Hotel €

(☏022 818 37 37; www.hotel-bel-esperance. ch; Rue de la Vallée 1; s/d/tr/q from Sfr110/170/210/250; ⊘reception 7am-10pm; @🛜) This two-star hotel is extraordinary value. Rooms are quiet and cared for, those on the 1st floor share a kitchen, and there are fridges for guests to store picnic supplies – or sausages – in! Ride the lift to the 5th floor to flop on its wonderful flower-filled rooftop terrace, complete with barbecue that can be rented (Sfr8).

City Hostel — Hostel €

(☏022 901 15 00; www.cityhostel.ch; Rue de Ferrier 2; dm/s/d from Sfr33/65/79; ⊘reception 7.30am-noon & 1pm-midnight; P@🛜) This clean, well-organised hostel near the train station feels more like a hotel than a hostel. Breakfast (Sfr6) is served in a nearby cafe and parking costs Sfr12 to Sfr14 per night.

Hotel Edelweiss — Hotel €€

(☏022 544 51 51; www.hoteledelweissgeneva. com; Place de la Navigation 2; d Sfr160-400; ❄@🛜) Plunge yourself into the heart of the Swiss Alps with this Heidi-style hideout, very much the Swiss Alps *en ville* with its fireplace, wildflower-painted pine bedheads and big, cuddly St Bernard lolling over the banister. Its chalet-styled restaurant is a key address among Genevans for traditional cheese fondue.

Hôtel Auteuil — Design Hotel €€

(☏022 544 22 22; www.hotelauteuilgeneva. com; Rue de Lausanne 33; d weekday/weekend from Sfr250/180, q Sfr450/320; P➡❄@🛜) The star of this crisp, design-driven hotel near Cornavin train station is its enviable collection of B&W photos of 1960s film stars in Geneva – Sean Connery during the filming of *Goldfinger,* Audrey Hepburn et al – strung on the walls.

Hôtel Les Armures — Historic Hotel €€€

(☏022 310 91 72; www.hotel-les-armures.ch; Rue du Puits St-Pierre 1; s/d from Sfr450/695; P❄@🛜) This intimate, refined 17th-century beauty slumbers in the heart of the Old Town.

Hôtel Beau-Rivage Historic Hotel €€€

(☎022 716 66 66; www.beau-rivage.ch; Quai du Mont-Blanc 13; d from Sfr515; P ❄ @ 📶) Run by the Mayer family for five generations, the Beau-Rivage is a 19th-century jewel dripping in opulence.

Eating

Geneva flaunts ethnic cuisines galore. If it's local and traditional you're after, dip into a cheese fondue or platter of pan-fried *filets de perche* (perch fillets). But beware: not all those cooked up are fresh from the lake. Many come frozen from Eastern Europe, so it's imperative to pick the right place to sample this simple Lake Geneva speciality.

PÂQUIS

There's a tasty line-up of more affordable restaurants on Place de la Navigation. For Asian-cuisine lovers without a fortune to blow, try a quick-eat joint on Rue de Fribourg, Rue de Neuchâtel, Rue de Berne or the northern end of Rue des Alpes. Hungry students can be found devouring half-chickens at the Pâquis branch of Vieille Ville institution, Chez Ma Cousine (p68).

Buvette des Bains Cafeteria €

(☎022 738 16 16; www.bains-des-paquis.ch; Quai du Mont-Blanc 30, Bains des Pâquis; mains Sfr14-16; ⏰7am-10.30pm) Meet Genevans at this earthy beach bar – rough and hip around the edges – at lakeside pool, Bains des Pâquis. Grab breakfast, a salad or the *plat du jour* (dish of the day), or dip into a *fondue au crémant* (Champagne fondue). Dining is self-service on trays and alfresco in summer. In summer pay Sfr2/1 per adult/child to access the canteen, inside the pub.

À Table Food Truck €

(☎022 731 68 57; www.a-table.ch; Place De-Grenus 4; pasta Sfr12-15; ⏰11.30am-2.30pm Mon-Fri) A hip and nippy little number, this *bar à pâtes* (pasta bar) cooks delicious homemade pasta and, occasionally, risotto loaded with fresh, seasonal produce. Nothing is industrially produced and gluten-free eaters can dine well, too. Eat at the bijou Place De-Grenus restaurant or on the move thanks to its two Piaggio trucks that are parked at different spots each day.

Cottage Café Mediterranean €

(☎022 731 60 16; www.cottagecafe.ch; Rue Adhémar-Fabri 7; tapas & mezze Sfr4-16; ⏰7.30am-midnight Mon-Fri, 9am-midnight Sat) Hovering near the waterfront, this quaint cottage hides in a park guarded by two stone lions and a mausoleum (Geneva's Brunswick Monument, no less). On clear days, views of Mont Blanc from its garden are swoon-worthy, and lunching or lounging inside

Interior of Cathédrale St-Pierre (p59)
SYLVAIN SONNET / GETTY IMAGES ©

is akin to hanging out in your grandma's book-lined living room.

Brasserie des Halles de l'Île — European €€

(☎ 022 311 08 88; www.brasseriedeshallesdelile.ch; Place de l'Île 1; mains Sfr20-50; ⏰ 10.30am-midnight Sun & Mon, to 1am Tue-Thu, to 2am Fri & Sat) At home in Geneva's old market hall on an island, this industrial-style venue cooks up a buzzing cocktail of after-work aperitifs with music, after-dark DJs and seasonal fare of fresh veggies and regional products (look for the Appellation d'Origine Contrôllée products flagged on the menu). Arrive early to snag the best seat in the house – a superb terrace hanging over the water.

Le Comptoir — Fusion €€

(☎ 022 731 32 37; www.lecomptoirdesign.com; Rue de Richemont 7-9; 2-/3-course lunch menu Sfr19/22, mains Sfr19.50-29.50; ⏰ noon-2pm & 6.30pm-1am Mon-Thu, 6.30pm-2am Fri & Sat Sep-Jul) To savour the real vibe of this U-shaped space, come at dusk or later when night lights twinkle on sideboards and the Counter's retro decor comes into its own. We love the faux sheepskins and crystal in the faintly kitsch Lola Bar lounge. The cuisine is a tasty mix of sushi, curries and wok-cooked dishes.

Les 5 Portes — Bistro €€

(☎ 022 731 84 38; http://les5portes.com; Rue de Zürich 5; mains Sfr28-44; ⏰ 9am-1am Mon-Thu, 9am-2am Fri, 5pm-2am Sat, 11am-11pm Sun) The Five Doors – with, indeed, five doors – is a fashionable Pâquis port of call that successfully embraces the gamut of moods and moments for eating and drinking. Its Sunday brunch is a particularly buzzing affair.

VIEILLE VILLE

Eateries crowd Place du Bourg-de-Four, Geneva's oldest square, in the lovely Old Town. Otherwise, head down the hill towards the river and Place du Molard, packed with tables and chairs for much of the year.

Chez Ma Cousine — Chicken €

(☎ 022 310 96 96; www.chezmacousine.ch; Place du Bourg-de-Four 6; mains Sfr14.90-17.40; ⏰ 11am-11.30pm Mon-Sat, 11am-10.30pm Sun) *'On y mange du poulet'* (we eat chicken) is the strapline of this student institution, which appeals for one good reason – gen-

Alfresco dining, Geneva

erously handsome and homely portions of chicken (half a chicken to be precise), potatoes and salad at a price that can't possibly break the bank. It has a second branch in **Pâquis** (Rue Lissignol 5; ⏱11am-3pm & 5.15-11.30pm Mon-Fri, 11am-11.30pm Sat).

RIVE & EAUX-VIVES

Le Relais d'Entrecôte
Steakhouse €€

(☎022 310 60 04; www.relaisentrecote.fr; Rue Pierre Fatio 6; steak & chips Sfr42; ⏱noon-2.30pm & 7-11pm) Key vocabulary at this timeless classic where everyone eats the same dish is *à point* (medium), *bien cuit* (well done) and *saignant* (rare). It doesn't even bother with menus, just sit down, say how you like your steak cooked and wait for it to arrive – two handsome servings (!) pre-empted by a green salad and accompanied by perfectly crisp, skinny fries.

Should you have room at the end of it all, the desserts are justly raved about. No advance reservations, so arrive sharp.

Le Décanteur
Italian €€

(☎022 700 67 38; www.ledecanteur.ch; Rue des Eaux-Vives 63; mains Sfr22-25; ⏱11am-3pm & 5.30pm-midnight Mon-Wed) No address is lovelier for fresh homemade *pâtes* (pasta), copious salads laced with fresh mozzarella, wafer-thin carpaccio and other true Italian dishes. Everything that's cooking is written with a flamboyant hand on the blackboard wall and seating is in the faintly industrial-styled interior or on the busy pavement terrace outside. After work, it morphs into a first-rate wine bar.

L'Adresse
Modern €€€

(☎022 736 32 32; www.ladress.ch; Rue du 31 Décembre 32; mains Sfr25-35; ⏱11am-midnight Tue-Sat) The Address is an urban loft with a fabulous rooftop terrace, at home in a hybrid fashion/lifestyle boutique and contemporary bistro fashioned out of old artists' workshops. It's the Genevan address for lunch (great value at Sfr18/24 for one/two courses), brunch or Saturday slunch – a 'tea-dinner' meal of cold and warm nibbles, sweet and savoury, shared over a drink or three around 5pm.

If You Like...
Ice Cream

Nothing like a lakeside stroll and ice. Count on paying Sfr3.50/6 for a one-/two-ball cornet at these Geneva institutions.

1 **GELATERIA ARLECCHINO** (www.larlecchino.ch; Rue du 31 Décembre 1; per scoop Sfr3.50) Left-bank choice: chocolate and ginger, honey, peanut cream and mango are among the 40 flavours at this lip-licking parlour.

2 **GELATOMANIA** (Rue des Pâquis 25; 1-/2-scoop cornet Sfr3.50/6; ⏱11.30am-11pm Sun-Thu, to midnight Fri & Sat May-Sep, noon-7pm Oct-Apr) Right-bank choice: a constant queue loiters outside this shop where ice-cream maniacs wrap their tongues around exotic flavours like carrot, orange and lemon, cucumber and mint, lime and basil or pineapple and basil.

3 **MÖVENPICK** (Place du Rhône; 1/2/3 scoops in cornet Sfr4.90/8.50/12; ⏱noon-11pm Mon-Sat, 2-11pm Sun Apr-Oct, noon-to 9pm Nov-Mar) The luxe address to sit down riverside and drool over the creamiest of Swiss ice cream topped with whipped cream, hot chocolate sauce and other decadent treats.

PLAINPALAIS

Omnibus
European €€

(☎022 321 44 45; www.omnibus-cafe.ch; Rue de la Coulouvrenière 23; mains Sfr33-40; ⏱11.30am-2.30pm & 6.30-10pm Mon, 11.30am-2.30pm & 6pm-midnight Tue-Fri, 6.30pm-midnight Sat) Don't be fooled or deterred by the graffiti-plastered facade of this Rhône-side, industrial-inspired bar, cafe and restaurant. Inside, a maze of retro, romantic and eclectic rooms seduces on first sight. Particularly popular is the back room (reservations essential) with carpet wall hangings and lots of lace. Its business card is a recycled bus ticket.

Café des Bains Modern European €€

(022 321 57 98; Rue des Bains 26; mains Sfr25-50; noon-2pm Mon-Sat, 7-10pm Tue-Sat) No brand labels, beautiful objects and an eye for design are trademarks of this fusion restaurant opposite the contemporary art museum where Genevan beauties flock. The summer patio with tables beneath trees and parasols is gorgeous.

Drinking & Nightlife

Summer ushers in dozens of scenic spots around the city where you can lounge in the sun over a mint tea or mojito – Place du Bourg-de-Four in the Old Town and Carouge are strewn with seasonal cafe terraces, as is the short riverside length of Place du Rhône.

La Buvette de Bateau Bar

(022 736 07 75; www.bateaugeneve.ch; Quai Gustave-Ador 1; 11.30am-midnight Tue-Sat mid-May–mid-Sep) Few terraces are as dreamy as this. Moored permanently by the quay near the Jet d'Eau, this fabulous belle époque paddle steamer sailed Lake Geneva's waters from 1896 until its retirement in 1974, and is now one of the busiest lounge bars in town in summer. Flower boxes festoon its decks and the cabin kitchen cooks tapas, bruschetta and other drink-friendly snacks.

Yvette de Marseille Bar

(Rue Henri Blanvalet 13; 5.30pm-midnight Mon & Tue, 5.30pm-1am Wed & Thu, 5.30pm-2am Fri, 6.30pm-2am Sat) No bar begs the question 'what's in the name?' more than this buzzy drinking hole. Urban and edgy, it occupies a mechanic's workshop once owned by Yvette. Note the garage door, the trap door in the floor where cars were repaired and the street number 13 (aka the departmental number of the Bouches-du-Rhône département, home to Marseille).

L'Atelier Cocktail Club Cocktail Bar

(Rue Henri Blanvalet 11; 5pm-2am Tue-Sat) Reputed to mix the best mojitos in town, this buzzing cocktail bar in Eaux-Vives is one of the city's hottest 'after work' spots. Its interior decor mixes classic bistro features with upcycled vintage, complete with leather armchairs to sink into and a piano to tinkle on between cocktails.

Buildings line the Rhône River, Geneva

KATARINA STEFANOVIC / GETTY IMAGES ©

Soleil Rouge
Wine Bar

(www.soleilrouge.ch; Bd Hélvetique 32; ⏰5-10pm Mon, 10am-11pm Tue & Wed, 10am-midnight Thu-Sat) The trendy address to sip Spanish wine on bar stools outside or in. Watch for flamenco, jazz and other great live sounds from 7pm some evenings.

Café des Arts
Cafe, Bar

(Rue des Pâquis 15; ⏰11am-2am Mon-Fri, 8am-2am Sat & Sun) As much a place to drink as a daytime cafe, this Pâquis hang-out lures a local crowd with its Parisian-style terrace and artsy interior. Food-wise, think meal-size salads, designer sandwiches and a great-value lunchtime *plat du jour*.

Marius
Wine Bar

(Place des Augustins 9; ⏰5.30pm-1.30am Mon-Fri) This doll's house–size *bar à vin* – an old butcher's shop, hence the tiles and ceramic – is a great little spot in Plainpalais to discover regional and natural wines. Pair your chosen vintage with a cold meat, cheese or antipasti platter for the perfect gourmet experience.

Mambo Club
Club

(☎079 901 02 02; www.mambo.ch; Rue de Monthoux 60; admission before/after midnight free/Sfr10; ⏰10pm-5am Thu, from midnight Fri & Sat) Deep house and mainstream sets Genevans dancing 'til dawn at this hybrid cocktail club, dance school and nightclub in Pâquis. Those in the know book a table in advance.

⭐ Entertainment

Palais Mascotte
Cabaret Bar

(☎022 741 33 33; www.palaismascotte.ch; Rue de Berne 43; dinner with show Sfr78, nightclub admission Thu/Fri & Sat Sfr10/15; ⏰11pm-5am Wed-Sat) This mythical address, around since 1887 and much-loved by the over 30-somethings, buzzes with atmosphere. Dine in the top floor Le Duc (reserve in advance), enjoy cabaret in the ground floor Le Mascotte, and take in concerts

---

♥ If You Like…
Lakeside Lounging

Genevan living is easy in summer when a constant crowd throngs to the city's manicured lakefront quays and grungier Rhône riverbanks to lounge in a bevy of fabulous pop-up terrace bars – alfresco, edgy and effortlessly cool.

1 LA TERRASSE
(www.laterrasse.ch; Quai du Mont-Blanc 31; ⏰8am-midnight Apr-Sep) With wooden tables inches from the water, this summertime cafe-bar on the water's edge gets packed out on warm days – especially at weekends and in the evenings.

2 TERRASSE LE PARADIS
(☎079 665 35 73; www.terrasse-paradis. ch; Quai Turrettini; sandwiches & salads Sfr10-14; ⏰10am-9pm Jun-Sep) On the right bank, this refreshingly casual, Rhône-side venue practically begs you to pull out a book and stay all day with its deck-chairs tumbing down steps to the water and beakers of homemade *citronnade* (lemonade). 'Paradise' does not serve alcohol, but the pots of green mint tea flow and the wholly affordable sandwiches, salads and legendary *taboulé* (Sfr13) hit the spot beautifully.

3 LE BATEAU LAVOIR
(Passerelle des Lavandières; ⏰11am-midnight Mon-Thu, 11am-2am Fri, 5pm-2am Sat May-Sep) Moored between the old market hall and Pont de la Coulouvrenière, this eye-catching boat with cabin-sized dining area inside, parasol-shaded seating on its roof, and hip edgy crowd is a winner with its 360-degree lake view.

4 LA BARJE
(Terrasse des Lavandières; www.labarje.ch; Promenade des Lavandières; ⏰11am-midnight Mon-Fri, 3pm-midnight Sat & Sun Apr-Sep) This summertime address is not a barge at all, but rather a vintage caravan with tin roof and candy-striped facade, parked up on the grassy banks of the Rhône near the Bâtiment des Forces Motrices. Proceeds go towards helping young people in difficulty.

followed by '90s dance music in the basement nightclub Le Zazou.

Orange Cinéma
Cinema

(www.orangecinema.ch; Quai Gustave-Ador; ☾ Jul & Aug) Glorious summertime open-air cinema with a screen set up on the lakeside.

Bâtiment des Forces Motrices
Performing Arts

(www.bfm.ch; Place des Volontaires 4) Geneva's one-time riverside pumping station (1886) is now a striking space for classical music concerts, dance and other performing arts.

Grand Théâtre de Genève
Opera

(www.geneveopera.ch; Bd du Théâtre 11) The city's lovely theatre hosts ballet too.

🛍 Shopping

Designer shopping is wedged between Rue du Rhône and Rue de Rive. **Globus** (Rue du Rhône 50; ☾ 9am-7pm Mon-Wed & Sat, to 9pm Thu, to 7.30pm Fri, food hall 7.30am-10pm Mon-Fri, 8.30am-10pm Sat) and **Manor** (Rue de Cornavin) are the main department stores.

Grand-Rue in the Old Town and Carouge boast artsy boutiques, or try Geneva's twice-weekly **flea market** (Plaine de Plainpalais; ☾ Wed & Sat).

Favarger
Chocolate

(☎ 022 738 18 26; www.favarger.ch; Quai des Bergues 19; ☾ 1-6pm Mon, 10am-6pm Tue-Fri, 9am-5pm Sat) A veteran on the Swiss chocolate scene, this respected *chocolatier* has a stylish lake-facing boutique near the spot where its first factory opened in 1826. A favourite for its vintage and contemporary design packaging, its speciality is Avelines, a super smooth cocktail of milk chocolate, almonds and hazelnuts bundled into glorious melt-in-the-mouth bites.

Caran d'Arche – Maison de Haute Ecriture
Arts & Crafts

(www.carandache.ch; Place du Bourg-de-Four 8; ☾ 11am-6pm Mon, 10am-6pm Tue-Thu, 10am-7pm Fri, 9.30am-6pm Sat) Beautifully designed boutique packed with a rainbow of pencils, pastels, paints and crayons crafted by Swiss colour maker Caran d'Aché in Geneva since 1915.

ℹ Information

Tourist Office (☎ 022 909 70 00; www.genevetourisme.ch; Rue du Mont-Blanc 18; ☾ 9am-6pm Mon-Sat, 10am-4pm Sun)

ℹ Getting There & Away

Air

Aéroport International de Genève (GVA; www.gva.ch) Geneva airport is 4km from the town centre.

Boat

CGN (Compagnie Générale de Navigation; ☎ 0848 811 848; www.cgn.ch) The Compagnie Générale de Navigation operates a steamer service from its Jardin Anglais jetty to other

Rooftops of Lausanne
ANTARES71 / GETTY IMAGES ©

villages on Lake Geneva. Some only sail from May to September. Those aged six to 16 pay 50% less; under six years sail for free.

Train

Trains to/from Annecy, Chamonix and other destinations in neighbouring France use Gare des Eaux-Vives (Av de la Gare des Eaux-Vives). More-or-less-hourly connections run from Geneva's central train station Gare de Cornavin (Place de Cornavin) to most Swiss towns. Left luggage lockers in the main hall cost Sfr4/6/8/10 per six hours for a small/medium/large/extra-large locker.

Bern (Sfr49, 1¾ hours)

Geneva Airport (Sfr2.50, 15 minutes)

Lausanne (Sfr21.80, 30 minutes)

Zürich (Sfr84, 2¾ hours)

🟢 Getting Around

To/From the Airport

The quickest way to/from Geneva airport is by train (Sfr2.50, 15 minutes, half-hourly); otherwise take bus No 10 from the Rive stop (Sfr2.50, 30 minutes, four to nine hourly). Arriving at the airport, before leaving the luggage hall, grab a free public transport ticket from the machine next to the information desk. A metered taxi into town costs Sfr35 to Sfr50.

Bicycle

Genèveroule (www.geneveroule.ch; Place du Rhône; 4hr free, then per hr Sfr2; ⊙9am-7pm May-Oct) To borrow a bike, show proof of ID and pay a Sfr20 cash deposit. Find other Genèveroule stands at Bains des Pâquis, Place de l'Octroi in Carouge, and Place de Montbrillant.

Boat

Yellow shuttle boats called Les Mouettes (known as 'Seagulls') cross the lake every 10 minutes between 7.30am and 6pm. Public-transport tickets from machines at boat bays are valid.

Car & Motorcycle

Much of the Old Town is off limits to cars and street parking elsewhere can be hard to snag; try public car park Parking du Mont Blanc (www.parkgest.ch; Quai du Général-Guisan; per 25 min Sfr1). Before leaving the car park, validate your parking ticket in an orange TPG machine to get one hour's free travel for two people on city buses, trams and boats.

Public Transport

Tickets for buses, trolley buses and trams run by TPG are sold at dispensers at stops and through the TPG office (www.tpg.ch; Rue de Montbrillant; ⊙7am-7pm Mon-Fri, 9am-6pm Sat) inside the main train station. A one-hour ticket for multiple rides in the city costs Sfr3.50 and a ticket valid for three stops in 30 minutes is Sfr2.

LAUSANNE

POP 130,400 / ELEV 495M

This hilly city (pronounced loh-*san*), Switzerland's fourth largest, enjoys a blessed lakeside location. The medieval centre is dominated by a grand Gothic cathedral and, among the museums, its unusual Art Brut collection stands out. Throughout the year Lausanne's citizens are treated to a busy arts calendar, while the lake drums up a plethora of activities on and out of the water. Strolling the lakeshore in picturesque Ouchy (once a lakeside village in its own right long since enveloped by the city) is a pure pleasure, as is a meander day or night around Flon, an area of formerly derelict warehouses rejuvenated as a hip urban centre with a cinema complex, art galleries and trendy shops, and restaurants and bars galore.

🔵 Sights & Activities

Downhill by the water in **Ouchy**, Lake Geneva (Lac Léman) is the source of many a sporting opportunity, including sailing, windsurfing, waterskiing and swimming; the tourist office has details. Seasonal stands in front of Château d'Ouchy rent pedalos and kayaks, and cycling and rollerblading are big on the silky-smooth waterfront promenades. West of Ouchy, **Plage de Vidy**, backed by thick woods and parklands, is one of Lake Geneva's few sandy beaches

MUDAC   Museum
(Musée de Design et d'Arts Appliqués Contemporains; www.mudac.ch; Place de la Cathédrale 6; adult/child Sfr10/free, 1st Sat of month free; ⊙11am-6pm, closed Mon Sep-Jun) This ode to modern design and applied arts hosts six intriguing temporary exhibitions each

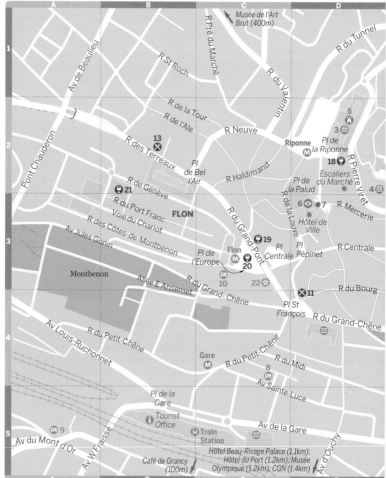

year. Find it opposite the cathedral's southern side.

Place de la Palud
Square

In the heart of the Vieille Ville (Old Town), this 9th-century medieval market square – pretty as a picture – was originally bogland. For five centuries it has been home to the city government, now housed in the 17th-century Hôtel de Ville (town hall). A fountain pierces one end of the square, presided over by a brightly painted column topped by the allegorical figure of Justice, clutching scales and dressed in blue.

Musée Historique de Lausanne
Museum

(☎ 021 315 41 01; www.lausanne.ch/mhl; Place de la Cathédrale 4; adult/child Sfr8/free, 1st Sat of month free; ☒ 11am-6pm Tue-Thu, to 5pm Fri-Sun) Until the 15th century, the city's bishops resided in this lovely manor across from the cathedral (after which it became a jail, then a court, then a hospital). Since 1918 it has devoted itself to evoking

Lausanne

Lausanne's heritage through paintings, drawings, stamps, musical instruments, silverware and so on. Don't miss the film featuring Lausanne in 1638.

Musée Cantonal des Beaux Arts
Museum

(☏ 021 316 34 45; www.mcba.ch; Place de la Riponne 6; adult/child Sfr10/free, 1st Sat of month free; ◷ 11am-6pm Tue-Thu, to 5pm Fri-Sun) **Palais de Rumine**, a bombastic neo-Renaissance pile (1904) where the Treaty of Lausanne (finalising the break up of the Ottoman Empire after WWI) was signed in 1923, safeguards the city's fine arts museum. Works by Swiss and foreign artists, ranging from Ancient Egyptian art to Cubism, are displayed, but the core of the collection is made up of works by landscape painter Louis Ducros (1748–1810). During temporary exhibitions (many with free admission), the permanent collection is often closed.

Musée de l'Art Brut
Museum

(☏ 021 315 25 70; www.artbrut.ch; Av des Bergières 11-13; adult/child Sfr10/free; ◷ 11am-6pm Tue-Sun) *Brut* means crude or rough, and that's what you get in this extraordinary gallery with its huge collection of works by untrained artists (many from the fringes of society or with a mental illness), put together by French artist Jean Dubuffet in the 1970s in what was a late-18th-century country mansion. Exhibits offer a striking

75

MARTIN MOXTER / GETTY IMAGES ©

⭐ Don't Miss
Cathédrale de Notre Dame

Lausanne's Gothic cathedral, Switzerland's finest, stands proudly at the heart of the Old Town. Raised in the 12th and 13th centuries on the site of earlier, humbler churches, it lacks the lightness of French Gothic buildings but is remarkable nonetheless. Pope Gregory X, in the presence of Rudolph of Habsburg (the Holy Roman Emperor) and an impressive following of European cardinals and bishops, consecrated the church in 1275.

Although touched up in parts in following centuries (notably the main facade, which was added to the original to protect the interior against ferocious winds), the cathedral remains largely as it was (thanks to today's constant conservation work). The most striking element is the elaborate entrance on the south flank of the church (which, unusually for Christian churches, was long the main way in). The painted statuary depicts Christ in splendour, the coronation of the Virgin Mary, the Apostles and other Bible scenes. Free 40-minute guided tours run July through September.

NEED TO KNOW

Place de la Cathédrale; ⊙9am-7pm Apr-Sep, to 5.30pm Oct-Mar

variety and, at times, surprising technical capacity, and an often inspirational view of the world. Take bus 2, 3 or 21 to the Beaulieu-Jomini stop.

Musée Olympique   Museum

(☎021 621 65 11; www.olympic.org/museum; Quai d'Ouchy 1; adult/child Sfr18/10; ⊙9am-6pm May–mid-Oct daily, 10am-6pm mid-Oct–Apr Tue-Sun) Lausanne's Musée Olympique is easily the city's most lavish museum and an essential stop for sports buffs (and kids). Following a thorough revamp of its facilities, the museum reopened in 2014, with its tiered landscaped gardens and site-specific scuptural works as inviting as ever. Inside, there is a fabulous cafe with a champion lake view from its terrace, and a state-of-the-art museum recounting the Olympic story from its inception to present-day through video, interactive displays, memorabilia and temporary themed exhibitions.

Tours

CGN — Boat Tour

(📞 0848 811 848; www.cgn.ch; Quai Jean-Pascal Delamuraz) Offers cruises of Lake Geneva, some aboard beautiful belle époque steamers.

Guides d'Accueil MDA — Walking Tour

(📞 021 320 12 61; www.lausanne.ch/visites; Place de la Palud; adult/child Sfr10/free; ⊙10am & 2.30pm Mon-Sat May-Sep) Walking tours of the Old Town, departing from in front of the Hôtel de Ville on Place de la Palud. Themed tours for up to five people on demand.

🛏 Sleeping

At check-in, your hotel will give you a free Lausanne Transport Card, covering unlimited use of public transport for the duration of your stay

Lhotel — Boutique Hotel €

(📞 021 331 39 39; www.lhotel.ch; Place de l'Europe 6; r from Sfr130; ✳🛜) This smart small hotel is ideally placed for the city's lively Flon district nightlife. Rooms are simple and startlingly white, and come with iPads; breakfast costs Sfr14. There's a fab rooftop terrace and your stay gives you access to the spa at five-star Lausanne Palace & Spa nearby for Sfr55.

Lausanne Guest House — Hostel €

(📞 021 601 80 00; www.lausanne-guesthouse.ch; Chemin des Épinettes 4; dm from Sfr37, s/d from Sfr90/107, with shared bathroom from Sfr80/96; ⊙reception 7.30am-noon & 3-10pm; 🅿@🛜) 🍃 An attractive mansion converted into

Lausanne Don't Miss List

NATHALIE NINI REY, LAUSANNE GUIDE

1 CATHÉDRALE DE NOTRE DAME
The cathedral of Lausanne is a masterpiece of early Gothic style: do not miss the painted portal dated 1235 and its impressive polychromatic sculptures, the rose window with its medieval symbolism, the new organ (2002) and its fantastic design.

2 CENTRE & MARKET
From the cathedral, a walk down 174 stairs leads you to Place de la Palud (p74). A must is the open-air market on Wednesday and Saturday morning. Features local products like cheese, charcuterie, pastry, and fruits and vegetables.

3 SAUVABELIN & HERMITAGE
A short bus ride (No 16; 15 minutes) from St-François square brings you to Sauvabelin, a 60-hectare forest in the northern part of Lausanne. Climb the wooden tower and its 150 steps for a 360-d breathtaking view. Walk downhill to the **Fondation de l'Hermitage** (📞 021 320 50 01; www.fondation-hermitage.ch; Route du Signal 2; adult/child Sfr18/free; ⊙10am-6pm Tue, Wed & Fri-Sun, to 9pm Thu), an exhibition of paintings in a beautiful 19th-century mansion.

4 LAVAUX VINEYARDS
The nearest Lavaux vineyards are easy to reach by train from Lausanne and are a fun day trip (p84). A 15-minute train ride to **Grandvaux** brings you to the steep terraces of this wine area; from there you can walk down to the picturesque village of **Lutry** on the lake in an hour.

5 ART BRUT MUSEUM
This very special museum (p75) shows the creative works of people living in psychiatric hospitals, in prisons or outside society. Paintings, sculptures, collage and patchworks made from all kinds of materials will astonish you.

quality backpacking accommodation near the train station. Many rooms have lake views and you can hang out in the garden or terrace. Parking is Sfr11 per day, there's a 24-hour laundry and room to leave your bike. Some of the building's energy is solar.

Hôtel Elite
Boutique Hotel €€

(☎ 021 320 23 61; www.elite-lausanne.ch; Av Sainte Luce 1; s/d/q Sfr200/275/420; P ❄@☎) The same family has run this lovely apricot townhouse of a hotel for three generations. A couple of sunloungers and tables dot the pretty handkerchief-sized garden, and inside at reception it's all fresh flower arrangements and soft background music. Rooms on the 4th floor look out to the lake and the best have a balcony, too.

Hôtel du Port
Hotel €€

(☎ 021 612 04 44; www.hotel-du-port.ch; Place du Port 5; s/d from Sfr145/175; ☎) A perfect location in Ouchy, just back from the lake, makes this a good choice. The better doubles look out across the lake (Sfr20 extra) and are spacious (23 sq metres). Some very good junior suites are situated on the 3rd floor.

Hôtel Beau-Rivage Palace
Historic Hotel €€€

(☎ 021 613 33 33; www.brp.ch; Place du Port 17-19; r from Sfr440; ❄@☎❋) Easily the most stunningly located hotel in town, this luxury lakeside address is sumptuous. A beautifully maintained early-19th-century mansion set in immaculate grounds, it tempts with magnificent lake and Alp views, a grand spa, and a number of bars and upmarket restaurants (including a superb gastronomic temple headed by Anne-Sophie Pic, the only French female chef with three Michelin stars).

 # Eating

Lausanne's dining scene is laidback. Its best addresses are stylish cafe-bars and bistros that morph, come dusk, into great places for drinks and tapas.

Holy Cow
Burgers €

(www.holycow.ch; Rue Cheneau-de-Bourg 17; burger with chips & drink Sfr20; ☺11am-10pm Mon & Tue, to 11pm Wed-Sat; 🚻) A Lausanne success story, with branches in Geneva, Zürich and France, burgers (beef, chicken or veggie) feature local ingredients, creative toppings and witty names. Grab an artisanal beer, sit at a shared wooden table, and wait for your burger and fab fries to arrive in a straw basket. A second outlet can be found at **Rue des Terreaux** (Rue des Terreaux 10; burger with chips & drink Sfr20; ☺11am-11pm Mon-Sat).

Café Romand
Swiss €

(☎ 021 312 63 75; www.cafe-romand.ch; Place St François 2; mains Sfr16-41.50; ☺8am-midnight Mon-Sat)

Ouchy harbour, Lausanne
IAN TROWER / GETTY IMAGES ©

Tucked away in an unpromising looking arcade, this Lausanne legend dating to 1951 is a welcome blast from the past. Locals pour into the broad, somewhat sombre dining area filled with timber tables to revel in fondue, raclette (Sfr8.50 per serve), *cervelle au beurre noir* (brains in black butter), tripe, *pied de porc* (pork trotters) and other feisty traditional dishes.

L'Éléphant Blanc   Modern European €€
(021 312 64 89; www.lelephantblanc.ch; Rue Cité-Devant 4; mains Sfr27-46; 11.30am-2.30pm & 6.30pm-midnight Tue-Sat) One of a handful of restaurants behind the cathedral, the White Elephant offers wonderful local market cuisine, and staggeringly good value with its lunchtime *plat du jour* (dish of the day, Sfr18.90).

Café St-Pierre   Modern European €€
(021 326 36 36; www.cafesaintpierre.ch; Place Benjamin Constant 1; 7.30am-midnight Tue & Wed, to 1am Thu, to 2am Fri, 11am-2am Sat, 11am-6pm Sun;) The fact that every table is snapped up by noon while friendly waiters zip between tables and that the telephone is constantly ringing says it all – this hip cafe-bar buzzes! Its interior is contemporary and relaxed, and the cuisine is modern European – think pasta, big salads and fish at lunchtime, creative tapas from 7pm, and brunch on weekends. Reserve in advance.

Café de Grancy   Modern European €€
(021 616 86 66; www.cafédegrancy.ch; Ave du Rond Point 1; mains Sfr18.50-42; 8am-midnight Mon-Fri, 10am-midnight Sat & Sun;) This place just to the south of the train station has floppy lounges for drinking in the front and creative cuisine for hip dining further back. An unbeatable value *pâte du jour* (pasta of the day) served with salad or soup is a lunchtime winner. Wednesday evening fondues, first Tuesday of the month themed dinners and great weekend brunches draw the crowds.

If You Like…
Bridge Bars

When there's a bridge, there's a bar. At least that's how it works in artsy Lausanne where the monumental arches of its bridges shelter the city's most happening summertime bars.

1 LES ARCHES
(www.lesarches.ch; Place de l'Europe; 11am-midnight Mon-Wed, to 1am Thu, to 2am Fri & Sat, 1pm-midnight Sun) Occupying four arches of Lausanne's magnificent Grand Pont (built between 1839 and 1940) above Place de l'Europe, this is the perfect port of call for that all-essential, after-work drink in the warm evening sun or for that final drink before bed.

2 BOURG PLAGE
(www.le-bourg.ch; 2pm-midnight Apr-Sep) Mid-evening, Lausanne's hipsters move to Bourg Plage, with pool table, table football, palm trees and deckchairs in one old stone arch of Pont Charles Bessières (built between 1908 and 1910); steps lead up to it from Rue Centrale and down to it from opposite MUDAC on Rue Pierre Veret.

Drinking & Nightlife

Eating venues Café St-Pierre and Café de Grancy are stylish drinking addresses, too, packed with a hip crowd year-round.

Caffè Bellini   Bar
(021 351 24 40; www.caffebellini.ch; Rue de la Barre 5; 11am-1am Mon-Thu, to 2am Fri & Sat) Lausanne's most charming terrace is tucked away in the Old Town and is *the* spot for summertime drinks, with fairy lights, a cool crowd and a retro-influenced interior. Antipasto platters and pizzas are good, and service chipper but occasionally forgetful. Call to reserve your spot.

Great Escape   Pub
(021 312 31 94; www.the-great.ch; Rue Madeleine 18; 11am-late) Everyone knows the Great Escape, a busy student pub with pub grub (great burgers) and an

enviable terrace with a view over Place de la Riponne. From the aforementioned square, walk up staircase Escaliers de l'Université and turn right.

MAD
Club

(📞021 340 69 69; www.mad.ch; Rue de Genève 23; 🕙11pm-4am Thu-Sun) With five floors of entertainment, four dance floors and a restaurant called Bedroom, MAD (Moulin á Danse de Lausanne) is a mad sort of place, going strong since 1985 in the Flon area. Music can be anything (reggaeton, mashup, hardcore), the dress code is snappy, and 3rd-floor Jetlag Club is only for partygoers aged over 26. Sunday is gay night.

Le D! Club
Club

(📞021 351 51 40; www.dclub.ch; Place Centrale; 🕙11pm-5am Wed-Sat) DJs spin house in all its latest sub-forms at this heaving club. Take the stairs down from Rue du Grand-Pont and turn right before descending all the way into Place Centrale.

⭐ Entertainment

Lausanne is among Switzerland's busier night-time cities; look for free listings mag **What's Up** (www.whatsup.ch) in bars. The rejuvenated warehouse quarter Flon, with its vast central square, is the heart of the city's nightlife scene.

Le Romandie
Live Music

(📞021 311 17 19; www.leromandie.ch; Place de l'Europe 1a; 🕙10pm-4am Tue & Thu-Sat) Lausanne's premier rock club resides in a post-industrial location within the great stone arches of the Grand Pont. Expect live rock, garage and even punk, followed by DJ sounds in a similar vein.

Opéra de Lausanne
Opera

(📞021 315 40 20; www.opera-lausanne.ch; Av du Théâtre 12; 🕙box office noon-6pm Mon-Fri) Opera and classical music concerts presented in a recently refurbished building.

ℹ Information

Tourist Office (📞021 613 73 73; www.lausanne-tourisme.ch; Place de la Gare 9; 🕙9am-7pm) A handy branch of the local tourist office. A second branch can be found lakeside in **Ouchy** (📞021 613 73 21; www.lausanne-tourisme.ch; Place de la Navigation 6; 🕙9am-7pm Apr-Sep, to 6pm Oct-Mar).

Canton de Vaud Tourist Office (📞021 613 26 26; www.lake-geneva-region.ch; Av d'Ouchy 60; 🕙8am-noon & 1-5.30pm Mon-Fri) Provides hiking- and cycling-route brochures.

ℹ Getting There & Away
Boat

CGN (Compagnie Générale de Navigation; www.cgn.ch) Runs passenger boats around the lake and over to France, including some grand old steamers.

Train

You can travel by train to and from the following:
Bern Sfr32, 70 minutes, one or two an hour
Geneva Sfr21.80, 30 to 50 minutes, up to six hourly
Geneva Airport Sfr26, 50 minutes, up to four hourly

ℹ Getting Around
Car & Motorcycle

Parking in central Lausanne is a headache. In blue zones you can park for free (one-hour limit) with a time disk. Most white zones are meter parking.

Savvy Travel

The seven-day **Regional Pass Lake Geneva-Alps** (adult/child Sfr130/65) provides free bus and train travel in the Lake Geneva region for three days in seven and half-price travel on the other four days. It also gives 50% off CGN boat services and 25% off some cable cars (including up to Les Diablerets glacier). A five-day version yielding two days of free travel costs Sfr105/50. Holders of one of the various Swiss rail passes get 20% discount off the Regional Pass. Buy it online at www.sbb.ch or at train stations.

Public Transport

Buses and trolley buses service most destinations; the m2 Métro line (single trip/day pass Sfr1.90/Sfr8.80) connects the lake (Ouchy) with the train station (Gare) and the Flon district.

AROUND LAUSANNE

Head out of Lausanne, and wine tasting and gastronomy suddenly become key dominators, be it westbound along La Côte (the Coast) or eastbound towards jazz-famed Montreux along a lakeshore pretty enough to be called the Swiss Riviera. For dedicated wine buffs, a tasting pilgrimage to Lavaux's Unesco-protected vineyards is essential.

La Côte

Fantasy castles, imposing palaces and immaculately maintained medieval villages sprinkle the Coast – the luxuriant lakeshore between Lausanne and Geneva where more than half of the Canton de Vaud's wine, mostly white, is produced.

The train line from Geneva follows the course of the lake here, but arriving by a CGN paddle steamer – try to catch one of the beautifully restored belle époque ones – is definitely the more romantic option.

MORGES

POP 15,250

Some 12km west of Lausanne, the first town of importance is the wine-growing village of **Morges** (www.morges-tourisme.ch). A real highlight is the town's **Fête de la Tulipe** (tulip festival), mid-April to mid-May, which turns lakeside Parc de l'Indépendence into a vivid sea of colour.

Sights

Château de Morges Chateau
(www.chateau-morges.ch; Place du Port; adult/child Sfr10/3; ◷10am-5pm Jul & Aug, 10am-noon & 1.30-5pm Tue-Fri, 1.30-7pm Sat & Sun Mar-Jun & Sep-Nov) Dominating Morge's bijou port is the squat, four-turreted 13th-century Château de Morges built by Savoy duke Louis in 1286 and home to four military-

GENEVA & THE WEST LA CÔTE

Detour:
Coppet

Midway between Nyon and Geneva, this tightly packed medieval village is a delight to meander through with its lakeside warren of hotels and restaurants bowing at the feet of hilltop, 18th-century **Château de Coppet** (www.chateaudecoppet.ch; adult/child Sfr8/6; ◷2-6pm Apr-Oct). The rose-coloured stately home belonged to the wily Jacques Necker, Louis XVI's banker and finance minister. The pile, sumptuously furnished in Louis XVI style, became home to Necker's daughter, Madame de Staël, after she was exiled from Paris by Napoleon. In her literary salons here she entertained the likes of Edward Gibbon and Lord Byron.

inspired museums today. Don't miss the 10,000 toy soldiers on parade in the Musée de la Figurine Historique.

Sleeping & Eating

La Maison d'Igor Boutique Hotel €€
(☎021 803 06 06; www.maison-igor.ch; Rue St-Domingue 2; s/d from Sfr160/180) Igor Stravinsky's elegant old digs have been reborn as Morges' most charming boutique hotel, with eight individually and stylishly themed rooms (some with lake and Alp views) combining period features with contemporary details, a charming restaurant with a Mediterranean-influenced menu (mains Sfr28 to Sfr42), manicured grounds, a vegetable garden and a generous dollop of charm throughout, plus lovely service.

Café de Balzac Cafe €
(☎021 811 02 32; www.balzac.ch; Rue de Louis-de-Savoie 37; plat du jour Sfr22, mains Sfr24-35; ◷8am-6.30pm Tue-Fri, 9am-5.30pm

Sat, 11am-5.30pm Sun) Lovers of exotic hot chocolate, teas and dishes with an Asian twist should make a pilgrimage to this gorgeous old-fashioned cafe, one block back from the lakeside promenade in the heart of the old centre.

Metropolis Café Bistro €€
(☏ 021 803 23 33; Rue de Louis-de-Savoie 20; mains Sfr26-39; ⏰ 7am-midnight Mon-Wed, to 1am Thu, to 2am Fri & Sat, 9am-midnight Sun; 🛜) Dine beneath parasols around an age-old stone fountain outside or on vintage flexi-plastic inside at this hybrid eating-drinking space that morphs into a happening bar after dark. Food is fusion and creative, and nicely done.

NYON

POP 19,200

Of Roman origin but with a partly Celtic name (the 'on' comes from *dunon,* which means fortified enclosure), Nyon is a pretty lake town pierced at its hilltop-heart by the gleaming white turrets of a fairy-tale château and a tasty lunch address.

Sights

Château de Nyon Chateau
(www.chateaudenyon.ch; Place du Château) Nyon's castle was started in the 12th century, modified 400 years later and now houses the town's **Musée Historique et des Porcelaines** (www.chateaudenyon.ch; Place du Château; adult/child Sfr8/free; ⏰ 10am-5pm Tue-Sun Apr-Oct, 2-5pm Tue-Sun Nov-Mar) and, in its old stone cellars, the **Caveau des Vignerons** (Place du Château; ⏰ 2-9pm Fri & Sat, 11am-8pm Sun) where you can taste different Nyon wines by local producers. Pay Sfr25 per person to sample two reds, two whites and one rosé with a plate of charcuterie, cheese and nibbles. Don't miss the sweeping view of Lake Geneva from the château terrace.

Left: Lavaux vineyards; **Below:** Place de la Palud (p74), Lausanne
(LEFT) ANTARES71 / GETTY IMAGES ©; (BELOW) INGOLF POMPE 84 / ALAMY ©

Eating

Hôtel-Restaurant de la Plage — Swiss €€

(☎022 364 10 35; www.hoteldelaplage.info; Chemin de la Falaise, Gland; mains Sfr37-86; ⏲noon-2pm & 7-9.30pm Tue-Sun Feb–mid-Dec; P 👪) This seemingly insignificant lakeside hotel 7km north of Nyon plays host to a packed dining room and terrace, thanks to a reputation for some of Lake Geneva's best *filets de perche*, pan-fried in a divinely buttery, herby secret-recipe sauce. Fries and a green salad are included and, unless you specify otherwise, you automatically get two (very large!) servings.

L'Auberge du Château — Italian €€

(☎022 361 00 32; www.aubergeduchateau.ch; Place du Château 8; mains Sfr28-50; ⏲8am-midnight, closed Sun Oct-Apr) Filling the pretty pedestrian square in front of Nyon's château, tables here look out on the *Sleeping Beauty* towers and lake beyond. Cuisine is Italian and creative – *taglierini* with figs, simple homemade gnocchi and authentic pizza cooked in a wood-fired oven.

Lavaux Wine Region

East of Lausanne, the mesmerising serried ranks of lush, pea-green vineyards that stagger up the steep terraced slopes above Lake Geneva form the Lavaux wine region – sufficiently magnificent to be a Unesco World Heritage site. One-fifth of the Canton de Vaud's wine is produced on these steep, gravity-defying slopes.

Walking between vines and wine tasting on weekends in local *caveaux* (wine cellars) are key reasons to explore the string of 14 villages beaded along this fertile and wealthy 40km stretch of shore. The tourist office in Montreux is the best place to pick up detailed information and maps.

LUTRY

POP 9500

This captivating medieval village, just 4km east of Lausanne, was founded in the 11th century by French monks. Its central **Église de St Martin et St Clément** was built in the early 13th century and there's a modest **château** a short way north. Stroll along the pretty waterfront and the slightly twee main street lined with art galleries, antique stores, the occasional cafe and wine cellar **Caveau des Vignerons** (📞078 661 26 25; Grand Rue 23; ☺5-9pm Tue-Fri, 11am-2pm & 5-9pm Sat) where you can taste wine by different local producers. The two main wine types are Calamin and Dézaley, and most of the whites (about three-quarters of all production) are made with the Chasselas grape.

Bus 9 links Lutry with Place St François in Lausanne. From Lutry a beautiful 5.5km **walking trail** winds east through vines and the tiny hamlets of **Le Châtelard** and **Aran** to the larger wine-making villages of **Grandvaux** and **Riex**. For staggering vine and lake views, hike up to **La Conversion** (3.8km) above Lutry and continue on the high trail to Grandvaux (4km).

CULLY

POP 1800

Lakeside Cully, 5km east of Lutry, is a lovely village for a waterfront meander and early evening mingle with *vignerons* (winegrowers) in its **Caveau des Vignerons** (www.caveau-cully.ch; Place d'Armes 16; tasting of 3 wines Sfr12; ☺5-9pm Thu-Sun Apr-Nov). Alternatively hike along the well-signposted walking trail uphill to the inland villages of **Riex** and **Epesses**, and have a tipple in a wine cellar there instead before looping back to Cully (4.4km).

Sleeping & Eating

Hotel Lavaux   Hotel €€

(📞021 799 93 93; www.hotellavaux.ch; Route Cantonal; s/d with lake view from Sfr164/210; 🅿🛜) Perfectly placed to take in views across the lake (south-facing rooms) or of the famous Lavaux vineyards (north-facing), Hotel Lavaux is the region's nattiest place to sleep. Rooms are sleekly simple and contemporary, and the restaurant a popular spot for local and seasonal fare. In summer, the outdoor terrace is a super spot to hang out with a sundowner.

Scenic Trips

The panorama of Lavaux vineyards staggering down to the lake is particularly fine from the back of a boat. CGN's daily Fabuleux Vignobles de Lavaux (Fabulous Lavaux Vineyards) cruise departs from Montreux and Vevey in the morning, with stops in Vevey, Lausanne, Lutry, Cully and Rivaz-St Saphorin. A Montreux circuit adult ticket costs Sfr50.

Another fun and easy way to lose yourself in green vines and blue lake views is aboard the **Lavaux Express** (www.lavauxexpress.ch; adult/child Sfr15/6; ☺Tue-Sun Apr-Oct), a tractor-pulled tourist train that chugs through Lavaux' vineyards and villages. Pick from two routes: Lutry CGN boat pier up to the wine-growing villages of Aran and Grandvaux (one hour return trip), or Cully pier to Riex, Espesses and Dézaley (1¼ hour).

In season, the **Train de Caveaux** (www.lavauxexpress.ch; adult/child Sfr25/6; ☺6.30pm Fri-Sun May–mid-Sep) chugs from Lutry to a local *caveau* (cellar bar) where you can taste wine. The **Lavaux Panoramic** (www.lavaux-panoramic.ch; ☺Sat & Sun Apr-Oct) is another train that runs twice-daily circular vineyard trips from Chexbres to St-Saphorin (adult/child Sfr12/6, 1½ hours) and Chardonne (adult/child Sfr15/6, two hours).

Detour:
Rivaz to Chardonne

Lavaux Vinorama (☎021 946 31 31; www.lavaux-vinorama.ch; Route du Lac 2; ⏱10.30am-8.30pm Mon-Sat, to 7pm Sun, closed Mon & Tue Nov-Jun), a thoroughly modern tasting and discovery centre 5km east of Cully in Rivaz, is the best place to discover the various appellations of the Lavaux vineyards. Opened in 2010, it sits in a designer bunker at the foot of a terraced vineyard by the lake and is fronted by a shimmering 15m-long bay window decorated with 6000 metallic pixels inspired by the veins of a vine leaf. Inside, a film evokes a year in the life of a wine-growing family and, in the state-of-the-art **Espace Dégustation**, you can sample dozens of different wines.

The region's most picturesque town is **St-Saphorin**, a medieval town with a church that dates from 1530 and with heavenly views over the lake. Grab a wine, coffee or full meal at **Auberge de l'Onde** (☎021 925 49 00; www.aubergedelonde.ch; menus Sfr85-150; ⏱noon-2pm & 7-9.30pm Wed-Sun).

Villa Le Lac (www.villalelac.ch; Route de Lavaux 21; adult/child Sfr12/6; ⏱10am-5pm Fri-Sun Jun-Sep), 2.8km east in Corseaux, was built by Le Corbusier between 1923 and 1924. The little white lakefront house with a functional rooftop sun deck and ribbon windows is the perfect overture to the world-renowned Swiss architect's better-known work. Each summer the house hosts a different exhibition.

From the village of **Chardonne**, uphill from Corseaux, there are some lovely **walking trails**, including the kid-easy **Boucle Chardonne** (2.8km) that starts and ends at the funicular station and swoops in a circle through pea-green vines.

If arriving by train, alight at Cully and head east on foot for 15 minutes, or catch a (less-frequent) train to Epesses.

Auberge du Raisin   Hotel €€

(☎021 799 21 31; www.aubergeduraisin.ch; Place de l'Hôtel de Ville 1; r from Sfr150) This grand old hotel-restaurant started taking in weary travellers in the 15th century. One of Lavaux' finest dining establishments, its rotisserie cooks up a lavish meaty meal and offers a creative take on fish dishes (mains Sfr35 to Sfr52). In summer, head to the terrace for superb views over the lake to France. Advance reservations are essential.

SWISS RIVIERA

Stretching east to Villeneuve, the Swiss Riviera rivals its French counterpart as a magnet for the rich and famous. Magnificent belle époque paddle steamers cruise the lake as they did in 1910, treating passengers to a banquet of gourmet views and paparazzi glimpses of otherwise-hidden lakeside properties, while trains saunter from the shore to perfect mountain scenes. All this barely an hour's drive from ski spots, in a climate so mild that palm trees and other subtropical flora flourish.

....

Vevey

POP 18,900

Lakeside Vevey exudes a certain under-stated swankiness with its tiny but perfect Old Town, lakeside central square and promenades, stylish dining, unusual museums and treasure trove of little boutiques made for post-lunch browsing. Don't miss Charlie Chaplin, signature 'little tramp' cane in hand, posing on the waterfront.

Sights

Alimentarium   Museum

(☎021 924 41 11; www.alimentarium.ch; Quai Perdonnet; adult/child Sfr12/free; ⏱10am-5pm Tue-Fri, to 6pm Sat & Sun) Nestlé's

Detour:
Aigle

An absolute must for anyone with a passion for wine or turreted castles, Aigle (population 9700), at the southeast end of Lake Geneva, is the capital of the Chablais wine-producing region in southeast Vaud. Grapes grown on the vines carpeting the gentle slopes here make some of Switzerland's best whites.

Two thousand years of wine-making is explored in the compelling **Musée de la Vigne et du Vin** (www.museeduvin.ch; Place du Château 1; adult/child Sfr11/5; ◷10am-6pm Jul & Aug, closed Mon Apr-Jun, Sep & Oct, 10am-4pm Tue-Sun Jan-Mar, Nov & Dec), a thoroughly modern and interactive wine museum inside Aigle's fairy-tale château. The six hands-on digital experiments – indulge in your own Chasselas grape harvest, make wine etc – in the 'lab' are particularly fun.

Afterwards, cross the castle courtyard to the 13th-century **Maison de la Dîme** and peek at whatever temporary exhibition is on upstairs (entry included in the wine museum ticket price).

There are several other equally atmospheric places to lunch in the narrow old-world lanes on the approach from Aigle's new town to the old, château-crowned part of Aigle known as the Quartier du Cloître. Nearing the château, the streets smell of red wine as you pass the cellars of local *vignerons*.

Aigle **tourist office** (☎024 466 30 00; www.aigle-tourisme.ch; Rue Colomb 5; ◷8.30am-noon & 1.30-6pm Mon-Fri, 8.30am-noon Sat Apr-Oct) is a 10-minute walk from the château, in the new town. Regular trains link Lausanne (Sfr15.60, 30 minutes) with Aigle via Montreux.

headquarters have been in Vevey since 1814, hence its presence in the form of this museum dedicated to nutrition and all things edible, past and present. Boring it is not. Its displays are clearly meant to entertain as well as inform, starting with the gigantic silver fork that sticks out of the water in front of the lakeside mansion (a great picnic spot thanks to the handful of wooden chairs screwed into the rocks here on the lakeshore).

✖ Eating & Drinking

Le Littéraire   Cafe €
(☎021 922 42 00; Quai Perdonnet 33; ◷9am-9pm; 🛜) Take the local town library, add a trendy cafe with ceiling-to-floor windows facing the lake and a summertime terrace, and you get this local favourite. Check the blackboard outside for the good-value *plat du jour* (Sfr18.50).

Le Mazot   Swiss €€
(☎021 921 78 22; Rue du Conseil 7; mains Sfr12-36; ◷11am-2pm & 6pm-midnight Mon, Tue & Thu-Sat, 6pm-midnight Sun) In the heart of the Old Town, this tiny restaurant with quintessential striped canopy and flower-box pavement terrace is an institution of classic local cooking. Steaks and horse meat fillets in a legendary house sauce (secret recipe) dominate the offerings.

Denis Martin   Molecular €€€
(☎021 921 12 10; www.denismartin.ch; Rue du Château 2; tasting menu from Sfr368; ◷from 7pm Tue-Sat, closed 3 weeks Jul-Aug & 2 weeks Dec-Jan) Charismatic and engaging, chef Denis Martin is one of the country's biggest names in Swiss contemporary cooking and molecular cuisine. His tasting menu – think Michelin-starred – is a thrilling succession of 20-odd different bite-sized taste sensations, served in a traditional 17th-century mansion a block from the lake. Reservations essential.

ℹ️ Information

Tourist Office (☏ 084 886 84 84; www.
montreux-vevey.com; Grande Place 29; ◷ 9am-
6pm Mon-Fri, to 3pm Sat, to 1pm Sun May-Sep,
9am-noon & 1-5.30pm Mon-Fri, 9am-1pm Sat
Oct-Apr) On the square in the former market
building.

ℹ️ Getting There & Away

Vevey is linked by train to Lausanne (Sfr10.60, 15
to 25 minutes) and Montreux (Sfr3.50, five to 10
minutes).

Montreux

POP 25,500

In the 19th century, writers, artists and
musicians (Lord Byron and the Shelleys
among them) flocked to this pleasing
lakeside resort and it has remained a
magnet ever since. Peaceful walks along
a lakeshore beaded with 19th-century
hotels, a mild microclimate, a hilltop Old
Town, the famous two-week **Montreux
Jazz Festival** (www.montreuxjazz.com) in
July, and a fabulous 13th-century fortress
are its main drawcards.

◉ Sights

Queen Studio Experience
Historic Site

(www.mercuryphoenixtrust.com; Rue du Théâtre
9, Casino Barrière de Montreux; ◷ 10.30am-
10pm) `FREE` Queen recorded seven albums
in this lovingly preserved studio (they also
owned the joint from 1979 to 1993), and
a visit here will give you a strong sense
of their oeuvre and relationship with the
town. Charming paraphernalia (handwritten lyric notes and the like) means this
shrine of sorts definitely has a kind of
magic.

The experience also offers the
possibility of mixing tracks and signing
the wall outside the studio's door, making
it a hands-on affair. Other luminaries who
have used the hallowed space include
David Bowie, Iggy Pop and the Rolling
Stones.

Freddie Mercury Statue
Monument

(Place du Marché) Year-round, fresh flowers
adorn the feet of this 3m-tall statue of
Freddie Mercury, 'lover of life, singer of
songs', in front of Montreux' old covered
market on the waterfront.

Lake Geneva boardwalk, Montreux

EXPRESSO / GETTY IMAGES ©

KEN WELSH / GETTY IMAGES ©

★ Don't Miss
Château de Chillon

From the waterfront in Montreux, the fairy-tale **Chemin Fleuri** (Flower Path) – a silky smooth promenade framed by flowerbeds positively tropical in colour and vivacity – snakes dreamily along the lake for 4km to the magnificent stone hulk of lakeside Château de Chillon. Occupying a stunning position on Lake Geneva, this oval-shaped 13th-century fortress is a maze of courtyards, towers and halls filled with arms, period furniture and artwork. The landward side is heavily fortified, but lakeside it presents a gentler face.

Chillon was largely built by the House of Savoy and taken over by Bern's governors after Vaud fell to Bern. Don't miss the medieval frescos in the **Chapelle St Georges** and the spooky Gothic **dungeons**.

The fortress gained fame in 1816 when Byron wrote *The Prisoner of Chillon*, a poem about François Bonivard, thrown into the dungeon for his seditious ideas and freed by Bernese forces in 1536. Byron carved his name into the pillar to which Bonivard was supposedly chained. Painters William Turner and Gustave Courbet subsequently immortalised the castle's silhouette on canvas, and Jean-Jacques Rousseau, Alexandre Dumas and Mary Shelley all wrote about it.

Count 45 minutes to walk from Montreux to Chillon, or take trolley bus 1. CGN boats and steamers – a wonderful way to arrive – call at Château de Chillon from Lausanne (adult return Sfr53, 1¾ hours), Vevey (Sfr23, 50 minutes) and Montreux (Sfr17, 15 minutes).

NEED TO KNOW
☏ 021 966 89 10; www.chillon.ch; Av de Chillon 21; adult/child Sfr12.50/6; ☉ 9am-7pm Apr-Sep, 9.30am-6pm Mar & Oct, 10am-5pm Nov-Feb, last entry 1hr before close

🛏 Sleeping & Eating

Tralala Hôtel Boutique Hotel €€
(📞 021 963 49 73; www.tralalahotel.ch; Rue du Temple 2; r/ste from Sfr110/200; ❄ @ 📶) This boutique references Montreux' extraordinary musical heritage and is perched up high above the lake in the old part of town. Rooms come in three sizes – S ('Small & Sexy'), L or XL – and each pays homage to a different artist, giving guests the chance to sleep with Aretha Franklin, David Bowie and 33 other famous musicians.

Hôtel La Rouvenaz Hotel €€
(📞 021 963 27 36; www.rouvenaz.ch; Rue du Maré 1; s/d/ste from Sfr180/260/420; @ 📶) A stylish family-run spot with its own tasty Italian restaurant downstairs and wine bar next door, you cannot get any closer to the lake or the heart of the action. Its six rooms are simple, but pleasant; most have at least a lake glimpse. Low season prices plummet.

Hôtel Masson Historic Hotel €€
(📞 021 966 00 44; www.hotelmasson.ch; Rue Bonivard 5; r from Sfr190; P 📶) In 1829 this vintner's mansion was converted into a hotel. The old charm has remained intact and the property, set in magnificent grounds, is on the Swiss Heritage list of the country's most beautiful hotels. It lies back in the hills southeast of Montreux, best reached by taxi.

Restaurant du Pont Brasserie €€
(📞 021 963 25 20; www.restaurantdupont.ch; Rue du Pont 12; mains Sfr28-42; ⏱ 11am-2.30pm & 5.30-11.30pm Wed-Sat, 11am-11.30pm Sun) Situated in a solid old building high up in the Old Town, the summer terrace here is a riot of blooms, and the soundtrack is that of water rushing down to the lake and the Golden Pass train. The menu specialises in brasserie staples, big salads and very good seafood dishes with a Portuguese touch.

ℹ Information

Tourist office (📞 084 886 84 84; www.montreux-vevey.com; Rue du Théâtre 5; ⏱ 9am-6pm Mon-Fri, 9.30am-5pm Sat & Sun) Staff here will help book hotels – a must at festival time.

ℹ Getting There & Away

From Lausanne, some three trains an hour (Sfr12.40, 20 to 35 minutes) serve Montreux. Montreux is also on the scenic Golden Pass route to the Bernese Oberland.

Bern, Basel & the Northwest

Easily one of the most charming capitals on the planet, Bern's 15th-century Old Town is fairy-tale-like with its terraced stone buildings, covered arcades, clock towers and cobbled streets. When Swiss politicians had to pick a capital it leapt out as the unthreatening choice: Geneva was too French, Zürich too German. Bern was just right.

Tucked up against the French and German borders in the northwest corner of the country, business-like Basel straddles the majestic Rhine. The town is home to top-flight art galleries and boasts an enchanting Old Town.

A far cry from the staggering Alpine scenes more readily associated with Switzerland, a gentle corner in the northwest remains a 'secret'. From the evocative medieval towns of Fribourg and Neuchâtel to gorgeous medieval villages like Gruyères, it proffers sights and scapes off the tourist track.

Château de Gruyères (p115)
CLAUDE-OLIVIER MARTI / GETTY IMAGES ©

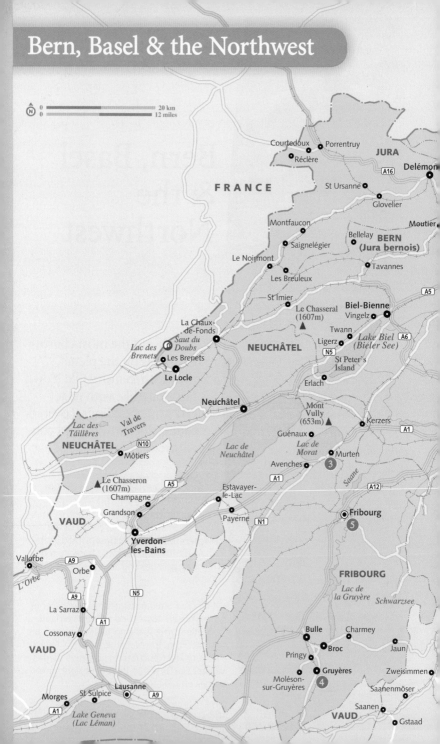

0
0
20 km
12 miles

Courtedoux
Porrentruy
JURA
Réclère
Delémont
A16
FRANCE
St Ursanne
Glovelier
Moutier
Montfaucon
Bellelay
BERN
Saignelégier
(Jura bernois)
Le Noirmont
Tavannes
Les Breuleux
St Imier
La Chaux-
de-Fonds
Le Chasseral
(1607m)
Biel-Bienne
Vingelz
Saut du
Doubs
NEUCHÂTEL
Twann
Lake Biel
A6
Lac des
Brenets
Les Brenets
Ligerz
(Bieler See)
N5
Le Locle
St Peter's
Island
Erlach
Neuchâtel
Mont
Vully
(653m)
Kerzers
A1
Lac des
Taillères
Val de
Travers
Guénaux
NEUCHÂTEL
N10
Lac de
Neuchâtel
Lac de
Morat
Murten
3
Môtiers
Avenches
A1
A12
Saane
Le Chasseron
(1607m)
A5
Estavayer-
le-Lac
Champagne
Fribourg
Grandson
Payerne
N1
5
VAUD
Yverdon-
les-Bains
Vallorbe
A9
Orbe
FRIBOURG
L'Orbe
A9
Lac de
la Gruyère
Schwarzsee
N5
La Sarraz
A1
Bulle
Charmey
Cossonay
Broc
Jaun
VAUD
Pringy
Zweisimmen
Moléson-
sur-Gruyères
Gruyères
4
Morges
St Sulpice
Lausanne
A9
Saanenmöser
Saanen
VAUD
A1
Lake Geneva
(Lac Léman)
Gstaad

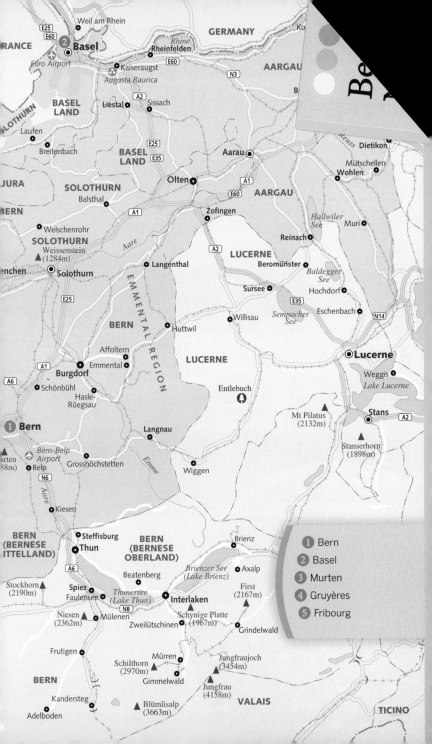

...ern, Basel & the Northwest's Highlights

Bern

Oddly overlooked by many, Switzerland's capital of Bern (p100) is a fantasyland of medieval buildings spilling down to the sinuous River Aare. Delightfully languid and laid-back, you can get lost for days in its 6km of covered arcades that squirrel away a bevy of boutique shops and galleries that mix modern commercial flair with the sort of deeply held conservatism you'd expect of the Swiss.

Basel

Greater Europe never feels closer to Switzerland than it does in Basel (p105), where France and Germany are a short toss of raclette away. International companies make their headquarters here and help support some excellent museums, including one of the nation's most-compelling, the Beyeler Foundation, which mixe media in both engaging and challenging ways. For more traditional pleasures, the Old Town is a gem. Left: *Fasnacht* celebrations (p11

CHRISTIAN KOBER / GETTY IMAGES ©

Murten

Like your best childhood fantasy, tiny Murten (p114) is an ancient walled town that seems almost toy-sized in scale. Yet it's the real deal: for various reasons, the locals never yanked down their defensive perimeter like most other European towns. The result is that you can dash back six centuries while exploring watchtowers, battlements and more. Go ahead, boil some oil.

Gruyères

The folks over in the Emmental region might object to us saying this, but Gruyères (p114) is the nearly namesake town for what could be the best Swiss cheese. And what a namesake it is! A beautiful downtown of ancient buildings tumbles down to its old streets where wheels echo on the cobblestones. Cheese factories and bistros serving fondue abound, and overlooking it all is a classic castle.

Above: Fondue, Gruyères

Fribourg

An exquisite Old Town peppered with lovely art museums and cafes ranging from historic to cutting-edge contemporary is what makes this small medieval town (p111) on the banks of the Sarine River so utterly and deeply appealing. The fact that locals on the west bank speak French, while those on the east bank speak Swiss German, only adds to the charm and originality.

Bern, Basel & the Northwest's Best...

Historic Spots

○ **Murten** A perfectly preserved jewel-box of an old walled town. (p114)

○ **Bern's Old Town** A warren of medieval covered arcades and old streets that tumble down towards the river. (p100)

○ **Château de Gruyères** A turreted beauty dating to the 15th century. Don't miss the dungeon. (p115)

○ **Basel's Old Town** Get lost on narrow 16th-century lanes. (p109)

Local Foods

○ **La Maison du Gruyère** Traditional factory for the namesake cheese. (p115)

○ **Fromagerie d'Alpage de Moléson** An even more old-fashioned Gruyère cheese dairy. (p115)

○ **Cailler** Another famous Swiss name offers factory tours and chocoate workshops. (p117)

Museums

○ **Fondation Beyeler** Brilliant and wide-ranging private collection, one of the country's best. (p106)

○ **Augusta Raurica** Remains of a large Roman town near Basel with an excellent museum. (p111)

○ **Zentrum Paul Klee** Eye-catching museum with thousands of stunning works by the prodigious artist. (p100)

○ **Historisches Museum Bern** Get to know Einstein at Bern's excellent history museum. (p101)

Need to Know

Outdoor Spots

o **Bärenpark** Bern's great attraction has several bears living in relative natural splendour. (p104)

o **Sentier des Fromageries** A beautiful trail amid the clanging cow bells of the dairy farms around Gruyères. See where the cheese comes from. (p116)

o **Neuchâtel** The town sits on the shores of its namesake lake, Switzerland's largest and noted for clear, fresh water. (p117)

Left: Basel Old Town (p105);
Above: Gruyères valley (p114)

ADVANCE PLANNING

o **Two months before** Start the diet as you'll be inundated with amazing chocolate and amazing cheese. Need we say more?

o **One month before** Give up on the diet and vow to start one *after* your trip. You don't want to skip on delicacies like Gruyère-filled fondue.

RESOURCES

o **Schweizer Mittelland Tourismus** (www.smit.ch) The tourist office for the region around Bern.

o **Pays de Fribourg** (www.pays-de-fribourg.ch) Provides info on Fribourg and the surrounding region.

o **La Gruyère** (www.gruyere.com) Everything you want to know about the delicious, hard, nutty cheese.

o **Lonely Planet** (www.lonelyplanet.com/switzerland/bern) The low-down on the capital.

GETTING AROUND

Train Frequent trains in all directions make getting around this part of Switzerland as easy as it is to tear off the wrapper on your chocolate bar. Bern is an excellent hub.

Car As always, a car will let you get off the beaten path and make visiting outlying attractions – like cheese and chocolate factories – that much easier.

BE FOREWARNED

o **Summer** Basel is often the warmest part of Switzerland in summer and can get almost sweaty on May days. Elsewhere, mild weather makes a visit ideal as you can hike around the verdant countryside, especially Gruyères and Neuchâtel.

o **Winter** Don't expect downhill skiing in this region but the Swiss are good at adopting the German love of Christmas markets, which can be found on central squares everywhere. Bern in particular has late fall and wintertime festivals starting with the legendary Onion Market on the fourth Monday in November.

Bern, Basel & the Northwest Itineraries

Some of Switzerland's best Old Towns are in this region (think Bern and Murten to start) along with some of the best local foods (think chocolate and cheese).

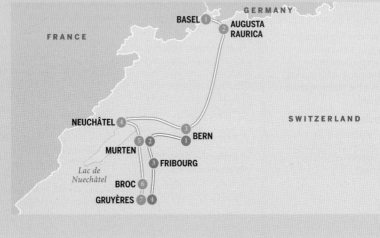

HISTORY & CHEESE
BERN TO GRUYÈRES

Start in Switzerland's surprising and enticing capital, ❶ **Bern** (p100). Wander the Old Town and say hello to its namesake bears in the Bärenpark (p104). Retrace the steps of Albert Einstein in the Einstein Haus (p103).

A quick train ride and you are in ❷ **Murten** (p114), a medieval town where you can spend half a day happily exploring its stone walls.

Stop in ❸ **Fribourg** (p111) to stroll its 12th-century Old Town (p111), admire wacky art creations in the Espace Jean Tinguely-

Niki de Saint Phalle (p111), and climb the 74m-tower of Cathédrale de St Nicolas de Myre (p112) for panoramic views.

End in ❹ **Gruyères** (p114) with a splendid castle and cheese as the star. Visit La Maison du Gruyère (p115) or Fromagerie d'Alpage de Moléson (p115) to see how the iconic Swiss cheese is made, taste, and walk afterwards along a spider's web of beautiful hiking paths.

A SWISS TASTE
BASEL TO GRUYÈRES

1 Basel (p105) combines old world allure with modern flash. Take in the sweep of the Rhine River and visit the Fondation Beyeler (p106) with its incredible art collection.

Take a train or drive to **2 Augusta Raurica** (p111) in Kaiseraugst, which preserves the ruins of a lare Roman town that originated more than 2000 years ago. From here hit **3 Bern** (p100), worth a day or more of your time. Admire the ancient Zytglogge, an ancient iconic clock tower and explore the centuries-old streets. Don't-miss museums include the Zentrum Paul Klee (p100), which exhibits many of the Cubist works by the master.

Train it over to **4 Neuchâtel** (p117) on the beautiful shores of its vast lake. Go for a stroll and try the local soft cheese. Nip back around the lake and wander along the old walls of **5 Murten** (p114). Maybe climb the steps a few extra times as you want to be hungry: first at **6 Broc**, where you can enjoy the famous Cailler chocolate factory (p117) and second at **7 Gruyères** (p114), which makes one of the world's most popular cheeses, a key ingredient of luscious Swiss fondue.

Roman ruins of Augusta Raurica (p111)

Discover Bern, Basel & the Northwest

At a Glance

○ **Bern** The Swiss capital is worthy of the honour thanks to its beautiful old architecture and parks.

○ **Basel** (p105) Museums and an old quarter good for exploring.

○ **Murten** (p114) Medieval town with a perfectly preserved wall.

○ **Gruyères** (p114) Almost as tasty as its namesake cheese.

○ **Fribourg** (p111) Experience Switzerland's French-German language divide.

Bern's Zytglogge

MERTEN SNIJDERS / GETTY IMAGES ©

BERN

POP 127,515 / ELEV 540M

Wandering its picture-postcard Old Town, with arcaded stone streets and a provincial, laid-back air, it is hard to believe that Bern (Berne in English and French) is the capital of Switzerland – but it is, plus a Unesco World Heritage site to boot.

Indeed, on the city's long, cobbled streets, lined with 15th-century terraced buildings and fantastical folk figures frolicking on fountains since the 16th century, you feel as if you're in some kind of dizzying architectural canyon.

◎ Sights

Zentrum Paul Klee Museum
(📞 031 359 01 01; www.zpk.org; Monument im Fruchtland 3; adult/child Sfr20/7, audioguide Sfr6; ◷10am-5pm Tue-Sun) Bern's answer to the Guggenheim, Renzo Piano's architecturally bold 150m-long wave-like edifice houses an exhibition space that showcases rotating works from Paul Klee's prodigious and often-playful career. Interactive computer displays and audioguides help interpret the Swiss-born artist's work. Next door, the fun-packed **Kindermuseum Creaviva** (📞 031 359 01 61; www.creaviva-zpk.org; Monument im Fruchtland 3; ◷10am-5pm Tue-Sun) **FREE** lets kids experiment with hands-on art exhibits or create original artwork with the atelier's materials during the weekend **Five Franc Studio** (www.creaviva-zpk.org/en/art-education/5-franc-studio; admission Sfr5; ◷10am-4.30pm Sat & Sun). Bus 12 runs from Bubenbergplatz direct to the museum.

Zytglogge
Clock Tower

(Marktgasse) Bern's most famous Old Town sight, this ornate clock tower once formed part of the city's western gate (1191–1256). Crowds congregate to watch its revolving figures twirl at four minutes before the hour, after which the chimes begin. Tours enter the tower to see the clock mechanism from May to October; contact the tourist office for details. The clock tower supposedly helped Albert Einstein hone his special theory of relativity, developed while working as a patent clerk in Bern.

Historisches Museum Bern
Museum

(Bern Historical Museum; ☎ 031 350 77 11; www.bhm.ch; Helvetiaplatz 5; adult/child Sfr13/4, incl Einstein Museum Sfr18/8; ⏰10am-5pm Tue-Sun) Tapestries, diptychs and other treasures vividly illustrate Bernese history from the Stone Age to the 20th century in this marvellous castle-like edifice, the best of several museums surrounding Helvetiaplatz. The highlight for many is the 2nd floor, devoted to a superb permanent exhibition on Einstein.

Münster
Cathedral

(www.bernermuenster.ch; Münsterplatz 1; tower adult/child Sfr5/2; ⏰10am-5pm Mon-Sat, 11.30am-5pm Sun May–mid-Oct, noon-4pm Mon-Fri, 10am-5pm Sat, 11.30am-4pm Sun rest of year) Bern's 15th-century Gothic cathedral boasts Switzerland's loftiest spire (100m); climb the dizzying 344-step spiral staircase for vertiginous views. Coming down, stop by the **Upper Bells** (1356), rung at 11am, noon and 3pm daily, and the three 10-tonne **Lower Bells** (Switzerland's largest). Don't miss the main portal's **Last Judgment**, which portrays Bern's mayor going to heaven, while his Zürich counterpart is shown into hell. Afterwards, wander through the adjacent **Münsterplattform**, a bijou clifftop park with a sunny pavilion cafe.

Kunstmuseum
Museum

(☎ 031 328 09 44; www.kunstmuseumbern.ch; Hodlerstrasse 8-12; adult/child Sfr7/free; ⏰10am-9pm Tue, to 5pm Wed-Sun) Bern's Museum of Fine Arts houses Switzerland's

Bern Don't Miss List

CHRISTINE LAUTERBURG, SINGER

1 MATTE
Matte is a lovely quarter near the River Aare with old houses and a lot of clubs and bars. We like to start at one and keep wandering, visiting many. It's pretty by day and very fun by night, and the river is right alongside.

2 REITHALLE
Everyone thinks Switzerland is so tidy and orderly but they haven't seen the **Reithalle** (www.reitschule.ch). It was built in 1897 as a riding school, so it has a huge indoor space. Later it was a squat and you can still find its wild past. Local people love it. Here you can see many concerts, theatre, other performances, film and pretty much anything that's experimental. It's not far from the main train station.

3 BREITENRAIN
Breitenrain is a quiet quarter with French flair and a real feel for the culture. It's on the east side of the river and it's fun to wander its quiet streets and visit one of the tempting restaurants.

4 MARZILIBAD
In summer we all take a dip in this **open-air swimming pool** (www.aaremarzili.ch; ⏰May-Sep) right beside the Aare River. We work on our tans and play on the huge lawns, foosball tables and other sports. You have to be a really strong swimmer to go in the river itself, so the pool is perfect – and it's free!

5 GURTEN
From Gurten, a hilly neighbourhood near Bern, you can see the whole city. It's a pretty place to walk and it's easy to get to. Catch a tram from the main station (direction: Wabern), exit at Gurtenbahn and walk on the top. There's also a little train that goes up the hill. Have dinner in the nice restaurant and then have a good stroll back down.

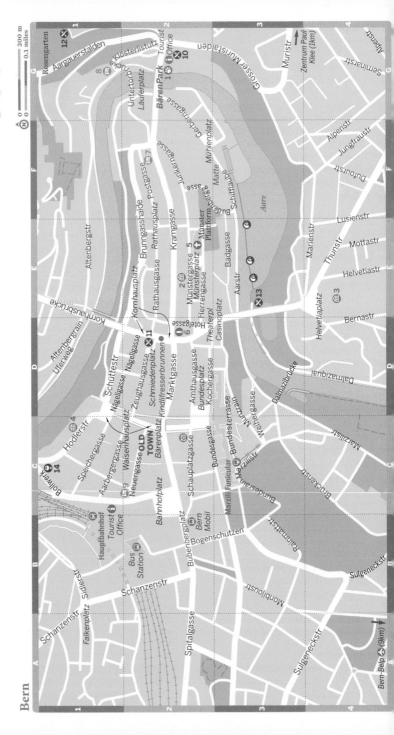

BERN, BASEL & THE NORTHWEST BERN

oldest permanent collection, ranging from an exquisite early Renaissance *Madonna and Child* by Fra Angelico to 19th- and 20th-century works by the likes of Hodler, Monet and Picasso.

Einstein-Haus Bern   Museum
(🕿 031 312 00 91; www.einstein-bern.ch; Kramgasse 49; adult/student Sfr6/4.50; ⊙10am-5pm Mon-Sat mid-Feb–Mar, 10am-5pm daily Apr–mid-Dec) Housed in the humble apartment that Einstein shared with his young family while working at the Bern patent office, this small museum includes a 20-minute biographical film telling Einstein's life story. Displays trace the development of Einstein's general equation $E=mc^2$ and the sometimes poignant trajectory of his family life.

🛏 Sleeping

Hotel Landhaus   Hotel €
(🕿 031 348 03 05; www.landhausbern.ch; Altenbergstrasse 4; dm Sfr38, s Sfr80-130, d Sfr120-180, q Sfr200-220; P ⊖ @ 🛜) Fronted by the river and Old Town spires, this well-known boho hotel offers a mix of stylish six-bed dorms, family rooms and doubles. Its buzzing ground-floor cafe and terrace attracts a cheery crowd. Breakfast (included with private rooms) costs Sfr8 extra for dorm-dwellers.

Hotel Belle Epoque   Hotel €€
(🕿 031 311 43 36; www.belle-epoque.ch; Gerechtigkeitsgasse 18; s Sfr170-200, d Sfr240-280; ⊖ @ 🛜) Conveniently situated along Bern's main arcaded thoroughfare is this romantic Old Town hotel with opulent art nouveau furnishings. TVs are tucked away

into steamer-trunk-style cupboards to preserve the belle époque design ethos.

Hotel Schweizerhof   Luxury Hotel €€€
(🕿 031 326 80 80; www.schweizerhof-bern.ch; Bahnhofplatz 11; s Sfr284-640, d Sfr364-790; P ✳ @ 🛜) This classy five-star offers lavish accommodation with excellent amenities and service. A hop, skip and a jump from the train station, it's geared for both business and pleasure.

✖ Eating

For a munch between meals, nothing beats the *Brezeln* (pretzels) smothered in salt crystals or sunflower, pumpkin or sesame seeds from kiosks at the train station.

Terrasse & Casa   Swiss, Italian €€
(🕿 031 350 50 01; www.schwellenmaetteli.ch; Dalmaziquai 11; mains Sfr21.50-48.50; ⊙Terrasse 9am-12.30am Mon-Sat, 10am-11.30pm Sun, Casa 11.45am-2.30pm & 6-11.30pm Tue-Fri, 6-11.30pm Sat, 11.45am-11pm Sun) Dubbed 'Bern's Riviera', this twinset of eateries enjoys a blissful Aare-side setting. Terrasse is a glass shoebox with wooden decking over the water, sun loungers overlooking a weir (illuminated at night) and comfy sofa seating, perfect for lingering over Sunday brunch, a drink, or midweek two-course lunch specials (Sfr25). Next door, Casa serves Italian delicacies in a cosy, country-style house.

Altes Tramdepot   Swiss €€
(🕿 031 368 14 15; www.altestramdepot.ch; Am Bärengraben; mains Sfr18-37; ⊙11am-12.30am) At this cavernous microbrewery, Swiss

TAMBAKO THE JAGUAR / GETTY IMAGES ©

⭐ Don't Miss
BärenPark

A popular etymological theory is that Bern got its name from the bear (Bär in German), when the city's founder, Berthold V, duke of Zähringen, snagged one here on a hunting spree. To the dismay of some, there was still a 3.5m-deep cramped bear pit in the city until 2009, when it was replaced by today's spacious 6000-sq-metre open-air riverside park dotted with trees and terraces, in which a number of bears now roam freely.

NEED TO KNOW

Bear Park; www.baerenpark-bern.ch; ⊙9.30am-5pm

specialities compete against wok-cooked stir-fries for your affection, and the microbrews go down a treat: sample three different varieties for Sfr10.80, or four for Sfr14.50.

Restaurant Rosengarten
Swiss, Mediterranean €€
(☎031 331 32 06; www.rosengarten.be; Alter Aargauerstalden 31b; mains Sfr19.50-43.50; ⊙9am-midnight) Panoramically perched on a hilltop adjacent to Bern's rose garden, this restaurant is nicest in warm weather, when you can enjoy the terrace seating. From grilled Provençal-style pork

cutlets to marinated lamb with tzatziki, the menu spans multiple culinary worlds.

Kornhauskeller Mediterranean €€€
(☎031 327 72 72; www.bindella.ch; Kornhaus-platz 18; mains Sfr24-55; ⊙11.45am-2.30pm & 6pm-12.30am) Fine dining takes place beneath vaulted frescoed arches at Bern's ornate former granary, now a stunning cellar restaurant serving Mediterranean cuisine. Beautiful people sip cocktails alongside historic stained-glass windows on the mezzanine; in its neighbouring cafe, punters lunch in the sun on the busy pavement terrace.

🍷 Drinking & Nightlife

Bern has a healthy drinking scene. Several spaces, such as Kornhauskeller and Altes Tramdepot, are as much drinking as dining spots.

Kapitel Bar, Club

(www.kapitel.ch; Bollwerk 41; ⏲11am-11.30pm Tue & Wed, to 3.30am Thu, to 5am Fri, 4pm-6am Sat) Starting as a restaurant where businesspeople come for light, healthy lunches, this award-winning venue morphs by evening into a bar, recognised around town for its savvy bartenders and unparalleled choice of cocktails. Come 11pm, it transforms again into one of Bern's hippest clubs, with international DJs spinning electronic music.

ℹ Information

Tourist Office (☏031 328 12 12; www.bern.com; Bahnhoftplatz 10a; ⏲9am-7pm Mon-Sat, to 6pm Sun) Street-level floor of the train station. City tours, free hotel bookings, internet access. There's also a branch near the bear park (☏031 328 12 12; www.bern.com; Bärengraben; ⏲9am-6pm Jun-Sep, 10am-4pm Mar-May & Oct, 11am-4pm Nov-Feb).

ℹ Getting There & Away

Train

By rail, there are services at least every hour to most major Swiss destinations, including Geneva (Sfr49, two hours), Basel (Sfr39, one hour),
Interlaken Ost (Sfr27, 55 minutes) and Zürich (Sfr49, one hour).

ℹ Getting Around

Bicycle

You can borrow a free bike, scooter or skateboard from Bern Rollt (☏031 318 93 50; www.bernrollt.ch; Milchgässli; first 4hr free, per additional hr Sfr1; ⏲8am-9.30pm), which you'll find adjacent to the train station. You'll need ID and Sfr20 as a deposit.

Bus, Tram & Funicular

Get around on foot or hop on a bus or tram run by Bern Mobil (www.bernmobil.ch; tickets 30min/1hr/1 day Sfr2.30/4.30/11.80). Tickets, available from machines at stops, cost Sfr2.30 for journeys up to six stops (valid 30 minutes) or Sfr4.20 for a single journey within zones 1 and 2 (valid one hour).

A funicular, the Drahtseilbahn Marzili (Drahtseilbahn Marzili; www.marzilibahn.ch; one way Sfr1.20; ⏲6.15am-9pm), descends from behind the parliament building to the riverside Marzili quarter.

BASEL

POP 165,566 / ELEV 273M

Tucked up against the French and German borders in Switzerland's northwest corner, businesslike Basel straddles the majestic Rhine. The town boasts top-flight art galleries, museums and avant-garde architecture, and an enchanting Old Town, all mostly concentrated in

---

Old Town Fountains

Bern's flag-festooned medieval centre is an attraction in its own right, with 6km of covered arcades and cellar shops and bars descending from the streets. After a devastating fire in 1405, the wooden city was rebuilt in today's distinctive grey-green sandstone.

Bern'S 11 decorative **fountains** (1545) depict historic and folkloric characters. Most are along Marktgasse as it becomes Kramgasse and Gerechtigkeitsgasse, but the most famous lies in Kornhausplatz: the **Kindlifresserbrunnen** (Ogre Fountain) of a giant snacking on children!

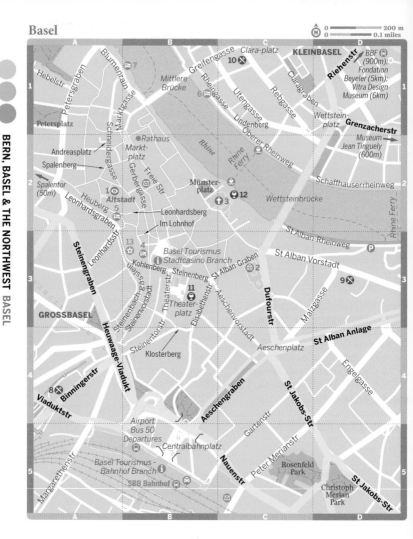

Grossbasel (Greater Basel) on the south bank of the Rhine.

Basel is also the closest Switzerland comes to having a seaport; the Rhine is navigable for decent-sized ships from this point until it reaches the North Sea in Holland.

◉ Sights

Note that most museums are closed on Monday. For more on the city's 30-plus museums and galleries, grab the relevant tourist office booklet or check out www.museenbasel.ch.

Fondation Beyeler   Museum
(061 645 97 00; www.fondationbeyeler.ch; Baselstrasse 101, Riehen; adult/child Sfr25/6; 10am-6pm, to 8pm Wed) This astounding private-turned-public collection, assembled by former art dealers Hildy and Ernst Beyeler, is housed in a long, low, light-filled, open-plan building, designed by Italian architect Renzo Piano. The varied exhibits juxtapose 19th- and 20th-

Basel

century works by Picasso and Rothko against sculptures by Miró and Max Ernst and tribal figures from Oceania. Take tram 6 to Riehen from Barfüsserplatz or Marktplatz.

Museum Jean Tinguely   Museum
(📞 061 681 93 20; www.tinguely.ch; Paul Sacher-Anlage 2; adult/child Sfr18/free; ⏰ 11am-6pm Tue-Sun) Built by leading Ticino architect Mario Botta, this museum showcases the playful, mischievous and downright wacky artistic concoctions of sculptor-turned-mad scientist Jean Tinguely. Push-buttons next to some of Tinguely's 'kinetic' sculptures allow visitors to set them in motion. It's great fun to watch them rattle, shake and twirl, with springs, feathers and wheels radiating at every angle, or to hear the haunting musical sounds produced by the gigantic *Méta-Harmonies* on the upper floor. Catch bus 31 from Claraplatz.

Vitra Design Museum   Museum
(www.design-museum.de; Charles-Eames-Strasse 1, Weil am Rhein; adult/child €10/free; ⏰ 10am-6pm) Pop across the German border to this dazzling design museum adjoining the factory complex of famous furniture manu-

facturer Vitra. The main building, designed by Guggenheim Bilbao architect Frank Gehry, is surrounded by an ever-expanding bevy of installations by other cutting-edge architects. Watch contemporary furniture being made (and purchase it) at the adjoining VitraHaus, or hurtle down Carsten Höller's whimsical, corkscrewing 38m-long **Vitra Slide**, inaugurated in 2014. Catch bus 55 from Kleinbasel's Claraplatz to the Vitra stop (25 minutes).

Münster   Cathedral
(Cathedral; www.baslermuenster.ch; Münsterplatz; ⏰ 10am-5pm Mon-Fri, to 4pm Sat, 11.30am-5pm Sun) Blending Gothic exteriors with Romanesque interiors, this 13th-century cathedral was largely rebuilt after an earthquake in 1356. Renaissance humanist Erasmus of Rotterdam (1466–1536), who lived in Basel, lies buried in the northern aisle. Groups of two or more can climb the soaring Gothic towers (per person Sfr5). Behind the church, leafy **Münster Pfalz** offers sublime Rhine views.

Kunstmuseum   Museum
(Museum of Fine Arts; 📞 061 206 62 62; www.kunstmuseumbasel.ch; St Alban-Graben 16; adult/child Sfr15/free; ⏰ 10am-6pm Tue-Sun) Undergoing a major overhaul in 2015/16, Basel's superb art museum houses the world's largest collection of Holbeins and a fine impressionist wing, among thousands of other works. A brand new modernist wing adjacent to the main museum is planned. In preparation for the grand reopening, the museum will close from February 2015 to April 2016; check the website for updates.

🛏 Sleeping

Book ahead if coming for a convention or trade fair. When you check in, remember to ask for your mobility ticket, which entitles you to free use of public transport.

Der Teufelhof   Boutique Hotel €€
(📞 061 261 10 10; www.teufelhof.com; Leonhardsgraben 49; s Sfr148-578, d Sfr174-648; 📶) Stylish and centrally located, 'The Devil's Court' fuses two hotels into

one: the nine-room Kunsthotel, with parquet floors and crisp white bedding, and the larger Galeriehotel annexe, in a former convent next door. Two excellent restaurants, the gourmet-caliber Bel Étage and the less formal **Atelier** (☎061 261 10 10; www.teufelhof.com/en/restaurants/atelier.html; Leonhardsgraben 49; weekday lunch specials Sfr27, 2-/3-/4-/5-course dinner menus Sfr59/77/95/113; ⏰noon-2pm & 6.30-10pm;), cap it all off.

Hotel Krafft Hotel €€

(☎061 690 91 30; krafftbasel.ch; Rheingasse 12; s Sfr110-150, d Sfr175-265;) Design-savvy urbanites will love this renovated historic hotel. Sculptural modern chandeliers dangle in the creaky-floored dining room overlooking the Rhine, and minimalist Japanese-style tea bars adorn each landing of the spiral stairs.

Au Violon Hotel €€

(☎061 269 87 11; www.au-violon.com; Im Lohnhof 4; s Sfr120-160, d Sfr140-180;) The doors are one of the few hints that quaint, atmospheric Au Violon was a prison from 1835 to 1995. Most of the rooms are two cells rolled into one and either look onto a delightful cobblestone courtyard or have views of the Münster. Sitting on a leafy hilltop, it also has a well-respected restaurant with outdoor seating in summer.

Les Trois Rois Luxury Hotel €€€

(☎061 260 50 50; www.lestroisrois.com; Blumenrain 8; s/d from Sfr350/570;) Indisputably Basel's most prestigious address, this classic riverfront hotel blends the dignified elegance of bygone times (waltz in the ballroom, anyone?) with indispensable mod cons, including sauna and gym access, and state-of-the-art Bang & Olufsen media centres in every room.

Eating

Basel's culinary culture benefits from the city's location against the French and German borders and its long history of immigration, especially from southern Europe.

Volkshaus Basel Brasserie, Bar €€

(☎061 690 93 11; volkshaus-basel.ch; Rebgasse 12-14; mains Sfr28-56; ⏰11.30am-2pm & 6-10.30pm Mon-Fri, 11.30am-10.30pm Sat) This stylish new Herzog & de Meuron–designed venue is part resto-bar, part gallery and part performance space. For relaxed dining, head for the atmospheric beer garden, in a cobblestoned courtyard decorated with columns, vine-clad walls and light-draped rows of trees. The menu ranges from brasserie classics (*steak-frites*) to more innovative offerings (shrimp and cucumber salad with sour cream lavender dressing). The bar is open 10am to 1am Monday to Saturday.

Acqua Italian €€€

(☎061 564 66 66; www.acquabasilea.ch; Binningerstrasse 14; 2-course menus Sfr45-72, 3-course Sfr62-89; ⏰noon-2pm & 7pm-midnight Tue-Fri, 7pm-midnight Sat;) A glam post-industrial atmosphere reigns at these converted waterworks, with brown-leather banquettes and chandeliers inside bare-stone and concrete walls, surrounded by candlelit outdoor patios. Build your own two- to three-course meal from the delectable menu of Tuscan-inspired meat, fish and vegetarian offerings. Basel's beautiful people drink in the attached lounge bar.

St Alban Stübli Swiss, Mediterranean €€€

(☎061 272 54 15; www.st-alban-stuebli.ch; St Alban Vorstadt 74; mains Sfr32-57; ⏰11.30am-3pm & 6pm-midnight Mon-Fri year-round, plus 6pm-midnight Sat Oct & Nov) Set in a quiet street, this cosy tavern is an exquisite haven for fine Swiss- and Mediterranean-themed cuisine. On any given night, the menu might feature smoked salmon and duck breast salad, gourmet burgers with Appenzeller cheese, a cold soup trilogy (gazpacho, melon-mint and tomato-basil), or veal cordon bleu with market vegetables and rösti.

Drinking & Nightlife

For good bar-hopping, explore the area between Barfüsserplatz and Klosterberg or the Rheingasse/Utengasse neighbourhood in Kleinbasel.

ARPAD BENEDEK / GETTY IMAGES ©

⭐ Don't Miss
Altstadt

Begin exploring Basel's delightful medieval Old Town in **Marktplatz**, dominated by the astonishingly vivid red facade of the 16th century **Rathaus** (above). From here, climb 400m west along Spalenberg through the former artisans' district to the 600-year-old **Spalentor** city gate, one of only three to survive the walls' demolition in 1866. Along the way, linger in captivating lanes such as Spalenberg, Heuberg and Leonhardsberg, lined by impeccably maintained, centuries-old houses.

Chill am Rhy   Bar
(www.chillamrhy.ch; unter dem Münster; ⊙5pm-1am late Jun-Aug) Backlit with neon colours and boasting incomparable Rhine views, this summer-only outdoor bar consists of a series of tents and tables dreamily straddling a cobblestoned terrace on the steep hillside below the Münster.

Campari Bar   Bar
(✆061 272 83 83; www.restaurant-kunsthalle.ch; Steinenberg 7; ⊙10am-midnight Mon-Thu, to 1am Fri & Sat, 12.30pm-midnight Sun) A soothing spot for an upscale cocktail moment, especially in warmer weather, when you can listen to the water play of the adjacent Tinguely Fountain.

⭐ Entertainment

For comprehensive entertainment listings, pick up the bi-weekly *Basel Live* brochure from the tourist office. In August, **Orange Cinema** (www.orangecinema.ch) brings nightly outdoor film screenings (most in English) to the cobblestones of Münsterplatz.

Bird's Eye Jazz Club   Jazz
(✆061 263 33 41; www.birdseye.ch; Kohlenberg 20; ⊙8-11.30pm Tue-Sat Sep-May, Wed-Sat Jun-Aug) One of Europe's top jazz dens attracts local and headline foreign acts. Concerts start at 8.30pm.

HANS-PETER MERTEN / GETTY IMAGES ©

⭐ Don't Miss
Fasnacht

Basel's renowned 72-hour carnival kicks off at 4am on the Monday after Ash Wednesday with the **Morgestraich**, when streetlights are extinguished and a procession winds through the central district. Participants wear elaborate costumes and masks. The main parades are on Monday and Wednesday afternoons. Tuesday is devoted to children and to an open-air display of colourful lanterns in Münsterplatz.

NEED TO KNOW
www.fasnachts-comite.ch

ℹ Information

Basel Tourismus (☎061 268 68 68; www.basel.com) SBB Bahnhof (SBB Bahnhof; ⏰8.30am-6pm Mon-Fri, 9am-5pm Sat, to 3pm Sun & holidays); Stadtcasino (Steinenberg 14; ⏰9am-6.30pm Mon-Fri, to 5pm Sat, 10am-3pm Sun & holidays) The Stadtcasino branch organises two-hour city walking tours (adult/child Sfr18/9, in English or French upon request) starting at 2.30pm Monday to Saturday May through October, and on Saturdays the rest of the year.

ℹ Getting There & Away

Air

EuroAirport (MLH or BSL; ☎+33 3 89 90 31 11; www.euroairport.com) serves Basel (as well as Mulhouse in France and Freiburg in Germany). Located 5km north in France, it has flights to numerous European cities.

Train

Basel has two main train stations: the Swiss/French train station SBB Bahnhof, in the city's south, and the German train station BBF (Badischer) Bahnhof, in the north.

Two trains an hour run from SBB Bahnhof via Olten to Geneva (Sfr73, 2¾ hours). As many as seven, mostly direct, leave every hour for Zürich (Sfr32, 55 minutes to 1¼ hours).

❶ Getting Around

Bus 50 runs every seven to 30 minutes from 5am to midnight between the airport and SBB Bahnhof (Sfr4.20, 20 minutes). Buy tickets at the machine outside the arrivals hall (bills, coins and credit cards accepted). The trip by taxi (📞 061 325 27 00, 061 444 44 44) costs around Sfr40.

If you're not staying in a hotel in town, tram and bus tickets cost Sfr2.10 for short trips (maximum four stops), Sf3.40 for longer trips within Basel and Sfr9 for a day pass.

CANTON DE FRIBOURG

Canton de Fribourg (population 273,200) tots up 1671 sq km on the drawing board. Pre-Alpine foothills rise grandly around its cold craggy feet; Gruyéres with its sprinkling of small mountain resorts pierces its heart; and Fribourg heads the canton up north, where pretty lakeside villages slumber between vineyards and fruit orchards.

What makes this canton fascinating is its *Röstigraben* (linguistic divide): west speaks French, east speaks German.

Fribourg

POP 36,633 / ELEV 629M

Nowhere is Switzerland's language divide felt more keenly than in Fribourg (Freiburg) or 'Free Town', a medieval city where inhabitants on the west bank of the Sarine River speak French, and those on the east bank of the Sanne speak German.

◎ Sights

Espace Jean Tinguely – Niki de Saint Phalle   Museum

(📞 026 305 51 40; www.mahf.ch; Rue de Morat 2; adult/child Sfr6/free; ⊙11am-6pm Wed & Fri-Sun, 11am-8pm Thu) FREE Jump on the button to watch the *Retable de l'Abondance Occidentale et du Mercantilisme Totalitaire* (1989–90) make its allegorical

Detour:
Augusta Raurica

By the Rhine east of Basel, the Roman ruins of **Augusta Raurica** (📞 061 552 22 22; www.augustaraurica. ch; ⊙10am-5pm) FREE in Kaiseraugst are Switzerland's largest. They're the last remnants of a colony founded in 43 BC, the population of which grew to 20,000 by the 2nd century AD. Today, restored features include an open-air theatre and several temples. There's also a **Römermuseum** (Roman Museum; Giebenacherstrasse 17; adult/reduced Sfr8/6; ⊙10am-5pm) with an authentic Roman house among its exhibits.

The train from Basel to Kaiseraugst takes 11 minutes (Sfr5.30); it's then a 10-minute walk to the site.

comment on Western opulence. Created in memory of Fribourg's modern artistic prodigy, Jean Tinguely (1925–91), in a tramway depot dating to 1900, this nifty space showcases his machines alongside the boldly out-there creations of French-American artist Niki de Saint Phalle (1930–2002) who worked with Tinguely from the 1950s until his death.

Old Town   Neighbourhood

The 12th-century Old Town was laid out in simple fashion, with Grand-Rue as the main street and parallel Rue des Chanoines/Rue des Bouchers devoted to markets, church and civic buildings. The settlement later spread downhill to the river: the bridges here – stone **Pont du Milieu** (Middle Bridge, 1720) and roof-covered **Pont du Berne** (1653) – proffer great views. Fribourg's famous **Tilleul de Morat**

(Morat Linden Tree) stands in front of the Renaissance **town hall** on Grand-Rue.

Musée d'Art et d'Histoire   Museum

(☎026 305 51 40; www.mahf.ch; Rue de Morat 12; adult/child Sfr8/free; ⊙11am-6pm Tue, Wed & Fri-Sun, to 8pm Thu) FREE Fribourg's art and history museum, with an excellent collection of late-Gothic sculpture and painting, is housed in Hôtel Ratzé. Gothic meets Goth in the underground chamber, where religious statues are juxtaposed with some of Tinguely's sculptural creations. Don't miss the museum's walled, bench-clad garden, pierced by a Niki de Saint Phalle sculpture – it's a beautiful picnic spot.

Cathédrale de St Nicolas de Myre   Cathedral

(www.cathedrale-fribourg.ch; Rue des Chanoines 3; tower adult/child Sfr3.50/1; ⊙9.30am-6pm Mon-Fri, 9am-4pm Sat, 2-5pm Sun, tower 10am-noon & 2-5pm Mon-Fri, 10am-4pm Sat, 2-5pm Sun

Apr-Oct) Before entering this brooding 13th-century Gothic cathedral, contemplate the main portal with its 15th-century sculptured portrayal of the Last Judgment. On your right upon entering, inside the Chapelle du Saint Sépulcre, is a sculptural group (1433) depicting Christ's burial with exceptional lifelikeness and movement.

A 368-step hike up the cathedral's 74m-tall **tower** affords its visitors wonderful views.

🛏 Sleeping & Eating

Hôtel du Faucon   Hotel €

(☎026 321 37 90; www.hotel-du-faucon.ch; Rue de Lausanne 76; s/d from Sfr100/125; ⊙reception 7.30am-9pm; 🛜) A golden falcon marks the spot. Well placed between boutiques on Fribourg's main pedestrian street, this contemporary hideout offers an exceptional price-quality ratio. Furnishings are modern and mod-cons are cleverly dotted throughout. Breakfast Sfr15.

Le Mondial
Cafe, Restaurant €

(☑ 026 321 27 72; www.cafelemondial.ch; Rue de l'Hôpital 39; mains Sfr17-25; ⏲ 8am-11pm Mon-Thu, 8am-midnight Fri, 9am-midnight Sat) This airy cafe-restaurant – a stylish mix of modern and vintage – gets packed at lunchtime and after work when students and suited businesspeople tuck into its house specialities, warm *tartines* (grilled toasts with extravagant toppings, and a salad) and moreish *ballons* (burger-style creations). Not to be missed between meals are its feisty homemade cakes.

Restaurant du Gothard
Bistro €€

(☑ 026 322 32 85; Rue du Pont Muré 16; mains Sfr23.50-36; ⏲ 9am-11.30pm Mon, Tue, Thu & Fri, 8am-11.30pm Sat & Sun) Tinguely's old eating haunt is a kitsch mix of 19th-century furnishings, Niki de Saint Phalle drawings and nostalgia-tinged bric-a-brac. Pick from the day's specials chalked on blackboards; fondues and horse steaks are firm favourites.

Auberge de la Cigogne
Modern European €€€

(☑ 026 322 68 34; www.aubergedelacigogne.ch; Rue d'Or 24; 2-/3-course lunch menu Sfr21/25, dinner menus Sfr38-90; ⏲ 10am-2.30pm & 6.45pm-midnight Tue-Sat) This highly revered establishment, in a beautiful riverside mansion from the 1770s, has some outstanding *prix fixe* menus, which feature stellar desserts such as *crème brûlée aux framboises parfumé à lavande* (with raspberries and perfumed with lavender). Lunch here is exceptional value.

❶ Information

Tourist Office (☑ 026 350 11 11; www.fribourgtourism.ch; Place Jean Tinguely 1, Equilibre; ⏲ 9am-6pm Mon-Fri year-round, 9am-3pm Sat May-Sep, 9-12.30pm Sat Oct-Apr) Mountains of information on Fribourg town and region, planted on the ground floor of Fribourg's most striking contemporary building (have no fear – it won't fall on your head). The tourist office also runs an information desk in the cathedral, open weekends too.

113

Detour:
Café Tivoli

The little town of Châtel-St-Denis, 45km south of Fribourg via the A12, warrants a visit solely for its legendary fondue *moitié-moitié* (made with Gruyére and Vacherin Fribourgeois) cooked up at **Café Tivoli** (☎021 948 70 39; www.cafetivoli.ch; Place d'Armes 18; fondue per person Sfr24; ⊙8am-11pm Sun-Thu, 8am-midnight Fri & Sat), a much-loved, family-run and very traditional restaurant. Expect to pay Sfr24 per person for your share of the caquelon's bounty.

ℹ Getting There & Away

Trains travel hourly to/from Neuchâtel (Sfr20.80, 55 minutes), and more frequently to Geneva (Sfr40, 1½ hours) and Bern (Sfr13.60, 20 minutes). Regular trains run to Lausanne (Sfr24, 45 to 55 minutes).

Murten
POP 6450 / ELEV 450M

This German-speaking medieval village on the eastern shore of Murten See (Lac de Morat) isn't called Murten (Morat) – derived from the Celtic word *moriduno* meaning 'fortress on the lake' – for nothing. In May 1476 the Burgundy duke Charles the Bold set off from Lausanne to besiege Murten – only to have 8000 of his men butchered or drowned in Murten Lake during the Battle of Murten. The fortifications that thwarted the duke (who escaped) create a quaint little lakeside town well worth a visit.

◉ Sights & Activities

Murten is a cobblestone three-street town crammed with arcaded houses. A string of hotel-restaurants culminating in

a 13th-century castle (closed to visitors) line Rathausgasse; shops and eateries stud parallel Hauptgasse, capped by the medieval **Berntor city gate** at its eastern end; while parallel Deutsche Kirchgasse and its western continuation, Schulgasse, hug the city ramparts.

Scale the wooden **Aufstieg auf die Ringmauer** (rampart stairs) behind the **Deutsche Kirche** (German Church; Deutsche Kirchgasse) to reach the covered walkway traversing part of the sturdy medieval walls. It's magical at sunset.

Late April to mid-October **Navigation Lacs de Neuchâtel et Morat** (☎032 729 96 00; www.navig.ch; ⊙Apr–mid-Oct) runs tours of Lake Murten (Sfr19, 70 minutes).

🛏 Sleeping & Eating

Hotel Murtenhof & Krone   Hotel €
(☎026 672 90 30; www.murtenhof.ch; Rathausgasse 1-5; s/d from Sfr120/160; ⊙restaurant 11am-10pm; 🛜) The Murtenhof, in a 16th-century patrician's house, is a spacious space to sleep. Its terrace restaurant (mains Sfr26 to Sfr42) cooks up dreamy lake views and traditional cuisine; local perch filets and fera are highlights.

ℹ Getting There & Around

From the train station (Bahnhofstrasse), 300m south of the city walls, hourly trains run to/from Fribourg (Sfr11.60, 30 minutes), Bern (Sfr13.60, 35 minutes) via Kerzers (Sfr4.60, nine minutes) and Neuchâtel (Sfr12.60, 25 minutes).

Navigation Lacs de Neuchâtel et Morat runs seasonal boats to/from Neuchâtel.

Gruyères
POP 1800 / ELEV 830M

Cheese and featherweight meringues drowned in thick cream are what this dreamy village is all about. Its heart is cobbled, a castle is its crowning glory and hard AOC Gruyère (the village is Gruyéres but the 's' is dropped for the cheese) has been made for centuries in its Alpine pastures.

YVES MARCOUX / DESIGN PICS / GETTY IMAGES ©

⭐ Don't Miss
Château de Gruyères

This bewitching turreted castle, home to 19 different Counts of Gruyères who controlled the Sarine Valley from the 11th to 16th centuries, was rebuilt after a fire in 1493. Inside, view period furniture, tapestries and modern 'fantasy art' and watch a 20-minute multimedia film. Don't miss the short footpath that weaves its way around the castle. A combined ticket covering the château and La Maison de Gruyères cheese dairy costs Sfr14.50 (no child combo ticket).

NEED TO KNOW

📞 026 921 21 02; www.chateau-gruyeres.ch; Rue du Château 8; adult/child Sfr10/3; ⊙ 9am-6pm Apr-Oct, 10am-4.30pm Nov-Mar

◉ Sights & Activities

La Maison du Gruyère
Cheese Dairy

(📞 026 921 84 00; www.lamaisondugruyere.ch; Place de la Gare 3; adult/child Sfr7/3; ⊙ 9am-7pm Jun-Sep, to 6pm Oct-May) The secret behind Gruyère cheese is revealed in Pringy, 1.5km from Gruyères. Cheesemaking takes place three to four times daily between 9am and 11am and 12.30pm to 2.30pm. A combined ticket to the dairy and Château de Gruyères costs Sfr14.50.

Fromagerie d'Alpage de Moléson
Cheese Dairy

(📞 026 921 10 44; www.fromagerie-alpage. ch; Moléson-sur-Gruyères; adult/child Sfr5/2; ⊙ 9am-7pm May-Sep) At this 17th-century *fromagerie d'alpage* (mountain dairy), 5km southwest of Gruyères in Moléson-sur-Gruyères (elevation 1100m), cheese is made in summer using old-fashioned methods – watch how they do it at 10am daily. The Alpine chalet also sells cheese and serves fondue, *soupe du chalet* (a thick and hearty vegetable and potato soup topped with Gruyère double cream

115

If You Like...
Cute Towns

If you like Murten, you'll love these other cute old towns:

1 LOTHURN
This enchanting little town with a mellow cobblestone centre has one very big cathedral: the imposing, 66m-tall facade of St Ursus. Fountains, churches and city gates bolster Solothurn's claim to be Switzerland's most beautiful baroque town. There are two trains per hour to Bern.

2 ST URSANNE
The most enchanting town in the Jura region is medieval St Ursanne with its 12th-century Église Collégiale, a grand Gothic church. Ancient houses, the 16th-century town gates, a lovely stone bridge and a bevy of eating options on miniature central square, Place Roger Schaffer, tumble towards the Doubs River. The train station is 1km east of the centre.

3 RHEINFELDEN
Rheinfelden, 24km east of Basel, has a pretty Old Town. Several medieval city gates, defensive towers and parts of the old walls still stand. It's a short train ride from Basel.

4 MÔTIERS
In the Val de Travers, this bewitching town has a pretty castle, absinthe distilleries and cafe-bars with absinthe on the menu. Get the train from Neuchâtel (Sfr3.60, 35 minutes).

and cheese) and other typical mountain dishes in its restaurant.

Sentier des Fromageries Walking
Cheese is still produced in a couple of traditional mountain chalets with traditional shingle roofs along the Sentier des Fromageries (Cheese Dairy Path), a 7.3km trail that takes walkers through cow-specked green Gruyères pastures. Ask at the Maison du Gruyère for the brochure outlining the two-hour walk.

🛏 Sleeping & Eating

Cheese fondue is the natural star of every menu, irrespective of season (locals only eat fondue in winter); *moitié-moitié* is a mix of Gruyère and soft local Vacherin.

La Ferme du Bourgoz B&B €
(☑ 026 921 26 23; www.lafermedubourgoz. ch; Chemin du Bourgo 14; s/d from Sfr80/100; P) You'll sleep well thanks to the cheese dreams that a stay at the Murith family's cheesemaking home encourages. Simple, cosy rooms and farm-fresh breakfasts, plus chunks of homemade Gruyère for sale. Find the farm a five-minute walk from Gruyères train station.

Le Chalet de Gruyères Swiss €€
(☑ 026 921 21 54; www.chalet-gruyeres.ch; Rue du Bourg 53; fondues & raclettes from Sfr30; ⏰ noon-10pm) A quintessential Gruyères address with all-day dining, this cosy wooden chalet strung with cow bells oozes Alpine charm – and fodder (fondue, raclette, grilled meats). There's a flower-bedecked terrace in the warmer months, too.

ℹ Information

Tourist Office (☑ 026 921 10 30; www. gruyeres.ch; Rue du Bourg 1; ⏰ 9.30am-5.30pm Jul & Aug, shorter hours rest of the year)

ℹ Getting There & Around

Gruyères can be reached by hourly bus or train (Sfr16.20, one hour) from Fribourg (via Bulle).

CANTON DE NEUCHÂTEL

The focus of this heavily forested 800 sq km canton (population 171,700), northwest of its Fribourg counterpart, is Lac de Neuchâtel – the largest lake entirely within Switzerland. Canton capital Neuchâtel sits plumb on its northern shore and the gentle Jura Mountains rise to the north and west.

Neuchâtel

POP 33,474 / ELEV 430M

Its Old Town sandstone elegance, the airy Gallic nonchalance of its cafe life and the gay lakeside air that imbues the shoreline of its lake makes Neuchâtel disarmingly charming.

◉ Sights

Old Town   Neighbourhood

The Old Town streets are peppered with 18th-century mansions and fanciful gold-leaf fountains topped by anything from a banner-wielding knight, **Fontaine du Banneret** (Rue Fleury), to a maiden representing Justice, **Fontaine de la Justice** (Rue de l'Hôpital); see a copy on the street and the original in the Musée d'Art et d'Histoire.

Heading uphill along Rue du Château, walk through the medieval city gate to the **Prison Tower** (Rue Jehanne de Hochberg 5; admission Sfr2; ◷8am-6pm Apr-Sep).

🛏 Sleeping & Eating

Local specialities include tripe and *tomme neuchâteloise chaude* (baked goat's-cheese starter). Rue des Moulins and nearby Rue des Chavannes in the commune are the places to imbibe.

L'Aubier   Hotel €€

(☎032 710 18 58; www.aubier.ch; Rue du Château 1; s/d with sink Sfr85/120, s/d/tr/q with shower & toilet Sfr130/180/240/320) ◢ Soulful sleeping above one of Neuchâtel's greenest eating spaces is what this lovely nine-room, 4th-floor cafe-hotel is all about. Find it in an old building with diagonal-striped shutters peeping down on a sword-wielding knight.

Hôtel DuPeyrou   French €€€

(☎032 725 11 83; www.dupeyrou.ch; Av DuPeyrou 1; mains Sfr54-58, menu with/without wine Sfr154/95; ◷noon-2pm & 7-10pm Tue-Sat) DuPeyrou presides like a mini-Versailles over manicured gardens, somewhat incongruously in the town centre. Built between 1765 and 1770, it regales with gastro-

nomic dining in an 18th-century ambience. Its leafy green terrace is simply gorgeous and come autumn, game dishes stun.

♥ If You Like...
Chocolate

If you like chocolate (and who doesn't?), you'll love visits to some of Switzerland's most famous chocolate brands:

1 Cailler

(☎026 921 59 60; www.cailler.ch; Rue Jules Bellet 7, Broc; adult/child Sfr10/free; ◷10am-6pm Apr-Oct, 10am-5pm Nov-Mar) Factory tours at Maison Cailler take visitors on an extravagant twirl through its history, ending with a sweet chance to taste and buy chocolate in the factory shop. Even more fabulous are Cailler's chocolate workshops – themed, one- to 2½ hours long, some designed for children. Workshops cost Sfr20 to Sfr75 including factory tour, and must be reserved in advance via email or telephone. The factory is 2km north of Gruyères, in Broc.

2 Chocolaterie Walder

(Grand-Rue 1; ◷7.30am-6.30pm Tue-Fri, 7am-5pm Sat) In the biz since 1919, this third-generation chocolate maker in Neuchâtel creates *éclats* (square tablets of milk or dark chocolate studded with caramelmelised pumpkin seeds or roasted hazelnuts perhaps, or unusually flavoured with coriander, lemongrass and dill, saffron, cinnamon or absinthe).

ⓘ Getting There & Away

Boat

Navigation Lacs de Neuchâtel et Morat (p114) runs boats late April to mid-October to/from Murten (Sfr24, 1¾ hours) and Biel (Bienne; Sfr36, 2½ hours).

Train

From the train station, a 10-minute walk northeast of the Old Town, hourly trains run to/from Geneva (Sfr40, 1¼ to 1½ hours), Bern (Sfr19.20, 30 to 50 minutes), Basel (Sfr37, 1½ hours) and other destinations.

Bernese Oberland & Central Switzerland

Whether you're hiking a trail with a jaw-dropping view that never quite seems real, carving virgin powder on a crisp winter's morning, or riding some improbable combination of railways and cable cars, the Swiss Alps don't get more beautiful than this. Nowhere are the resorts more chocolate box, the peaks higher, the glaciers grander. Fittingly watched over by Mönch (Monk) and Jungfrau (Virgin), the Bernese Oberland sends spirits soaring to heaven. Meanwhile the dreamy city of Lucerne has old-world charm, a buoyant cultural scene and a stunning setting on the lake that bears its name. Ringing the town are fabled peaks like Mt Pilatus and Mt Rigi just waiting for you to ascend.

Mt Pilatus (p158)
PAWEL TOCZYNSKI / GETTY IMAGES ©

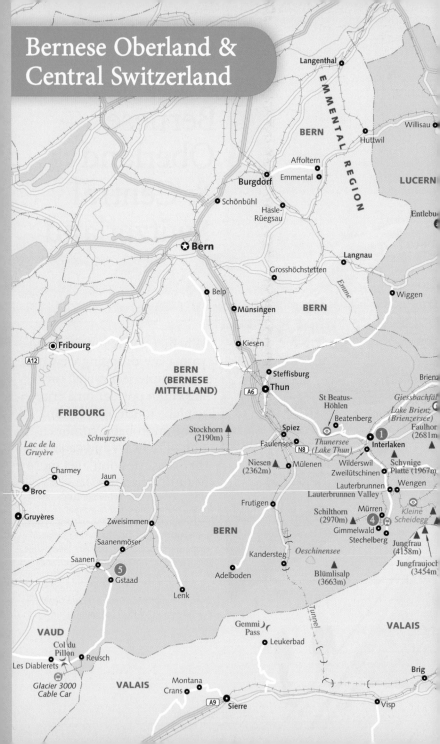

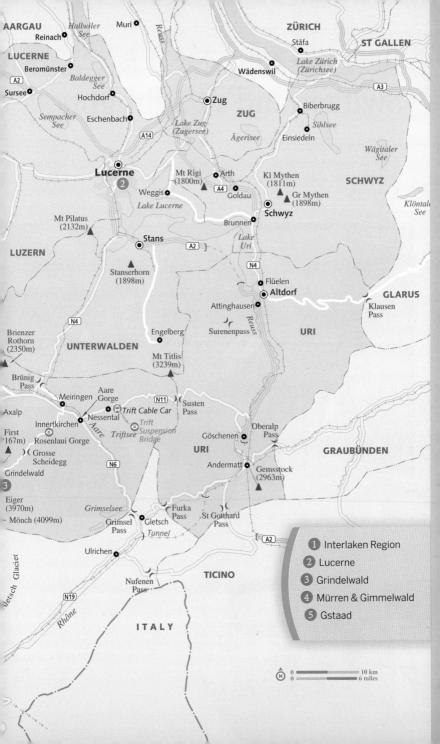

Bernese Oberland & Central Switzerland's Highlights

Interlaken Region

Just arriving on the train in this charming tourism outpost (p128) is a reward, with its views of the surrounding lakes. But those Alps looming large are Interlaken's raison d'être. This popular town is the gateway to the Jungfrau region, one of the most beautiful places on the planet.

2 Lucerne Outdoors

Cute as all hell is one description for Lucerne (p151) you're unlikely to challenge. And as you wander its Old Town you'll keep finding yet another reason to stay outside exploring its bridges, plazas and promenades. Before long you'll find yourself drawn along the aqua lake and to the surrounding peaks.

Grindelwald

Smaller than Interlaken but also quainter, Grindelwald (p135) is the forward outpost to the Jungfrau Alps. It has a wide range of adventure sports, and is well linked to any vista that captures your fancy. Red flowers spill out of window boxes and the chalet-style lodgings have the requisite woodsy quality and views of glaciers and iconic peaks that keep you transfixed for days.

ROBERTO SONCIN GEROMETTA / GETTY IMAGES ©

INGOLF POMPE / LOOK-FOTO / GETTY IMAGES ©

Mürren & Gimmelwald

Just reaching these two mountainside villages is fun. Cable cars and oddball trains combine to get you up from the valley below but also elevate you to something far better. Mürren (p143) has grandstand views of Eiger, Mönch and Jungfrau, while a short cow path away, Gimmelwald (p144) is a timeless vision of rural Switzerland.

Gstaad

Another one of those familiar Swiss resort names that conjures images of wealth and exclusivity, Gstaad (p149) is firstly simply a great place to hit the snow; secondly it boasts its own contingent of paparazzi all winter long. You can always find a stretch somewhere along the 220km of slopes where the crowds are a distant memory.

Bernese Oberland & Central Switzerland's Best…

Mountain Peaks

- **Jungfraujoch** Top of the heap for summit visits. The views go on and on. (p140)

- **Schilthorn** You'll recognise it from an old Bond movie; the ride up is pure fun. (p145)

- **Mt Titlis** Views of the Eiger, Mönch, Jungfrau and more. (p156)

Hikes

- **Grindelwald** Trails fan out across the Alps in all directions. Go for an hour or a week. (p135)

- **Kleine Scheidegg** More Alpine trails: up, down and all around. (p140)

- **Lauterbrunnen** Glaciers melt and the water crashes down in waterfalls you can hike to through beautiful forests. (p142)

- **Mürren** Meadows of wildflowers and impossibly beautiful vistas await. (p143)

Skiing

- **Jungfrau Region** Some 214km of prepared runs and 44 (and counting) ski lifts in one of the world's best settings spread over several gorgeous Alpine towns. (p134)

- **Gstaad** A chic and celebrity-filled setting with more than 250km of ski runs. (p149)

- **Kandersteg** More than 50km of cross-country ski trails in a beautiful river valley. (p149)

Need to Know

Nightlife

o **Interlaken** Daredevil adventurers, ski bums everywhere and vista-seeking visitors combine for year-round fun. (p128)

o **Lucerne** The cultured class of the region has remarkable concerts and chic bars – and yet you can still hear the odd cowbell. (p151)

o **Gstaad** Famed for highbrow food and drink, a place where half the people are used to seeing their names in bold type. (p149)

Left: Hikers embark on the Panoramaweg (p134); **Above:** Evening in Gstaad (p149)

ADVANCE PLANNING

o **Two months before** Sort out your accommodation in the major ski areas if travelling from mid-December to March; do the same for the Jungfrau region and Lucerne from June to September.

o **One month before** Book adventure sports activities with operators from May to September. The same goes for extreme winter sports in winter. If driving to car-free Wengen and Mürren, book the Interlaken train station garage.

RESOURCES

o **Swiss Panorama** (www.swisspanorama.com) See conditions at top peaks across the Alps.

o **Lucerne Hotels** (www.luzern-hotels.ch) Good local source for lodging in a popular city.

o **Jungfrau Region** (www.jungfrau.ch) Resort info, rail tickets and timetables, accommodation, webcams and more.

GETTING AROUND

o **Trains** From regular to rack, railways add to the fun of exploring the region.

o **Cable Cars** Where the rails end, cables arc up to the peaks, usually with gravity-defying views on the way.

o **Boats** From Lucerne, you can get boats to towns with links to the summits.

o **Walking** Hoofing it between Alpine spots is the reason for many a trip.

BE FOREWARNED

o **Seasons** Many businesses in the Alps close in April and from mid-October to mid-December.

o **Weather** Whether it's skiing, hiking or making an expensive summit journey, check the weather right up until the last minute and have a Plan B ready if nature isn't ready for you.

o **Passes** A Swiss or Eurail Pass alone will take you only so far into the Jungfrau region.

Bernese Oberland & Central Switzerland Itineraries

These itineraries take you to the heart of the Alps and their most jaw-dropping sights.

SWITZERLAND

LUCERNE 1 — Lake Lucerne

MT PILATUS 3 (2132M)

MT TITLIS 2 (3239M)

Brienzersee (Lake Brienz)

Thunersee (Lake Thun)

INTERLAKEN 1

WENGEN 6 5 — GRINDELWALD 2

LAUTERBRUNNEN 6

SCHILTHORN 8 (2970M) 7 MÜRREN

KLEINE SCHEIDEGG 3

JUNGFRAUJOCH (3454M) 4

3 DAYS

LUCERNE GLORIES
LUCERNE TO LUCERNE

Is there a more genteel city in Switzerland than ❶ **Lucerne** (p151)? Start by walking over one of its iconic wooden bridges. Then wander through the tidy streets to Lake Lucerne, which laps the heart of the city. Follow the north shore east for views of snow-clad Alps across the ice-blue waters. After a visit to the Verkehrshaus (p153), a fabulous museum dedicated to the country's incredibly diverse transportation, stop by Museum Sammlung Rosengart (p151) to revel in the beauty of painters from the impressionists onwards. After a night of music at a concert or lounge, set off in the morning for ❷ **Mt Titlis** (p156), one of the most breathtaking

Swiss peaks. A train to Engelberg is followed by four cable cars to the top (including one that spins). Here you'll find a fantasyland of glaciers and jagged peaks. Look southwest to see the backsides of the fabled Jungfrau peak and its mates.

Back in Lucerne for another day, board a lake steamer to start a fun-filled journey that includes a cog railway (a train that uses gears to climb) and puts you atop the comparatively modest ❸ **Mt Pilatus** (p158), where all of Lucerne and its lake stretch out before you.

BEST OF THE ALPS

INTERLAKEN TO SCHILTHORN

Look across the calming waters of Lakes Thun and Brienz from the ideally located **①Interlaken** (p128) as a sort of sensory respite from what's to come. Catch the train to **②Grindelwald** (p135) and plan your assault on the Alps, which loom almost overhead. Get a morning train up to **③Kleine Scheidegg** (p140), a barren crossroads 2000m up. Change to the legendary train through the mountain to **④Jungfraujoch** (p140), which at 3454m is one of the most famous high spots on the planet; glacier-clad peaks spread out before you.

Back in Kleine Scheidegg, ditch the train for the winding hiking path down the mountain to **⑤Wengen** (p143), a cliffside village with surrounding Alps in all directions. Spend a night or two and wander the myriad trails. Take a train down to **⑥Lauterbrunnen** (p142) and see glacier-fed waterfalls. Now head right back up another mountain by cable car to Grütschalp where you change to a mountain train to **⑦Mürren** (p143). Settle in here for another angle on the earth's most beautiful pageant. Finally take cable cars up to **⑧Schilthorn** (p145) where, on a clear day, you can see everywhere you've just been.

The Alpine village of Wengen (p143)

Discover Bernese Oberland & Central Switzerland

At a Glance

○ **Interlaken** Gateway city and hub to a world of Alpine adventures.

○ **Lucerne** (p151) Switzerland's most beautiful lakeside city has Alpine views, fine museums and excellent nightlife.

○ **Wengen** (p143) Prime location in a theatre of Alps.

○ **Titlis** (p156) Famed cable car ride brings you to sensational views amid glaciers.

Paraglider, Wengen (p143)
SASIPA MUENNUCH / GETTY IMAGES ©

INTERLAKEN

POP 5659 / ELEV 570M

Once Interlaken made the Victorians swoon with mountain vistas from the chandelier-lit confines of grand hotels; today it makes daredevils scream with adrenalin-loaded adventures. Straddling the glittering Lakes Thun and Brienz and dazzled by the pearly whites of Eiger, Mönch and Jungfrau, the scenery here is mind-blowing. Particularly, some say, if you're abseiling waterfalls, thrashing white water or gliding soundlessly above 4000m peaks.

Though the streets are filled with enough yodelling kitsch to make Heidi cringe, Interlaken still makes a terrific base for exploring the Bernese Oberland.

◎ Sights

Cross the turquoise Aare River for a mooch around Interlaken's compact and quiet old quarter, Unterseen.

Harder Kulm   Mountain
(www.harderkulm.ch) For far-reaching views to the 4000m giants, ride the **funicular** (adult/child return Sfr28/14; ⏱every 30 min 8.10am-6.25pm late Apr-Oct, plus 7-8.30pm Jul & Aug) to 1322m Harder Kulm. Many hiking paths begin here, and the vertigo-free can enjoy the panorama from the **Zweiseensteg** (Two Lake Bridge) jutting out above the valley. The wildlife park near the valley station is home to Alpine critters, including marmots and ibex.

Tourist Museum   Museum
(Obere Gasse 26; adult/child Sfr5/2; ⏱2-5pm Tue-Sun May–mid-Oct) This low-key museum sits on a cobbled, fountain-dotted square in Unterseen. The permanent exhibition presents

a romp through tourism in the region with costumes, carriages and other curios.

Heimwehfluh — Mountain

(www.heimwehfluh.ch; funicular adult/child return Sfr16/8, toboggan Sfr9/7; ⏲10am-5pm mid-Apr–late Oct) A nostalgic funicular trundles up to family-friendly Heimwehfluh for long views across Interlaken. Kids love the bob run down the hill – lay off the brakes to pick up speed.

🏃 Activities

Tempted to hurl yourself off a bridge, down a cliff or along a raging river? You're in the right place. Switzerland is the world's second-biggest adventure-sports centre and Interlaken is its busiest hub.

Almost every heart-stopping pursuit you can think of is offered here. You can white-water raft on the Lütschine, Simme and Saane Rivers, go canyoning in the Saxetet, Grimsel or Chli Schliere gorges, and canyon jump at the Gletscherschlucht near Grindelwald. If that doesn't grab you, there's paragliding, glacier bungee jumping, skydiving, ice climbing, hydrospeeding and, phew, much more.

Sample prices are around Sfr120 for rafting or canyoning, Sfr140 for hydrospeeding, Sfr130 to Sfr180 for bungee or canyon jumping, Sfr170 for tandem paragliding, Sfr180 for ice climbing, Sfr220 for hang-gliding, and Sfr430 for skydiving. A half-day mountain-bike tour will set you back around Sfr25.

Most excursions are without incident, but there's always a small risk and it's wise to ask about safety records and procedures.

The major operators able to arrange most sports from May to September include Alpinraft, Outdoor Interlaken and Swissraft. Advance bookings are essential.

Alpinraft — Adventure Sports

(☏033 823 41 00; www.alpinraft.com; Hauptstrasse 7; ⏲8am-6pm) Can arrange most sports, including canyoning, bungee jumping, rafting and ice climbing.

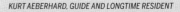

Local Knowledge

Interlaken Region Don't Miss List

KURT AEBERHARD, GUIDE AND LONGTIME RESIDENT

1 WATERFALLS

Take the Alpine train to Lauterbrunnen. Be impressed by the Staubbach Falls (p141), the highest waterfall in the Swiss Alps, and walk behind the falls. Continue travelling by a short bus ride to the spectacular **Trümmelbach** waterfalls (p141). Travel back to Interlaken by train, then take a **paddle steamer** (www.bls.ch) to **Giessbach** and you'll see more waterfalls on the way.

2 HIKING ON THE ETERNAL ICE

Three cogwheel trains transport you in about two hours from **Interlaken** (567m) to **Lauterbrunnen** (800m) to **Kleine Scheidegg** (2060m) to **Jungfraujoch** (3454m). From here, hike for one hour to the heart of the Swiss Alps, the **Mönchsjoch** hut at around 3700m.

3 FIVE CASTLE VISIT

From Interlaken take a **paddle steamer** to **Thun**. You'll see five castles, some dating back to the 15th century. Stop off at **Oberhofen** and/or **Spiez castles**: you can climb their watchtowers for good views. Back down at the lakeside, enjoy the beach and admire the swans.

4 IN & ABOVE THE CAVE

At **Beatus Caves** (www.beatushoehlen. ch) a fascinating underground world opens with lakes, wild water flows and impressive stalagmites; every few steps there's another surprise. Take a bus for a few minutes and change to a funicular to **Beatenberg**. Now catch a cable car to the **Niederhorn**, a great viewpoint nearly 2000m high; you'll see the turquoise waters of **Lake Thun** and the Alps behind. An easy one-hour walk brings you 100m higher to the **Gemmenalphorn**. Here you are surrounded by mountain flowers, ibexand cows. It's an Alpine dream.

129

Interlaken

Interlaken

⊙ Sights
1 Heimwehfluh Funicular.......................A5
2 Tourist Museum..................................A2

⊕ Activities, Courses & Tours
3 Alpinraft..D4
4 Outdoor Interlaken..........................D4
5 Skydive Switzerland – Scenic
   Air..D4
6 Vertical Sport.................................C3

⊜ Sleeping
7 Arnold's B&B....................................D3
8 Backpackers Villa Sonnenhof...........D3
9 Rugenpark B&B..................................A5
10 Victoria-Jungfrau Grand Hotel
   & Spa..C2

⊗ Eating
11 Benacus..A2
12 Sandwich Bar..................................B3
13 WineArt..C3

Outdoor Interlaken Adventure Sports

(📞033 826 77 19; www.outdoor-interlaken.
ch; Hauptstrasse 15; ⏰8am-7pm) One-stop
adventure sports shop.

Skydive Switzerland –
Scenic Air Scenic Flights

(📞033 821 00 11; www.skydiveswitzerland.
com; Hauptstrasse 26; ⏰7.30am-5pm Mon-
Fri; phone enquiries 7.30am-9pm Mon-Sat,
9am-9pm Sun) Arranges scenic flights,
skydiving and other activities.

🛏 Sleeping

Ask your hotel for the useful Interlaken
Guest Card for free bus transport as
well as discounts on various attractions
and sports facilities. Call ahead during
the low season, as some places close.

Rugenpark B&B B&B €

(📞033 822 36 61; www.rugenpark.ch;
Rugenparkstrasse 19; s Sfr87, d Sfr100-130, tr
Sfr126-165, q Sfr154-200; P🛜) Chris and
Ursula have worked magic to trans-
form this into an incredibly sweet B&B.
Rooms remain humble, but the place is
spotless and has been enlivened with
colourful butterflies, beads and travel
trinkets. our knowledgeable hosts are
always ready to help with local tips.

Backpackers Villa
Sonnenhof Hostel €

(📞033 826 71 71; www.villa.ch; Alpenstrasse
16; dm Sfr39.50-47, s Sfr69-79, d Sfr110-148;
P@🛜) Sonnenhof is a slick combination of ultramodern chalet and elegant art
nouveau villa. Dorms are immaculate, and
some have balconies with Jungfrau views.
There's also a relaxed lounge, a well-
equipped kitchen, a kids' playroom and a
leafy garden for mountain gazing. Special
family rates are available.

Sunny Days B&B €

(📞033 822 83 43; www.sunnydays.ch; Helveti-
astrasse 29; d Sfr120-180; P🛜) A little ray
of sunshine indeed, this chalet-style B&B
set in pretty gardens has sweet, simple
rooms – the pick of which have balconies
facing the Jungfrau. Tanja and her dad,
Dave, serve up generous breakfasts and

💗 If You Like…
Extreme Activities

If you like high adventure like the
plethora of activities you'll find in
Interlaken, consider some of these outfits
that can help you find pulse-pounding
experiences across the Alps:

1 Paragliding Jungfrau
(📞079 779 90 00; www.paragliding-jungfrau.
ch) Call ahead to organise your jump from First
at a height of 2150m (from Sfr180) or above the
Staubbach Falls (Sfr170).

2 Doris Hike
(📞033 855 42 40; www.doris-hike.ch) Doris'
informative guided hikes include glacier, waterfall and
high-alpine options. Call ahead for times and prices.

3 Swiss Adventures
(📞033 748 41 61; www.swissadventures.ch;
Alpinzentrum Gstaad) Organises guided climbs (Sfr108
to Sfr145) and vie ferrate (Sfr125), rafting (Sfr105),
canyoning (Sfr125) and, in winter, igloo building
(Sfr145) and snowshoe trekking (Sfr98 to Sfr125).

4 Vertical Sport
(http://verticalsport.ch; Jungfraustrasse
44; ⏰9am-noon & 1.30-6pm Mon-Fri, 9am-4pm
Sat) This rock-climbing store sells and rents out
top-quality climbing gear and is run by expert
mountaineers who can give sound advice.

hand out invaluable tips for making the
most out of the region.

Arnold's B&B B&B €

(📞033 823 64 21; www.arnolds.ch; Parkstrasse
3; s Sfr60-70, d Sfr100-130; P🛜) Frills are
few but the welcome from Beatrice and
Armin is warm at this family-run B&B.
The light, home-style rooms are housed
in a converted 1930s villa.

Walter's B&B B&B €

(📞033 822 76 88; www.walters.ch; Oelestrasse
35; s/d/tr/q Sfr50/66/99/112; 🛜) Walter is
a real star with his quick smile, culinary
skills and invaluable tips. Sure, the rooms

are a blast from the 1970s, but they are super-clean and you'd be hard pushed to find better value in Interlaken. Breakfast (Sfr7) is copious and the fondue dinner, which includes wine and dessert, a bargain at Sfr19 per person.

Hôtel du Lac Hotel €€
(033 822 29 22; www.dulac-interlaken.ch; Höheweg 225; s/d Sfr160/240; P) Smiley old-fashioned service and a riverfront location near Interlaken Ost make this 19th-century hotel a solid choice. It has been in the same family for generations and, despite the mishmash of styles, has kept enough belle époque glory to remain charming.

Victoria-Jungfrau Grand Hotel & Spa Luxury Hotel €€€
(033 828 26 10; www.victoria-jungfrau.ch; Höheweg 41; d Sfr400-800, ste Sfr600-1000; P @) The reverent hush and impeccable service here (as well as the prices) evoke an era when only royalty and the seriously wealthy travelled. A perfect melding of well-preserved art nouveau features and modern luxury make this Interlaken's answer to Raffles – with plum views of Jungfrau, three first-class restaurants and a gorgeous spa to boot.

Eating

Sandwich Bar Sandwiches €
(Rosenstrasse 5; snacks Sfr4-9; 7.30am-7pm Mon-Fri, 8am-5pm Sat) Choose your bread and get creative with fillings like air-dried ham with sun-dried tomatoes and brie with walnuts. Or try the soups, salads, toasties and locally made ice cream.

WineArt Mediterranean €€
(033 823 73 74; www.wineart.ch; Jungfraustrasse 46; mains Sfr24-59, 5-course menu Sfr59; 4pm-12.30am Mon-Sat) This is a delightful wine bar, lounge, restaurant and deli rolled into one. High ceilings, chandeliers and wood floors create a slick, elegant backdrop for season-driven Mediterranean food. Pair one of 600 wines with dishes as simple as buffalo mozzarella

Left: Mountain vista, Interlaken; **Below:** Market shopping, Interlaken
(LEFT) JORDAN LYE / GETTY IMAGES ©; (BELOW) INGOLF POMPE / LOOK-FOTO / GETTY IMAGES ©

and rocket salad and corn-fed chicken with honey-glazed vegetables – quality and flavour is second to none.

Benacus International €€
(☎ 033 821 20 20; www.benacus.ch; Kirchgasse 15; mains Sfr38-66; ☉11.30am-1.30pm & 5pm-12.30am Tue-Fri, 5pm-12.30am Sat) Super-cool Benacus is a breath of urban air with its glass walls, wine-red sofas, lounge music and street-facing terrace. The menu swings from creative tapas to Med-style flavours like monkfish bouillabaisse. The two-course lunch is good value at Sfr19.

🚹 Information

Tourist Office (☎ 033 826 53 00; www.interlakentourism.ch; Höheweg 37; ☉8am-7pm Mon-Fri, to 5pm Sat, 10am-4pm Sun Jul & Aug, 8am-noon & 1.30-6pm Mon-Fri, 9am-noon Sat rest of year) Halfway between the stations. There's a hotel booking board outside.

🚹 Getting There & Away

Interlaken has two train stations: Interlaken West and Interlaken Ost; each has bike rental, money-changing facilities and a landing stage for boats on Lake Thun and Lake Brienz.

Trains to Lucerne (Sfr31, two hours), Brig via Spiez (Sfr44, one hour) and Montreux via Bern or Visp (Sfr71, 2½ to three hours) depart frequently from Interlaken Ost train station.

The A8 freeway heads northeast to Lucerne and the A6 northwest to Bern, but the only way south for vehicles without a big detour round the mountains is to take the car-carrying train from Kandersteg, south of Spiez.

🚹 Getting Around

You can easily get around Interlaken on foot, but taxis and buses are found at each train station. Alternatively, pick up bikes, e-bikes, scooters, cars and quads for zipping around town at

Daniel's Fun Rental (www.daniels-fun-rental-interlaken.ch; Hauptstrasse 19; ☉9am-9pm), among others.

133

HENRY GEORGI / GETTY IMAGES ©

⭐ Don't Miss
Skiing the Jungfrau Region

Whether you want to slalom wide, sunny slopes at the foot of the Eiger or ski the breathtakingly sheer 16km Inferno run from Schilthorn to Lauterbrunnen, there's a piste that suits in the Jungfrau region. Grindelwald, Männlichen, Mürren and Wengen have access to some 214km of prepared runs and 44 ski lifts. A one-day ski pass for either Grindelwald–Wengen or Mürren–Schilthorn costs Sfr62/31 per adult/child, while a seven-day ski pass for these regions will set you back Sfr291/146. Ski passes for the whole Jungfrau ski region cost Sfr129 for adults and Sfr65 for children for a minimum two days, but switching between ski areas by train can be slow and crowded.

AROUND INTERLAKEN

Schynige Platte

The must-do day trip from Interlaken is Schynige Platte, a 1967m plateau where the **Alpengarten** (www.alpengarten. ch; ⏱8.30am-6pm Jun-Oct) **FREE** nurtures 600 types of Alpine blooms, including snowbells, arnica, gentian and edelweiss. The biggest draw up here, however, is the hiking. The **Panoramaweg** is an easy two-hour circuit. If you're here in July or

August, don't miss the **moonlight hikes** that follow the same route.

You reach the plateau on a late 19th-century **cog-wheel train** (www. schynigeplatte.ch; one way/return Sfr34/63; ⏱7.25am-4.45pm late May-late Oct) from Wilderswil. Trains run up to Schynige Platte at approximately 40- to 50-minute intervals until around 5pm.

JUNGFRAU REGION

If the Bernese Oberland is Switzerland's Alpine heart, the Jungfrau region is where yours will skip a beat. Presided over by glacier-encrusted monoliths Eiger, Mönch and Jungfrau (Ogre, Monk and Virgin), the scenery is positively uplifting. Hundreds of kilometres of walking trails allow you to capture the landscape from many angles, but it never looks less than astonishing.

The 'big three' peaks have an enduring place in mountaineering legend, particularly the 3970m Eiger, whose fearsome north wall has claimed many lives and remained unconquered until 1938. Reaching great heights is easier today; it takes just hours to whizz up by train to Jungfraujoch (3454m), the highest station in Europe.

Staying in resorts entitles you to a Gästekarte (Guest Card), good for discounts throughout the entire region.

❶ Getting There & Around

Getting around the Jungfrau region by train and mountain railway is a breeze, but it's worth bearing in mind that summit journeys are only really worth making on clear days. Check the webcams on www.jungfraubahn.ch and www. swisspanorama.com before you leave.

Hourly trains depart for the region from Interlaken Ost station. Sit in the front half of the train for Lauterbrunnen or the back half for Grindelwald. The two sections of the train split up where the two valleys diverge at Zweilütschinen.

The Swiss Half-Fare Card is valid within the entire region. There are some good-value travel passes available, such as the Berner Oberland Regional Pass, the six-day Jungfraubahnen Pass and the three-day Jungfrau VIP Pass.

Without a money-saving pass, sample fares include the following: Interlaken Ost to Grindelwald Sfr10.80; Grindelwald to Kleine Scheidegg Sfr31; Kleine Scheidegg to Jungfraujoch Sfr120 (return); Kleine Scheidegg to Wengen Sfr23; Wengen to Lauterbrunnen Sfr6.60; and Lauterbrunnen to Interlaken Ost Sfr7.40.

Many of the cable cars close for servicing in late April and late October.

Detour:
Spiez

Hunched around a horseshoe-shaped bay, with a medieval castle rising above emerald vineyards, the oft-overlooked town of Spiez makes a great escape. The vibe is low-key but the setting magical, with views to conical Niesen (2362m) and a fjord-like slither of the lake. Its vines yield crisp, lemony riesling and Sylvaner white wines.

The turreted medieval **Schloss Spiez** (www.schloss-spiez.ch; Schlossstrasse 16; adult/child Sfr10/2; ⏱2-5pm Mon, 10am-5pm Tue-Sun Easter–mid-Oct) is filled with oil paintings of its former masters, the influential von Bubenburg and von Erlach families. But it's the view that will grab you, whether from the lofty tower (which also sports 13th-century graffiti) or the banqueting hall.

From Interlaken West, trains run very frequently to Spiez (Sfr10, 20 minutes). By boat it's Sfr20 from Thun and Sfr27 from Interlaken West.

Grindelwald
POP 3761 / ELEV 1034M

Grindelwald's sublime natural assets are film-set stuff – the chiselled features of Eiger north face, the glinting tongues of Oberer and Unterer Glaciers and the crown-like peak of Wetterhorn will make you stare, swoon and lunge for your camera. Skiers and hikers cottoned onto its charms in the late 19th century, which makes it one of Switzerland's oldest resorts. And it has lost none of its appeal over the decades, with geranium-studded

Grindelwald

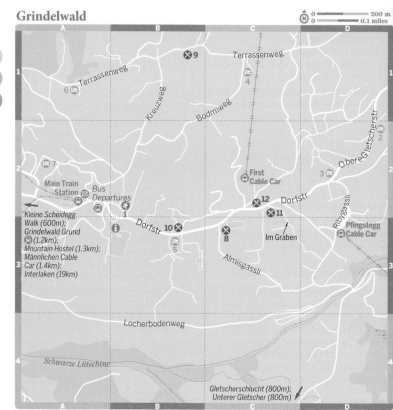

Grindelwald

Alpine chalets and verdant pastures set against an Oscar-worthy backdrop.

⊙ Sights & Activities

SUMMER ACTIVITIES

Grindelwald is outstanding hiking territory, veined with trails that command arresting views to massive north faces, crevassed glaciers and snow-capped peaks. High-altitude walks – around Männlichen, First and Pfingstegg – can be reached by taking cable cars up from the village.

Midway between First and Grindelwald is **Bort**, where you can rent scooters to zip back down to the valley on a 4.5km trail. Scooter rental costs Sfr30/22 for adults/children.

Gletscherschlucht
Glacier

(Glacier Gorge; adult/child Sfr7/3.50; ⏱10am-5pm May-Oct, to 6pm Jul & Aug) Turbulent waters carve a path through this craggy glacier gorge, a 30-minute walk south of the centre. A footpath weaves through tunnels hacked into cliffs veined with pink and green marble. It's justifiably a popular spot for canyon and bungee jumping expeditions.

Kleine Scheidegg Walk
Hiking

One of the region's most stunning day hikes is this 15km trek from Grindelwald Grund to Wengen via Kleine Scheidegg, which heads up through wildflower-freckled meadows to skirt below the Eiger's north face and reach Kleine Scheidegg, granting arresting views of the 'Big Three.' Allow around 5½ to six hours. The best map is the SAW 1:50,000 Interlaken (Sfr22.50).

Grindelwald Sports
Adventure Sports

(☎033 854 12 80; www.grindelwaldsports.ch; Dorfstrasse 103; ⏱8.30am-6.30pm, closed Sat & Sun in low season) Opposite the tourist office, this outfit arranges mountain climbing, ski and snowboard instruction, canyon jumping and glacier bungee jumping at the Gletscherschlucht. It also houses a cosy cafe and sells walking guides.

WINTER ACTIVITIES

Stretching from Oberjoch at 2486m right down to the village, the region of First presents a fine mix of cruisy red and challenging black ski runs. From Kleine Scheidegg or Männlichen there are long, easy runs back to Grindelwald, with Eiger demanding all the attention.

🛏 Sleeping

Grindelwald brims with characterful B&Bs and holiday chalets. Pick up a list at the tourist office, or log onto www.wir-grindelwalder.ch for a wide selection of holiday apartments.

Local buses, tourist office guided walks and entry to the sports centre are free with the Guest Card.

Hotel Tschuggen
Hotel €

(☎033 853 17 81; www.tschuggen-grindelwald.ch; Dorfstrasse 134; s Sfr85-102, d Sfr110-200, f Sfr230-310; P 🛜) Monika and Robert extend a warm welcome at this dark-wood chalet in the centre of town. The light, simple rooms are spotlessly clean; opt for a south-facing double for terrific Eiger views.

Naturfreundehaus
Hostel €

(☎033 853 13 33; www.nfh.ch/grindelwald; Terrassenweg 18; dm Sfr35-40, s Sfr57-58, d Sfr94-96; P 🛜) Vreni and Heinz are your welcoming hosts at this wood chalet, picturesquely perched above the village.

Pfingstegg cable car, Grindelwald
GLENN VAN DER KNIJFF / GETTY IMAGES ©

Creaking floors lead up to cute pine-panelled rooms with check curtains, including a shoebox single that's apparently Switzerland's smallest. Downstairs there's an old curiosity shop of a cafe and a garden granting wonderful views to the Eiger and Wetterhorn.

Mountain Hostel   Hostel €

(☎ 033 854 38 38; www.mountainhostel.ch; Grundstrasse 58; dm Sfr37-51, d Sfr94-122; P 🛜) Near Männlichen cable-car station, this is an ideal base for sports junkies, with well-kept dorms and a helpful crew. There's a beer garden, ski storage, TV lounge and mountain and e-bike rental.

Alpenblick   Hotel €

(☎ 033 853 11 05; www.alpenblick.info; Obere Gletscherstrasse 16; dm Sfr35-50, d Sfr100-180; P 🛜) In a quiet corner of town, 10 minutes' stroll from the centre, Alpenblick is a great budget find, with squeaky-clean, pine-filled rooms. Basement dorms are jazzed up with bright duvets. There's a diner-style restaurant and a terrace with glacier views.

Gletschergarten   Historic Hotel €€

(☎ 033 853 17 21; www.hotel-gletschergarten.ch; Obere Gletscherstrasse 1; s Sfr130-170, d Sfr230-300; P 🛜) The sweet Breitenstein family makes you feel at home in their rustic timber chalet, brimming with heirlooms from landscape paintings to snapshots of Elsbeth's grandfather who had 12 children (those were the days...). Decked out in pine and flowery fabrics, the rooms have balconies facing Unterer Gletscher at the front and Wetterhorn (best for sunset) at the back.

Hotel Bodmi   Hotel €€

(☎ 033 853 12 20; www.bodmi.ch; Terrassenweg 104; s Sfr185-215, d Sfr260-386, f Sfr369-435; P 🛜) Wake up to memorable Eiger views and creamy goat's cheese – courtesy of the resident herd – at this postcard-perfect chalet. Surrounded by meadows, the hotel sits above First cable car station and is a great base for summer hiking and winter skiing. Unwind in the spa or in the restaurant (mains Sfr25 to Sfr45) dishing up market-fresh Alpine fare.

Mountainside restaurant, Grindelwald

Romantik Hotel Schweizerhof

Historic Hotel €€€

(033 854 58 58; www.hotel-schweizerhof.com; Dorfstrasse; s incl half board Sfr240-360, d Sfr360-700; P 🛜 🏊) The grand dame of Grindelwald, this plush art nouveau hotel has stylish rooms with gleaming slate-floored bathrooms. The spa is a big draw, with massage jets, treatment rooms, a teeth-chattering ice grotto and a pool with wide-screen mountain vistas. The restaurant (mains Sfr26 to Sfr44) uses home-grown vegetables and herbs.

🍴 Eating

Bars, restaurants, bakeries and super-markets line central Dorfstrasse.

Cafe 3692

Cafe €

(www.cafe3692.ch; Terrassenweg 61; snacks & light meals Sfr6.50-21; ⏰8.30am-6pm Sun-Tue, 8.30am-midnight Fri & Sat) Run by dream duo Myriam and Bruno, Cafe 3692 is a delight. Bruno is a talented carpenter and has let his imagination run riot – a gnarled apple tree is an eye-catching artwork, a minecart trolley cleverly transforms into a grill, the ceiling is a wave of woodwork. Garden herbs and Grindelwald-sourced ingredients are knocked up into tasty day specials.

The Alpine teas are superb as are Heidi's delectable pastries and pralines. The minecart is wheeled out for barbecues every Friday and Saturday night in summer. Puzzled about the name? It refers to the local summit of Wetterhorn (3692m).

Pizzeria da Salvi

Pizza €

(033 853 89 89; Dorfstrasse 189; pizza Sfr18-24.50; ⏰11.30am-11pm) This cheerful Italian in Hotel Steinbock rolls out delicious wood-fired pizza. There are 110 different kinds of grappa on the menu.

Onkel Tom's Hütte

Pizza €

(033 853 52 39; Im Graben 4; pizzas Sfr13-33; ⏰6pm-midnight Thu, noon-midnight Fri-Tue) Tables are at a premium in this incredibly cosy barn-style chalet. Yummy pizzas are prepared fresh in three sizes to suit

Discount Travel Passes

You can save francs with the **Berner Oberland Regional Pass** (www.regiopass-berneroberland.ch; 4-/6-/8-/10-day pass Sfr230/290/330/370; ⏰May-Oct), which allows unlimited travel on most trains, buses, boats, mountain railways and cable cars, as well as discounts on local sights and attractions (for instance a 50% reduction on tickets to Jungfraujoch). The Junior Card (Sfr30) allows kids to travel free with their parents; unaccompanied they pay half price.

A good alternative is the **Jungfraubahnen Pass** (www.jungfrau.ch; adult/child Sfr250/75; ⏰May-Oct), which provides six days of unlimited travel throughout the region (Sfr185 with Swiss Pass, Swiss Card or Half-Fare Card), though you still have to pay Sfr58 from Eigergletscher to Jungfraujoch.

The three-day **Jungfrau VIP Pass** (adult/child Sfr235/70; ⏰May-Oct) covers unlimited travel on the Jungfrau Railways network, including the return journey from Eigergletscher to Jungfraujoch.

any appetite. The encyclopaedic wine list flicks from Switzerland to South Africa.

Memory

Swiss €€

(033 854 31 31; Dorfstrasse 133; mains Sfr17-36; ⏰9am-11.30pm) Always packed, the Eiger Hotel's unpretentious restaurant rolls out tasty Swiss grub like rösti, raclette and fondue, as well as – titter ye not – 'horny' chicken with a spicy 'Christian' sauce. Try to bag a table on the street-facing terrace.

C & M

Swiss €€

(033 853 07 10; Almisgässli 1; snacks Sfr5-9, mains Sfr29-49; ⏰8.30am-11pm Wed-Mon) Just as appetising as the menu are the stupendous views to Unterer Gletscher from this gallery-style cafe's sunny terrace. Enjoy a salad, coffee and cake, or seasonally inspired dishes such as homesmoked salmon and river trout with herb butter.

ℹ Information

The **tourist office** (☎ 033 854 12 12; www.grindelwald.ch; Dorfstrasse 110; ☻8am-noon & 1.30-6pm Mon-Fri, 9am-noon & 1.30-5pm Sat & Sun; 🛜) in the Sportzentrum hands out brochures and and hiking maps, and has a free internet terminal and wi-fi. There's an accommodation board outside or you can ask them to book rooms for you.

ℹ Getting There & Around

Grindelwald is off the A8 from Interlaken. A smaller road continues from the village over the Grosse Scheidegg Pass (1960m). It's closed to private traffic, but from mid-June to early October postal buses (Sfr50, 2 ¼hours) travel this scenic route to Meiringen roughly hourly from 8am to 5pm.

....

Around Grindelwald

KLEINE SCHEIDEGG

Eiger, Mönch and Jungfrau soar almost 2000m above you at Kleine Scheidegg (2061m), where restaurants huddle around the train station. Most people only stay for a few minutes while changing trains for Jungfraujoch, but it's worth lingering to appreciate the dazzling views, including those to the fang-shaped peak of Silberhorn.

Kleine Scheidegg is a terrific base for hiking. There are short, undemanding trails, one hour apiece, to Eigergletscher, down to Wengernalp, and up the Lauberhorn behind the village. These areas become intermediate ski runs from December to April. Alternatively, you can walk the spectacular 6km **Eiger Trail** from Eigergletscher to Alpiglen (two hours) for close-ups of the mountain's fearsome north face.

JUNGFRAUJOCH

Sure, everyone else wants to see Jungfraujoch (3454m) and yes, tickets are expensive, but don't let that stop you. It's a once-in-a-lifetime trip that you need to experience first-hand. And there's a reason why two million people a year visit Europe's highest train station. The icy wilderness of swirling glaciers and 4000m turrets that unfolds at the top is staggeringly beautiful.

The last stage of the train journey from Kleine Scheidegg burrows through the heart of Eiger before arriving at the sci-fi Sphinx meteorological station. Opened in 1912, the tunnel took 3000 men 16 years to drill. Within the weather station, there's an **Ice Palace** gallery of otherworldly ice sculptures, restaurants, indoor viewpoints and a souvenir shop.

Good weather is essential for this journey; check on www.jungfrau.ch or call ☎033 828 79 31. Don't forget to take warm clothing, sunglasses and sunscreen, as there's snow and glare up here all year.

Outside there are views of the moraine-streaked 23km tongue of the **Aletsch Glacier**, the longest glacier in the European Alps and a Unesco World Heritage site. The views across rippling peaks stretch as far as the Black Forest in Germany on cloudless days.

When you tire (as if!) of the view, you can zip across the frozen plateau on a flying fox (adult/child Sfr20/15), dash downhill on a sled or snow disc (adult/child Sfr15/10), or enjoy a bit of tame skiing or boarding (adult/child Sfr35/25) at the **Snow Fun Park**. A day pass covering all activities costs Sfr45 for adults and Sfr25 for children.

If you cross the glacier along the prepared path, in around an hour you reach the **Mönchsjochhütte** (☎033 971 34 72; www.moenchsjoch.ch; dm/incl half-board Sfr28/64; ☻late Mar–mid-Oct) at 3650m. Here you'll share your dinner table and dorm with hardcore rock climbers, psyching themselves up to tackle Eiger or Mönch.

From Interlaken Ost, the journey time is 2½ hours each way and the return fare is Sfr197.60. The last train back sets off at 5.45pm in summer and 4.45pm in winter. However, from May through to October

JORG GREUEL / GETTY IMAGES ©

★ Don't Miss
Waterfalls

Especially in the early-morning light, it's easy to see how the vaporous, 297m-high Staubbach Falls captivated prominent writers with its threads of spray floating down the cliffside. What appears to be ultra-fine mist from a distance, however, becomes a torrent when you walk behind the falls. Be prepared to get wet and wear sturdy shoes.

The glacier falls of Trümmelbachfälle are more of a bang-crash spectacle. Inside the mountain, up to 20,000L of water per second corkscrews through ravines and potholes shaped by the swirling waters. The 10 falls drain from 24 sq km of Alpine glaciers and snow deposits. A bus (Sfr3.40) from the Lauterbrunnen train station takes you to the falls.

NEED TO KNOW

Staubbach Falls (⊙8am-8pm Jun-Oct)
Trümmelbachfälle (www.truemmelbachfaelle.ch; adult/child Sfr11/4; ⊙9am-5pm)

there's a cheaper Good Morning Ticket costing Sfr145 if you take the first train (which departs at 6.35am from Interlaken Ost) and leave the summit by 1pm.

Getting these early trains is easier if your starting place is deeper in the region. Stay overnight at Kleine Scheidegg to take advantage of the excursion-fare train at 8am. From here, a return Good Morning Ticket is Sfr95.

Even the ordinary return ticket to Jungfraujoch is valid for one month, so you can use that ticket to form the backbone of your trip, venturing as far as Grindelwald and stopping for a few days' hiking, before moving on to Kleine Scheidegg, Jungfraujoch, Wengen and Lauterbrunnen.

LAUTERBRUNNEN

POP 2470 / ELEV 796M

Lauterbrunnen's wispy Staubbach Falls inspired both Goethe and Lord Byron to pen poems to their ethereal beauty. Today the postcard-perfect village, nestled deep in the valley of 72 waterfalls, attracts a less highfalutin crowd. Laid-back and full of chalet-style lodgings, Lauterbrunnen is a great base for nature-lovers wishing to hike or climb, and a magnet to thrill-seeking BASE jumpers.

Hikes heading up into the mountains from the waterfall-laced valley include a 2½-hour uphill trudge to Mürren and a more gentle 1¾-hour walk to Stechelberg. In winter, you can glide past frozen waterfalls on a well-prepared 12km cross-country trail.

Sleeping

Valley Hostel   Hostel €

(☎ 033 855 20 08; www.valleyhostel.ch; Fuhren; dm Sfr28, s Sfr43, d 66-76, tr 99-140; P 🛜) This relaxed, family-run hostel has an open-plan kitchen, a garden with tremendous views of the Staubbach Falls, a laundry and free wi-fi. Most of the spacious, pine-clad dorms have balconies. The friendly team can help organise activities from paragliding to canyoning.

Eating

Airtime   Cafe €

(☎ 033 855 15 15; www.airtime.ch; snacks & light meals Sfr6-15.50; ⏰9am-7pm; 🛜) Inspired by their travels in New Zealand, Daniela and Beni have set up this funky cafe, book exchange, laundry service and extreme sports agency. Munch wraps, sandwiches and homemade cakes (try the chocolate-nut special) as you use the free wi-fi to check your email. You can book adrenalin-fuelled pursuits like ice climbing, canyoning and bungee jumping here.

Flavours   Cafe €

(www.flavours.ch; snacks & light meals Sfr8-15; ⏰9.30am-6pm Wed Sun) Whether you fancy a slap-up egg-and-bacon breakfast, homemade cakes with locally roasted coffee or a freshly pressed juice, Flavours is the go-to place. Housed in the former bakery, the cafe opens onto a terrace with beanbags and a nicely chilled vibe.

ℹ Information

The **tourist office** (☎ 033 856 85 68; www.mylauterbrunnen.com; Stutzli 460; ⏰8.30am-noon & 2-6.30pm Jun-Sep, shorter hours rest of year) is opposite the train station.

If you're travelling to the car-free resorts of Wengen and Mürren, there's a multistorey **car park** (☎ 033 828 74 00; www.jungfraubahn.ch; per day/week Sfr17/82) by the station, but it's advisable to book ahead. There is also an open-air car park by the Stechelberg cable-car station, charging Sfr5 for a day.

Lauterbrunnen village
JASON MAEHL / GETTY IMAGES ©

WENGEN

POP 1300 / ELEV 1274M

Photogenically poised on a mountain ledge, Wengen's 'celestial views' have lured Brits here since Edwardian times. The fact you can only reach this chocolate-box village by train gives it romantic appeal. From the bench in front of the church at dusk, the vista takes on watercolour dreaminess, peering over to the misty Staubbach Falls, down to the Lauterbrunnen Valley and up to glacier-capped giants of the Jungfrau massif. In winter, Wengen morphs into a ski resort with a low-key, family-friendly feel.

The highlight in Wengen's calendar is the world-famous **Lauberhornrennen** (www.lauberhorn.ch) downhill ski race in mid-January, where pros reach speeds of up to 160km/h.

Skiing is mostly cruisy blues and reds, though experts can brave exhilarating black runs at Lauberhorn and the aptly named 'Oh God'.

The same area is excellent for hiking in the summer. Some 20km of paths stay open in winter, too. The hour-long forest trail down to Lauterbrunnen is a sylvan beauty.

😴 Sleeping

Expect summer rates to be roughly 30% cheaper than in winter high season.

Hotel Berghaus   Hotel €€
(🞄 033 855 21 51; www.berghaus-wengen.ch; d Sfr160-324; 🛜) Sidling up to the forest, this family-run chalet is a five-minute toddle from the village centre. Rooms are light, spacious and pin-drop peaceful – ask for a south-facing one for dreamy Jungfrau views. Call ahead and they'll pick you up from the train station.

Hotel Caprice   Boutique Hotel €€€
(🞄 033 856 06 06; www.caprice-wengen.ch; d Sfr310-435; 🛜) If you're looking for design-oriented luxury in the Jungfrau mountains, this boutique gem delivers with discreet service and authentically French cuisine. Don't be fooled by its cute Alpine trappings; inside it exudes Scandinavian-style simplicity with chocolate-cream colours, slick rooms and a lounge with an open fire.

🍴 Eating & Drinking

Santos   Cafe €
(🞄 078 67 97 445; snacks Sfr6-9; 🕙10am-7pm Mon, 10am-midnight Tue-Sun) This Portuguese TV-and-tiles place is the real deal. Mrs Santos whips up burgers, calamari, sandwiches and divine *pastéis de nata* (custard tarts).

Café Gruebi   Cafe €
(🞄 033 855 58 55; snacks & mains Sfr8-17.50; 🕙9am-6pm Mon-Sat, 11am-6pm Sun) Run by a husband-and-wife team, Gruebi offers cheap eats like rösti, cheese tarts, soups and goulash. The yummy homemade cakes are baked almost daily. Sit on the terrace when the sun's out.

Restaurant Schönegg   Swiss €€€
(🞄 033 855 34 22; www.hotel-schoenegg.ch; mains Sfr44-58; 🕙6.30-9pm) Chef Hubert Mayer serves seasonally inspired dishes like home-smoked salmon with apple horseradish and saddle of venison in port wine jus. The pine-clad, candlelit dining room is wonderfully cosy in winter and the mountain-facing terrace perfect for summertime dining.

ℹ️ Information

Next to Männlichen cable car is the **tourist office** (🞄 033 856 85 85; www.wengen.ch; 🕙9am-9pm Mon-Fri, 9am-noon & 1.30-9pm Sat & Sun, closed Sat & Sun Nov & Mar-Apr) You can rent e-bikes here for Sfr40/50 per half-/full day.

MÜRREN

POP 430 / ELEV 1650M

Arriving on a clear evening, as the train from Grütschalp floats along the horizontal ridge towards Mürren, the peaks across the valley feel so close that you could reach out and touch them. And that's when you'll think you've died and gone to Heidi heaven. With its low-slung wooden chalets and spellbinding views of Eiger, Mönch and Jungfrau, car-free Mürren is storybook Switzerland.

In winter, there are 53km of prepared ski runs nearby, mostly suited to intermediates, and a **ski school** (☎033 855 12 47; www.muerren.ch/skischule; ⏱9am-12.30pm & 1.30-5pm Mon-Fri, 9am-noon & 3-5pm Sat & Sun) charging Sfr50 for a two-hour group lesson. Mürren is famous for its hell-for-leather **Inferno Run** (www.inferno-muerren.ch) down from Schilthorn in late January. Daredevils have been competing in the 16km race since 1928 and today the course attracts 1800 intrepid amateur skiers. It's also the reason for all the devilish souvenirs.

In summer from Mürren, the **Allmendhubel funicular** (www.schilthorn.ch; one way/return Sfr6.40/12.60; ⏱every 20 min 9am-5pm) takes you above Mürren to a panoramic restaurant, the Skyline Chill relaxation area and an adventure playground. From here, you can set out on many walks, including the famous **Northface Trail** (1½ hours), via Schiltalp to the west, leading through wildflower-strewn meadows with views to the glaciers and waterfalls of the Lauterbrunnen Valley and the monstrous Eiger north face – bring binoculars to spy intrepid climbers. There's also a kid-friendly **Adventure Trail** (one hour).

🛏 Sleeping & Eating

In summer, rates are up to 30% cheaper than the high-season winter prices given below.

Hotel Eiger　　　　　Hotel €€
(☎033 856 54 54; www.hoteleiger.com; s Sfr178-270, d Sfr285-460; 🐾🏊) This huge wooden chalet harbours sleek and contemporary rooms. The service is first rate, as are the views from the swimming pool, with picture-windows perfectly framing the Eiger, Mönch and Jungfrau. The restaurant (mains Sfr21 to Sfr58) is one of Mürren's best.

Eiger Guesthouse　　Guesthouse €€
(☎033 856 54 60; www.eigerguesthouse.com; r Sfr110-220; 🐾) Run by a fun-loving, on-the-ball team, this central pick offers great value. Besides clean, spruced-up rooms (the best have Eiger views), there is a downstairs pub serving tasty grub and a good selection of draught beers.

Hotel Jungfrau　　　Hotel €€
(☎033 856 64 64; www.hoteljungfrau.ch; d Sfr180-280, q apt Sfr550; 🐾) Set above Mürren and overlooking the nursery slopes, this welcoming family-run hotel dates to 1894. Despite '70s traces, rooms are tastefully decorated in warm hues; south-facing ones have Jungfrau views. Downstairs there's a beamed lounge with an open fire.

Restaurant La Grotte　　Swiss €€
(☎033 855 18 26; mains Sfr13.50-43; ⏱11am-2pm & 5-9pm) Brimming with cowbells, cauldrons and Alpine props, this kitsch-meets-rustic mock cave of a restaurant is touristy but fun. Fondues and flambées are good bets.

GIMMELWALD

POP 130 / ELEV 1370M

If you think Mürren is cute, wait until you see Gimmelwald. This pipsqueak of a village has long been a hideaway for hikers and adventurers tiptoeing away from the crowds. The secret is out, though, and this mountainside village is swiftly becoming known for its drop-dead-gorgeous scenery, rural authenticity and sense of calm.

The surrounding hiking trails include one down from Mürren (30 to 40 minutes). Cable cars are also an option (Mürren or Stechelberg Sfr5.80).

🛏 Sleeping & Eating

Esther's Guest House　　Guesthouse €
(☎033 855 54 88; www.esthersguesthouse.ch; Kirchstatt; s/d Sfr60/140, apt Sfr170-250; 🐾) Esther runs this charming B&B with love. Drenched with piny light, the rooms are spotless, while the apartments are ideal for families. The attic room is a favourite with its slanted roof and star-gazing window. For an extra Sfr15, you'll be served a delicious breakfast of homemade bread, cheese and yoghurt.

Hotel Mittaghorn Guesthouse €
📞 033 855 16 58; Poeschenried 39; d/tr/q
Sfr100/140/170, half board per person Sfr15; 🛜)
Staring in wonder at the mountains is the main pursuit at this stunningly situated wooden chalet, run by the irrepressible Walter and his sidekick, Tom. Creaking floors and doors lead to simple, cosy rooms. Dinners are hearty, jovial affairs. It's a 10-minute uphill walk from the cable-car station.

SCHILTHORN

There's a tremendous 360-degree panorama from the 2970m **Schilthorn** (www.schilthorn.ch), best appreciated from the **Skyline** view platform or **Piz Gloria** revolving restaurant. On a clear day, you can see from Titlis around to Mont Blanc, and across to the German Black Forest.

Yet some visitors seem more pre-occupied with practising their delivery of the line, 'The name's Bond, James Bond', because a few scenes from *On Her Majesty's Secret Service* were shot here in 1968–69. The new **Bond World 007** interactive exhibition gives you the chance to pose for photos secret-agent style and relive movie moments in a helicopter and bob sled.

From Interlaken, take a Sfr121.80 excursion trip (Half-Fare Card and Swiss Card 50% off, Swiss Pass 65% off) going to Lauterbrunnen, Grütschalp, Mürren, Schilthorn and returning through Stechelberg to Interlaken. A return from Lauterbrunnen (via Grütschalp) and Mürren costs Sfr107 as does the return journey via the Stechelberg cable car. A return from Mürren is Sfr77. Ask about discounts for early-morning trips.

THE LAKES

Anyone who travels to Interlaken for the first time from Bern will never forget the moment they clap eyes on Thunersee (Lake Thun). As the train loops past pastures and tidy villages on the low southern shore, some people literally gasp at the sight of the Alps rearing above the startlingly turquoise waters.

Bordering Interlaken to the east, Brienzersee (Lake Brienz) has just as many cameras snapping with its unbelievably aquamarine waters and rugged mountain backdrop.

Viewing platform, Schilthorn

FERGUS KENNEDY / GETTY IMAGES ©

Steamers ply both lakes from late May to mid-September. There are no winter services on Brienzersee, whereas special cruises continue on Thunersee. For more information contact **BLS** (☎058 327 48 10; www.bls.ch). A day pass valid for both lakes costs Sfr66 from Tuesday to Sunday, Sfr39 on Monday; children pay half-price. Eurail Passes, the Regional Pass and the Swiss Pass are valid on all boats, and InterRail and the Swiss Half-Fare Card get 50% off.

Thun

POP 42,735 / ELEV 559M

Ringed by mountains, hugging the banks of the aquamarine Aare River and topped by a turreted castle, medieval Thun is every inch your storybook Swiss town. History aside, the town is infused with a young spirit, with lively crowds sunning themselves at riverside cafes and one-of-a-kind boutiques filling the unusual arcades.

◎ Sights & Activities

It's a pleasure to wander Thun's attractive riverfront Old Town, where plazas and lanes are punctuated by 15th- and 16th-century townhouses. A stroll takes in the 300-year-old Untere Schleusenbrücke, a covered wooden bridge that is a mass of pink and purple flowers in summer. Nearby is the split-level, flag-bedecked Obere Hauptgasse, whose arcades conceal boutiques and galleries. At the street's northern tip is cobblestone Rathausplatz, centred on a fountain and framed by arcaded buildings.

The tourist office's one-and-a-half-hour guided tours (Sfr15 per person), every Wednesday and Saturday from May to October, take in the Altstadt and castle.

For a magical 360-degree view of Thun, the lake and the glaciated Jungfrau mountains, walk 20 minutes south of the centre to Jakobshübeli viewpoint.

Schloss Thun
Castle

(www.schlossthun.ch; Schlossberg 1; adult/child Sfr10/3; ⊙10am-5pm) Sitting on a hilltop and looking proudly back on 900 years of history, Schloss Thun is the castle of your wildest fairy-tale dreams, crowned by a riot of turrets and affording tremendous views of the lake and Alps. It once belonged to Duke Berchtold V of the powerful Zähringen family. Today it houses a **museum**, showcasing prehistoric and Roman relics, tapestries, majolica and plenty of shining armour.

🛏 Sleeping

Zunfthaus zu Metzgern
Historic Hotel €

(☎033 222 21 41; www.zumetzgern.ch; Untere Hauptgasse 2; s/d/tr without bathroom Sfr55/110/165) Sitting on Thun's prettiest square is this 700-year-old guild house. Bold artworks glam up the well-kept, parquet-floored rooms. Downstairs the chef uses local organic ingredients to prepare dishes like lamb with caramelised apricots and poached rainbow trout with fig-vanilla sauce (mains Sfr24 to Sfr44).

🍴 Eating & Drinking

Kaffee und Kuchen
Cafe €

(☎079 79 254 02; Obere Hauptgasse 34; snacks & light meals Sfr6.50-21; ⊙9am-11.30pm Tue-Thu, 9am-12.30am Fri & Sat, 10am-7pm Sun) This stone-vaulted, candlelit cellar has an arty vibe and invites lazy days spent reading, guzzling coffee and lingering over brunch. The homemade food – from wraps and salads to rich chocolate-chilli cake – is delicious.

Fluss
Fusion €€

(☎033 222 01 10; Mühleplatz 9; mains Sfr27-58; ⊙11am-12.30am, closed Sun winter) Right on the banks of the Aare River, this contemporary glass-walled lounge restaurant attracts a young crowd who come for the

147

beautifully prepared sushi, sashimi and herb-infused grill specialities. The olive-tree-dotted waterfront deck is perfect for sundowners and people-watching.

Information

Tourist Office (☏ 033 225 90 00; www.thun.ch; Bahnhofplatz; ⏱ 9am-6.30pm Mon-Fri, to 4pm Sat, plus to 1pm Sun Jul & Aug)

❶ Getting There & Away

Thun is on the main north–south train route from Frankfurt to Milan and beyond. Frequent trains run to Interlaken West (Sfr15.60, 30 minutes). Boats glide across the lake to Interlaken Ost (Sfr42) and Spiez (Sfr20).

Brienz

POP 3019 / ELEV 566M

Quaint and calm, Brienz peers across the exquisitely turquoise waters of its namesake lake to rugged mountains and thick forests beyond. The deeply traditional village has a stuck-in-time feel with its tooting steam train and woodcarving workshops. In town, mosey down postcard-perfect Brunngasse, a curving lane dotted with stout wooden chalets, each seemingly trying to outdo its neighbour with window displays of vines, kitsch gnomes and billowing geraniums.

◎ Sights & Activities

Kids can splash around in the water playground on the tree-fringed lake promenade.

Rothorn Bahn Railway

(www.brienz-rothorn-bahn.ch; one way/return Sfr54/84; ⏱ hourly 7.30am-4.30pm Jun-late Oct) This is the only steam-powered cog-wheel train still operating in Switzerland, climbing 2350m, from where you can set out on hikes or enjoy the long views over Brienzersee to snow-dusted 4000m peaks. Walking up from Brienz takes around five hours.

Schweizer Holzbildhauerei Museum Museum

(Hauptstrasse 111; adult/child Sfr5/free; ⏱ 9am-6pm May-Sep, shorter hours rest of year) Several woodcarvers open their attached workshops, including Jobin, which has been in business since 1835. You can see its intricately carved sculptures, reliefs and music boxes in this museum.

❶ Getting There & Away

From Interlaken Ost, Brienz is accessible by train (Sfr8, 20 minutes) or boat (Sfr29, April to mid October). The scenic Brünig Pass (1008m) is the road route to Lucerne.

Steam train, Brienz
INMACOR / GETTY IMAGES ©

WEST BERNESE OBERLAND

At the western side of the Jungfrau are Simmental and Frutigland, dominated by two wildly beautiful river valleys, the Simme and the Kander. Further west is Saanenland, famous for the ritzy ski resort of Gstaad.

Kandersteg

POP 1236 / ELEV 1176M

Turn up in Kandersteg wearing anything but muddy boots and you'll attract a few odd looks. Hiking is this town's raison d'être, with 550km of surrounding trails. An amphitheatre of spiky peaks studded with glaciers and jewel-coloured lakes creates a sublime natural backdrop to the rustic village of dark-timber chalets.

Jagged mountains frame the impossibly turquoise **Oeschinensee** (www.oeschinensee.ch; cable car one way/return Sfr18/26; ☉ cable car 8am-6pm), where you can fish, stroll, swim or hire a row boat. A cable car takes you to within 20 minutes of the lake by foot. Once there, it takes an hour to hike back down to Kandersteg.

Kandersteg has some first-rate hiking in its wild backyard on the cantonal border with Valais. A superb trek is the high-level **Gemmi Pass** (2314m) to Leukerbad, involving a steep descent. Alternatively, you could walk through flower-strewn pastures in the wildlife-rich Üschenetäli. For more of a challenge, test the 3½-hour *via ferrata* at **Allmenalp**. Equipment can be hired at the valley station for Sfr25.

In winter there are more than 50km of **cross-country ski** trails, including the iced-over Oeschinensee.

🛏 Sleeping & Eating

Kandersteg's popularity with hikers means there's lots of cheaper accommodation, but many places close between seasons. Ask for the Guest Card for reductions on activities.

The Hayloft   B&B €
(☎ 033 675 03 50; www.thehayloft.ch; Altes Bütschels Hus; s/d/tr Sfr60/100/120) Picture a dark-wood, 500-year-old chalet snuggled against the hillside, flower-strewn meadows where cows graze placidly, views of waterfalls and glaciers – ahhh...this place sure is idyllic! The farm-turned-B&B is in the capable hands of Peter and Kerry, who welcome guests like members of the family and serve delicious breakfasts and dinners (Sfr30).

Anchor the dog and Snorkel the cat are a throwback to the pair's round-the-world sailing venture in 1993. See the website for directions.

ℹ Information

The **tourist office** (☎ 033 675 80 80; www.kandersteg.ch; Äussere Dorfstrasse 26; ☉ 8am-noon & 1.30-6pm Mon-Fri, 8.30am-noon & 3-6pm Sat Jun-Sep, shorter hours rest of year) can suggest hiking routes and other activities in the area.

ℹ Getting There & Away

Kandersteg is at the northern end of the Lötschberg Tunnel, through which trains trundle to Goppenstein (30km from Brig) and onwards to Iselle in Italy. See www.bls.ch/autoverlad for more details.

Gstaad

POP 3600 / ELEV 1100M

Synonymous with the glitterati and fittingly twinned with Cannes, Gstaad appears smaller than its reputation – too little for its designer ski boots, as it were. While the principal competitive sports are celebrity-spotting and gazing wistfully into Gucci-filled boutiques, others might enjoy the fine hiking and skiing.

🏃 Activities

WINTER ACTIVITIES

Gstaad Mountain Rides' 220km of ski slopes cover a good mix of blues, reds and blacks, and include neighbouring resorts like Saanen, Saanenmöser, St Stephan and Zweisimmen. Beginners can test out the snow on gentle, tree-lined runs at Wispile and Eggli, while more proficient skiers can cruise challenging reds at Les Diablerets. A day ski pass costs Sfr66 for an adult and Sfr37 for a child, and under nine year olds ski free. Snowboarders tackle the curves, bowls and jumps at the ski-cross slope at Riedenberg.

Non skiers and families are in their element in Gstaad, with off-piste fun including ice skating, curling, horse-drawn trap rides, winter hiking on 30 trails, snowshoeing, airboarding at Saanenmöser and snow golf at Wispile.

SUMMER ACTIVITIES

Hiking is the main summer pursuit and the opportunities are boundless, with 300km of marked trails threading through the region. A scenic three-hour hike takes you from Wispile to Launensee, a crystalline Alpine lake, with views of the craggy Wildhorn massif en route. Wispile is the best bet for families, with a dairy trail, a petting zoo and a downhill scooter trail (adult/child Sfr15/8) from its middle station.

🛏 Sleeping

Expect discounts of 30% to 50% in summer. The tourist office has a list of self-catering chalets. Many places close from mid-October to mid-December and from April to mid-June.

Hotel Alphorn   Hotel €€
(033 748 45 45; www.gstaad-alphorn.ch; Gsteigstrasse 51; s Sfr117-142, d Sfr212-282; P) A traditional Swiss chalet with a 21st-century twist, the Alphorn has smart rooms with plenty of warm pine, chunky beds and balconies with country views. Downstairs there's a cosy restaurant (mains Sfr27 to Sfr38), a sauna and a whirlpool big enough for two.

Gstaad Palace   Luxury Hotel €€€
(033 748 50 00; www.palace.ch; Palacestrasse 28; s Sfr440-720, d Sfr690-1120; P ✳ @ ☎) Opulent, exclusive and – in case you happen to be wondering – accessible by

helicopter, this hilltop fairy-tale palace has attracted celebrity royalty like Michael Jackson, Robbie Williams and Liza Minnelli. Lavish quarters, a luxurious spa, several gourmet restaurants and an Olympic pool justify the price tag. Retro disco Green Go is also up here.

🍴 Eating & Drinking

If Gstaad's ritzy restaurants aren't for you, head for the mountain chalet restaurants at the summit stations of the cable cars.

Michel's Stallbeizli   Swiss €
(033 744 43 37; www.stallbeizli.ch; Gsteigstrasse 38; snacks & fondue Sfr16-22; 9.30am-6pm mid-Dec–Mar;) Dining doesn't get more back-to-nature than at this converted barn. In winter, you can feast away on fondue, drink Alpine herbal tea, or munch home-cured meat and cheese, with truly moo-ving views (pardon the pun) to the cud-chewing cows and goats in the adjacent stable. Kids love it.

Wasserngrat   Swiss €€
(033 744 96 22; mains Sfr20-50; 10am-4.30pm Thu-Sun Aug & mid-Dec–Mar) Marvel at views of Les Diablerets glacier and Gstaad from the slope-side perch of Wasserngrat, where a fire crackles in the rustic-chic restaurant and skiers warm up over fondue on the sunny terrace. Top ingredients like truffles and foie gras flavour classic Alpine dishes.

ℹ Information

The **tourist office** (033 748 81 81; www.gstaad.ch; Promenade 41; 8.30am-6.30pm Mon-Fri, 9am-noon & 1.30-5pm Sat & Sun Jul-Aug & Dec-Mar, shorter hours rest of year) has stacks of info on the area.

ℹ Getting There & Away

Gstaad is on the Golden Pass route between Montreux (Sfr25, 1½ hours) and Spiez (Sfr26, 1½ hours; change at Zweisimmen). There is an hourly service to Geneva airport (Sfr53, three hours) via Montreux.

LUCERNE

POP 59,500 / ELEV 435M

Recipe for a gorgeous Swiss city: take a cobalt lake ringed by mountains of myth, add a well-preserved medieval Altstadt (Old Town) and a reputation for making beautiful music, then sprinkle with covered bridges, sunny plazas, candy-coloured houses and waterfront promenades. Lucerne is stunning, and deservedly popular since the likes of Goethe, Queen Victoria and Wagner savoured her views in the 19th century. Legend has it that an angel with a light showed the first settlers where to build a chapel in Lucerne, and today it still has amazing grace.

Though the shops are still crammed with what Mark Twain so eloquently described as 'gimcrackery of the souvenir sort', Lucerne doesn't only dwell on the past, with a roster of music gigs keeping the vibe upbeat. Carnival capers at Fasnacht, balmy summers, golden autumns – this 'city of lights' shines in every season.

◎ Sights

Museum Sammlung Rosengart   Museum

(☏ 041 220 16 60; www.rosengart.ch; Pilatus-strasse 10; adult/student Sfr18/16; ⊙ 10am-6pm Apr-Oct, 11am-5pm Nov-Mar) Lucerne's blockbuster cultural attraction is the Sammlung Rosengart, occupying a graceful neoclassical pile. It showcases the outstanding stash of Angela Rosengart, a Swiss art dealer and close friend of Picasso. Alongside works by the great Spanish master are paintings and sketches by Cézanne, Klee, Kandinsky, Miró, Matisse and Monet. Standouts include Joan Miró's electric-blue *Dancer II* (1925) and Paul Klee's childlike *X-chen* (1938).

Kapellbrücke   Bridge

(Chapel Bridge) You haven't really been to Lucerne until you have strolled the creaky 14th-century Kapellbrücke, spanning the Reuss River in the Old Town. The octagonal water tower is original, but its

---

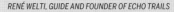

> **Local Knowledge**

Lucerne Outdoors Don't Miss List

RENÉ WELTI, GUIDE AND FOUNDER OF ECHO TRAILS

1   **WALK THE MUSEGG WALL**
As you walk along this 14th-century Lucerne fortification (p153) and go up the self-guided historic towers you are rewarded with the best views of town, the lake and the mountains.

2   **DO THE PILATUS MOUNTAIN**
Pilatus (p158) features friendly dragon playgrounds for kids, rope parks, dragon cave walks, a secure Alpine flower path and Swiss Alps as far as you can see. Hear your own echo, enjoy delicious food and luxurious accommodation, all accessible by the world's steepest cogwheel railway, aerial trams, gondolas and boats.

3   **SWIM LAKE LUCERNE**
Cool off at the many Lake Lucerne swimming facilities and savour Alpine scenery while you swim in crystal-clear waters that start in the Gotthard Pass and flow down the Ruess river. (Tribschen, the lakeside swimming facility run by the city of Lucerne, is my favourite.)

4   **HIKE THE SWISS PATH**
If you want to understand how Switzerland was founded, walk and hike segments of the 35km scenic **Swiss Path** (Weg der Schweiz; www.weg-der-schweiz.ch). It circles Lake Uri and begins at the Rütli, in Seelisberg, 35km east of Lucerne. Take the Tell bus from the Lucerne train station to Altdorf (runs Mondays to Saturdays) and a local bus to the Swiss trailhead.

5   **E-BIKE TO KUESNACHT**
Hop on a Swiss-built Flyer electric bike (ask at the tourist office) and ride from Lucerne through villages and farms on signposted paths. About 15km east along the lake, **Kuesnacht's Hohle Gasse** (www.hohlegasse.ch) offers displays on Switzerland's national hero, William Tell.

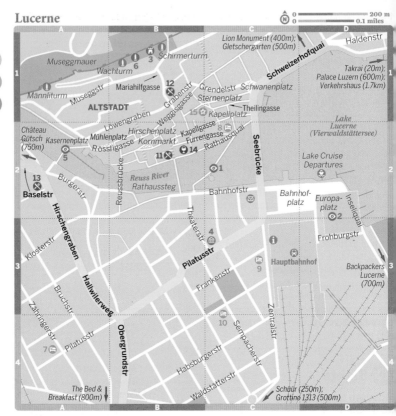

Lucerne

Lucerne

gabled roof is a modern reconstruction, rebuilt after a disastrous fire in 1993. As you cross the bridge, note Heinrich Wägmann's 17th-century triangular roof panels, showing important events from Swiss history and mythology. The icon

is at its most photogenic when bathed in soft golden light at dusk.

Lion Monument   Monument
(Löwendenkmal; Denkmalstrasse) By far the most touching of the 19th-century sights that lured so many British to Lucerne is

the Lion Monument. Lukas Ahorn carved this 10m-long sculpture of a dying lion into the rock face in 1820 to commemorate Swiss soldiers who died defending King Louis XVI during the French Revolution. Mark Twain once called it the 'saddest and most moving piece of rock in the world'. For Narnia fans, it often evokes Aslan at the stone table.

Spreuerbrücke
Bridge

(Spreuer Bridge; btwn Kasernenplatz & Mühlenplatz) Downriver from Kapellbrücke, this 1408 structure is darker and smaller but entirely original. Lore has it that this was the only bridge where Lucerne's medieval villagers were allowed to throw *Spreu* (chaff) into the river. Here, the roof panels consist of artist Caspar Meglinger's movie-storyboard-style sequence of paintings, *The Dance of Death,* showing how the plague affected all levels of society.

Museggmauer
Fortress

(City Wall; ⊙8am-7pm Apr-Oct) FREE For a bird's-eye view over Lucerne's rooftops to the glittering lake and mountains beyond, wander the medieval ramparts. A walkway is open between the Schirmerturm (tower), where you enter, and the Wachturm, from where you have to retrace your steps. You can also ascend and descend the **Zytturm** or Männliturm (the latter not connected to the ramparts walkway).

Verkehrshaus
Museum

(Swiss Museum of Transport; ☎041 370 44 44; www.verkehrshaus.ch; Lidostrasse 5; adult/child Sfr30/15; ⊙10am-6pm Apr-Oct, to 5pm Nov-Mar; ⊕) A great kid-pleaser, the fascinating interactive Verkehrshaus is deservedly Switzerland's most popular

museum. Alongside space rockets, steam locomotives, bicycles and dugout canoes are hands-on activities such as flight simulators and broadcasting studios.

The museum also shelters a **planetarium** (adult/child Sfr15/9), Switzerland's largest **3D cinema** (www.filmtheater.ch; adult/child daytime Sfr18/14, evening Sfr22/19), and its newest attraction: the **Swiss Chocolate Experience** (adult/child Sfr15/9), a 20-minute ride that whirls visitors through multimedia exhibits on the origins, history, production and distribution of chocolate, from Ghana to Switzerland and beyond.

Kultur und Kongresszentrum
Arts Centre

(KKL; ☎tour reservations 041 226 79 50; www.kkl-luzern.ch; Europaplatz; guided tour adult/child Sfr15/9) French architect Jean Nouvel's waterfront arts and convention centre is a postmodern jawdropper in an otherwise historic city. Inside, the tall, narrow concert hall, partly built below the lake's surface, is surrounded by a reverberation chamber and has an adjustable

Lion Monument, Lucerne
LUISMIX / GETTY IMAGES ©

suspended ceiling, all creating a bubble of silence that results in near perfect acoustics. Countless accolades showered upon the hall have raised the profile of the tripartite Lucerne Music Festival, increasingly one of the highlights on the global music calendar.

🛏 Sleeping

Most hotels offer winter discounts – sometimes up to one-third off, but you'll be lucky to get a bed (or any kip for that matter) at Fasnacht, so book well ahead.

ALTSTADT

The Bed & Breakfast B&B €
(☎ 041 310 15 14; www.thebandb.ch; Taubenhausstrasse 34; d Sfr190, s/d/tr/q with shared bathroom Sfr85/130/180/220; P @ 🛜) This friendly B&B feels like home – with stylish, contemporary rooms, crisp white bedding and scatter cushions. Unwind in the garden or with a soak in the old-fashioned tub. Book ahead for the room under the eaves with private bathroom; all others share facilities. Take bus 1 to Eichhof.

Hotel des Alpes Hotel €€
(☎ 041 417 20 60; www.desalpes-luzern.ch; Furrengasse 3; s Sfr140-170, d Sfr218-268; 🛜) Facing the river and directly overlooking Kapellbrücke, the location is this hotel's biggest draw. The rooms are turn-of-the-21st-century comfy, though light sleepers may find them noisy.

CENTRAL LUCERNE

Hotel Waldstätterhof Hotel €€
(☎ 041 227 12 71; www.hotel-waldstaetterhof.ch; Zentralstrasse 4; s Sfr190, d Sfr290-315; P 🛜) Opposite the train station, this hotel with faux-Gothic exterior offers smart, modern rooms with hardwood-style floors and high ceilings, plus excellent service.

Hotel Alpha Hotel €€
(☎ 041 240 42 80; www.hotelalpha.ch; Zähringerstrasse 24; d Sfr154, s/tw/tr with shared bathroom Sfr84/122/163; @ 🛜) Easy on the eyes and wallet, this hotel is in a quiet residential area 10 minutes' walk from the Old Town. Rooms are simple, light and spotlessly clean; cheaper rooms on each floor share bathroom facilities.

Rooftops of Lucerne

The Hotel   Hotel €€€

(☎ 041 226 86 86; www.the-hotel.ch; Sempacherstrasse 14; s/d ste from Sfr425/455; ✳@🛜) This shamelessly hip hotel, bearing the imprint of architect Jean Nouvel, is all streamlined chic, with refined suites featuring stills from movie classics on the ceilings. Downstairs, Bam Bou is one of Lucerne's hippest restaurants, and the gorgeous green park across the street is a cool place to idle.

AROUND CENTRAL LUCERNE

Backpackers Lucerne   Hostel €

(☎ 041 360 04 20; www.backpackerslucerne.ch; Alpenquai 42; dm/d from Sfr33/78; ⏱reception 7-10am & 4-11pm; @🛜) Could this be backpacker heaven? Just opposite the lake, this is a soulful place to crash with art-slung walls, bubbly staff, a well-equipped kitchen and immaculate dorms with balconies. It's a 15-minute walk southeast of the station. There's no breakfast, but guests have kitchen access.

Palace Luzern   Hotel €€€

(☎ 041 416 16 16; www.palace-luzern.ch; Haldenstrasse 10; r from Sfr450) This luxury belle époque hotel on the lakefront is sure of its place in many a heart. Inside it's all gleaming marble, chandeliers, airy rooms and turn-of-the-20th-century grandeur.

Château Gütsch   Hotel €€€

(☎ 041 289 14 14; www.chateau-guetsch.ch; Kanonenstrasse; d Sfr330-570, ste Sfr445-1260; 🛜) The setting is incomparable at this Russian-owned, fairy-tale hilltop palace. Many rooms and suites enjoy sweeping aerial perspectives over Lake Lucerne, as do the bar and breakfast terrace. From the station, take a taxi or catch bus 12 to Kanonenstrasse (10 minutes, plus 10-minute uphill walk).

✗ Eating

Wirtshaus Galliker   Swiss €€

(☎ 041 240 10 01; Schützenstrasse 1; mains Sfr21-51; ⏱11.30am-2pm & 5-10pm Tue-Sat, closed Jul–mid-Aug) Passionately run by the Galliker family for over four generations, this old-style, wood-panelled tavern at-

---

---

tracts a lively bunch of regulars. Motherly waitresses dish up Lucerne soul food (rösti, *chögalipaschtetli* and the like) that is batten-the-hatches filling.

Grottino 1313   Italian €€

(☎ 041 610 13 13; www.grottino1313.ch; Industriestrasse 7; 2-course lunch menu Sfr20, 4-course dinner menu Sfr64; ⏱11am-2pm & 6-11.30pm Mon-Fri, 6-11.30pm Sat, 9am-2pm Sun) Offering a welcome escape from Lucerne's tourist throngs, this relaxed yet stylish eatery serves ever-changing 'surprise' menus featuring starters like chestnut soup with figs, creative pasta dishes, meats cooked over an open fire and scrumptious desserts. The gravel-strewn, herb-fringed front patio is lovely on a summer afternoon, while the candlelit interior exudes sheer cosiness on a winter's evening.

Brasserie Bodu   French €€

(☎ 041 410 01 77; www.brasseriebodu.ch; Kornmarkt 5; mains Sfr25-58; ⏱11.30am-11pm) Banquettes, wood panelling and elbow-to-elbow tables create a warm ambience at

BERNARD VAN DIERENDONCK / LOOK-FOTO / GETTY IMAGES ©

⭐ Don't Miss
Mt Titlis

With a name that makes English speakers titter, Titlis is Central Switzerland's tallest mountain, has its only glacier and is reached by the world's first revolving cable car, completed in 1992. However, that's the last leg of a breathtaking four-stage journey. First, you glide up to Gerschnialp (1300m), then Trübsee (1800m). Transferring to a large gondola, you head for Stand (2450m) to board the Rotair for the head-spinning journey over the dazzling **Titlis Glacier**. As you twirl above the deeply crevassed ice, peaks rise like shark fins ahead, while tarn-speckled pastures, cliffs and waterfalls lie behind.

A glacial blast of air hits you at Titlis station (3020m) but the genuine oohs and aahs come when you step out onto the **terrace**, where the panorama of glacier-capped peaks stretches to Eiger, Mönch and Jungfrau in the Bernese Oberland. It's a 45-minute hike to the 3239m summit (wear sturdy shoes). Otherwise, enjoy the snowboarding and skiing.

The return trip to Titlis (45 minutes each way) costs Sfr86 from Engelberg. However, in fine weather, you can walk some sections. Between Stand and Trübsee, the Geologischer Wanderweg is open from July to September; it takes about two hours up and 1½ hours down. From Trübsee up to Jochpass (2207m) takes about 1½ hours, and down to Engelberg takes around the same time.

Reductions on all fares are 50% for Swiss, Eurail and InterRail pass holders.

Engelberg is at the end of a train line, about an hour from Lucerne (Sfr16.40). If on a day trip, check the Lucerne tourist office's Mt Titlis excursion tickets.

NEED TO KNOW
www.titlis.ch

this classic French-style bistro, where diners huddle around bottles of Bordeaux and bowls of *bouillabaisse* (fish stew) or succulent sirloin steaks.

KKL World Café International €

(📞 041 226 71 00; www.kkl-luzern.ch/en/cuisine; Europaplatz 1; mains Sfr17-22.50; ⊙8.30am-9pm) Salads and sandwiches fill the display cases at the KKL's slick bistro-cum-cafeteria; there are also wok dishes at lunch and dinner.

Jazzkantine Cafe €

(📞 041 410 73 73; www.jazzkantine.ch; Grabenstrasse 8; pasta Sfr16, sandwiches Sfr7-14; ⊙9am-12.30am Mon-Sat) With its long bar, sturdy wooden tables and chalkboard menus, this arty haunt serves tasty Italian dishes and good coffee. Regular jazz workshops and gigs take place downstairs.

Takrai Thai €

(📞 041 412 04 04; www.takrai.ch; Haldenstrasse 9; mains Sfr14.50-22.50; ⊙11am-2.15pm & 5-10pm Mon-Fri, 11am-10pm Sat) This pint-sized Thai joint emphasises local organic produce in its generously portioned cur-

ries. If you can't nab a table, order take-away and chow down lakeside.

🍷 Drinking & Nightlife

Rathaus Bräuerei Brewery

(📞 041 410 52 57; www.braui-luzern.ch; Unter den Egg 2; ⊙11.30am-midnight Mon-Sat, to 11pm Sun) Sip home-brewed beer under the vaulted arches of this buzzy tavern near Kapellbrücke, or nab a pavement table and watch the river flow.

⭐ Entertainment

Schüür Live Music

(www.schuur.ch; Tribschenstrasse 1; ⊙7pm-late) Live gigs are the name of the game here: think everything from metal, garage, pop, electro, Cuban and world, plus theme nights with DJ-spun Britpop and '80s classics.

Stadtkeller Traditional Music

(📞 041 410 47 33; www.stadtkeller.ch; Sternenplatz 3; ⊙lunch/dinner show 12.15/8pm) Alphorns, cowbells, flag throwing, yodelling – name the Swiss cliché and you'll find it at this tourist-oriented club with regular lunch and dinner folklore shows.

Restaurant on the Rathausquai, Lucerne

🔒 Shopping

Mosey down Haldenstrasse for art and antiques or Löwenstrasse for vintage threads and souvenirs.

ℹ️ Information

Tourist Information

Tourist Office (☎ 041 227 17 17; www.luzern. com; Zentralstrasse 5; ⏰ 9am-7pm Mon-Sat, 9am-5pm Sun May-Oct, 8.30am-5.30pm Mon-Fri, 9am-5pm Sat, 9am-1pm Sun Nov-Apr) Reached from Zentralstrasse or platform 3 of the Hauptbahnhof. Offers city walking tours. Call for hotel reservations.

ℹ️ Getting There & Away

Frequent trains connect Lucerne to Interlaken West (Sfr56, two hours), Bern (Sfr36, one hour), Lugano (Sfr56, 2½ hours), Geneva (Sfr74, three hours) and Zürich (Sfr23, one hour).

The departure points are the quays around Bahnhofplatz and Europaplatz.

ℹ️ Getting Around

Should you be going further than the largely pedestrianised Old Town, city buses leave from outside the Hauptbahnhof at Bahnhofplatz. Tickets cost Sfr2.20 for a short journey, Sfr3 for one zone and Sfr4.20 for two. Ticket dispensers indicate the correct fare for each destination. A zone 101 day ticket (Sfr6) covers the city centre and beyond; Swiss Pass holders travel free. There's an underground car park at the train station.

LAKE LUCERNE

Majestic peaks hunch conspiratorially around Vierwaldstättersee – which twists and turns as much as the tongue does when pronouncing it. Little wonder English speakers use the shorthand Lake Lucerne!

To appreciate the views, ride up to Mt Pilatus, Mt Rigi or Stanserhorn. When the clouds peel away or you break through them, precipitous lookout points reveal a crumpled tapestry of green hillsides and shimmering cobalt waters below, with glaciated peaks beyond. It's especially atmospheric in autumn, when fog rises like dry ice from the lake, and in winter, when the craggy heights are dusted with snow.

ℹ️ Getting Around

From Lucerne, destinations include Alpnachstad (one way/return Sfr25/42, 1¾ hours). Longer trips are relatively cheaper than short ones, and you can alight as often as you want. An SGV day ticket costs Sfr66 for adults and Sfr33 for children. Swiss and Eurail passes (on days selected for travel only) are valid on scheduled boat trips, while InterRail entitles you to half-price tickets.

Mt Pilatus

Rearing above Lucerne from the southwest, **Mt Pilatus** (www.pilatus. com) rose to fame in the 19th century when Wagner

Lake Lucerne, viewed from Mt Pilatus

waxed lyrical about its Alpine vistas. Legend has it that this 2132m peak was named after Pontius Pilate, whose corpse was thrown into a lake on its summit and whose restless ghost has haunted its heights ever since. Poltergeists aside, it's more likely that the moniker derives from the Latin word *pileatus,* meaning cloud covered – as the mountain frequently is.

From May to October, you can reach Mt Pilatus on a classic 'golden round-trip'. Board the lake steamer from Lucerne to Alpnachstad, then rise with the world's steepest cog railway to Mt Pilatus. From the summit, cable cars bring you down to Kriens via Fräkmüntegg and Krienseregg, where bus 1 takes you back to Lucerne. The reverse route (Kriens–Pilatus–Alpnachstad–Lucerne) is also possible. The return trip costs Sfr91 (less with valid Swiss, Eurail or InterRail passes).

Mt Pilatus is fantastic for **walking**. Hikes include a steep, partially roped 2.8km scramble (June to September) from Fräkmüntegg to the summit.

In winter, try **sledging** 6km through snowy woodlands from Fräkmüntegg to Kriens. A return ticket between Kriens and Fräkmüntegg by cable car costs Sfr38 for adults and Sfr19 for children. Free sledge hire is available at Fräkmüntegg station.

Mt Rigi

Blue, no red, no dark…Turner couldn't quite make up his mind about how he preferred 1797m **Rigi** (www.rigi.ch), so in 1842 the genius painted the mountain in three different lights to reflect its changing moods. On a clear day, there are impressive views to a jagged spine of peaks including Mt Titlis and the Jungfrau giants. The sunrises and sunsets viewed from the summit are the stuff of bucket lists.

The 33-room **Rigi Kulm Hotel** (041 880 18 88; www.rigikulm.ch; s Sfr148-203, d Sfr228-318; 🛜) is the only major establishment at the summit and commands stirring views. The natty streamlined rooms mix old and new furnishings and boast immaculate

Detour:
Brunnen

Tucked into the mountains, where Lake Lucerne and Lake Uri meet at right angles, Brunnen enjoys mesmerising views south and west. English artist Joseph Turner was so impressed that he painted *The Bay of Uri from Brunnen* (1841). As the wind rushes down from the mountains, it creates perfect conditions for sailing and paragliding.

The **Swiss Knife Valley Museum** (041 820 60 10; www.swissknifevalley.ch; Bahnhofstrasse 3; ⏱10am-6.30pm Mon-Fri, to 5pm Sat & Sun; 👪) gives an insight into the country's most famous of exports - the Victorinox Swiss Army Knife. Should you so wish, you can construct your own in 15 minutes flat.

By far the most pleasant way to reach Brunnen is to take a boat from Lucerne (Sfr37, 1¾ hours).

bathrooms, plus there's a good restaurant and stylishly decorated self-service cafeteria for those not staying the night.

For recommended hiking routes, check www.rigi.ch. There are several easy walks (one to two hours) down from Rigi Kulm to Rigi Kaltbad, with wonderful views.

Two rival railways carry passengers to the top. One runs from Arth-Goldau (one way/return Sfr40/64), the other from Vitznau (one way/return Sfr45/72). The Vitznau track gives the option of diverting at Rigi Kaltbad and taking the cable car to or from Weggis instead. Holders of Swiss, Eurail and InterRail passes receive a 50% discount on fares, and children under 16 travel free when accompanied by a parent.

Valais & Zermatt

Valais landscapes leave you dumbstruck: from the unfathomable Matterhorn (4478m) to the Rhône Valley's tapestry of vineyards and shimmering 23km Aletsch Glacier. With such backdrops, how can any hike, bike or ski tour be anything but great?

The Valais tale is of rags to riches, of changing seasons and celebrities, of an outdoors so wonderful it never goes out of fashion. Wedged in a remote corner of southern Switzerland, this is where farmers were so poor they didn't have two francs to rub together a century ago, where today luminaries sip champagne cocktails in the posh winter playground of Verbier.

As earthy as a vintner's boots in September and as clean as the aesthetic in Zermatt's lounge bars, this canton can be fickle. The west speaks French, the east German, united in matters of cantonal pride by fine wine and glorious cheese.

The famed Matterhorn rises above the town of Zermatt
AYMONDCHAN PHOTO / GETTY IMAGES ©

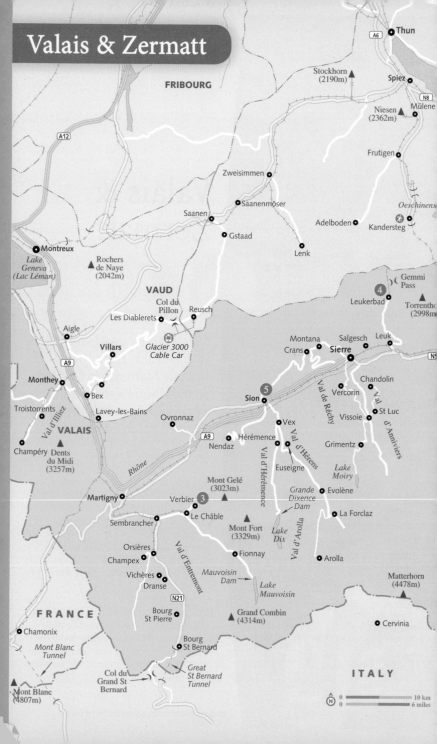

Valais & Zermatt

Valais & Zermatt's Highlights

Zermatt

The first time the Matterhorn (p178) pops into view never fails to thrill excited passengers aboard the red train up to the car-free ski resort of Zermatt (p178). Bewitching and charismatic, it's an iconic prima donna of a mountain, impossible not to ogle at from every last angle. Sit back, ski or hike, or admire aboard a cogwheel railway or cable car and get set to become hopelessly obsessed. Below: Europe's highest cogwheel railway, Gornergratbahn (p179)

Aletsch Glacier

Fittingly, this 23km-long ribbon of ice – Europe's longest glacier – is a Unesco World Heritage site. Streaming like a six-lane superhighway around the 4195m peak of Aletschhorn, the glacier (p186) makes compelling viewing on summertime hikes and winter ski sprees. The icing on the snow-white cake: the twinset of bijou, car-free mountain villages, accessed by cable car from the valley, from which to stride out in this magnificent glacial wilderness.

Verbier

Heidi may be fictional, but her Alpine village life style isn't. And there is no finer address to experience it than glitzy Verbier (p172) where Swiss history comes to life in a storybook sweep of ancient log chalets strung with springtime geraniums, walking trails sprinkled with wild flowers, shimmering ski pistes, and swish bars and clubs – staunchly 21st century – where celebrities hobnob at the end of every wonderful day.

Leukerbad

In a country renowned for its spas, Leukerbad (p178) stands out. Water heated at untold depths of the earth bubbles forth at a toasty 36°C into a series of soaking and therapy pools - looked down on by soaring mountain peaks criss-crossed with hiking trails, ski pistes and the mythical Gemmi mountain pass. Saunas, whirlpools and a bevy of alpine-flower wraps and grape-seed baths only add to the invigorating, soul-cleansing pleasure.

Sion

Few towns are as gourmet as this. Thanks to the glittery Rhône River weaving its way through the centre of town, Sion (p175) can readily quench the thirst of its surrounding vineyards. A quick ramble and you can taste some of Switzerland's finest whites. Or march on either of two castles that surmount meandering little lanes lined with outdoor cafes where, yes, you can enjoy more of the local vintages.

Valais & Zermatt's Best...

Skiing

○ **Verbier** More than 400km of runs served by almost 100 lifts. (p172)

○ **Zermatt** The Matterhorn is a backdrop for 350km of ski runs for every taste and skill level. (p178)

○ **Saas Fee** Excellent snow on the slopes around a lovely old traditional town. (p183)

○ **Bettmeralp** Family-friendly skiing on the dramatic edge of the Aletsch Glacier. (p187)

Mountain Panoramas

○ **Gornergratbahn** Europe's highest open-air cogwheel railway, in Zermatt. (p179)

○ **Matterhorn Glacier Paradise** Sweeping glacial panorama pierced by the Matterhorn, atop Zermatt's celebrity cable car. (p182)

○ **Médran Cable Car** Watch the sun rise from the top of Verbier's Mont Fort. (p173)

○ **Allalin** Glorious 360-degree views of Saas Fee's 4000m glacial giants. (p183)

Easy Hikes

○ **Zermatt** One of Switzerland's best places to hike with oodles of well-marked trails. (p178)

○ **Salgesch** Wineries linked by a beautiful 6km walk through vineyards. (p174)

○ **Fiesch** Begin hikes here with the spectacle of the Aletsch Glacier. (p186)

○ **Bettmeralp** Catch a cable car up to beautiful walks with glacier views. (p187)

Extraordinary Dines

o **Chez Vrony** Celebrity mountain address with organic cuisine and Matterhorn view. (p181)

o **Café du Midi** Cheese fondue in Martigny. (p171)

o **Le Namasté** Mountain cabin with traditional Swiss cuisine on Verbier's slopes. (p174)

o **Spielboden** Saas Fee mountain chic. (p185)

o **Au Cheval Blanc** Bistro fare and Valaisan wine. (p177)

Need to Know

ADVANCE PLANNING

o **Five months before** If travelling to any of the top ski resorts like Zermatt or Verbier during peak season (Christmas to March), nail accommodation.

o **Three months before** For summertime Matterhorn excursions, beat the crowds by lining up your ideal Zermatt room early.

RESOURCES

o **Valais Tourism** (www.valais.ch) The region's tourism authority.

o **Verbier Booking** (www.verbierbooking.com) Book early during peak winter skiing season.

o **Ski Zermatt** (www.ski-zermatt.com) Skiing info plus live cams of the Matterhorn.

o **Ski Suisse** (www.ski-suisse.com) Book ski accommodation.

GETTING AROUND

o **Train** The major towns are all connected by efficient train service. Zermatt is also the western terminus for the popular Glacier Express train, which runs east all the way to St Moritz.

o **Car** Travelling around the Valais is a grandiose experience thanks to the astonishing road links – high mountain passes, snowbound in winter, and masterfully engineered tunnels – it shares with neighbouring Italy. For exploring intriguing hidden valleys, you'll want a car.

BE FOREWARNED

o **Parking** Zermatt, gateway to the Matterhorn, is car-free and you have to leave your car in valley car parks below and catch a train up.

o **Peak Seasons** Christmas to March and July and August are busy, busy, busy any place that's beloved for winter skiing or hiking under azure blue summer skies. Plan accordingly. (Locals in the know suggest the golden, uncrowded days of September for enjoying the green outdoors.)

Valais & Zermatt Itineraries

The Matterhorn serves as a sentinel to these tours, which feature a spectacular glacier that leads back to the Jungfrau region, and the best of Valais.

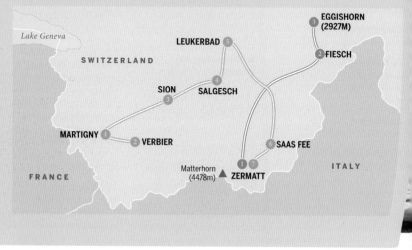

3 DAYS

MATTERHORN
ZERMATT TO EGGISHORN

It's the Matterhorn baby! And the lure of this Swiss icon rightfully draws people to **①Zermatt** (p178). From this car-free village, you can wander myriad trails in summer and ski myriad runs in winter. Spend a couple of nights here to explore the celebrity resort and its gargantuan mountains at an appropriate go-slow pace. Ride the cable car up to Matterhorn Glacier Paradise (p182), an icy landscape with spectacular views of dozens of peaks over 4000m. Second day, chug up to the top of Gornergrat aboard Europe's oldest cogwheel railway, the Gornergratbahn (p179), or take the Sunnegga Express up to Sunnegga

and stroll down through wild flower-strewn meadows (summer) or ski (winter) down to Chez Vrony (p181) for lunch on the terrace with unforgettable Matterhorn views.

Third day, ride the train from Zermatt down to Täsch in the valley, then catch a train to the bijou village of **②Fiesch** (p186). From here catch a cable car and gondola up to **③Eggishorn** (p186) and clamp your hand over your mouth so nothing will fly in when your jaw drops – the views of the 23km Aletsch Glacier, which curves in a huge ribbon of ice back towards Jungfrau, are simply magnificent.

5 DAYS

MARTIGNY TO ZERMATT

Start your outdoorsy Valais adventure in the home of St Bernard dogs, ❶ **Martigny** (p170). The Musée et Chiens du Saint-Bernard (p171) honours the brandy-proffering, drooling pooch of lore. It's a short ride by train and bus or car to ❷ **Verbier** (p172), a posh ski resort that fully justifies the hype with spectacular powder in winter.

Back in the valley, pause for a vineyard ramble from spring to autumn at the wineries around ❸ **Sion** (p175). The Bisse de Clavau is a centuries-old canal that today waters the grapes and leads to restaurants amid the vines. ❹ **Salgesch** (p174) is another fine place to enjoy local wine: stroll the 6km-long Sentier Viticole trail through vineyards.

Take a restorative break at ❺ **Leukerbad** (p178), a thermal spa set up high amid staggering Alpine beauty. Return to the valley and head east to car-free ❻ **Saas Fee** (p183). Thirteen peaks and nine glaciers create a festival of natural beauty. From here, it's a short jaunt over to ❼ **Zermatt** (p178) and the essential prospect of the Matterhorn.

Gazing over the Aletsch Glacier (p186) near Fiesch
CHRIS SCHMID / GETTY IMAGES ©

Discover Valais & Zermatt

At a Glance

○ **Verbier** (p172) Glitzy ski resort with some of Europe's best powder

○ **Sion** (p175) Walk, dine fine, drink amid Valaisan vineyards.

○ **Leukerbad** (p178) Europe's largest thermal resort is pure drama.

○ **Zermatt** (p178) Chic, car-free ski resort & gateway to the iconic Matterhorn peak.

○ **Aletsch Glacier** (p186) Staggering, 23km Unesco-listed river of ice.

Thermal spring path, Leukerbad (p178)
STEFANO CELLAI / GETTY IMAGES ©

LOWER VALAIS

Stone-walled vineyards, tumbledown castle ruins and brooding mountains create an arresting backdrop to the meandering Rhône valley in western Valais. Running west to east, the A9 motorway links towns such as Roman-rooted Martigny and vine-strewn Sion, where the French influence shows not only in the lingo but also in the locals' passion for art, wine and pavement cafes.

....

Martigny

POP 16,785 / ELEV 476M

Once the stomping ground of Romans in search of wine and sunshine en route to Italy, small-town Martigny is Valais' oldest town. Look beyond its concrete high-rises to enjoy a world-class art gallery, Roman amphitheatre and a posse of droopy St Bernard dogs to romp up the surrounding mountains with.

◎ **Sights & Activities**

Fondation Pierre Gianadda   Gallery
(☏ 027 722 39 78; www.gianadda. ch; Rue du Forum; adult/10-25yr Sfr20/12; ⏰ 9am-7pm) Set in a concrete edifice, this renowned gallery harbours a stunning art collection with works by Picasso, Cézanne and van Gogh, occasionally shifted to make space for blockbuster exhibitions such as 'Matisse en son siècle' (Matisse in his Century). Equally outstanding is the garden (with cafe and picnic area) where Henry Moore's organic sculptures, Niki de Saint Phalle's buxom *Bathers* and César's *Le Sein* (The Breast) pop out among the foliage. The Fondation

also hosts classical music recitals (tickets Sfr30 to Sfr120).

Musée et Chiens du Saint-Bernard
Museum

(☏027 720 49 20; www.museesaintbernard.ch; Rte du Levant 34; museum adult/child Sfr12/7, with dog-walking Sfr35/10; ☺10am-6pm) A tribute to the lovably dopey St Bernard, this museum opposite Martigny's **Roman amphitheatre** includes real-life fluff bundles in the kennels. In July and August you can join the dogs for a 1½-hour walk in nearby woods; reserve in advance. Upstairs an exhibition traces the role of St Bernards in hospice life, on canvas and in film.

🛏 Sleeping & Eating

Hôtel Beau Site
Hotel €

(☏027 722 81 64; www.chemin.ch; Chemin-Dessus; s/d/q Sfr110/150/190; ☺Jun-Aug, rest of year advance reservation only; 📶) 🌿 Perched high above town at 1211m, this ecofriendly art-nouveau house from 1912 is an oasis of peace amid walking trails. Rooms are simple with shared bathroom, and vegetarian meals (Sfr30) are sourced from the veggie patch. From Martigny, follow signs for Col des Planches and Chemin-sur-Martigny, driving uphill for 7km through Le Bourg and Chemin-Dessous to the hamlet of Chemin-Dessus.

Café du Midi
Cafe €

(☏027 722 00 03; www.cafedumidi.ch; Rue des Marronniers 4; fondue Sfr21-24; ☺noon-11pm Wed-Mon) Guzzle Trappist brews and gorge on as much raclette as you can handle or dip into one of 10 different fondues – including with tomato, mushrooms or à la bière (beer fondue) – at this shabby-chic cafe with buzzing pavement terrace. Unusual is the fondue made from melted chèvre (goat's cheese).

La Vache qui Vole
Bistro €€

(☏027 722 38 33; www.lavachequivole.ch; Place Centrale 2b; plat du jour Sfr25-27, mains Sfr28-48; ☺10.30am-1am Mon-Sat; 📶) The Flying Cow is a gallery-style wine bar with an angelic cow strung from its ceiling and a Virgin Mary collection upstairs. World

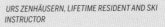

Local Knowledge

Valais Outdoors Don't Miss List

URS ZENHÄUSERN, LIFETIME RESIDENT AND SKI INSTRUCTOR

1 ALETSCH GLACIER
As a landscape of extraordinary beauty, the Jungfrau-Aletsch Region in the Swiss Alps was included in the list of Unesco World Natural Heritage sites. Vacations in the Aletsch Glacier area are vacations in untouched nature and in an attractive hiking area. From the summit of the **Eggishorn**, at 2927m, you can enjoy beautiful views over the whole length of the Aletsch Glacier (p186) and the mighty peaks of the Eiger, Mönch and Jungfrau and as far as the Matterhorn.

2 HIGHEST REVOLVING RESTAURANT
Don't miss the highest revolving restaurant in the world on the **Mittelallalin** (3500m), which offers a 360-degree panorama and the highest and largest Ice Pavilion in the world, containing ice sculptures and an exhibition about glacier formation. It's all above the car-free resort of **Saas Fee** (p183), one of the most attractive in Valais.

3 VERBIER
As soon as the first snow falls, Verbier (p172) becomes a winter sports paradise. 'Les 4 Vallées' (Four Valleys) is the name of this immense ski resort with 412 km of piste and more than 90 lifts and railways linking the train stations of Verbier, Nendaz, Veysonnaz, Thyon and La Tzoumaz. It's a fine winter playground, and in summer it's a place for hiking.

4 PORTES DU SOLEIL
Between Switzerland and France discover the **Portes du Soleil** (www.portesdusoleil. com), the largest linked international ski area containing the mountain resorts of Champéry, Val-d'Illiez-Les Crosets-Champoussin, Morgins and Torgon. You could spend years exploring the myriad runs here.

cuisine is its culinary stomping ground – creative salads, pasta and risotto jostle for tastebud time with curries and raw fish – and the wine list is packed with Valais wines by small producers. End with lemon-lime sorbet doused in limoncello.

ℹ Information

Tourist Office (027 720 49 49; www.martignytourism.ch; Ave de la Gare 6; ⏰9am-6.30pm Mon-Fri, to 5pm Sat, 10am-3pm Sun Jul & Aug, reduced hours Sep-Jun) Ask the tourist office about vineyard walks and cycling trails in Martigny's terraced, green surrounds.

ℹ Getting There & Away

Martigny is on the main train line running from Lausanne (Sfr23, 50 minutes) to Brig (Sfr25, 55 minutes).

From Martigny the panoramic **Mont Blanc Express** (www.mont-blanc-express.com) goes to Chamonix (Sfr33, 1½ hours) in France.

Verbier

POP 3000 / ELEV 1500M

Ritzy Verbier is the diamond of the Valaisian Alps: small, stratospherically expensive and cut at all the right angles to make it sparkle in the eyes of accomplished skiers and piste-bashing stars. Yet despite its ritzy packaging, Verbier is that rare beast of a resort – all things to all people. It swings from schnapps-fuelled debauchery to VIP lounges, bunker hostels to design-oriented hotels, burgers to Michelin stars. Here ski bums and celebs slalom in harmony on powder that is legendary.

Unlike smaller resorts, Verbier scarcely shuts between seasons. Bar a couple of weeks in May and October, there's always something happening.

🎯 Activities

Something of a recreation mecca, there is an activity to suit every outdoor urge. For an overview and on-the-ground guidance, hook up with a local mountain guide at **Les Guides de Verbier** (027 775 33 70; www.guideverbier.com; Rue de Médran 41). For a one-stop shop online go to www.verbier-booking.com.

SKIING

Verbier's skiing is justifiably billed as some of Europe's finest. The resort sits at the heart of the Quatre Vallées (Four Valleys), comprising a cool 412km of runs and 94 ski lifts. A regional ski pass costs Sfr70 per day.

HIKING

The walking here is superb, with 500km of signposted trails – several suitable for families are mapped in the 55-page *Hiking* brochure available at the tourist office. Notable shorter strolls include the **Sentier des Sculptures**, a sculpture path with works of arts sculpted in wood with a chainsaw by ex-Valaisain ski champ William Besse; the art-endowed **Verbier 3D Parc de Sculptures** between Les Ruinettes and La Chaux; and the two-hour trail from Les Ruinettes along the irrigation channel **Bisse du Levron**.

BIKING

Verbier-La Tzoumaz Bike Park
Mountain Biking

(027 775 33 63, 027 775 25 11; www.verbier-bikepark.ch; adult/child day pass Sfr34/17; ⏰8am-5.30pm Jul-Sep, 9am-12.30pm & 1.30-4.30pm Mon-Fri, 9am-4.30pm Sat & Sun Jun & Oct) Ride the Médran cable car from Verbier up to Les Ruinettes to pick up dozens of downhill trails between trees in Verbier's first-class bike park. Trails range from dead easy to super-hard with 2m jumps, and three are equipped with a timing system. There is also a mountain-bike school.

Trottinettes
Scooter Rental

(027 775 25 11; 1 descent Sfr20; ⏰8am-5pm Jul & Aug, reduced hours Jun, Sep & Oct) Hugely popular with families, *trottinettes* (downhill scooters) are one way of getting down the mountain from Les Ruinettes. Buy your ticket at the ticket office on Place de Médran then ride the Médran cable car up to Les Ruinettes to collect your scooter and helmet. Children under eight years

NEIL EMMERSON / GETTY IMAGES ©

★ Don't Miss
Mont Fort at Sunrise

Nothing stirs the soul quite like seeing the sun rise from the top of Mont Fort, at a panoramic 3330m. The Médran cable car departs on Thursdays in July at 4.45am and in August at 5am. The trip costs Sfr60/38 per adult/child, covers unlimited travel on cable cars for the rest of the day, and includes an early bird breakfast in the giant igloo-shaped Les Gentianes restaurant (2950m) on the Col des Gentianes. Reserve at least 24 hours in advance at the Médran ticket office on Place de Médran in Verbier.

must ride with an adult. Count on one hour for the descent.

🛌 Sleeping

Verbier is doable for ski bums on a budget with pre-planning. Rates nosedive by 30% to 50% in July and August.

Les Touristes   Hotel €
(☎ 027 771 21 47; www.hoteltouristes-verbier.ch; Rte de Verbier; s Sfr75-90, d Sfr150-180; P 🛜; 🚠 Fromagerie) An authentic original, Les Touristes opened to summer tourists in 1933, well before skiing took off. Today it is a 15-minute walk downhill from the hip hub of modern Verbier, next to a *fromage-*

rie (cheese dairy) and fourth-generation bakery in the old village of Verbier. Its 16 rooms are basic with pine trappings, floral bedding, washbasins and shared showers in the corridor.

Chez Angèle   B&B €€
(☎ 027 771 48 19; Chemin de la Crête 20; d Sfr140-220; 🚠 Fromagerie) From the ginger cat that slumbers on the windowsill to the carved wooden shutters, brass door bell and balcony overflowing with summertime geraniums, this B&B offers unadulterated Alpine charm. Rooms are traditional chalet-style and its picture-postcard surrounds are enchanting. Find it a 15-minute

173

Detour:
Salgesch & Sierre

As dreamy as a Turner watercolour in the golden autumn light, the winegrowing hamlet of Salgesch produced the first-ever Swiss grand cru in 1988. Blessed with chalky soil and sunshine, Salgesch yields spicy Pinot noirs, fruity dôles and mineral Fendants. Many cellars open their doors for tastings.

A real must for wine buffs is the scenic **Sentier Viticole** (wine trail; 6km) that leads through vineyards from the wine museum inside Sierre's gourmet **Château de Villa** (☎ 027 455 18 96; www.chateaudevilla.ch; Rue Ste Catherine 4; fondue Sfr23-26, mains Sfr25-40; ⏱11.30am-2pm & 6-10.30pm) to the gabled **Weinmuseum** (Wine Museum; ☎ 027 456 45 25; adult/child Sfr6/free, with Sierre wine museum ticket free; ⏱2-5pm Tue-Sun Apr-Nov) in Salgesch – allow 2½ hours for the walk, which takes in 80 explanatory panels about the vines, local winegrowing techniques, the harvest and so on. Complete the trip with dinner and an overnight in a wine barrel at themed **Hotel Arkanum** (☎ 027 451 21 00; www.hotelarkanum.ch; s/d from Sfr103/178; P 🛜). Hourly trains link Salgesch and Sierre (Sfr3, three minutes), in the geographic centre of Valais.

walk downhill from Verbier Station, behind the church in the old village of Verbier.

W Hotel
Design Hotel €€€
(☎ 027 472 88 88; www.wverbier.com; Rue de Médran 70, Place Blanche; d from Sfr300) From the coffee tables on each balcony, fashioned from cut-off tree trunks on wheels, to the five-star spa, this sophisticated hotel near the Médran cable car is sensational. At home in four contemporary chalet-style buildings linked by glass corridors, design is the driver here.

🍴 Eating & Drinking

Fer à Cheval
Pizzeria €
(☎ 027 771 26 69; Rue de Médran; pizza Sfr18-23, mains Sfr25-40; ⏱11.30am-midnight) Thank goodness for the Horseshoe, an affordable, down-to-earth pizzeria with sunny terrace, electric atmosphere and fabulous food any hour. Find it footsteps from Place Centrale, towards the Médran cable-car station. Our favourite 'table': the wooden cart.

Le Namasté
Swiss €
(☎ 027 771 57 73; www.namaste-verbier.ch; Les Planards; mains Sfr15-25; ⏱daily mid-Dec–Easter & mid-Jul–Aug, Thu-Sun mid-May–Jun, Sep & Oct) Its name means 'Welcome' in

Tibetan and it's always packed. Jean-Louis – a metal sculptor who creates fantastical beasts from old tools – and his wife Annick are the creative energy behind this cosy mountain cabin at 1937m with traditional Swiss kitchen. Ski to it from Savoleyres or, come nightfall, skidoo up and sledge down.

Le Bec
Brasserie €
(☎ 027 775 44 04; www.brasserielebec.com; Rue de Médran 77, Place Blanche; mains Sfr16-25; ⏱8.30am-6.30pm Jul-Apr; 🛜 👶) This Verbier hipster, with big bold windows and stylish outside seating on Place Blanche, is the place to be seen. Its modern kitchen cooks up quinoa-style salads, bacon burgers with handcut fries and other contemporary brasserie fare. Top marks to the chef for the salmon and cod fishcakes with mint-scented pea mash, homemade basil lemonade (and complimentary organic carrot purée for babies!).

ℹ Information

Tourist Office (☎ 027 775 38 88; www.verbier.ch; Place Centrale; ⏱8.30am-7pm Dec-Apr, reduced hours May-Nov)

ℹ️ Getting There & Away

Swish St-Bernard Express trains from Martigny run hourly year-round to Le Châble (Sfr10.80, 30 minutes) from where you can board a Verbier-bound bus (Sfr6, 30 minutes) or – in season – the **Le Châble-Verbier cable car** (📞 027 775 25 11; www.televerbier.ch; adult one way/return Sfr10/15, child Sfr5/8; ⏱7am-4.45pm Nov, to 7.30pm Dec-Apr, Jul & Aug), across from the train station.

....

Sion

POP 32,170 / ELEV 490M

French-speaking Sion is bewitching. The serpentine Rhône River bisects Sion and a twinset of 13th-century hilltop châteaux play guard atop a pair of craggy rock hills.

Sion moves to a relaxed beat, with winemaking (and tasting) playing an essential role in the town's mantra and pavement cafes lining the helter-skelter of quaint lanes that thread sharply downhill from its castles to medieval Old Town.

◎ Sights

Château de Tourbillon   Chateau
(Rue des Châteaux; ⏱10am-6pm May-Sep, 11am-5pm mid-Mar–Apr & Oct–mid-Nov)
FREE Lording it over the fertile Rhône Valley from its hilltop perch above Sion, the crumbling remains of this medieval stronghold, destroyed by fire in 1788, are worth the stiff trudge for the postcard views alone; wear solid shoes as the rocky path is hairy in places.

Château de Valère   Chateau
(Rue des Châteaux; adult/child Sfr8/4; ⏱11am-6pm Jun-Sep, to 5pm Oct-May) Slung on a hillock opposite Château

de Tourbillon is this 11th- to 13th-century château that grew up around a fortified basilica. The church interior reveals beautifully carved choir stalls, a frescoed apse and the world's oldest playable organ from 1440; summertime concerts on Saturday (4pm) are magical. The château also hosts the **Musée Cantonal d'Histoire** (📞 027 606 47 15; adult/child Sfr8/4; ⏱11am-6pm Jun-Sep, to 5pm Tue-Sun Oct-May) and nestles a lunchtime cafe with view within its walls.

🏃 Activities

What makes trails in this part of the Rhône Valley so unique are the *bisses* – miniature canals built from the 13th century to irrigate the steeply terraced vineyards and fields.

Best known is the **Bisse de Clavau**, a 550-year-old irrigation channel that carries water to the thirsty, sun-drenched vineyards between Sion and St Léonard. Vines, planted on narrow terraces supported by drystone retaining walls, are devoted to the production of

VALAIS & ZERMATT SION

Château de Tourbillon
DIANA HEALEY / GETTY IMAGES ©

ARCHITECT: JEAN-PIERRE EMERY / IMAGE COURTESY OF NICOLA WILLIAMS ©

⭐ Don't Miss
Fondation Pierre Arnaud

Don't miss this stunning art gallery with mountain peaks looming large on its dazzling mirrored facade and silver-leafed edelweiss in the Alpine rooftop garden. Inside is equally brilliant, with the gallery hosting two contemporary art exhibitions each year. End with lunch in L'Indigo, the museum bistro with wooden-decking terrace looking across the serene water of Lake Louché to the mountains beyond. Take bus No 353 from La Poste bus stop in Crans-Montana to Lens (Sfr4.40, 20 minutes).

Ensure you make time for a circular stroll around the lake to admire the gallery's striking sustainable architecture. The 84 photovoltaic solar panels that make up the 250 sq metre facade provide thermic insulation for the art works inside as well as creating a brilliant reflection of the museum's staggeringly beautiful surrounds.

NEED TO KNOW

📞027 483 46 10; www.fondationpierrearnaud.ch; Route de Crans 1, Lens; adult/child Sfr18/free, Sun brunch with/without museum Sfr58/45; 🕑10am-7pm Tue, Wed & Fri-Sun, to 9pm Thu late Dec-Sep

highly quaffable Valaisian dôle (red) and Fendant (white) wines. Taste them alone or with lunch at **Le Cube** (📞079 566 95 63; www.verone.ch; Bisse de Clavau; mains Sfr20-40; 🕑11am-9pm Sat, to 6pm Sun May-Oct), an old winegrower's hut once used to store tools and now transformed into a fabulously stylish address in the vines to wine and dine. The Cube sits on the Bisse de Clavau footpath (7.5km, 2½ hours), part of the Chemin du Vignoble.

 Sleeping & Eating

Food and wine are big reasons to linger. Rue du Grand-Pont, so-called because of the river that runs beneath its entire length, is peppered with tasty places to eat well and drink fine Valais wine.

Hôtel Elite
Hotel €

(☏ 027 322 03 27; www.hotelelite-sion.com; Ave du Midi 6; s/d/tr/q Sfr111/150/210/285; ℗ 🛜) Aptly named, this bright, modern two-star address just off the main street is the best place to stay in town. Rooms, painted soft apricot hues, are not quite as bold as the pillar-box-red reception.

Au Cheval Blanc
Swiss €€

(☏ 027 322 18 67; www.au-cheval-blanc.ch; Rue du Grand-Pont 23; mains Sfr29-59, beef Sfr36-51; 🕙10am-midnight Tue-Fri, 11am-midnight Sat) A local institution for its great food and convivial vibe, this traditional bistro with leafy pavement terrace on Rue du Grand-Pont uses the best local produce. The icing on the cake is its Val d'Hérens beef prepared just as you like it – as tartare, carpaccio, with vinaigrette, as a *tagliata di filetto* or *en rossini*.

Restaurant Damien Germanier
Modern Swiss €€€

(☏ 027 322 99 88; www.damiengermanier.ch; Rue du Scex 33; lunch/dinner menus from Sfr65/100; 🕙11.30am-2pm & 7-9pm Tue-Sun) At Chez Damien Germanier, dedicated gourmets can plump for the Valaisian chef's surprise menu or treat tastebuds to a magnificent 10-course symphony of tastes and experiences with his feast of a '5 Senses' menu. Dining is white table-cloth and unadulterated gastronomic.

ℹ Information

Tourist Office (☏ 027 327 77 27; www.siontourism.ch; Place de la Planta; 🕙9am-6pm Mon-Fri, to 12.30pm Sat; 🛜)

ℹ Getting There & Around

Train

All trains on the express route between Lausanne (Sfr30, 50 to 80 minutes) and Brig (Sfr9.60, 25 to 35 minutes) stop in Sion.

❤ If You Like…
Hidden Valleys

If you like the off-the-beaten path charm of Val d'Héremance, there are other hidden little valleys tucked away deep in between jutting peaks:

1 VAL D'HÉRENS
This thickly wooded valley hides many peculiarities and pastures mown by silky black Hérens cattle. The road wriggles up from Sion through Vex and then Euseigne, passing the wondrous Gaudí-esque rock pinnacles Pyramides d'Euseigne.

2 VAL D'ENTREMONT & VAL FERRET
The St Bernard Express train from Martigny to Orsières branches south at Sembrancher, chugging along the Val d'Entremont to the Italian border. Orsières marks the beginning of pine-brushed Val Ferret. It's a 1¾-hour walk to Champex (1471m), a mountain village with a beautiful glassy lake.

3 VAL D'ANNIVIERS
Brushed with pine and larch, scattered with dark-timber chalets and postcard villages and set against glistening 4000m peaks, this strikingly beautiful, little-explored valley beckons skiers eager to slalom away from the crowds and hikers seeking big nature. The road south from Sierre corkscrews precipitously past postage-stamp orchards and vineyards, arriving after 13km in the medieval village of Vissoie, a valley crosroads for five ski stations.

Val d'Héremance

Out of earshot of tourist footsteps, this valley remains mystifyingly unknown, despite harbouring one of the world's greatest hydraulic marvels, the 285m-high **Grande Dixence dam**. From Sion, follow the signs for this valley and the Val d'Hérens, which share the same road as far as Vex, where you branch right and follow a twisting road 30km to the dam.

From the dam base, it's a 45-minute hike or a speedier **cable car** (www.theytaz-excursions.ch; adult/child return Sfr10/5;

Detour:
Leukerbad

The road that zigzags 14km up from the medieval hillside hamlet of **Leuk,** past breathtakingly sheer chasms and wooded crags, is a spectacular build-up to Leukerbad. Gazing up to an amphitheatre of towering rock turrets and canyon-like spires, Europe's largest thermal spa resort is pure drama.

Walliser Alpentherme & Spa Leukerbad (☎027 472 10 10; www.alpentherme. ch; Dorfplatz; thermal baths 3hr/day Sfr23/28, with sauna village Sfr39/53, Roman-Irish bath with/without soap-brush massage Sfr74/54; ⏱pools 9am-8pm, sauna village & Roman-Irish baths 10am-8pm) offers a twinset of pools – one in, one out, both 36°C – with whirlpools, jets, Jacuzzi and dramatic mountain view. To lounge in the traditional Valais Sauna Village – all wood and rustic cartwheels, with several saunas, mill, ice-cold stream and herbal steam rooms – you must be naked. Equally invigorating is the Roman-Irish bath, a two-hour nude bathing ritual.

Hourly postal buses link Leukerbad with Leuk (Sfr11.40, 30 minutes) and Visp (Sfr19.40, one hour); the bus station adjoins Leukerbad's **tourist office** (☎027 472 71 71; www.leukerbad.ch; Ratplatz; ⏱9am-noon & 1.15-6pm Mon-Fri & Sun, 9am-6pm Sat).

⏱every 10min 10.05am-12.15pm & 1.15-5.15pm Jun–mid-Oct) ride to the top. Before boarding, book a 1¼-hour guided **tour** (www.grande-dixence.ch; guided tour adult/child Sfr10/6, with return cable car Sfr15/7; ⏱11.30am, 1.30pm, 3pm & 4.30pm mid-Jun–Sep) of the dam at the information point at the bottom. Framed by snow-dusted crags, the milky-green waters abruptly vanish like a giant infinity pool. Collecting the meltwater of 35 glaciers, weighing 15 million tonnes and supplying a fifth of Switzerland's energy, the dam is sure to impress.

UPPER VALAIS

In a xylophone-to-gong transition, the soothing loveliness of vineyards in the west gives way to austere beauty in the east of Valais. Bijou villages of woodsy chalets stand in collective awe of the drum-roll setting of vertiginous ravines, spiky 4000m pinnacles and monstrous glaciers. The effervescent thermal waters of Leukerbad, the dazzling 23km Aletsch Glacier and the soaring pyramid of Matterhorn are natural icons.

Zermatt

POP 6000 / ELEV 1605M

You can almost sense the anticipation on the train from Täsch: couples gaze wistfully out of the window, kids fidget and stuff in Toblerone, folk rummage for their cameras. And then, as they arrive in Zermatt, all give little whoops of joy at the pop-up book effect of one-of-a-kind **Matterhorn** (4478m). Trigonometry at its finest, topographic perfection, a bloody beautiful mountain – call it what you will, Matterhorn is hypnotic.

Since the mid-19th century, Zermatt has starred among Switzerland's glitziest resorts. British climber Edward Whymper reached the top of the Matterhorn in 1865 and plucky souls have come here ever since to climb, hike and ski, spellbound by the scenery.

◉ Sights

It pays to meander away from main strip **Bahnhofstrasse** with its flashy boutiques and stream of horse-drawn sleds or carriages and electric taxis. Head towards the noisy gushing river along **Hinterdorfstrasse**, crammed with archetypal Valaisian timber storage barns propped up on stone discs and stilts to keep out the rats.

Gornergratbahn
Railway

(www.gornergrat.ch; Bahnhofplatz 7; one way adult/child Sfr42/21; ⏱7am-9.50pm) Europe's highest cogwheel railway has climbed through picture-postcard scenery to **Gornergrat** (3089m) – a 30-minute journey – since 1898. Sit on the right-hand side of the little red train to gawp at the Matterhorn. Tickets allow you to get on and off en route; there are restaurants at Riffelalp (2211m) and Riffelberg (2582m). In summer an extra train runs once a week at sunrise and sunset – the most spectacular trips of all.

Matterhorn Museum
Museum

(🕿027 967 41 00; www.matterhornmuseum. ch; Kirchplatz; adult/child Sfr10/5; ⏱11am-6pm Jul-Sep & mid-Dec-Apr, 3-6pm Oct-mid-Dec) This crystalline, state-of-the-art museum provides fascinating insight into Valaisian village life, mountaineering, the dawn of tourism in Zermatt and the lives the Matterhorn has claimed. Short films portray the first successful ascent of the Matterhorn on 13 July 1865 led by Edward Whymper, a feat marred by tragedy on the descent when four team members crashed to their deaths in a 1200m fall down the North Wall. The infamous rope that broke is exhibited. No credit cards.

Mountaineers' Cemetery
Cemetery

(Kirchstrasse) A walk in Zermatt's twinset of cemeteries – the Mountaineers' cemetery in the garden of Zermatt's **St Mauritius Church** (Kirchplatz) and the main cemetery across the road – is a sobering experience. Numerous gravestones tell of untimely deaths on Monte Rosa, the Matterhorn and Breithorn.

🏃 Activities

An essential stop in activity planning is **Snow & Alpine Center** (🕿027 966 24 60; www.alpincenter-zermatt.ch; Bahnhofstrasse 58; ⏱9am-noon & 3-7pm Mon-Fri, 4-7pm Sat & Sun mid-Nov-Apr, 9am-noon & 3-7pm Jul-Sep), home to Zermatt's ski school and mountain guides. In winter buy lift passes

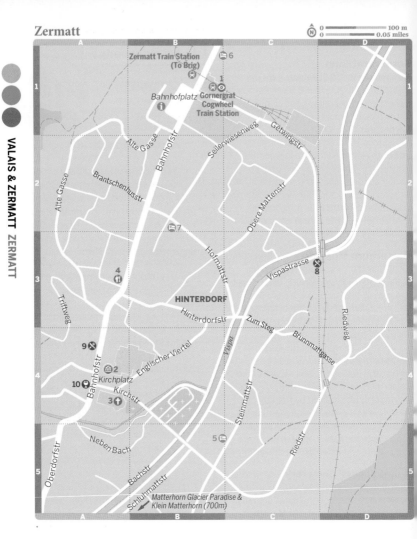

here (Sfr79/380 for a one-/six-day pass excluding Cervinia in neighbouring Italy, Sfr92/434 including Cervinia).

SKIING

Zermatt is cruising heaven, with mostly long, scenic red runs, plus a smattering of blues for ski virgins and knuckle-whitening blacks for experts. The main skiing areas in winter are **Rothorn**, **Stockhorn** and **Klein Matterhorn** – 350km of ski runs in all with a link from Klein Matterhorn to the Italian resort of

Cervinia and a freestyle park with half-pipe for snowboarders.

Summer skiing (20km of runs) and boarding (gravity park at Plateau Rosa on the Theodul glacier) is Europe's most extensive.

HIKING

Zermatt is a hiker's paradise in summer with 400km of trails through some of the most incredible scenery in the Alps – the tourist office has trail maps. For menacing Matterhorn close-ups, nothing beats the highly dramatic **Matterhorn Glacier Trail** (two hours, 6.49km) from Trockener Steg to Schwarzsee; 23 information panels en route tell you everything you could possibly need to know about glaciers and glacial life.

🛏 Sleeping

Book well ahead in winter, and bear in mind that nearly everywhere closes from May to mid- or late June and October to November or early December.

Hotel Bahnhof   Hotel €
(🕿 027 967 24 06; www.hotelbahnhof.com; Bahnhofstrasse; dm Sfr40-45, s/d/q from Sfr80/110/235; ⏰ reception 8-11.30am & 4-7pm, closed May & Oct; 🛜) Opposite the train station, these five-star budget digs have comfy beds, spotless bathrooms and family-perfect rooms for four. Dorms (Sfr5 liner obligatory) are cosy and there's a stylish lounge with armchairs to flop in and books to read. No breakfast, but feel free to prepare your own in the snazzy, open-plan kitchen.

Chesa Valese   Chalet €€
(🕿 027 966 80 80; www.chesa-valese.ch; Steinmattstrasse 2; s/d/q Sfr165/260/505) This traditional burnt-red wood chalet with slate-roof conservatory and flowery garden is romantic, charming and ablaze

with red geraniums in summer. Cosy rooms are country-style and the very best stare brazenly at the Matterhorn. Rates include access to the Wellness Centre with sauna, steam bath and Jacuzzi.

Vernissage
Backstage Hotel   Design.Hotel €€€
(🕿 027 966 69 70; www.backstagehotel.ch; Hofmattstrasse 4; s Sfr180-450, d Sfr250-600; 🛜) Crafted from wood, glass and the trademark creativity of local artist Heinz Julen, this 19-room lifestyle hotel is effortlessly cool – the type of place where bathtubs have legs and practically every bit of furniture is a unique piece. Cube loft rooms are just that: a loft room with a giant glass cube in their centre with bed on top, and bathroom and kitchenette inside. Fabulous.

Eating

Snowboat   International €
(🕿 027 967 43 33; www.snowboat.ch; Vispastrasse 20; mains Sfr19-26; ⏰ noon-midnight) This hybrid eating-drinking, riverside address with marigold-yellow deckchairs sprawled across its rooftop sun terrace, is a blessing. When fondue tires, head here for barbecue-sizzled burgers (forget beef, try a lamb and goat's cheese or Indonesian chicken satay burger), super-power creative salads (the Omega 3 buster is a favourite) and great cocktails. The vibe? 100% fun and funky.

Chez Vrony   Swiss €€
(🕿 027 967 25 52; www.chezvrony.ch; Findeln; breakfast Sfr28, mains Sfr23-45; ⏰ 9.15am-5pm Dec-Apr & mid-Jun–mid-Oct) Ride the Sunnegga Express to 2288m then ski down blue piste 6 or summer-hike 15 minutes to Zermatt's tastiest slope-side address in the hamlet of Findeln. Keep snug in a cream blanket or lounge on a sheepskin-cushioned chaise longue and revel in the effortless romance of this century-old farmhouse with potted Edelweiss on the tables, first-class Matterhorn views and exceptional organic cuisine.

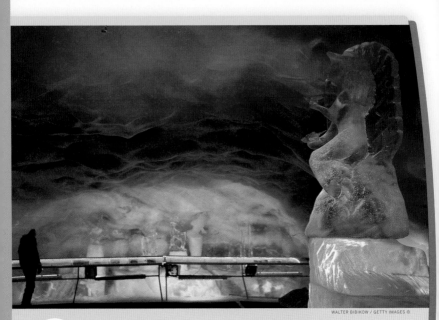

WALTER BIBIKOW / GETTY IMAGES ©

Don't Miss
Matterhorn Glacier Paradise

Views from Zermatt's cable cars are all remarkable, but the Matterhorn Glacier Paradise is the icing on the cake. Ride Europe's highest-altitude cable car to 3883m and gawp at 14 glaciers and 38 mountain peaks over 4000m from the **Panoramic Platform** (only open in good weather). Don't miss the **Glacier Palace**, an ice palace complete with glittering ice sculptures and an ice slide to swoosh down bum first. End with some exhilarating **snow tubing** outside in the snowy surrounds.

NEED TO KNOW
www.matterhornparadise.ch; adult/child Sfr99/49.50; ◷8.30am-4.20pm

---

Whymper Stube   Swiss €€
(☏027 967 22 96; www.whymper-stube.ch; Bahnhofstrasse 80; raclette Sfr9, fondue Sfr25-48; ◷11am-midnight Nov-Apr & Jun–mid-Oct) This cosy bistro opposite Zermatt's historic Zermathof Hotel is legendary for its excellent raclette and fondues, cheese and meat. The icing on the cake is a segmented pot bubbling with three different cheese fondues. Service is relaxed and friendly, tables are packed tightly together, and the place – all inside – buzzes come dusk. End with decadent meringue and cream.

🍷 Drinking

Still fizzing with energy after schussing down the slopes? Zermatt pulses in party-mad après-ski huts, suave lounge bars and Brit-style pubs. Most close (and some melt) in low season.

Elsie Bar   Wine Bar
(www.elsiebar.ch; Kirchplatz 16; ◷4pm-midnight) This elegant, old-world wine bar across from the church has taken in walkers and climbers since the 1950s.

Vernissage Bar Club
Bar

(☎ 027 966 69 70; www.vernissage-zermatt.ch; Hofmattstrasse 4; ☉ 5pm-midnight Tue-Thu & Sun, to 2am Fri & Sat) The ultimate après-ski antithesis, Vernissage exudes grown-up sophistication. Local artist Heinz Julen has created a theatrical space with flowing velvet drapes, film-reel chandeliers and candlelit booths. Catch an exhibition, watch a movie, pose in the lounge bar.

❶ Information

Tourist Office (☎ 027 966 81 00; www.zermatt.ch; Bahnhofplatz 5; ☉ 8.30am-6pm; 🛜) A wealth of information, iPads to surf on and free wi-fi.

❶ Getting There & Away

Car

Zermatt is car-free. Motorists have to park in the **Matterhorn Terminal Täsch** (☎ 027 967 12 14; www.matterhornterminal.ch; Täsch; day/subsequent day Sfr14.40/13.50; ☉ 6am-10pm) and ride the Zermatt Shuttle train (adult/child Sfr8/4, 12 minutes, every 20 minutes from 6am to 9.40pm) the last 5km to Zermatt.

Train

Trains to Täsch depart roughly every 20 minutes from Brig (Sfr32, 1½ hours), stopping at Visp en route. Zermatt is also the starting point of the Glacier Express to Graubünden, one of the most spectacular train rides in the world.

....

Saas Fee

POP 1760 / ELEV 1800M

Hemmed in by a magnificent amphitheatre of 13 implacable peaks over 4000m and backed by the threatening tongues of nine glaciers, this village looks positively feeble in the revealing light of summer.

Today Saas Fee is a chic, car-free resort where every well-to-do skier and hiker wants to be. Modern chalets surround the village but its commercial heart, well-endowed with old timber chalets and barns on stilts (once used to store hams and grain), retains a definite old-world, Heidi-style charm.

◉ Sights & Activities

Allalin
Glacier

(Saas Fee–Allalin one way/return Sfr53/72) Year-round, the underground Mittelallin

Saas Fee

MICHAEL WHITEHEAD / GETTY IMAGES ©

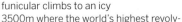

Below: Matterhorn viewed from Findeln; **Right:** Diners at Zermatt restaurant

(BELOW) PIERRE HANQUIN PHOTOGRAPHIE / GETTY IMAGES ©; (RIGHT) INGOLF POMPE / LOOK-FOTO / GETTY IMAGES ©

funicular climbs to an icy 3500m where the world's highest revolving restaurant on the Allalin glacier basks in glorious 360-degree views of Saas Fee's 4000m glacial giants. Wrap up warm to visit the subzero **Eispavillion** (ice cave), hollowed out 10m below the ice surface, or soar down Feegletscher's 20km of summer ski slopes. To reach the glacier, ride the Alpin Express cable car to Felskinn (3000m), then the funicular.

Abenteuerwald   Adventure Sports

(Adventure World; ☎ 027 958 18 58; Hochseilgarten; discovery/grand tour adult Sfr23/33, child Sfr18/23; ☾10am-7pm Mon-Sat Jul & Aug, noon-6pm Tue-Sat Jun & Sep–mid-Oct; 🚼) Known far and wide among local outdoor types, this tree climbing course is one of the most spectacular in the Swiss Alps. Two courses take wannabe Janes and Tarzans across suspension bridges, monkey nets and various other obstacles strung up

high between trees. It is the two zip wires that cross the Fee Gorge, however, that really stun. Not for the vertigo-prone or children under 115cm in height.

Swiss Ski & Snowboard School   Skiing

(☎ 027 957 23 48; www.skischule-saas-fee. ch; Dorfplatz 1; ☾9am-noon & 3-6pm Mon-Fri, 3-6pm Sat & Sun) Book lessons with the main ski school on the central church square.

Feeblitz   Luge

(Panoramastrasse; 1/6/10 descents adult Sfr6.50/36.50/59, child Sfr4.50/25/40; ☾10am-6pm Jul & Aug, noon-5.30pm Sep, 1-6pm Nov school holidays & mid-Dec–Apr) Cross the bridge over the river and turn left along Mischistrasse to reach Saas Fee's speedfiend luge track, next to the Alpin Express cable car. Kids under eight or 110cm ride for free with a parent.

184

🛏 Sleeping & Eating

During the winter ski season (December to April) many hotels only offer half-board. Most close in May and November. Irrespective of season, hotel guests get a free Visitor's Card which yields a bonanza of savings, including on car parking fees, cable cars and so on.

WellnessHostel 4000   Hostel €

(📞027 958 50 50; www.wellnesshostel4000.ch; Panoramastrasse 1; dm/s/d incl breakfast from Sfr43/106/127; ⏱reception 7am-10pm Jun-Apr; 🍽❄@📶🏊) This striking, modern building wedged between mountain-peak view and 17th-century granaries on stilts is possibly Switzerland's loveliest hostel. A new breed, it adjoins a pool and spa with gym, various saunas and steam baths, phone- and tablet-free zone, and tea station. Sharp and stylish rooms range from six-bed dorms to swanky family rooms

and doubles, and standard rates include the pool.

Pricier 'Experience4000plus' rates throw in the gym and spa, too.

Spielboden   Swiss €€

(📞027 957 22 12; www.spielboden.ch; Spielboden; mains Sfr32-46, 3-/4-course menu Sfr65/85; ⏱10am-4pm mid-Dec–Apr & mid-Jun–Sep) This stylish *bergrestaurant,* next to the cable car station of the same name at 2450m, is a real treat. Its unassuming exterior hides a striking 'mountain chic' interior with contemporary wooden furnishings, appealing bar area and – the icing on the cake – bijou terrace with chaises longues to lounge on over coffee and staggering mountain panoramas. Cuisine is contemporary and delicious.

La Gorge   Swiss €€

(📞027 958 16 80; www.lagorge.ch; Blomattenweg 1; mains Sfr15-39; ⏱8am-11.30pm Mon-Sat; 👶) Head to the Gorge to feast on incredible aerial views of glacial white water racing in the Fee Gorge far below; a second terrace offers views to the Allalin glacier. Two stone knight-in-shining-armour turrets complete the unusual setting. Cuisine is predicatable Swiss, with some great choices for young appetites.

ℹ Information

Tourist Office (☏ 027 958 18 58; www.saas-fee.ch; Obere Dorfstrasse 2; ⏰ 8.30am-noon & 2-6pm Mon-Fri, 8am-6pm Sat, 9am-noon & 3-6pm Sun)

ℹ Getting There & Away

Buses depart half-hourly from Brig (Sfr19, 1¼ hours) and Visp (Sfr16.80, 45 minutes).

Saas Fee is car-free; park at the village entrance (Sfr19/14 per day winter/summer) and walk or pay around Sfr25 for an **electric taxi** (☏ 079 220 21 37) to take you to your hotel.

Aletsch Glacier

As you approach the source of the mighty Rhône and gain altitude, the deep valley narrows and the verdure of pine-clad mountainsides and south-facing vineyards that defines the west of the canton switches to rugged wilderness. Along the way is a string of bucolic villages of geranium-bedecked timber chalets and onion-domed churches.

Out of view from the valley floor lies the longest and most voluminous glacier in the European Alps. The Aletsch Glacier (Aletschgletscher) is a seemingly never-ending, 23km-long swirl of deeply crevassed ice that slices past thundering falls, jagged spires of rock and pine forest. It stretches from Jungfrau in the Bernese Oberland to a plateau above the Rhône and is, justly so, a Unesco World Heritage site.

FIESCH & EGGISHORN

Most people get their first tantalising glimpse of Aletsch Glacier from Jungfraujoch, but picture-postcard riverside Fiesch on the valley floor is the best place to access it. From the village, ride the **cable car** (www.eggishorn.ch) up to **Fiescheralp** – a hot spot for paragliding – and continue up to **Eggishorn** (2927m). Nothing can prepare you for what awaits on exiting the gondola. Streaming down in a broad curve around the Aletschhorn (4195m), the glacier is just like a frozen five-lane superhighway. In the distance, to the north, rise the glistening summits of Jungfrau (4158m), Mönch (4107m), Eiger (3970m) and Finsteraarhorn (4274m). To the west of the cable-car exit, spy Mont Blanc and the Matterhorn.

Marmot
TAMBAKO THE JAGUAR / GETTY IMAGES ©

BETTMERALP & RIEDERALP

This twinset of family-friendly car-free hamlets, accessible only by cable car, is the stuff of Swiss Alpine dreams. Paved with snow December to March, kids are pulled around on traditional wooden Davos sledges and skis are the best way to get to the local supermarket. With the run at the top of the Bettmerhorn cable car (2647m) skirting the edge of the Aletsch Glacier, skiing here is a sensationally picturesque and dramatic affair – 104km of intermediate or easy ski runs in the so-called **Aletsch Arena** (www. aletscharena.ch) ski area, with a one-day ski pass costing Sfr55 (Sfr59 including cable car up from the valley).

Hiking in the summer is equally as mind-blowing. From **Bettmeralp** (1950m) take the cable car to **Bettmerhorn** for a dramatic bird's-eye glacier view. Exit the station and follow the wooden walkway through cinematically oversized boulders to the so-called *Eis Terrasse* (Ice Terrace) where information panels tell you about the glacier and several marked footpaths start.

Sleeping & Eating

Villa Cassel   Historic Hotel €€
(027 928 62 20; www.pronatura-aletsch.ch/vacations; Riederfurka; dm incl breakfast/half-board Sfr50/70, d Sfr170/210; mid-Jun–mid-Oct) Short but sweet is the season at this fabulous mountainside villa, the stunning summer pad of wealthy Englishman Ernest Cassel who – so the story goes – had to pay local farmers to stuff the bells of their cows with hay after their incessant ringing upset one of his house guests – a young Winston Churchill no less. Rooms today are simple pine with shared bathrooms.

Chüestall   Swiss €€
(027 927 15 91; www.chuestall-blausee.ch; Riederalp; mains Sfr20-40; 10am-4.45pm Jun-Oct & Dec-Apr) 'Cowshed' is what its name means and that is exactly what this thoroughly modern address on the slopes

---

Family Fave: Marmot Spotting

They spend nine-tenths of their lives underground, but come the warm sunny days of July, marmots pop out of their painstakingly dug burrows beneath the slopes to take in some sun and unwittingly entertain walkers.

The rocky southern-facing slopes above the tree line in **Spielboden** (2443m) shelter colonies of the small alpine mammal known for its shrill whistle. Atypically unfearful of humans, these Valaisian marmots happily eat carrots, peanuts and bread from your hand – the boldest let you pet and cuddle them.

Ride the bright-orange Spielbodenbahn cable car from Talsation Längflue to mid-station Spielboden (single/return Sfr24/34) and buy *marmeltierfutter* (marmot food, aka small plastic bags of chopped carrot, bread chunks and peanuts in shells, which the marmots shell themselves) for Sfr4.50 from the Spielboden (p185) restaurant by the cable car station. Then amble downhill keeping your eyes peeled. It's a 2½ hour walk to Saas Fee village.

---

at 2207m was until 1961. In summer look out for flyers advertising raclette evenings, Sunday brunches etc. Walk or ski to it from the top of the Moosfluh cable car in Riederalp or Bettmeralp's Blausee (Blue Lake – yes, it's by a lake) chairlift.

Getting There & Away

The base stations for these resorts – Mörel (for Riederalp), Betten (Bettmeralp) and Fiesch – are on the train route between Brig and Andermatt. Cable-car departures (Sfr9.40) are linked to train arrivals.

Zürich, Lake Constance & the Northeast

Switzerland's biggest city, Zürich, is not only efficient, it's also hip. The locals are hard-working early risers but, come clock-off time, they throw themselves wholeheartedly into a festive vortex. Much of the ancient centre, with its winding lanes and tall church steeples, has been kept intact. Winterthur, just to the northeast, is a cultural powerhouse, with major museums.

Northeastern Switzerland is the place to tiptoe off the map and back to nature for a few days. Here country lanes unravel like spools of thread, weaving through Appenzell's patchwork meadows and past the fjord-like waters of Walensee.

From the thunderous Rheinfall to the still waters of Lake Constance, nature is on a grand scale here. Completing the storybook tableau are castle-topped towns like Stein am Rhein and Schaffhausen, their facades festooned with frescos; while in St Gallen, the abbey library literally catches your breath with its rococo splendour.

Zürich

Zürich, Lake Constance & the Northeast

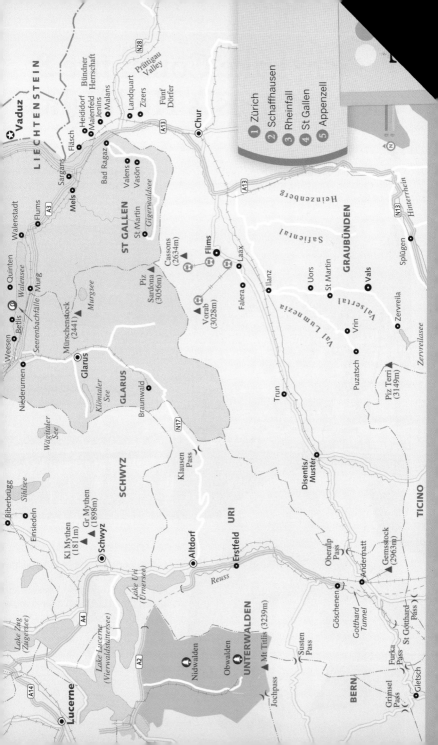

Zürich, Lake Constance & the Northeast's Highlights

Zürich

Switzerland's number one city, Zürich (p198) has an image of suited bankers so conservati°
that they could be from another era. And while partly true, those suits do come off and the
locals certainly know how to enjoy themselves. Cutting-edge bars, restaurants and boutiqu°
can be found across town.

1

2 Schaffhausen's Swiss Food

Who doesn't like cheese? A pot of lightly
simmering fondue is one of the core
pleasures of Switzerland. Raclette – th°
heated (often by flame) cheese you er°
joy with fresh potatoes – is another lo°
cal favourite that can warm the chillie°
bones on a frosty night. Schaffhause°
(p214) and the surrounding region ar°
dotted with ageless traditional havens
for Swiss food. Left: Raclette with potatoes an°
gherkins

STOCKFOOD / GETTY IMAGES ©

Thundering Rheinfall

3

Watched over by castles, Rheinfall (p217) always surprises: northeastern Switzerland is not that hilly yet here is a long pounding waterfall that throws up enough spray to grow a rainforest. Walk out on platforms that put you in the midst of the gravity-fed fury and *feel* the thundering power. Summertime ferries get you close to the pounding action.

St Gallen's Stiftsbibliothek

4

In *A World Lit Only by Fire*, the historian William Manchester writes about how the facts of the ancient world survived to the modern age. One of the places where monks tirelessly wrote out mankind's knowledge to pass on to future generations was right here in St Gallen's extraordinary Stiftsbibliothek (p222). Amid Unesco-recognised rococo splendour you can see some of the 150,000 surviving books on display.

Appenzell

5

Even the name is melodic: Appenzell. This lovely little town (p225), surrounded by Alpine beauty, harmoniously blends a rainbow of pastel-coloured vintage buildings in its Old Town. At the centre of town is the Landsgemeindeplatz, an all-star of a main square, where one of the nation's purest forms of democracy is practised. Pick any trail leading out of town and soon you'll be in glorious mountains.

Zürich, Lake Constance & the Northeast's Best…

Museums

○ **Stiftsbibliothek** St Gallen's star attraction was a repository for knowledge in medieval times. (p222)

○ **Schloss Kyburg** Try on a suit of armour at this castle overlooking Winterthur. (p213)

○ **Kunsthaus** A huge and deep collection that reflects Zürich's wealth. (p202)

○ **Schweizerisches Landesmuseum** A wonderful romp through Swiss history. (p198)

Old Towns

○ **Appenzell** Beautiful Old Town with colourful buildings around a square lined with cafes. (p225)

○ **Stein am Rhein** Cobblestone streets and gingerbread houses are among the details that yell 'cute' and 'quaint'! (p217)

○ **Werdenberg** A 13th-century town with the oldest Swiss collection of timber houses. (p227)

○ **Schaffhausen** Tidy streets dating from the 16th to 18th centuries make this a stroller's dream. (p214)

Outdoor Fun

○ **Lake Constance Ferries** Hop around the lake aboard boats that offer beautiful views. (p220)

○ **Bodensee-Radweg** A 273km easy-peasy bike and walking path around Lake Constance. (p219)

○ **Rhine Cycling** Several routes take you past ancient treasures and natural wonders.

○ **Lake Zürich** Join bankers removing their pinstripes for a dip in the crystal-clear waters right in the centre. (p199)

Need to Know

Natural Wonders

○ **Rheinfall** Huge falls never fail to stun first-time visitors. (p217)

○ **Lake Constance** A vast lake bordering Switzerland, Germany and Austria mirrors the Alps and is lined with sights. (p219)

○ **Seerenbachfälle** A series of three massive waterfalls tumble down in a beautful remote setting near Walensee. (p228)

○ **Braunwald** A car-free town with mountain and meadow views. (p229)

ADVANCE PLANNING

○ **Two months before** Check for any blockbuster exhibitions in Zürich and buy tickets.

RESOURCES

○ **Zürich** (www.zuerich. com) Full details on the big city.

○ **Züritipp** (www.zueritipp. ch) Jammed with info on what's on in Zürich.

○ **Art in Zürich** (www. artinzurich.ch) What's up and on in the city's museums.

○ **Ostschweiz Tourismus** (Eastern Switzerland Tourism; www.ostschweiz. ch) From St Gallen to Appenzell and beyond.

○ **Lonely Planet** (www. lonelyplanet.com/ switzerland/zurich) Reader tips and more.

GETTING AROUND

○ **Train** All the main towns are well-linked to each other and Zürich.

○ **Ferry** Lake Constance is criss-crossed by a web of ferries, many of which hop along the shore from one stop to the next, so you can sit back on deck and enjoy a cruise. On foggy days there's a touch of mystery and drama as a cute little village materialises in the mist.

○ **Cable Cars** The Galurs Alps, an hour east of Zürich, are threaded by all manner of peak-seeking cable cars.

BE FOREWARNED

○ **Christmas** The region draws fully on its Germanic heritage as every town has a delightful Christmas market on its main square. Zürich has several, including a great one in the main station you can pop through between trains.

○ **Summer** People pour outside and central squares are filled with cafes, while special events – like fireworks – happen in the countryside and along the lakeshore.

Left: Rheinfall (p217); **Above:** Medieval streetscape, Stein am Rhein (p217)

Zürich, Lake Constance & the Northeast Itineraries

Whether you're fresh off a plane or train, Zürich is an excellent starting point for tours around the region.

SCHAFFHAUSEN
RHEINFALL
KREUZLINGEN
KONSTANZ
Lake Constance (Bodensee)
GERMANY
WINTERTHUR
ST GALLEN
ZÜRICH
APPENZELL
SÄNTIS
AUSTRIA
SWITZERLAND
Zürichsee (Lake Zürich)
WALENSEE
WERDENBERG
LIECHTENSTEIN
Walensee

3 DAYS

OLD SWITZERLAND
ZÜRICH TO ST GALLEN

Start your ❶ **Zürich** (p198) day with a stroll around the namesake lake. Watch bankers officiously heading to work and revel in the knowledge that you're on holiday. Wander the Old Town, popping into the Fraumünster (p198), the 13th-century cathedral. Soak up some of the city's rich culture at museums such as Schweizerisches Landesmuseum (p198), Museum für Gestaltung (p199) and Museum Rietberg (p199). Laze away in a tidy cafe before having a hearty Swiss meal in one of Zürich's traditional restaurants. In summer, head out to a lakeside place for a drink under the stars.

Catch a quick and early train to nearby ❷ **Winterthur** (p212) and make the walk up to Schloss Kyburg (p213), a classic old castle with good views. Consider visits to some of the fine local museums or head right on to pretty ❸ **Schaffhausen** (p214), where you can make an easy transfer to see the thundering wonder that is ❹ **Rheinfall** (p217), a 150m-wide waterfall on the Rhine River. Continue on to ❺ **St Gallen** (p221), one of Switzerland's finest Old Towns, where you can enjoy a delicious dinner. In the morning be ready for the rococo confection that is the Unesco-listed Stiftsbibliothek (p222), a medieval treasure worthy of all the accolades.

ZÜRICH TO WALENSEE

Whirl through ❶**Zürich's** Old Town (p198), buy something shamelessly expensive in the luxe shops and head out for ❷**Schaffhausen** (p214). Soak up the ancient charms of the walkable centre, then get spray in your face at the waterfall spectacular at ❸**Rheinfall** (p217). Now that you're damp, you're in the right mood for the silvery blue beauty of Lake Constance. Cross over from ❹**Kreuzlingen** (p221) to the beautiful medieval German town of ❺**Konstanz** (p219). Catch one of the lake boats at this water transport hub and go exploring the lake.

Spend a restful night in ❻**St Gallen** (p221) and ponder the magnificence of the Stiftsbibliothek (p222), which was the western world's equivalent of a mainframe back in the day. ❼**Appenzell** (p225) is a good place for a long lunch; in fact, you might just slow down, stay the night and enjoy an invigorating morning hike into the surrounding Alps.

Timeless 13th-century houses line the little lanes of ❽**Werdenberg** (p227). Get a gander over it all from the peak at ❾**Säntis** (p226) and then settle back along beautiful ❿**Walensee** (p227).

View over Säntis (p226)

Discover Zürich, Lake Constance & the Northeast

ZÜRICH

Zürich is an enigma. A savvy financial centre with possibly the densest public transport system in the world, it also has a gritty, post-industrial edge that always surprises. The nation's largest city has an evocative old town and lovely lakeside location. It's museums, shops and myriad restaurants can easily keep you busy for a few days.

◉ Sights

The city spreads around the northwest end of Zürichsee (Lake Zürich), from where the Limmat river runs further north still, splitting the medieval city centre in two. The narrow streets of the Niederdorf quarter on the river's east bank are crammed with restaurants, bars and shops. The central areas around the lake, especially Niederdorf, are best explored on foot.

Fraumünster Church
(www.fraumuenster.ch; Münsterhof; ⊙9am-6pm Apr-Oct, 10am-4pm Nov-Mar) The 13th-century cathedral is renowned for its stunning, distinctive stained-glass windows, designed by the Russian-Jewish master Marc Chagall (1887–1985). He did a series of five windows in the choir stalls in 1971 and the rose window in the southern transept in 1978. The rose window in the northern transept was created by Augusto Giacometti in 1945.

Schweizerisches Landesmuseum Museum
(Swiss National Museum; www.musee-suisse.ch; Museumstrasse 2; adult/child Sfr10/free; ⊙10am-5pm Tue, Wed & Fri-Sun, 10am-7pm Thu) Inside a purpose-built cross between a mansion and a castle sprawls this eclectic and

Fraumünster, Zürich
JOHN BORTHWICK / GETTY IMAGES ©

imaginatively presented museum. The permanent collection offers an extensive tour through Swiss history, with exhibits ranging from elaborately carved and painted sleds to household and religious artefacts to a series of reconstructed historical rooms spanning six centuries. The museum remains open while undergoing a major expansion; the new archaeology section and brand-new wing are slated to open in 2016.

Museum Für Gestaltung Museum
(Design Museum; ☑043 446 67 67; www.museum-gestaltung.ch; Ausstellungstrasse 60; adult/child Sfr12/free; ☺10am-8pm Wed, 10am-5pm Tue & Thu-Sun) Consistently impressive and wide-ranging, the revolving exhibitions at this design museum include anything from works by classic photographers such as Henri Cartier-Bresson to advertising for design furniture of yesteryear. Graphic and applied arts dominate the permanent collections. Take trams 4, 13 or 17.

Museum Rietberg Gallery
(☑044 415 31 31; www.rietberg.ch; Gablerstrasse 15; adult/child Sfr18/free; ☺10am-5pm Tue & Thu-Sun, 10am-8pm Wed) Set in three villas in a leafy park and fronted by a striking emerald-glass entrance, this museum houses the country's only assembly of African, Oriental and ancient American art. The permanent collection is frequently complemented by temporary exhibitions. Take tram 7.

Cabaret Voltaire Gallery
(☑043 268 57 20; www.cabaretvoltaire.ch; Spiegelgasse 1; exhibition & film screening Sfr5; ☺12.30-6.30pm Tue-Sun) Birthplace of the zany Dada art movement, this bar-cum-art-space came back to life in 2004 as a hotbed of contentious art exhibitions and socially critical artistic ferment. Watch a 30-minute film about the history of Dada downstairs (Sfr5) or head for the cafe upstairs (free admission and longer hours).

Grossmünster Church
(www.grossmuenster.ch; Grossmünsterplatz; ☺10am-6pm Mar-Oct, 10am-5pm Nov-Feb) Founded by Charlemagne in the 9th

Local Knowledge

Zürich Don't Miss List

JANINA BARUTH, ZÜRICH RESIDENT AND MEDIA EXECUTIVE

1 LAKE ZÜRICH
One of the most beautiful spots during summertime is **Seebad Enge** (www.seebadenge.ch; Mythenquai 9; admission Sfr7; ☺9am-7pm May & Sep, 9am-8pm Jun-Aug). By day you can swim in Lake Zürich while looking at the Alps. It gets packed during the weekend when it's sunny. In the afternoon the bar is open, plus there are many events such as readings and little concerts. It's a 10-minute walk from the tram station Bürkliplatz.

2 UETLIBERG: ZÜRICH'S MOUNTAIN
Only a few minutes away by S-Bahn from the main station (No 10, station: Uetliberg) you get a break from the urban stress and still have the feeling of being in the city. From the **Uetliberg** hill you have a beautiful view all over the city and lake. Thewre's a great restaurant, too.

3 LANGSTRASSE IN KREIS 4 & 5
In Zürich's most colourful and lively area you'll find bars, restaurants and clubs. Arthouse movies are big here, including the summertime **Kino Röntgenplatz** (www.sommerkinoröntgenplatz.ch), an open-air cinema showing classics. It's free but a hat is passed around.

4 LAKESIDE ZÜRICH
A walk along the lake from **Bellevue** to **Zürichhorn** is one of the most impressive things to do in Zürich. It takes maybe 45 minutes and you'll pass by musicians, BBQ places, people having a picnic, and ice-cream vendors. Take a tram to Bellevue.

5 SHOPPING IN NIEDERDORF
For shopping that's not like everywhere else, go to the Niederdorf area. Here you find little shops, wine and chocolate shops, clothes and shoe shops, art ateliers, jewellery stores and great bars, hotels and restaurants, theatres, arthouse cinemas...

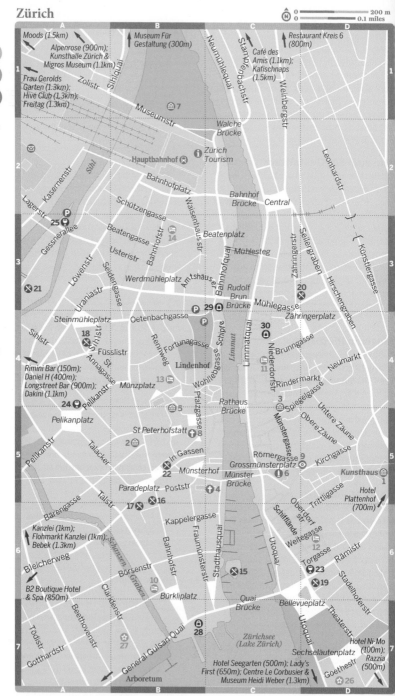

Zürich

Zürich

century (but heavily reworked since), Zürich's twin-towered landmark cathedral sits directly across the river from Fraumünster. The interior showcases stained-glass work by Augusto Giacometti. For nice views, climb the southern tower, the **Karlsturm** (adult/child Sfr4/2; ⊙10am-4.45pm).

Firebrand preacher Huldrych Zwingli (1484–1531) began speaking out against the Catholic Church here in the 16th century, and thus brought the Reformation to Zürich. **Zwingli's house** (Kirchgasse 13), where he lived and worked, is nearby.

St Peterskirche
Church

(St Peter's Church; St Peterhofstatt; ⊙8am-6pm Mon-Fri, 8am-4pm Sat) From any position in the city, it's hard to overlook the 13th-century tower of this church. Its prominent clock face, 8.7m in diameter, is the largest in Europe. Inside, the choir stalls date from the 13th century but the rest of the church is largely an 18th-century remake. Just below is one of Zürich's most picturesque spots: St Peterhofstatt, a lovely cobbled square surrounding a graceful old tree.

Kunsthalle Zürich
Gallery

(⏩044 272 15 15; www.kunsthallezurich.ch; Limmatstrasse 270; adult/child Sfr12/free, after Thu 5pm free, combined ticket with Migros Museum Sfr20; ⊙11am-6pm Tue, Wed & Fri, 11am-8pm Thu, 10am-5pm Sat & Sun) Upstairs from the Migros Museum, the 'Art Hall' features changing exhibitions of contemporary art, spread over two floors.

Migros Museum
Museum

(⏩044 277 20 50; www.migrosmuseum.ch; Limmatstrasse 270; adult/child Sfr12/free, after Thu 5pm free, combined ticket with Kunsthalle Sfr20; ⊙11am-6pm Tue, Wed & Fri, 11am-8pm Thu, 10am-5pm Sat & Sun) Housed in the newly renovated Löwenbräu brewery, this well-funded contemporary art museum focuses on innovative work from the past few decades. Take tram 4, 13 or 17 to Dammweg.

Beyer Museum
Museum

(⏩043 344 63 63; www.beyer-ch.com/uhrenmuseum; Bahnhofstrasse 31; adult/child Sfr8/free; ⊙2-6pm Mon-Fri) Inside the premises of a purveyor of fine timepieces is this little jewel of a small museum, which chronicles the rise of timekeeping, from striated medieval candles to modern watches. To see short videos of the most creative pieces in

⭐ Don't Miss
Kunsthaus

Zürich's impressive fine arts gallery boasts a rich collection of largely European art that stretches from the Middle Ages through a mix of Old Masters to Alberto Giacometti stick-figure sculptures, Monet and Van Gogh masterpieces, Rodin sculptures and other 19th- and 20th-century art. The museum is free on Wednesdays.

NEED TO KNOW

Museum of Fine Arts; ☎044 253 84 84; www.kunsthaus.ch; Heimplatz 1; adult/child Sfr15/free; ⏰10am-8pm Wed-Thu, to 6pm Tue & Fri-Sun

action (Moses striking a rock with his staff to bring forth water, a magician who lifts cups to reveal ever-changing geometric shapes), ask staff for a loaner iPad.

Centre Le Corbusier & Museum Heidi Weber   Museum

(www.centrelecorbusier.com; Höschgasse 8; adult/child Sfr12/8; ⏰noon-6pm Wed-Sun Jul-Sep) Set in parkland on the eastern lakeshore, the last item designed by iconoclastic Swiss-born architect Le Corbusier looks like a 3D Mondrian painting set. Completed after Le Corbusier's

death, it contains many of his architectural drawings, paintings, furniture and books – collected by fan and friend Heidi Weber. It's 1.2km south of Bellevueplatz. ZürichCard and Swiss Museum Pass not accepted.

James Joyce Foundation   Museum

(☎044 211 83 01; www.joycefoundation.ch; Augustinergasse 9; ⏰10am-5pm Mon-Fri) FREE James Joyce spent much of WWI in Zürich and wrote *Ulysses* here. This foundation, which boasts Europe's largest Joyce collection, hosts regular English-language readings of his work on Monday, Tuesday and Thursday afternoons.

Activities

Zürich comes into its own in summer, when the parks lining the lake are overrun with bathers, sun seekers, in-line skaters, footballers, lovers, picnickers, party animals and preeners. Police even patrol on rollerblades!

From May to mid-September, official swimming areas known locally as *Badis* open around the lake and up the Limmat river. There are also plenty of free, unofficial places to take a dip. Official swimming areas are usually wooden piers with a pavilion and most offer massages, yoga, saunas and snacks. Admission is Sfr7, and swimming areas are generally open from 9am to 7pm in May and September and 9am to 8pm from June to August.

Tours

Sweet Zurich   Food Tour
(www.sweetzurich.ch; tours Sfr85; ⏰2pm Tue-Fri) Kerrin Rousset shares her passion for Zürich's sweeter side on these two-and-a-half-hour chocolate-lovers' tours of the city, which include insights into history and production along with ample tasting opportunities.

Sleeping

Prices sometimes head north for various major trade fairs (including those in Basel).

Kafischnaps   Hotel €
(☏043 538 81 16; www.kafischnaps.ch; Kornhausstrasse 57; r Sfr88-118) Set in a one-time butcher's shop, this cool, bustling neighbourhood cafe has a collection of five cheerful little rooms upstairs, each named and decorated after a fruit-based liquor. Book ahead online; they fill up fast. The bar (8am or 9am to midnight daily) is grand for a coffee, beer or brunch. Take tram 11 or 14 to Schaffhauserplatz.

Zürich with Children

In summer, spending time having a dip in the **Limmat river** or lake is a pleasant investment for the whole family. A walk along the Planetenweg in **Uetliberg** combines views with exercise and education on the planets. Uetliberg is on a 870m mountain top at the namesake stop on the S10 line.

Parents wanting a one-stop lesson in Swiss history should take their children to the **Schweizerisches Landesmuseum** (p198), a clever and attractively laid out museum with interactive screens, book corners and even a short slide from the highest part of the history section down to the beginning. With its garden setting, the **Museum Rietberg** (p199) can also be a clever compromise between art and the outdoors.

Dakini   B&B €
(☏044 291 42 20; www.dakini.ch; Brauerstrasse 87; s/d from Sfr100/160; 🚶@📶) Run by multilingual and well-travelled artist Susanne Seiler, this relaxed Züri-West B&B attracts a bohemian crowd. Four double rooms and four singles, each with its own colour scheme and two with balconies, are spread across three floors, sharing the kitchen and bathroom on each. A scrumptious and filling breakfast is served at the family-style table. Take tram 8 to Bäckeranlage.

City Backpacker   Hostel €
(☏044 251 90 15; www.city-backpacker.ch; Niederdorfstrasse 5; dm/s/d Sfr37/77/118; ⏰reception closed noon-3pm; @📶) Extremely well located in the Altstadt, this private hostel with a youthful party vibe is friendly and well equipped, if a trifle cramped. In summer, you can always overcome the claustrophobia by hanging out on the rooftop terrace.

Hotel Otter
Hotel €

(☎044 251 22 07; www.hotelotter.ch; Oberdorfstrasse 7; s/d/apt from Sfr125/155/200; ⎚) Offering one of Zürich's best price-to-location ratios, this small hotel on a Niederdorf back street has 17 rooms with a variety of colour schemes, including some studio apartment–style units with kitchen. It's only a five-minute walk from several major attractions, including the Fraumünster, the Opernhaus, the Kunsthaus, the Limmat River and the Zürichsee.

Townhouse
Boutique Hotel €€

(☎044 200 95 95; www.townhouse.ch; Schützengasse 7; s Sfr195-395, d Sfr225-425; ⎚) With luxurious wallpapers, wallhangings, parquet floors and retro furniture, the 21 rooms in these stylish digs come in an assortment of sizes from 15 sq metres to 35 sq metres. Located close to the main train station, the hotel offers friendly service and welcoming touches including a DVD selection and iPod docking stations.

Lady's First
Hotel €€

(☎044 380 80 10; www.ladysfirst.ch; Mainaustrasse 24; s Sfr230-325, d Sfr290-395; ⎚) At this attractive hotel near the opera house and lake, the immaculate and generally spacious rooms provide a pleasant mixture of traditional parquet flooring and designer furnishings. The hotel spa and its accompanying rooftop terrace are for female guests only.

Hotel Ni-Mo
B&B €€

(☎044 370 30 30; hotel-nimo.ch; Seefeldstrasse 16; s Sfr180-250, d Sfr230-270; ⎚) Gregarious film producer Eva Stiefel took over this 10-room B&B near the opera house in 2013 and has turned it into one of Zürich's most welcoming small hotels. Minimalist modern rooms with all-wood flooring and tiled bathrooms are complemented by a tony downstairs breakfast room hung with local artwork. A Zürich native, Eva enjoys helping guests discover the city.

Hotel Plattenhof
Design Hotel €€

(☎044 251 19 10; www.plattenhof.ch; Plattenstrasse 26; s Sfr175-375, d Sfr255-405; P☎) This trendy design hotel in a quiet residential area has low Japanese-style beds, Molteni furniture and oak parquet floors, plus mood lighting in some rooms. It's cool without being pretentious, and even the 'old' rooms are stylishly minimalist. Downstairs in the same building is a hip cafe.

Hotel Seegarten
Hotel €€

(☎044 388 37 37; www.hotel-seegarten.ch; Seegartenstrasse 14; s Sfr205-405, d Sfr295-405; ☎) Rattan furniture and vintage tourist posters give this place an airy Mediterranean atmosphere, which is reinforced by its proximity to the lake and the on-site restaurant, Latino.

B2 Boutique Hotel & Spa
Boutique Hotel €€€

(☎044 567 67 67; www.b2boutiquehotels.com; Brandschenkestrasse 152; s/d from Sfr330/380; @☎) A stone's throw from Google's European headquarters, this quirky newcomer in a renovated brewery is filled with seductive features. Topping the list are the stupendous rooftop Jacuzzi pool, the spa and the fanciful library-lounge, filled floor to ceiling with an astounding 30,000 books (bought from a local antiquarian) on 13m-high shelves. Spacious rooms sport modern decor (including the odd bean-bag chair).

From the Hauptbahnhof, take tram 13 to Enge and walk five minutes west.

Hotel Widder
Hotel €€€€

(☎044 224 25 26; www.widderhotel.ch; Rennweg 7; s/d from Sfr470/650; P✳@☎) A supremely stylish hotel in the equally grand district of Augustiner, the Widder is a pleasing fusion of modernity and traditional charm. Rooms and public areas across the eight individually decorated townhouses that make up this place are stuffed with art and designer furniture.

205

Baur au Lac
Hotel €€€

(044 220 50 20; www.bauraulac.ch; Talstrasse 1; s/d from Sfr540/870; P ❄ @) This family-run lakeside jewel is set in a private park and offers all imaginable comforts and a soothing sense of privacy. Rooms are decorated in classic colours, adding to the sense of quiet well-being. Throw in the spa, restaurants and faultless service and you can see why VIPs flock here.

🍴 Eating

Denizens of Zürich have the choice of an astounding 2000-plus places to eat and drink. Traditional local cuisine is very rich, as epitomised by the city's signature dish, *Zürcher Geschnetzeltes* (sliced veal in a creamy mushroom sauce).

Haus Hiltl
Vegetarian €

(044 227 70 00; hiltl.ch; Sihlstrasse 28; per 100g takeaway/cafe/restaurant Sfr3.50/4.50/5.50; ⏰6am-midnight Mon-Sat, 8am-midnight Sun; 🍴) Guinness-certified as the world's oldest vegetarian restaurant (established 1898), Hiltl proffers an astounding smorgasbord of meatless delights, from Indian and Thai curries to Mediterranean grilled veggies to salads and desserts. Browse to your heart's content, fill your plate and weigh it, then choose a seat in the informal cafe or the spiffier adjoining restaurant (economical takeaway service is also available).

Bebek
Middle Eastern €

(044 297 11 00; bebek.ch; Badenerstrasse 171; snacks & mains Sfr6-22; ⏰7am-midnight Mon-Fri, 8am-midnight Sat & Sun; 🍴) Grab a spot on the sidewalk terrace or sit inside beneath sparkling chandeliers on beautiful Moroccan-tiled floors. Either way this recently opened eatery is a wonderfully casual place to enjoy late breakfasts (Swiss or Middle Eastern, till 4pm daily), delicious *mezes* (Sfr6 to Sfr9.50 for vegan/veggie options, Sfr10.50 to Sfr16 for meat, Sfr25 to Sfr31 for full-on platters) and glasses of fresh mint tea.

Bauschänzli
Cafeteria, Beer Garden €

(www.bauschaenzli.ch; Stadthausquai 2; mains Sfr13-26; ⏰11am-11pm Apr-Sep) Location is the big draw at this beer garden/cafeteria-style eatery built atop 17th-century fortifications that jut into the middle of the Limmat River. Watch swans, boats and passersby as you nosh on bratwurst, grilled trout, Wiener schnitzel, chips and cold mugs of beer. In October and November, it hosts Zürich's month-long version of Oktoberfest.

Café Sprüngli
Sweets €

(044 224 46 46; www.spruengli.ch; Bahnhofstrasse 21; sweets Sfr7.50-16; ⏰7am-6.30pm Mon-Fri, 8am-6pm Sat, 9.30am-5.30pm Sun) Sit down for cakes, chocolate, coffee or ice cream at this epicentre of sweet Switzerland, in business since 1836. You can have a light lunch too, but whatever you

Outdoor dining, Zürich

do, don't fail to check out the heavenly chocolate shop around the corner on Paradeplatz.

Alpenrose Swiss €€

(☎044 271 39 19; alpenrose.me; Fabrikstrasse 12; mains Sfr26-42; ⊙11am-midnight Wed-Fri, 6.15-11pm Sat & Sun) With its timber-clad walls, 'No Polka Dancing' warning and multiregional Swiss cuisine, the Alpenrose exudes cosy charm. Specialities include Ticinese risotto and *Pizokel*, a savoury kind of *Spätzli* from Graubünden – as proudly noted on the menu, they've served over 20,000kg of the stuff over the past 20 years! Save room for creamy cognac parfait and other scrumptious desserts.

Zeughauskeller Swiss €€

(☎044 220 15 15; www.zeughauskeller.ch; Bahnhofstrasse 28a; mains Sfr19-35; ⊙11.30am-11pm; 🖉) The menu (in eight languages) at this huge, atmospheric beer hall with ample sidewalk seating offers more than a dozen varieties of sausage, along with numerous other Swiss specialities, including some vegetarian options.

Restaurant Kreis 6 Swiss, Mediterranean €€

(☎044 362 80 06; www.restaurantkreis6.ch; Scheuchzerstrasse 65; mains Sfr30-47; ⊙noon-2.30pm Mon-Fri, 6pm-midnight Mon-Sat) Whether beneath the whitewashed vaulting or the shady pergola in the summer garden, this makes a charming and romantic spot for a range of Mediterranean dishes in warmer weather and Swiss comfort meals in winter. Trams 10 and 15 run close by.

Giesserei Swiss €€

(☎044 205 10 10; www.diegiesserei.ch; Birchstrasse 108; mains Sfr26-38; ⊙11.30am-2pm Mon-Fri, 5.30pm-midnight Mon-Sat year-round, 10am-2.30pm Sun Sep-May) This former factory in Oerlikon is a winner with its scuffed post-industrial atmosphere and pared-down menu (three starters, three mains and three desserts). The abundant Sunday Champagne brunch (Sfr55; September through May) is renowned across town. Take tram 11 to Regensbergbrücke.

Restaurant Reithalle Swiss, International €€

(☎044 212 07 66; www.restaurant-reithalle.ch; Gessnerallee 8; mains Sfr22-40; ⊙11am-midnight Mon-Fri, 6pm-midnight Sat, 6-11pm Sun) Fancy eating in the stables? At these boisterous, converted barracks, the walls are still lined with the cavalry horses' feeding and drinking troughs, but straw has been replaced by a Swiss/international menu, including vegetarian options. Lunch specials go for Sfr20 to Sfr26.

If You Like... Swiss Food

If you like the hearty cheesy Swiss fare at restaurant's like Zürich's Alpenrose and Raclette Stube, you'll like the great local food at these places:

1 **Gerberstube**
(☎052 625 21 55; www.gerberstube.ch; Bachstrasse 8, Schaffhausen; mains Sfr30-49; ⊙11.30am-11.30pm Mon-Sat) Behind its 1708 rococo facade, Gerberstube serves carefully prepared traditional cooking in opulent dining rooms. In medieval times it was a guildhall; today it's a tempting setting to tuck into rich oxtail soup with port wine, or less-traditional curry scampi.

2 **Burg Hohenklingen**
See p219 for details on this 12th-century hilltop fortress in Stein am Rhein.

3 **Appenzeller Schaukäserie**
(www.showcheese.ch; Stein; iPad tour & tasting adult/child Sfr10/5; ⊙8.30am-6.30pm May-Oct, 8.30am-5.30pm Nov-Apr) Cheese-lovers should pop into this Stein-based dairy, which runs through the manufacturing process, explaining how cheeses like the famous Räss get their sweaty-socks smell (a coating of herbs and brine). From Appenzell, there is a frequent bus service to Stein (Sfr7.20, 12 minutes).

Raclette Stube
Swiss €€

(☎ 044 251 41 30; www.raclette-stube.ch; Zähringerstrasse 16; mains Sfr28-44; ☻6-11pm) For the quintessential Swiss cheese experiences – fondue and raclette – pop by this warm and welcoming restaurant, which has three branches around town.

Razzia
International €€€

(☎ 044 296 70 70; razzia-zuerich.ch; Seefeldstrasse 82; mains Sfr32-55; ☻11.30am-2.30pm Mon-Fri, 6.30pm-midnight Mon-Sat) Chandeliers, neoclassical friezes and frescoed ceilings create an elegant backdrop in this stunningly restored theatre, opened as a restaurant in 2014. The atmosphere and dinner prices are decidedly upscale (in keeping with the Seefeldstrasse address), but nine daily lunch menus (Sfr26 to Sfr50) offer the same setting and international cuisine – from lobster, avocado and grapefruit salad to sesame-beef teriyaki – without breaking the bank.

Kronenhalle
Brasserie €€€

(☎ 044 262 99 00; www.kronenhalle.ch; Rämistrasse 4; mains Sfr45-69; ☻noon-midnight) A haunt of city movers and shakers in suits, the Crown Hall is a brasserie-style establishment with an old-world feel, white tablecloths and lots of dark wood. Impeccably mannered waiters move discreetly below Chagall, Miró, Matisse and Picasso originals, serving a daily-changing menu that regularly crosses international borders, from gazpacho to tuna sashimi to Chateaubriand in Béarnaise sauce.

Coco
European €€€

(☎ 044 211 98 98; www.coco-grill.ch; Bleicherweg 1a am Paradeplatz; 2-course lunch menu Sfr25-45, 5-course dinner menu Sfr100-120; ☻11.30am-2pm Mon-Fri, 6.30-9.30pm Mon-Sat) Secreted down a short alley just off Paradeplatz, Coco features an ever-changing five-course 'surprise menu' in the evenings, revolving around the restaurant's trademark charcoal-grilled meat and fish. The atmosphere is romantic, with a teeny front bar, good for a pre-dinner wine, and an almost conspiratorial dining area out back. At lunchtime, more affordable two-course menus are available.

Kaufleuten nightclub

🍷 Drinking & Nightlife

Options abound across town, but the bulk of the more animated drinking dens are in Züri-West, especially along Langstrasse in Kreis 4 and Hardstrasse in Kreis 5.

Generally dress well at clubs and expect to pay Sfr15 to Sfr30 admission.

Frau Gerolds Garten   Bar
(www.fraugerold.ch; Geroldstrasse 23/23a; ⏱11am-midnight Mon-Sat, noon-10pm Sun Apr-Oct, closed in bad weather; 🚻) Hmm, where to start? The wine bar? The margarita bar? The gin bar? Whichever poison you choose, this wildly popular recent addition to Zürich's summertime drinking scene is pure unadulterated fun. Over-hung with multicoloured streamers and sandwiched between cheery flower beds and a screeching railyard, its outdoor seating options range from picnic tables to pillow-strewn terraces to a second-floor sundeck.

Rimini Bar   Bar
(www.rimini.ch; Badweg 10; ⏱7.15pm-midnight Sun-Thu, 6.45pm-midnight Fri, 2pm-midnight Sat Apr-Oct) Secluded behind a fence along the Sihl River, this bar at the Männerbad public baths is one of Zürich's most inviting open-air drinking spots. Its vast wood deck is adorned with red-orange party lights, picnic tables and throw cushions for lounging, accompanied by the sound of water from the adjacent pools. Open in good weather only.

Café Odeon   Bar
(🕿044 251 16 50; www.odeon.ch; Am Belle-vueplatz; ⏱7am-late Mon-Fri, 8am-3am Sat, 9am-1am Sun) This one-time haunt of Lenin and the Dadaists is still a prime people-watching spot. Come for the art nouveau interior, the OTT chandeliers and a whiff of another century.

Longstreet Bar   Bar
(🕿044 241 21 72; www.longstreetbar.ch; Lang-strasse 92; ⏱6pm-late Wed-Fri, 8pm-4am Sat) In the heart of the Langstrasse action, the Longstreet is a music bar with a varied roll call of DJs. Try to count the thousands of light bulbs in this purple-felt-lined one-time cabaret.

Café des Amis   Cafe
(www.desamis.ch; Nordstrasse 88; ⏱8am-midnight Mon-Fri, 9am-midnight Sat, 9am-6pm Sun) A good weekend brunch stop (until 4pm), this is, above all, a popular place to hang out and drink – anything from coffee to cocktails. In summer, spread out on the generous, cobbled terrace.

Rio Bar   Bar
(www.riozurich.ch; Gessnerallee 17; ⏱8am-midnight Mon-Fri, from 9am Sat, 10am-10pm Sun) With its outdoor terrace and prime location near the Hauptbahnhof, this tiny bar on an island in the Sihl river makes a tempting stop any time.

Hive Club   Club
(🕿044 271 12 10; www.hiveclub.ch; Gerold-strasse 5; ⏱11pm-late Thu-Sat) Electronic music creates the buzz at this artsy, alternative club adjacent to Frau Gerolds Garten in Kreis 5. Enter through an alley strung with multicoloured umbrellas, giant animal heads, mushrooms and watering cans. Big-name DJs keep things going into the wee hours three nights a week.

Kanzlei   Club
(🕿044 291 63 11; www.kanzlei.ch; Kanzleistrasse 56; ⏱11pm-late Thu-Sat) What is a school playground by day morphs by night into an outdoor bar and underground club. Reggae, dancehall, hip-hop and more appear regularly on the varied calendar.

Kaufleuten   Club
(🕿044 225 33 22; www.kaufleuten.com; Pelikanplatz; ⏱11pm-late Tue-Sun) An opulent art deco theatre with a stage, mezzanine floor and bars arranged around the dance floor, Zürich's 'establishment' club plays house, hip hop and Latin rhythms to a slightly older crowd.

GAY & LESBIAN VENUES

Zürich has a lively gay scene, which includes Café Odeon.

Daniel H
Bar

(☑044 241 41 78; www.danielh.ch; Müller-strasse 51; ☾5pm-midnight Tue-Thu, to 2am Fri, 7pm-2am Sat) An easygoing lounge-bar arrangement (with a tiny courtyard at the side), the 'Dani H' is a cruisy place to start the night. It is hetero-friendly.

☆ Entertainment

CULTURAL CENTRES

Rote Fabrik
Live Music

(☑for music 044 485 58 68, for theatre 044 485 58 28; www.rotefabrik.ch; Seestrasse 395) With a fabulous lakeside location, this multi-faceted performing arts centre stages rock, jazz and hip-hop concerts, original-language films, theatre and dance performances. There's also a bar and a restaurant. Take bus 161 or 165 from Bürkliplatz.

LIVE MUSIC

Aside from the high-brow stuff, Zürich has an effervescent live-music scene. Many of the bars and clubs mentioned earlier in Zürich offer occasional gigs.

Moods
Live Music

(☑044 276 80 00; www.moods.ch; Schiffbaus-trasse 6; ☾7.30pm-late Mon-Sat, from 6pm Sun) This is one of Zürich's top jazz spots, although other musical genres, includ-ing funk, hip-hop, swing, Latin and world, also grab the occasional spot on its busy calendar.

Tonhalle
Classical Music

(☑044 206 34 34; www.tonhalle-orchester. ch; Claridenstrasse 7) An opulent venue used by Zürich's orchestra and chamber orchestra.

Opernhaus
Opera

(www.opernhaus.ch; Falkenstrasse 1) The city's premier opera house enjoys a worldwide reputation.

☖ Shopping

For high fashion, head for Bahnhofstrasse and surrounding streets. Across the river funkier boutiques are dotted about the lanes of Niederdorf. For grunge, preloved gear and some none-too-serious, fun, young stuff, have a stroll along Lang-strasse in Kreis 4.

The leading markets include the flea market at **Bürkliplatz** (☾8am-4pm Sat May-Oct), the year-round **Flohmarkt Kanzlei** (www.flohmarktkanzlei.ch; Kanzleistrasse 56; ☾8am-4pm Sat) and **Rosenhof** (www. rosenhof.ch; Rosenhof; ☾10am-8pm Thu, 10am-5pm Sat Mar-Dec), but the tourist office has details of more options.

Freitag
Accessories

(☑043 366 95 20; www.freitag.ch; Gerold-strasse 17; ☾11am-7.30pm Mon-Fri, 10am-6pm Sat) The Freitag brothers recycle colourful truck tarps into water-resistant, carry-all-chic in their factory. Every item, from purses to laptop bags, is original. Their outlet is pure whimsy – a pile of shipping containers that's been dubbed Kreis 5's first skyscraper. Shoppers can climb to the rooftop terrace for spectacular city views. Take the train from Hauptbahnhof to Hardbrücke.

Heimatwerk
Souvenirs

(☑044 222 19 55; www.heimatwerk.ch; Urani-astrasse 1; ☾9am-8pm Mon-Fri, 9am-6pm Sat) Good-quality, if touristy, souvenirs are found here, including fondue pots, forks, toys and classy handbags.

ⓘ Information

Discount Card

ZürichCard (www.zuerichcard.ch; adult/child 24hr Sfr24/16, 72hr Sfr48/32) Available from the tourist office and the airport train station, this provides free public transport, free museum admission and more.

Tourist information

Zürich Tourism (☑044 215 40 00, hotel reservations 044 215 40 40; www.zuerich.com; train station; ☾8am-8.30pm Mon-Sat, 8.30am-6.30pm Sun)

ⓘ Getting There & Away

Air

Zürich Airport (ZRH; ☑043 816 22 11; www. zurich-airport.com) is 9km north of the centre, with flights to most European capitals as well as some in Africa, Asia and North America.

Train

Direct trains run to Stuttgart (Sfr64, three hours), Munich (Sfr97, 4¼ hours), Innsbruck (Sfr77, 3½ hours) and other international destinations. There are regular direct departures to most major Swiss towns, such as Lucerne (Sfr24, 45 to 50 minutes), Bern (Sfr49, one to 1¼ hours) and Basel (Sfr32, 55 minutes to 1¼ hours).

ⓘ Getting Around

To/From the Airport

Up to nine trains an hour go to/from the Hauptbahnhof between around 6am and midnight (Sfr6.60, nine to 14 minutes).

Boat

Lake cruises (Zürichsee-Schifffahrtsgesell-schaft; ☏ 044 487 13 33; www.zsg.ch) run between April and October. They leave from Bürkliplatz. A small circular tour *(kleine Rundfahrt)* takes 1½ hours (adult/child Sfr8.40/4.20) and departs every 30 minutes between 11am to 7.30pm. A longer tour *(grosse Rundfahrt)* lasts four hours (adult/child Sfr25/12.50). Pick tickets up at ZVV (local transport) ticket windows.

Riverboats (adult/child Sfr4.20/2.90, every 30 minutes Easter to mid-October) run by the same company head up the Limmat river and do a small circle around the lake (one hour). Board riverboats at the Schweizerisches Landesmuseum stop.

Car & Motorcycle

Parking is tricky. The two most useful car-parking garages (www.parkhaeuser.ch; up to Sfr43 a day) are at Sihlquai 41 near the train station and at Uraniastrasse 3.

Public Transport

Zürich's ZVV (www.zvv.ch) public transport system of buses, S-Bahn suburban trains and trams is completely integrated. Services run from 5.30am to midnight, and tickets must be bought in advance. Every stop has a dispenser. Either type in the four-figure code for your destination or choose your ticket type: a short single-trip *Kurzstrecke* ticket valid for five stops (Sfr2.60), a single ticket for greater Zürich valid for an hour (Sfr4.20) or a 24-hour city pass for the centre, Zone 10 (Sfr8.40).

Bürkliplatz flea market, Zürich

AROUND ZÜRICH

Winterthur

POP 105,461 / ELEV 447M

Switzerland's sixth-largest city gave its name to one of Europe's leading insurance companies and is equally known for its high-quality museums.

⊙ Sights

Winterthur owes much of its eminence as an art Mecca to collector Oskar Reinhart, a scion of a powerful banking and insurance family. His collection was bequeathed to the nation and entrusted to his hometown when he died in 1965.

Ask the tourist office about the Winterthur Museum Pass (Sfr25 for one day, Sfr35 for two), which gives you entry to almost all the sights.

Sammlung Oskar Reinhart am Römerholz   Gallery

(☎058 466 77 40; www.roemerholz.ch; Haldenstrasse 95; adult/child Sfr15/free; ☉10am-5pm Tue & Thu-Sun, 10am-8pm Wed) The collection, housed in a charming country estate, is particularly fascinating in the way it seeks to bridge the gap between traditional and modern art, juxtaposing the likes of Goya, Rembrandt, Bruegel and Rubens with Cézanne, Monet, Picasso, Renoir and Van Gogh. There's a pleasant cafe (mains Sfr21 to Sfr25) next door. Catch the Museumsbus, or take bus 3 to Spital and walk 10 minutes uphill.

Museum Oskar Reinhart am Stadtgarten   Museum

(☎052 267 51 72; museumoskarreinhart. ch; Stadthausstrasse 6; adult/child Sfr15/ free; ☉10am-5pm Tue-Sun) Reinhart's 500-strong collection of Swiss, German and Austrian works of art from the 18th, 19th and 20th centuries is displayed in a museum on the edge of the central city's park.

Fotomuseum   Museum

(☎052 234 10 60; www.fotomuseum.ch; Grüzenstrasse 44 & 45; adult/child Sfr10/free; ☉11am-6pm Tue & Thu-Sun, 11am-8pm Wed) The vast collection at Winterthur's outstanding photography museum features great names and styles from the 19th century to the present. Additional photo shows are staged across the street in the museum's two partner institutions, the Fotostiftung and Zentrum für Fotografie. Buy a Kombi ticket (Sfr19) to visit all three.

Kunstmuseum   Museum

(☎052 267 51 62; www. kmw.ch; Museumstrasse 52; adult/child Sfr15/free; ☉10am-8pm Tue, 10am-5pm Wed-Sun) For a satisfying

Performer, Schloss Kyburg
NATALI GLADO / GETTY IMAGES ©

stroll through a solid collection of the 19th- and 20th-century classics, head to Winterthur's city art museum. Many of the standard suspects, from Klee to Monet, are represented, along with an impressive slew of contemporary creators.

Technorama   Museum
(☏052 244 08 44; www.technorama.ch; Technoramastrasse 1; adult/child Sfr27/16; ☺10am-5pm Tue-Sun) Had enough art? What about a science session? Technorama is an extraordinary voyage into the multiple worlds of hands-on science. Encompassing four jam-packed floors of exhibits, it offers some 500 interactive experiences (explained in English, French, German and Italian) that can't fail to fascinate kids, and plenty of adults too. Take bus 5 from the Hauptbahnhof. Swiss Museum Pass not accepted.

Schloss Kyburg   Castle
(☏052 232 46 64; www.schlosskyburg. ch; adult/child Sfr9/4; ☺10.30am-5.30pm Tue-Sun) Just outside the city, Kyburg weaves interactive fun into the texture of its ancient castle buildings; try on a suit of armour – but not the torture instruments... Take the S-Bahn to Effretikon, then bus 655 to Kyburg. Ask for timetables at the tourist office. The journey takes 30 minutes each way.

SLEEPING & EATING

Taverne zum Kreuz   Hotel €€
(☏052 269 07 20; www.taverne-zum-kreuz.ch; Stadthausstrasse 10b; s Sfr126-146, d Sfr156-176) Near the train station, this charmingly lopsided half-timbered tavern from the 18th century has cosy rooms full of character. Downstairs is an equally warm restaurant and bar. Prices are shaved somewhat at weekends.

Akazie   Mediterranean €€
(☏052 212 17 17; restaurant-akazie.ch; Stadthausstrasse 10; mains Sfr29-47; ☺11am-11pm Tue-Sat) Decked out in timber, this inviting, cosy location serves up creative nouvelle Mediterranean cuisine that

If You Like…
Castles

If you like big old castles such as Winterthur's Schloss Kyburg, you'll enjoy these other old fortresses scattered about the northeast of Switzerland:

1 SCHLOSS ARBON
This 16th-century castle watches over the historic centre of Arbon. The castle's **Historisches Museum** (http://museum-arbon. ch; Alemannenstrasse 4; adult/child Sfr6/free; ☺2-5pm Tue-Sun May-Sep, shorter hours rest of year) races you through 5500 years of history, from the Stone Age to the 18th-century linen trade. On one lane, centuries-old houses display frescos depicting trades of yore. Arbon is on the train line between Zürich and Rorschach.

2 SCHLOSS WARTEGG
You can stay the night at this magnificent fantasy palace (☏071 858 62 62; http://wartegg. ch; Rorschacherberg; s Sfr165, d Sfr265-290; P @) 🖉, a 10-minute drive from central Rorschach on the hillside above town. This 16th-century former royal Austrian castle is set in leafy grounds with towering sequoias and Lake Constance views.

comes in old-fashioned portions, washed down with wines from as far off as Sardinia.

ℹ Information
Tourist Office (☏052 267 67 00; www. winterthur-tourismus.ch; Hauptbahnhof; ☺8.30am-6.30pm Mon-Fri, 8.30am-4pm Sat)

ℹ Getting There & Around
Four to five trains an hour run to Zürich (Sfr12.40, 20 to 30 minutes). The A1 freeway goes from Zürich, skirts Winterthur and continues to St Gallen and Austria.

A Museumsbus minivan shuttle (Sfr5 round-trip) leaves the train station hourly between 9.45am and 4.45pm for the Sammlung Oskar Reinhart am Römerholz, the Museum Oskar Reinhart am Stadtgarten and the Kunstmuseum.

SCHAFFHAUSEN CANTON

Cyclists love touring this relatively flat region, and lower-end accommodation is booked up swiftly on weekends. Excellent public transport and manageable distances make it an easy day trip from Zürich too.

Schaffhausen

POP 35,413 / ELEV 404M

Schaffhausen is the kind of quaint medieval town one more readily associates with Germany – no coincidence, given how close it is to the border. Ornate frescoes and oriel bay windows grace the pastel-coloured houses lining the pedestrian-only **Altstadt** (Old Town).

◉ Sights

Opening hours are given for high season (April through October); many sights have reduced hours at other times.

Vorstadt *Neighbourhood*

Schaffhausen is often nicknamed the *Erkerstadt* because of its 171 *Erker* (oriel bay windows), once a status symbol of rich merchants. Some of the most impressive line up along Vorstadt, including the 17th-century **Zum Goldenen Ochsen** (Vorstadt 17), whose frescoed facade displays an eponymous Golden Ox. The frescos of the 16th-century **Zum Grossen Käfig** (Vorstadt 45) present an extraordinarily colourful tale of the parading of Turkish sultan Bajazet in a cage by the triumphant Mongol warrior leader Tamerlane.

Fronwagplatz *Square*

At the very heart of the Altstadt lies this square, flanked by ornate facades. The 16th-century **Mohrenbrunnen** (Moor Fountain) marks the north of the old market place, while at the southern end stands the **Metzgerbrunnen** (Butcher's Fountain), a William Tell–type figure and a large clock tower. Facing the latter is the late baroque **Herrenstube** (Fronwagplatz 3),

built in 1748, which was once the drinking hole of quaffing nobles.

Allerheiligen Münster *Cathedral*

(All Saints' Cathedral; Münsterplatz; ⏰10am-noon & 2-5pm Tue-Sun, cloister 7.30am-8pm Mon-Fri, 9am-8pm Sat & Sun) Completed in 1103, Schaffhausen's cathedral is a rare, largely intact specimen of the Romanesque style in Switzerland. It opens to a beautifully simple **cloister**. The herb garden has been lovingly tended since the Middle Ages and is a tranquil spot for contemplation. Walk through the cloister to reach the **Museum zu Allerheiligen** (www.allerheiligen.ch; Klosterstrasse 16; adult/child Sfr12/free; ⏰11am-5pm Tue-Sun), showcasing treasures from Schaffhausen fossils to Etruscan gold jewellery. The art collection contains works by Otto Dix, Lucas Cranach the Elder and contemporary Swiss artists.

Herrenacker *Square*

Framed by pastel-coloured houses with steep tiled roofs, this is one of Schaffhausen's prettiest squares. In August it's an atmospheric backdrop for music fest **Stars in Town** (www.starsintown.ch); Amy Macdonald and Status Quo were headliners in 2014.

Munot *Fortress*

(⏰8am-8pm May-Sep, 9am-5pm Oct-Apr) `FREE` Steps lead up through vineyards to this fine specimen of a 16th-century fortress. The unusual circular battlements were built with forced labour following the Reformation and conceal an atmospheric vaulted casemate. Climb the spiral staircase for views over a patchwork of rooftops and spires to the Rhine and wooded hills fringing the city.

🤸 Activities

Rhybadi *Swimming*

(www.rhybadi.ch; Rheinuferstrasse; adult/child Sfr3/1.50; ⏰8am-7pm Mon-Fri, 9am-6pm Sat & Sun May-Sep) If you're itching to leap into the Rhine, do it at this rickety 19th-century wooden bathhouse. There are diving boards and old-fashioned changing rooms reminiscent of an era when 'proper' folk bathed fully clothed.

Altstadt Walks
Walking Tour

(adult/child Sfr14/7; ☺10am Tue, 2pm Sat May–mid-Oct) These one-hour tours of the Old Town kick off at the tourist office. The well-informed guides speak German, English and French.

Untersee und Rhein
Boat Tour

(☎052 634 08 88; www.urh.ch; Freier Platz; one way Sfr47; ☺Apr-Oct) The 45km boat trip from Schaffhausen to Konstanz via Stein am Rhein and Reichenau is one of the Rhine's more beautiful stretches. The journey takes 3¾ hours downstream to Schaffhausen and 4¾ hours the other way. See the website for timetables.

🛏 Sleeping

Hotel Kronenhof
Hotel €€

(☎052 635 75 75; www.kronenhof.ch; Kirch-hofplatz 7; s Sfr150-170, d Sfr190-220, ste Sfr280; ☎) A guesthouse since 1489, the Kro-nenhof has welcomed the likes of Goethe and Tsar Alexander. A recent makeover has spruced up the historic interior, with the best rooms now flaunting dark wood

floors, crimson walls and bold art. You can wind down with a steam in the petite spa or a steak in the Ox bistro.

Park Villa
Hotel €€

(☎052 635 60 60; www.parkvilla.ch; Parkstrasse 18; s/d Sfr169/229, without bathroom Sfr98/130; P ☎) The eclectic furniture in this faintly Gothic house resembles a private antiques collection, with an array of four-poster beds, Persian carpets, chandeliers, patterned wallpaper and fake Ming vases in rooms. Dine in Louis XVI splendour in the banquet room.

Fischerzunft
Boutique Hotel €€

(☎052 632 05 05; www.fischerzunft.ch; Rhein-quai 8; s/d Sfr210/295; ☎) The sloping tiled roof and creamy-pink exterior of this low-slung Rhine-side mansion contain this charming boutique hotel, known above all for its gourmet restaurant. Rooms are individually decorated, often with lashings of chintzy floral fabrics.

🍴 Eating

Stadthausgasse is takeaway street, rolling out quick eats from pizza to Thai.

Schaffhausen Altstadt

Head to Fronwagplatz for bakeries, delis, gelaterias and alfresco cafes.

Café Vordergasse
Cafe €

(📞 052 625 42 49; Vordergasse 79; snacks & light meals Sfr10-20; ⏰6am-7pm Mon-Fri, 7am-5pm Sat, 10am-5pm Sun) This art nouveau–style tearoom spills onto an ever-popular pavement terrace. Try sandwiches, salads and quiches with a homemade lemonade or smoothie.

Wii am Rii
Bistro €€

(📞 079 259 92 47; www.wiiamrii.ch; Fischerhäuserstrasse 57; mains Sfr27.50-45.50; ⏰5-10.30pm Wed-Sat) Slow food is the watchword at this bistro down by the Rhine, which has a vintage-cool air and a wonderfully laid-back vibe. The good-natured staff pair regional, season-driven specialities, such as filet of veal with chanterelles and venison schnitzel, with a well-edited selection of local and Italian wines.

Oberhof
Swiss €€

(📞 052 632 07 70; www.oberhof-schaffhausen.ch; Stadthausgasse 15; mains Sfr26-69; ⏰11.30am-11pm Mon-Fri, 4-11pm Sat) There's always a buzz at Oberhof, which hides a slick, contemporary interior behind its historic facade. The menu skips from creative salads and Thai curries to surf and turf and vegan dishes – everything is super-fresh, nicely presented and served with a smile.

Fischerzunft
Gourmet €€€

(📞 052 632 05 05; www.fischerzunft.ch; Rheinquai 8; mains Sfr60-78; ⏰noon-2pm & 7-9pm Wed-Sun) André Jaeger and Jana Zwesper entice with European-Asian taste sensations at this Michelin-starred restaurant by the Rhine, with an elegant beamed dining room and riverside terrace. Match perfectly spiced fish dishes and handmade desserts with top wines from the cellar.

ℹ Information

Tourist Office (📞 052 632 40 20; www.schaffhausen-tourismus.ch; Herrenacker 15; ⏰1.30-6pm Mon, 9.30am-6pm Tue-Fri, 9.30am-3pm Sat, 9.30am-2pm Sun, shorter hours in winter) Hands out brochures and stocks cycling maps and guides. There is also a *vinothek* selling locally produced wines.

Stein am Rhein

BUENA VISTA IMAGES / GETTY IMAGES ©

⭐ Don't Miss
Rheinfall

Ensnared in wispy spray, the thunderous Rheinfall might not give Niagara much competition in terms of height (23m), width (150m) or even flow of water (700 cu metre per second in summer), but it's a stunning sight nonetheless.

Most views of the falls are free, but to get close up to the rushing waters on the south side of the falls, you pay an entry fee at the Schloss Laufen souvenir shop to descend the staircase to the Känzeli viewing platform.

During summer, ferries flit in and out of the water at the bottom of the falls. Some merely cross from Schloss Laufen to Schlössli Worth, but the round-trip that stops at the tall rock in the middle of the falls, where you can climb to the top and watch the water rush all around you, is far more fun.

To get to the Rheinfall, you can catch bus 1, 6 or 9 from Schaffhausen train station to Neuhausen Zentrum (Sfr3, 13 minutes), then follow the yellow footprints.

NEED TO KNOW

Rheinfall (Rhine Falls; www.rheinfall.ch; 🚃1, 6 or 9 to Neuhausen; get off one stop after Migross in the centre, then follow signs leading to north bank of river); **ferries** (www.maendli.ch; Schloss Laufen to Schlössli Worth adult/child Sfr2/1, round-trip Sfr8/4)

ℹ Getting There & Away

Direct trains run half-hourly to Zürich (Sfr22, 40 minutes) and Stein am Rhein (Sfr8.60, 24 minutes). Frequent trains to St Gallen (Sfr29, 1½ to two hours) usually involve a change at Winterthur or Romanshorn.

Stein am Rhein

POP 3286 / ELEV 407M

Stein am Rhein looks as though it has leaped out of the pages of a Swiss fairy-tale, with its miniature steam train, leafy river promenade and gingerbready houses. The effect is most overwhelming in its cobblestone Rathausplatz, where houses of all shapes and sizes, some half-timbered, others covered in frescoes line up for a permanent photo op. Why isn't this place on Unesco's World Heritage list?

Sights & Activities

Look out for daredevil kids diving from the bridge into the Rhine as you wander along the leafy river promenade.

Rathausplatz   Square

Often hailed as Switzerland's most beautiful town square (no mean feat!), the elongated Rathausplatz is picture-book stuff. The fresco-festooned **Rathaus** (town hall) soars above the 16th-century houses named according to the pictures with which they are adorned, such as *Sonne* (Sun) and *Der Weisse Adler* (The White Eagle).

Museum Lindwurm   Museum

(www.museum-lindwurm.ch; Unterstadt 18; adult/child Sfr5/3; ⊘10am-5pm Mar-Oct) A four-storey house has been converted into this museum, whose living rooms, servants' quarters and kitchen replicate the conditions enjoyed in the mid-19th century by a bourgeois family.

Klostermuseum St Georgen   Museum

(adult/child Sfr5/3; ⊘10am-5pm Tue-Sun Apr-Oct) This monastery museum sits between the Rathaus and the Rhine. A Benedictine monastery was built here in 1007, but what you see today, including the cloister and magnificent *Festsaal* (grand dining room), is largely a late-Gothic creation.

Sleeping & Eating

Half-timbered houses serving Swiss grub line the Rhine, but the quality can be hit or miss.

B&B Stein am Rhein   B&B €

(☎052 741 45 44; Bollstieg 22; s/d/f Sfr70/120/170; ☞) Huddled away in a green, quiet corner of town is this charming B&B. The kindly Keller family make you feel instantly at home in their chalet with bright, well-kept rooms kitted out with pine furnishings. Families are *herzlich wilkommen*, and cycling, mountain-biking and kayaking tours can be arranged on request. It's a 10-minute stroll east of the historic centre.

SYHA Hostel   Hostel €

(☎052 741 12 55; www.youthhostel.ch/stein; Hemishoferstrasse 87; dm Sfr32-34, s/d/q Sfr52/100/152; ☞) On the banks of the Rhine, this neat-and-tidy hostel has attractive gardens, a barbecue area

Rathaus (town hall), Stein am Rhein
ANDY CHRISTIANI / GETTY IMAGES ©

A Spin of the Lake

Hopping across the Swiss–German border from Kreuzlingen brings you to the high-spirited, sunny university town of **Konstanz** (www.konstanz.de), well worth a visit for its Romanesque cathedral, pretty Old Town and tree-fringed harbour. Edging north of Konstanz, you reach the Unesco-listed Benedictine monastery of **Reichenau** (www.reichenau.de), founded in AD 724. Close by is **Insel Mainau** (www.mainau.de; adult/child €18/10.50; ☺dawn-dusk), a pleasantly green islet with 45 hectares of Mediterranean-style gardens, including rhododendron groves, a butterfly house and a waterfall-strewn Italian garden.

Stepping across to the lake's northern flank you arrive in the wine-growing town of **Meersburg** (www.meersburg.de), where cobbled lanes thread past half-timbered houses up to the perkily turreted medieval castle. Just east of here is **Friedrichshafen**, forever associated with the Zeppelin, the early cigar-shaped craft of the skies, which made its inaugural flight in 1900. The **Zeppelin Museum** (www.zeppelin-museum.de; adult/child €8/3; ☺9am-5pm) traces the history of this bombastic, but ill-fated, means of air transport. Still on German turf is the postcard-perfect island town of **Lindau** (www.lindau.de), with its lavishly frescoed houses, palm-speckled promenade and harbour watched over by a lighthouse and Bavarian lion.

Lindau sits just a few kilometres north of Austria and the town of **Bregenz** (www.bregenz.ws). Rising dramatically above the town is the Pfänder (1064m). A **cable car** (www.pfaenderbahn.at; Steinbruchgasse 4, Bregenz; adult/child return €11.80/5.90; ☺8am-7pm) glides to the summit, where panoramic views of Lake Constance and the not-so-distant Alps unfold.

Even if you don't have your own car, getting around by bike or boat is a breeze. Well-signposted and largely flat, the 273km **Bodensee-Radweg** (www.bodensee-radweg.com) encircles the lake, weaving through fields of ripening wheat, vineyards, orchards and shady avenues of chestnut and plane. Most train stations in the region rent out bikes.

and playground. It's a 15-minute stroll northwest of Rathausplatz.

La P'tite Crêperie
Creperie €

(Unterstadt 10; crêpes Sfr7-13; ☺11am-7pm) Feast away on fabulously light crêpes with cheese and *Bündnerfleisch* (air-dried beef), maple syrup or – what could be more Swiss? – Toblerone at this hole-in-the-wall place with a boho feel. It's closed Tuesdays and Wednesdays during low season.

Burg Hohenklingen
Swiss €€

(☎052 741 21 37; www.burghohenklingen.ch; Hohenklingenstrasse 1; mains Sfr30.50-55; ☺10am-10pm Tue-Sun) For medieval atmosphere, you can't beat this 12th-century hilltop fortress, with superb views over Stein am Rhein. Tuck into Swiss classics such as beef braised in Pinot noir in the Rittersaal (Hall of Knights). It's a 30-minute uphill walk from the Old Town.

ⓘ Getting There & Away

Stein am Rhein is on the direct twice hourly train route to Schaffhausen (Sfr8.60, 26 minutes) and St Gallen (Sfr20.60, 1½ hours).

LAKE CONSTANCE

Before package holidays began whisking the locals and their beach towels abroad in the '70s and '80s, Lake Constance (Bodensee) was the German

219

Below: Buildings along Hauptgasse, Appenzell; **Right:** Countryside, Appenzell Canton

(BELOW) STUART DEE / GETTY IMAGES ©; (RIGHT) PHIL / GETTY IMAGES ©

Mediterranean, with its mild climate, flowery gardens and palm trees. The 'Swabian Sea', as it's nicknamed, is Central Europe's third largest lake, straddling Switzerland, Germany and Austria. It's a relaxed place to wind down for a few days, whether cycling through apple orchards and vineyards, heron-spotting in the lake's wetlands, or taking to its glassy waters by canoe.

Come in spring for blossoms, summer for lazy beach days and autumn for new wine. Almost everything shuts from November to February.

Information

The Bodensee Erlebniskarte (www.bodensee-erlebniskarte.de; 3/7/14 days Sfr86/114/160) discount card is sold from mid-April to mid-October. In its most expensive version, it entitles the holder to free unlimited ferry travel, entrance to many museums and attractions, including the Zeppelin Museum in Friedrichshafen and Insel Mainau, and a return journey up the Säntisbahn.

Getting There & Away

Frequent rail services link Zürich to Konstanz (Sfr31, 80 minutes) and Munich (Sfr97, 4¼ hours) in Germany. Trains (Sfr8, 19 minutes) run between Bregenz in Austria and St Margrethen in Switzerland.

Getting Around

Various ferry companies, including Switzerland's **SBS Schifffart** (www.sbsag.ch), Austria's **Vorarlberg Lines** (www.bodenseeschifffahrt. at) and **Germany's BSB** (www.bsb-online. com), travel across, along and around the lake from mid-April to late October, with the more-frequent services starting in late May. A Swiss Pass is valid only on the Swiss side of the lake.

Trains tend to be the easiest way to get around on the Swiss side, buses on the German bank.

Kreuzlingen

POP 20,349 / ELEV 404M

Kreuzlingen, in the Swiss canton of Thurgau, is often eclipsed by its prettier, more vivacious sister, Konstanz in Germany. That said, its lakefront location is charming, as is its **SYHA hostel** (☏071 688 26 63; www.youthhostel.ch/kreuzlingen; Promenadenstrasse 7; dm Sfr32, d Sfr74-80, q Sfr160-164; ☻Mar-Nov; @☎), which occupies an art nouveau villa and offers canoe and kayak rental. Should you need more details, try the **tourist office** (☏071 672 38 40; www.kreuzlingen-tourismus.ch; Sonnenstrasse 4; ☻10am-12.30pm Mon-Sat & 1.30-6pm Mon-Fri May-Sep, shorter hours in winter). Direct trains run every 30 minutes between Kreuzlingen and Schaffhausen (Sfr17.80, 55 minutes).

The lakeside road between Kreuzlingen and Stein am Rhein is dotted with quaint half-timbered Thurgau villages, such as Gottlieben, Steckborn and Berlingen. Near the latter is **Schloss Arenenberg** (www.napoleonmuseum.tg.ch; Salenstein; adult/child Sfr12/5; ☻10am-5pm), the handsome lakefront mansion where France's Napoleon III grew up.

ST GALLEN & APPENZELL CANTONS

The cultural high point of a journey around the extreme northeast of the country is a visit to St Gallen's legendary abbey, with its extraordinary rococo library.

Locals go to great lengths to preserve their heritage and this green, hilly region is sprinkled with beautiful, timeless villages. Both cantons are criss-crossed by endless hiking, cycling and mountain-biking trails.

St Gallen

POP 74,111 / ELEV 670M

St Gallen's history as the 'writing room of Europe' is evident in its principal attraction today: the sublime rococo library of its huge Catholic abbey, which

ENGEL & GIELEN / LOOK-FOTO / GETTY IMAGES ©

⭐ **Don't Miss**
Stiftsbibliothek

St Gallen's 16th-century library is one of the world's oldest and the finest example of rococo architecture in Switzerland. Along with the rest of the monastery complex surrounding it, the library forms a Unesco World Heritage site.

Filled with priceless books and manuscripts painstakingly handwritten by monks during the Middle Ages, it's a dimly lit confection of ceiling frescos, stucco, cherubs and parquetry. Only 30,000 of the total 150,000 volumes are in the library at any one time, and only a handful in display cases, arranged into special exhibitions. If there's a tour guide in the library at the time, you might see the monks' filing system, hidden in the wall panels.

NEED TO KNOW

Stiftsbibliothek (www.stiftsbibliothek.ch; Klosterhof 6d; adult/child Sfr12/9; ⊙10am-5pm Mon-Sat, 10am-4pm Sun)

rises gracefully above a fountain-dotted courtyard.

Local lore has it that St Gallen began with a bush, a bear and an Irish monk who should have watched where he was going. In AD 612, the tale goes, itinerant Gallus fell into a briar and considered the stumble a calling from God. After a fortuitous encounter with a bear, in which he persuaded it to bring him a log, take

some bread in return and leave him in peace, he used the log to begin building the hermitage that would one day morph into St Gallen's cathedral.

 Sights

Many houses of Old St Gallen boast elaborate *Erker* (oriel bay windows), especially around Gallusplatz, Spisergasse,

Schmiedgasse and Kugelgasse. The city's tourism folk have counted them all up and reckon there are 111 oriel windows! Some bear the most extraordinary timber sculptures – a reflection of the wealth of their one-time owners, mostly textile barons.

Multilingual guided tours of the Old Town (Sfr20 per person) kick off at the tourist office at 2pm Monday to Saturday from May to October.

Dom
Cathedral

(Klosterhof; ⏰9am-6pm Mon, Tue, Thu & Fri, 10am-6pm Wed, 9am-4pm Sat, noon-5.30pm Sun) The twin-towered cathedral is only slightly less ornate than the library, with dark and stormy frescos and aqua-green stucco embellishments. Oddly, entry is by two modest doors on the north flank – there is no door in the main facade, which is actually the cathedral's apse. Concerts are sometimes held – consult www.kirchenmusik.ch. The cathedral is closed during services.

St Laurenzen-Kirche
Church

(Zeughausgasse; tower adult/child Sfr5/2.50; ⏰9.30-11.30am & 2-4pm Mon, 9.30am-4pm Tue-Sat) St Gallen's cathedral gets all the attention, but this Protestant neo-Gothic church is also beautiful, with its mosaic-tiled roof, delicate floral frescos and star-studded ceiling resembling a night sky. Climb the **tower** for views over the town's terracotta rooftops and spires.

Textilmuseum
Museum

(www.textilmuseum.ch; Vadianstrasse 2; adult/child Sfr12/free; ⏰10am-5pm) St Gallen has long been an important hub of the Swiss textile industry, and this is the most interesting of the town's several museums. Butterflies dance across the purple walls of the museum's lounge bar, a fashionable coffee spot.

🛏 Sleeping

St Gallen is a business town, which can make beds scarce and prices high.

Annahaus
B&B €

(☏071 244 02 42; www.annahaus.ch; Langgasse 126; s/d Sfr75/Sfr130; P🛜) This sweet, petite B&B is 2km north of town. It's one of St Gallen's better budget picks, with a friendly welcome, a lounge with games, table tennis and a lending library, and bicycle storage. Two of the fresh, light rooms can accommodate families (a child's bed costs an extra Sfr30). Buses 3, 9 and 12 stop close by.

SYHA Hostel
Hostel €

(☏071 245 47 77; www.youthhostel.ch/st.gallen; Jüchstrasse 25; dm/s/d/q Sfr35/71/99/153; @🛜) Nestled in leafy grounds, this modern hillside hostel is only a 15-minute walk from the Old Town – or take the Trogenerbähnli (S21) from the train station to Birnbäume.

Hotel Dom
Boutique Hotel €€

(☏071 227 71 71; www.hoteldom.ch; Webergasse 22; s Sfr155-195, d Sfr225-255, tr Sfr275-305; 🛜) An almost startlingly modern hotel, plonked in the middle of the Old Town. The room decor is razor-sharp with clean lines, backlit walls and bold colours. A generous breakfast buffet sweetens the deal.

Einstein Hotel
Historic Hotel €€€

(☏071 227 55 55; www.einstein.ch; Berneggstrasse 2; s Sfr170-280, d Sfr270-460, ste Sfr490-2500; P@🛜) Silk curtains, cherry-wood furnishings and plush lambwool rugs grace the spacious rooms at this grand 19th-century pile. Relax with a swim in the strikingly lit atrium pool or a massage in the spa. The panoramic rooftop restaurant (mains Sfr24 to Sfr49) emphasises regional cuisine.

🍴 Eating & Drinking

St Gallen is noted for its *Erststock-Beizli*, traditional taverns situated on the 1st floor of half-timbered houses.

Focacceria
Cafe €

(☏071 220 16 15; www.focacceria.ch; Metzgergasse 22; foccacia Sfr7-15; ⏰11am-11pm Mon-Thu, 11am-midnight Fri, 10am-midnight Sat) Join the midday crowds for delicious focaccia prepared with homemade antipasti and spreads, speciality teas and coffees.

Metzgerei Gemperli
Sausages €

(Schmiedgasse 34; sausages from Sfr6.50; ◷8am-6.30pm Mon-Fri, 7am-5pm Sat) Bite into the best OLMA bratwurst, served plain in a *Bürli* (bun), at this butcher/sausage stand combo.

Wirtschaft Zur Alten Post
International €€

(☎071 222 66 01; www.apost.ch; Gallusstrasse 4; mains Sfr23-48; ◷11.30am-2pm & 5.30-10.30pm Tue-Sat) Things are a little ritzy at this upmarket but historical *Beizl* (tavern), where St Gallen specialities like fat veal sausages with rösti are complemented by more-original creations such as French corn-fed chicken with lemon-herb risotto.

Am Gallusplatz
Swiss €€

(☎071 223 33 30; www.gallusplatz.ch; Gallusstrasse 24; mains Sfr30-50; ◷11.30am-2.30pm Tue-Fri, 6-11.30pm Tue-Thu, 6pm-midnight Fri & Sat) Dine below atmospheric vaults at this tavern opposite the cathedral, which was a horse stable in a former life and still has a whiff of late medieval charm about it. The menu plays up meaty classics such as beef stroganoff and Wiener schnitzel, with a superb selection of wines to match.

Bäumli
Swiss €€

(☎071 222 11 74; www.weinstube-baeumli.ch; Schmiedgasse 18; mains Sfr22-47; ◷10am-midnight Tue-Sat) A late-medieval building housing an atmospheric wood-panelled, candlelit restaurant that showcases all the typical 1st-floor specialities, from bratwurst with fried onions to lamb cutlets, Wiener schnitzel, cordon bleu (pork schnitzel stuffed with ham and cheese) and *Geschnetzeltes* (a sliced pork or veal dish).

Trüffelschnüffler
Cafe

(Zeughausgasse 14; ◷1.30-6.30pm Wed-Fri, 10am-5pm Sat) 'Truffle sniffer' is the name of this arty cafe-cum-craft-shop. Stop by for drinks and handmade gifts, from groovy printed bags to wood-carved Swiss army knives.

Chocolaterie
Cafe

(www.chocolateriesg.ch; Gallusstrasse 20; ◷1-6.30pm Mon, 9am-6.30pm Tue-Fri, 9am-5pm Sat) For smooth, cocoa-rich hot or cold chocolate, this half-timbered place opposite the cathedral is surely the devil's work.

Families walk through the Barfusspfad (barefoot trail), near Appenzell

ℹ️ Information

Tourist Office (☏ 071 227 37 37; www.st-gallen-bodensee.ch; Bahnhofplatz 1a; ⏱9am-6pm Mon-Fri) There's another self-service information point, where you can pick up brochures, in the Chocolaterie.

ℹ️ Getting There & Away

St Gallen is a short train or bus ride from Romanshorn (Sfr9.40, 25 minutes). There are also regular trains (only four of them direct) to Bregenz in Austria (Sfr18, 35 to 50 minutes), Chur (Sfr34, 1½ hours) and Zürich (Sfr29, 65 minutes via Winterthur).

Appenzell

POP 5661 / ELEV 785M

Appenzell is a feast for both the eyes and the stomach. Behind the gaily decorative pastel-coloured facades of its traditional buildings lie cafes, *confiseries* (sweets and cake shops), cheese shops, delicatessens, butchers and restaurants offering local specialities. It's absolutely perfect for a long lunch and a lazy wander along the crystal-clear Sitter river.

◎ Sights & Activities

Countless hiking trails thread up into the Alps from Appenzell; see www.appenzell.info for inspiration. A great family walk is the 5km Barfusspfad (barefoot trail), which skips through meadows and over mountain brooks to Gonten.

Opening hours are given for high season; many sights have reduced hours from November to March.

Altstadt　　　　　Neighbourhood

The centrepiece of the Old Town is photogenic **Landsgemeindeplatz**, with elaborately painted hotels and restaurants around its edges. The open-air parliament takes place on this square on the last Sunday of April, with locals wearing traditional dress and voting (in the case of the men, by raising a short dagger).

The buildings along **Hauptgasse** are also noteworthy. The village **church** has

gold and silver figures flanking a baroque altar.

Brauerei Locher　　　　　Brewery

(www.appenzellerbier.ch; Brauereiplatz 1; visitor centre admission free, beer tasting Sfr8.50; ⏱10am-12.15pm Tue-Fri, 1-5pm Mon-Fri, 10am-5pm Sat & Sun) Pure local spring water goes into the refreshing Appenzeller Bier that's brewed here. The hands-on visitor centre whisks you through brewing history and processes. At the front you can buy beers such as hoppy Vollmond (full moon) and alcohol-free Leermond (empty moon). Beer tastings take place at 1pm every Monday.

Appenzell Museum　　　　　Museum

(Hauptgasse 4; adult/child Sfr7/3; ⏱10am-noon & 2-5pm) Beside the tourist office, this museum fills you in on traditional customs with its collection of 15th-century flags and banners, embroidery, folk art and (more grimly) historic torture instruments.

🛏️ Sleeping & Eating

The tourist office can advise on B&Bs, holiday apartments and farmstays in the area.

Gasthaus Hof　　　　　Guesthouse €

(☏ 071 787 40 30; www.gasthaus-hof.ch; Engelgasse 4; s/d/tr/q Sfr85/130/180/220; 🛜) Just off Landsgemeindeplatz, this cheap-sleep option has simple but spacious rooms with timber-clad walls. The old-school restaurant comes with plenty of local bonhomie.

Hotel Appenzell　　　　　Hotel €€

(☏ 071 788 15 15; www.hotel-appenzell.ch; Landsgemeindeplatz; s/d Sfr135/230; 🅿@🛜) With its broad, brightly decorated facade, this typical Appenzeller building houses generously sized rooms with wooden beds. Decor combines gentle pinks and blues with frilly lace on the picture windows. The restaurant offers a wide-ranging seasonal menu that includes vegetarian dishes.

Detour:
Säntis

Small in Swiss terms, the jagged Säntis peak (2503m) is the highest in this part of Switzerland. It offers a marvellous panorama encompassing Lake Constance, Zürichsee, the Alps and the Vorarlberg Mountains. From Schwägalp, the **Säntisbahn** (www.saentisbahn.ch; one-way/return Sfr32/45; ⊙7.30am-6pm Mon-Fri, 7.30am-6.30pm Sat & Sun late May–mid-Oct, 8.30am-5pm rest of year) glides to the summit every 30 minutes.

From Säntis, you can walk along the ridge to the neighbouring peak of **Ebenalp** (1640m) in about 3½ hours. At Wildkirchli on Ebenalp there are prehistoric caves showing traces of Stone Age habitation.

The descent to the jewel-coloured **Seealpsee** on foot takes 1½ hours. Alternatively, a **cable car** runs between the summit and Wasserauen approximately every 30 minutes. Wasserauen and Appenzell are connected by rail. By the lake, family-run dairy Seealpkäse sells delicious cheese specialities, including varieties made with wild garlic and chilli. For a glowing complexion, you can bathe in whey in a wooden bathtub (Sfr45) and gaze up at the mountains.

Back in Schwägalp, you can bed down for the night at Berghotel Schwägalp, a rustic mountain hotel with cosy pine-clad rooms and big mountain views.

Marktplatz — International €€

(☎071 787 12 04; www.marktplatz-appenzell.ch; Kronengarten 2; mains Sfr23.50-55; ⊙11am-11pm Fri-Tue; 🖪) Sit on the terrace on one of Appenzell's prettiest squares or in the intricately wood-carved interior of this restaurant. The menu has strong Italian overtones, as simple as spot-on roast lamb drizzled with rosemary, and beef medallions with saffron risotto. There's a Sfr13 children's menu.

Gasthaus Linde — Swiss €€

(☎071 787 13 76; Hauptgasse 40; mains Sfr18-30; ⊙noon-2pm & 7-10pm Fri-Wed) This warm, wood-panelled tavern oozes local character and does excellent Appenzell beer fondue. More adventurous diners can tuck into offal specialities.

🛈 Information

The **tourist office** (☎071 788 96 41; www.appenzell.ch; Hauptgasse 4; ⊙9am-noon & 1.30-6pm Mon-Fri, 10am-noon & 2-5pm Sat & Sun Apr-Oct, shorter hours rest of year) has details on the Appenzell Ferienkarte, which entitles you to free use of public transport and most cable cars, access to local museums and pools, plus one day's free bike hire (summer) or sled/cross-country ski hire (winter) when you stay in town three nights or more.

🛈 Getting There & Away

From St Gallen, the narrow-gauge train to Appenzell (Sfr7.20, 45 minutes) leaves from the front and to the right of the main train station. Departures from St Gallen are approximately every half-hour, via Gais or Herisau (where you must occasionally change trains).

Around Appenzell

Scattered with Alpine dairy farms and quaint villages, the countryside surrounding Appenzell makes for some highly scenic driving along narrow winding roads.

🔘 Sights & Activities

Volkskunde Museum — Museum

(www.appenzeller-museum-stein.ch; Stein; adult/child Sfr7/3.50; ⊙10am-5pm Tue-Sun) This folksy museum provides an overview of Appenzell life, its collection spanning everything from pastoral paintings to cheesemaking traditions.

Werdenberg   Village
Blink and you'll miss this village and that would be a shame! Founded in 1289, it is said to be the oldest settlement of timber houses in Switzerland. The huddle of some 40-odd houses lies between an oversized pond and a grapevine-covered hill topped by a castle.

Wildhaus   Village
Sitting pretty between the shark fin–like peaks of the Churfirsten range and Säntis is the family-friendly village of Wildhaus. This is a relaxed base for hiking in summer and skiing on 60km of pistes in winter at **Toggenburg** (www.toggenburg.ch; day pass adult/child Sfr 57/26). Activities such as guided donkey walks and llama trekking keep kids amused.

ⓘ Getting There & Away
Trains run from St Gallen to Buchs (Sfr20.60, 55 minutes), where you can pick up local buses to Werdenberg.

Walensee
Walensee is a long finger of a lake along the A3 freeway (and railway line) that connects Zürich with Graubünden. The limestone Churfirsten mountains rise spectacularly above its north flank, occasionally interrupted by a coastal hamlet or upland pasture and, about halfway along the lakefront, seemingly cracked open by Switzerland's highest waterfall.

◉ Sights & Activities

Flumserberg   Mountain
(www.flumserberg.ch) For a little Alpine fun, take the winding mountain road to Flumserberg, perched high above the lake and facing the impenetrable rock wall of the Churfirsten range. The mountain is the starting point for high-Alpine hikes like the 13km **7-Gipfel Tour**, taking in seven peaks and affording mind-blowing views of the Swiss Alps and Walensee. Allow roughly 6½ hours for the round-trip hike. For families, there are buggy-friendly footpaths, adventure playgrounds and a toboggan run, Floomzer.

Guesthouses perch on the Säntis mountainside

MARKUS KELLER / GETTY IMAGES ©

Seerenbachfälle   Waterfall

This series of three colossal waterfalls, thundering 585m from top to bottom, is fuelled by underground rivers running through the mountain rock from as far away as the peak of Säntis. The middle waterfall, a 305m drop, is considered Switzerland's highest. The closest you can reach by car is Betlis, a 30-minute hike from the road.

Weesen   Village

Petite and pretty, Weesen is the perfect base for exploring the lake, with a Geneva-style fountain shooting high into the air. A path along Walensee's north shore links Weesen to Walenstadt (about 6½ hours) or vice versa. The walk takes you along the lake shore, through dense forest and meadows.

Murgsee   Hiking

A challenging, classic Alpine trail leads from Maschgenkamm top station to the inky blue Murgsee lakes. You'll hike through silent pastures cloaked in wildflowers, and forests of chestnuts and pines. The round trek takes around seven hours (not including stops).

Schiffsbetrieb Walensee   Boat Tour

(www.walenseeschiff.ch) Boats regularly cross Murg and Quinten. From April to mid-October there are also regular boats between Weesen and Walenstadt, calling in at various spots along the way (including Betlis and Quinten).

🛏 Sleeping & Eating

Flyhof   Hotel €

(☏ 055 616 12 30; www.flyhof.ch; Betliserstrasse 16; s/d Sfr90/135; P 🛜) Sitting in mature gardens that slope picturesquely down to the lake, family-run Flyhof is a delight. Antique furniture and beams lend character to the quiet, comfy rooms. Regional ingredients are given a pinch of Mediterranean flavour in the wood-panelled restaurant in dishes like smoked trout with apple-celery salsa and braised lamb with chanterelles and apricots (mains Sfr25 to Sfr52).

Lofthotel Murg   Boutique Hotel €€

(☏ 081 720 35 75; www.lofthotel.ch; Murg; s Sfr140-180, d Sfr220-280; P 🛜) A 19th-century cotton mill has been reincarnated as the Lofthotel, affording fine views of the Churfirsten mountains and Walensee. Clean lines, polished concrete and bold artworks define the industrial-chic rooms. Farm-fresh produce and homemade preserves are served at breakfast.

Fischer-stube   Swiss €€

(☏ 055 616 16 08; www.fischerstubeweesen.ch; Marktgasse 9, Weesen; mains Sfr40-78; ⏱ 11.45am-2.30pm & 6-9.30pm Thu-Tue) Snowy white linen and bottle-green wood panelling create a refined backdrop for well-

Braunwald
CHRIS TOBIN / GETTY IMAGES ©

Detour:
Braunwald

The attractive car-free mountain resort of Braunwald perches on the side of a steep hill, gazing up to the snowcapped Tödi Mountain (3614m) and down to the pastures and fir forests spreading below.

The **Braunwaldbahn** (one-way/return Sfr7.20/14.40) climbs the hill from the Linthal Braunwaldbahn station. **Braunwald Tourism** (📞055 653 65 65; www.braunwald.ch; Dorfstrasse 2; ⏰8am-noon Mon-Sat, 1.30-5pm Mon-Fri) is on the top floor of the funicular station.

Braunwald is a terrific base for hiking in summer – one fine walk leads to the Oberblegisee, a glittering Alpine lake. If you're up for a challenge, tackle the five-hour *via ferrata* at Eggstock. In winter the resort has family appeal, with moderate skiing and off-piste fun from sledding to snow-tubing.

A converted grand Victorian fairy-tale hotel, the **Märchenhotel Bellevue** (📞055 653 71 71; www.maerchenhotel.ch; Dorfstrasse 24; d incl half board Sfr370-450, f Sfr390-510; 🅿🏊) combines elegant modern rooms with saunas and bars for adults and all manner of playthings for children. Parents can relax in the rooftop spa area while kids are looked after in the play area.

Less than two minutes from the funicular station, **Hostel Adrenalin** (📞079 347 29 05; www.adrenalin.gl; r per person Sfr29-64) is the hub of the young snowboarding and adventure-sports community in winter, with video games and lots of parties. Breakfast costs an extra Sfr8, and be prepared to fork out an extra Sfr5 for towels/bed linen respectively.

Trains run hourly from Linthal Braunwaldbahn to Zürich (Sfr25.80, 1½ hours) via Ziegelbrücke (Sfr13.80, 40 minutes). It's a 1¼-hour drive from Zürich along the A3.

executed fish dishes. Pair fine wines with local whitefish and perch.

🛈 Getting There & Away

By train from Zürich, get off at Ziegelbrücke (Sfr25.80, 45 minutes), a 15-minute walk from central Weesen, or change for trains on to Walenstadt.

GLARUS CANTON

The spiky, glacier-capped peaks of the Glarus Alps rise above stout wooden farmhouses and lush pastures in this little-explored canton, linked to the centre of the country by the vertiginous Klausenpass. Its northern boundary touches Walensee and provides much of the Alpine beauty that can be observed from the lake's north shore. For more information, contact **Glarner Tourismus** (📞055 610 21 25; www.glarus.ch; Niederurnen; ⏰8.15am-noon & 1.30-5.30pm Mon-Fri, 8am-5.30pm Sat, 8am-1pm Sun).

St Moritz, Graubünden & the Southeast

While you've probably heard about St Moritz' glamour, Davos' sensational downhill skiing and the tales of Heidi (fictionally born here), vast swathes of Graubünden remain little known and ripe for exploring. Strike into the Alps on foot or follow the lonesome passes that corkscrew high into the mountains, where only the odd marmot or chamois and your own little gasps of wonder break the silence. The Ticino Alps are as magnificent as elsewhere in Switzerland, but here you can admire them while sipping a full-bodied merlot at a pavement cafe, enjoying a hearty lunch at a chestnut-shaded *grotto* (rustic Ticino-style inn or restaurant), or floating in the mirror-like lakes of Lugano and Locarno. The southeast tempers its classic Alpine looks with Italian good-living.

Marina, Lake Maggiore (p261)

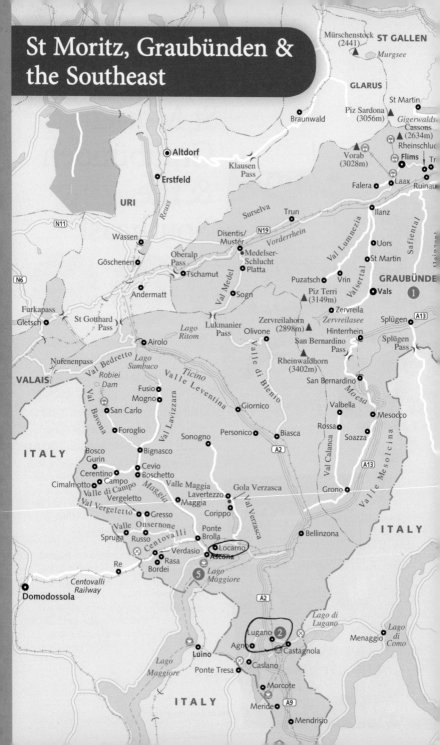

LIECHTENSTEIN

AUSTRIA

Sulzfluh
(2817m)

Fläsch
Maienfeld
Bündner
Herrschaft
Malans
Landquart
Zizers
Fünf
Dörfer
A13
N28 Küblis
Klosters
Selfranga
Gotschnagrat
(2285m)
Weissfluh
(2844m)
Wolfgang
Davos 4
Piz Buin
(3312m)
Pischahorn
(2980m)
Bos-cha
Guarda
Lavin
N27
Motta
Naluns
Ftan Scuol
Vulpera
Schloss
Tarasp
Untergadin
Inn River

Chur
Domat/Ems
Reichenau
Weisshorn
(2653m)
Domleschg
Hörnli (2496m)
Arosa
Jakobshorn
(2590m)
N28
Flüela
Pass
Sagliains
Susch
Ardez
A13
Valbella
Lenzerheide
Parpaner
Rothorn
(2865m)
Schiesshorn
(2605m)
Rinerhorn
(2528m)
Zernez
Chamanna
Cluozza
Il Fuorn
Ofen
Pass
N28
Müstair

Thusis
Via
Mala
Tiefencastel
Zillis
Andeer
Lenz
Wiesen
Filisur
Monstein
Bergün
Albula
Pass
Savognin
Parc
Ela
N3
Albulatal
Oberengadin
N27
Swiss
National
Park
Val Müstair

Avers Valley
Piz Nair
(3057m)
St Moritz
Julier Pass
Bivio
Silvaplana
Surlej
Juf
Sils-Maria
Septimber
Pass
Maloja
Casaccia
Val
Bregaglia
Maloja
Pass
N3
Soglio
Stampa
Castasegna
Promontogno
Chiavenna
Pizzo Badile
(3308m)

Celerina
Samedan
Muottas Muragl (2453m)
Piz Languard (3262m)
Val Bernina
Pontresina
Morteratsch
Piz Lagalb
(2959m)
ITALY
Val Fex
Diavolezza
(2973m)
N29
Bernina
Pass
Alp Grüm
(2091m)
Piz
Corvatsch
(3451m)
Piz
Bernina
(4049m)
Val Poschiavo
Poschiavo
Lago di
Poschiavo
Brusio

S-chanf
Zuoz
La Punt
Alp
Trupchun

ITALY

1 Graubünden
2 Lugano
3 St Moritz
4 Davos
5 Lago Maggiore

N 0   10 km
   0   6 miles

St Moritz, Graubünden & the Southeast's Highlights

Graubünden Outdoors

Hundreds of miles of ski runs lace the mountains of this vertiginous canton, and no skill or desire is not catered for. Resorts include the fabled Klosters (p250) and Laax (p248), which is one of the top Swiss resorts for snowboarders. In summer, the country's only national park (p245) offers natural wonder. Rhine Gorge

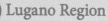

2 Lugano Region

Italian flair is never far away in the canton of Ticino (p254) and that's especially true in its main city of Lugano (p257). With sun-washed villas lining its namesake lake, Lugano makes a good starting point for excursions across the water and over the mountains of the region.
Lugano city

Skiing St Moritz

The world's original ski resort hasn't lost a step (or should we say a slalom) over the decades. St Moritz (p240) continues to draw the famous but it's still a place where they rub shoulders with humbler folks just there for the incredible skiing. After dark, the nightlife is some of the best in the country.

Winter Davos

Every January, Davos (p251) makes the news when world luminaries gather to think big thoughts and make proclamations. Important stuff, yes, but everyone would have more fun if they did the smart thing and hit the slopes. Davos may not have quite the fabled rep as its resort sibling St Moritz but it counters with some of the best ski runs in a nation of incredible ski runs.

Lago Maggiore

Most of the beautiful waters of Lake Maggiore (p261) stretch into Italy but right at the top is Locarno. Here you can stroll the Città Vecchia, the city's Old Town, and easily mistake it for Lombardy to the south. Head out on the water and enjoy views of palm trees along the sun-drenched shore. Back on land, tuck into the region's fine cuisine.

St Moritz, Graubünden & the Southeast's Best...

Natural Spots

○ **Müstair** Hidden away near the Italian border is this Unesco-listed treasure. (p244)

○ **Swiss National Park** See the raw, natural side of Switzerland. (p245)

○ **Lago di Lugano** Cruise the beautiful lake by boat while spotting palm trees on the shore. (p261)

○ **Klosters** More than 700km of footpaths radiate out through one perfect Alpine vista after another. (p250)

Food & Drink

○ **Lugano** You'll be spoiled for choice, but lake fish with Italian flavours are tops with regional wines. (p257)

○ **Locarno** The place for Italian-flavoured fare; try anything with polenta. (p262)

○ **St Moritz** In season the range of cafes, restaurants and bars is dizzying – and it's not the altitude. (p240)

○ **Davos** Draws Italian inspiration from Ticino plus there are plenty of hearty mountain meals that are perfect post-ski. (p251)

Skiing

○ **St Moritz** Famous for being famous, and also for fantastic skiing. (p240)

○ **Davos** If you can take your eyes off the fabled powder, you'll see magnificent scenery in all five ski areas. (p251)

○ **Pontresina** Shares many of St Moritz' pistes but also has its own stunners. (p243)

○ **Madrisa** The sweet spot of the region's skiing is accessible from Davos and Klosters. (p250)

Need to Know

Beautiful Towns

○ **Bellinzona** Fortresses and castles dominate this strategic old town at the confluence of valleys. (p254)

○ **Pontresina** Lovely old 13th-century town a beautiful train ride away from St Moritz. (p243)

○ **Chur** Old fortress towers still protect the Old Town and its cobblestone streets. (p246)

○ **Klosters** What a Swiss mountain village should look like – and it's authentically so. (p250)

ADVANCE PLANNING

○ **Four months before** Book your rooms for peak-season winter sports fun at the big-name resort towns like St Moritz, Klosters and Davos. Otherwise, the region is so relaxed that you can just turn up and enjoy.

RESOURCES

○ **Graubünden Tourism** (www.graubuenden.ch) Tourism info across the canton.

○ **Ticino Tourism** (www.ticino.ch) Tourism info covering the area.

○ **Wine** A big part of the Ticino experience is wine; get the *Le Strade del Vino* map-guide at tourist offices, which details wineries around the canton.

GETTING AROUND

○ **Train** Some of Switzerland's most famous and beautiful railways can be found in this region, including Rhätische Bahn's Glacier Express and the Bernina Express over the Bernina Pass. Otherwise, all the main towns are well-served by trains.

○ **Cable Cars & Gondolas** Like their brethren to the north, the Alps in this region are laced by cables conveying people to dizzying heights for dizzying views as well as superb hiking and skiing.

BE FOREWARNED

○ **Shoulder season** When it's not summer and prime time for hiking and other outdoor pleasures, or winter sports time (December to April), resort towns such as St Moritz all but shut down (May and November can be very quiet). A few places in St Moritz stay open for people arriving off the Glacier Express.

Left: Graubünden walnut pastry; **Above:** Laax area ski fields (p248)

St Moritz, Graubünden & the Southeast Itineraries

Spend days exploring Ticino, then enjoy Graubünden, whose raw beauty is punctuated by world-famous resorts.

3 DAYS

TICINO

BELLINZONA TO LOCARNO

The Italian accent *and* flavour of Ticino will come as a very lovely surprise for many who think of Switzerland in purely Germanic terms. Start in ❶**Bellinzona** (p254), which is dominated by fortresses that date back to Roman times. Head up the suitably named Castelgrande (p255; Grand Castle!) and survey your domain. Next up is Castello di Montebello (p255), which ticks off every necessary castle feature right down to the drawbridge. Finally hike up to the most formidable castle: Castello di Sasso Corbaro (p255).

Next up is ❷**Lugano** (p257). Beautifully set on its namesake lake, its sinuous streets are ideal for wandering, punctuated by the odd little square with cafes. Stop and get drawn into the richly detailed frescoes at Chiesa di Santa Maria degli Angioli (p259), then board a boat for a trip on the water. When the spirit moves you, pause for some delicious local fare.

Finally, don't even bother counting the palm trees in ❸**Locarno** (p262) – it's just about the sunniest Swiss destination and the perfect place to put your motor in neutral.

GRAUBÜNDEN

CHUR TO ST MORITZ

5 DAYS

Viewing Alps all around you is reason enough to visit ①**Chur** (p246). The evocative Old Town is just a bonus. Given you're on holiday, you could spend a relaxed afternoon bubbling away at the spa at ②**Bad Ragaz** (p251). Whether it's winter or summer, you'll find plenty to hold you in ③**Klosters** (p250): the skiing and hiking here and at nearby ④**Davos** (p251) are legendary. While Davos is renowned for its high-profile World Economic Forum (if you see anarchists it must be late January), Klosters retains a rural Swiss mountain-chalet flavour with an overlay of posh.

Leave the luxe behind and head over the Flüela Pass to little ⑤**Zernez** (p244). This tidy rural village is the gateway to the ⑥**Swiss National Park** (p245), where you can get as close as possible to raw Alpine nature in this beautiful but seemingly manicured country.

Once you've had your fill of marmots, you can shift gears entirely and make the short jaunt to possibly the most fabled Swiss resort of them all: ⑦**St Moritz** (p240). The myriad pleasures range from the natural to the sybaritic. Enjoy!

Castello di Sasso Corbaro (p255), Bellinzona
ANDREAS STRAUSS / LOOK-FOTO / GETTY IMAGES ©

Discover St Moritz, Graubünden & the Southeast

ST MORITZ

POP 5147 / ELEV 1856M

Switzerland's original winter wonderland and the cradle of Alpine tourism, St Moritz has been luring royals, celebrities and moneyed wannabes since 1864. With its shimmering aquamarine lake, emerald forests and aloof mountains, the town looks a million dollars.

Yet despite the string of big-name designer boutiques on Via Serlas and celebs bashing the pistes (Kate Moss and George Clooney included), this resort isn't all show. The real riches lie outdoors with superb carving on Corviglia, hairy black runs on Diavolezza and miles of hiking trails when the snow melts. Speaking of snow, the resort is gearing up to host the FIS Ski World Cup in 2017.

🏃 Activities

Segantini
Museum   Museum

(www.segantini-museum.ch; Via Somplaz 30; adult/child Sfr10/3; ⏰10am-noon & 2-6pm Tue-Sun, closed May & Nov) Housed in an eye-catching stone building topped by a cupola, this museum showcases the paintings of Giovanni Segantini (1858–99). The Italian artist beautifully captured the dramatic light and ambience of the Alps on canvas.

WINTER ACTIVITIES

With 350km of slopes, ultramodern lifts and spirit-soaring views, skiing in St Moritz is second to none, especially for confident intermediates. For groomed slopes with big mountain vistas, head to **Corviglia** (2486m), accessible by funicular from Dorf. From Bad a cable car goes to **Signal**

Lakeside St Moritz
HANS GEORG EIBEN / GETTY IMAGES ©

(shorter queues), giving access to the slopes of Piz Nair. There's varied skiing at **Corvatsch** (3303m), above nearby Silvaplana, including spectacular glacier descents and the gentle black run Hahnensee. Silhouetted by glaciated four-thousanders, **Diavolezza** (2978m) is a must-ski for freeriders and fans of jaw-dropping descents. A general ski pass that covers all the slopes, including Silvaplana, Sils-Maria, Celerina, Zuoz, Pontresina and Diavolezza, costs Sfr148/365 for two/six days in high season. Visit the website www.engadin. stmoritz.ch for the low-down on skiing facilities and services.

The first Swiss ski school was founded in St Moritz in 1929. Today you can arrange skiing or snowboarding tuition for Sfr120/85 per day for adults/children at the **Schweizer Skischule** (📞081 830 01 01; www.skischool.ch; Via Stradas 14; ⏲8am-noon & 2-6pm Mon-Sat, 8-9am & 4-6pm Sun).

SUMMER ACTIVITIES

In summer, get out and stride one of the region's excellent hiking trails, such as the Corvatsch *Wasserweg* (water trail) linking six mountain lakes. Soaring above St Moritz, **Piz Nair** (3057m) commands views of the jewel-coloured lakes that necklace the valley below.

Clean Energy Tour   Hiking

(www.clean-energy.ch) Beginning at Piz Nair, this eco-friendly 2½-hour hike presents different kinds of renewable energy in natural settings. You'll hike down from Chantarella along the flower-speckled Heidi Blumenweg, then Schellenursliweg past Lord Norman Foster's eco-sound, wood-tiled **Chesa Futura**.

Medizinisches Therapiezentrum Heilbad   Spa

(📞081 833 30 62; www.heilbad-stmoritz.ch; Plazza Paracelsus 2; mineral bath Sfr35; ⏲8am-7pm Mon-Fri, to 12.30pm Sat) After exerting yourself on the slopes, rest in a mineral bath or with an Alpine herb pack here.

> **Local Knowledge**

Graubünden Outdoors Don't Miss List

GIERI SPESCHA, GRAUBÜNDEN NATIVE WHO SPEAKS ROMANSCH

1 WILDLIFE WATCHING
Take a walk on the wild side in the ruggedly Alpine Swiss National Park (p245), which is Switzerland's only national park and one of the best-protected natural environments in Europe. Autumn is prime time for watching deer, especially in **Val Trupchun**.

2 RIDING THE GLACIER EXPRESS
Ready-made postcard views of peaks, glaciers, meadows and rivers unfold as the panoramic **Glacier Express** (www.glacierexpress.ch; one way adult/child Sfr145/73) train glides smoothly through Switzerland's Alpine heartland from St Moritz to Zermatt.

3 RHINE GORGE
A real treat for nature lovers and white-water river rafting enthusiasts, this imposing limestone gorge is often called Switzerland's **Little Grand Canyon**; it's about 5km north of Laax.

4 LAAX: FREESTYLE PARADISE
Hone your existing skills and try out new ones in areas geared to every skill at **Laax's mountain bike areas**. In winter Laax more than lives up to its winter sports reputation. In addition to Europe's first Freestyle Indoor Base, there are **four snowparks** offering something for all ability levels. Everything is possible – be it initial attempts in the Beginner Park, maxing out in the Ils Plauns Park or perfecting style.

5 HORSE-DRAWN CARRIAGE RIDE
Enjoy a fun horse-drawn carriage ride through the **Klosters countryside**. It's especially romantic in winter to snuggle up under blankets beneath the night sky and then enjoy a fondue afterwards.

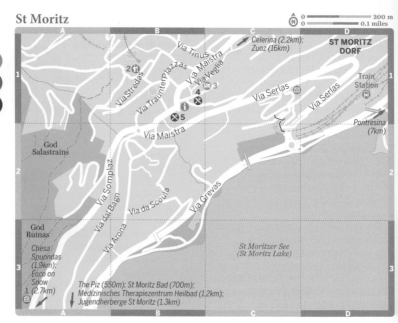

Celerina (2.2km); Zuoz (16km)

ST MORITZ DORF

Train Station

Pontresina (7km)

God Salastrains

Via Maistra

Via Somplaz

God Ruinas

Chesa Spuondas (1.9km); Ecco on Snow (2.7km)

The Piz (550m); St Moritz Bad (700m); Medizinisches Therapiezentrum Heilbad (1.2km); Jugendherberge St Moritz (1.3km)

St Moritzer See (St Moritz Lake)

🛏 Sleeping

Jugendherberge St Moritz
Hostel €

(☎081 836 61 11; www.youthhostel.ch/st.moritz; Via Surpunt 60; dm/s/d/q Sfr42.50/138/164/222; 🛜) On the edge of the forest, this hostel has clean, quiet four-bed dorms and doubles. There's a kiosk, children's toy room, bike hire and laundrette. Bus 9 stops in front of the hostel in high season.

Chesa Spuondas
Hotel €€

(☎081 833 65 88; www.chesaspuondas.ch; Via Somplaz 47; s/d/f incl half board Sfr155/282/318; P🛜) This family hotel nestles amid meadows at the foot of forest and mountains. Rooms are in keeping with the Jugendstil villa, with high ceilings, parquet floors and the odd antique. Kids are the centre of attention here, with dedicated meal times, activities, play areas and the children's ski school a 10-minute walk away. Bus 1 from St Moritz stops nearby.

The Piz
Hotel €€

(☎081 832 11 11; www.piz-stmoritz.ch; Via dal Bagn 6; s Sfr110-170, d Sfr190-310, apt Sfr280-570; 🛜) Splashes of crimson, hardwood floors and clean lines define this contemporary B&B in St Moritz Bad. Fitted with rain showers and flat-screen TVs, the wood-floored rooms are sleek and comfy. The sauna and steam room invite relaxation after a day on the trails or slopes.

Hotel Eden
Hotel €€

(☎081 830 81 00; www.edenstmoritz.ch; Via Veglia 12; s Sfr171-262, d Sfr341-528; P🛜) Right in the heart of town, the Eden centres on an attractive central atrium and antique-strewn lounge where a fire crackles in winter. The old-style, pine-panelled rooms are cosy and those on the top floor afford terrific lake and mountain views.

🍴 Eating

Hanselmann
Cafe €

(Via Maistra 8; pastries & cakes Sfr3-6, snacks & light meals Sfr12-24; ⏱7.30am-7pm Mon-Sun) You can't miss the lavishly frescoed fa-cade of St Moritz' celebrated bakery and

St Moritz

tea room, famous for its caramel-rich, walnut-studded Engadine nut tart.

Chesa Veglia Italian €€
(☎ 081 837 28 00; www.badruttspalace.com; Via Veglia 2; mains Sfr42-60, pizza Sfr23-36, menus Sfr45-70; ⊙noon-11.30pm) This slate-roofed, chalk-white chalet restaurant dates from 1658. The softly lit interior is all warm pine and creaking wood floors, while the terrace affords lake and mountain views. Go for pizza or regional specialities like *Bündner Gerstensuppe* (creamy barley soup) and venison medallions with *Spätzli* (egg noodles).

Ecco On Snow Gourmet €€€
(☎ 081 836 63 00; www.giardino-mountain. ch; Via Maistra 3, Giardino Mountain; menus Sfr142-208; ⊙7pm-midnight Wed-Sun) The pinnacle of St Moritz' dining scene, two-Michelin-starred Ecco On Snow is where chef Rolf Fliegauf gives flight to culinary fantasy when the flakes fall in winter. A sublime gold-and-white interior is the backdrop for exquisitely presented dishes with strong, assured flavours that revolve around primary ingredients – Wagyu beef and horseradish, lime, caramel, fig, and the like.

ⓘ Information

Uphill from the lakeside train station on Via Serlas is the post office and five minutes further on is the tourist office (☎ 081 837 33 33; www.stmoritz. ch; Via Maistra 12; ⊙9am-6.30pm Mon-Fri, to 6pm Sat). The website has details of the free St Moritz iPhone app.

ⓘ Getting There & Away

St Moritz Bad is about 2km southwest of the main town, St Moritz Dorf. Local buses and postal buses shuttle between the two.

The Glacier Express (p256) links St Moritz to Zermatt via the 2033m Oberalp Pass. The majestic route takes 7½ hours to cover the 290km and crosses 291 bridges. Seat reservation costs an additional Sfr33 in summer and Sfr13 in winter.

Regular trains, as many as one every 30 minutes, run from Zürich to St Moritz (Sfr73, 3½ hours) with one change (at Landquart or Chur). Postal buses run frequently in high season from St Moritz southwest to Maloja (Sfr11.40, 40 minutes) with stops at Silvaplana (Sfr5.40, 20 minutes) and Sils-Maria (Sfr8.20, 30 minutes).

BERNINA PASS ROAD

Bare, brooding mountains and glaciers that sweep down to farmland give the landscape around the Bernina Pass (2323m; Passo del Bernina in Italian) austere grandeur. The road twists spectacularly from Celerina southeast to Tirano in Italy, linking Val Bernina and Val Poschiavo.

From St Moritz, as many as 10 trains run via Pontresina (Sfr5.40, 10 minutes) direct to Tirano (Sfr30, 2½ hours) in northern Italy. This stretch of track, known as the **Bernina Line** (www.rhb-unesco.ch), was added to the Unesco World Heritage list in 2008 along with the Albula Pass. Constructed in 1910, it is one of the world's steepest narrow-gauge railways, negotiating the highest rail crossing in Europe and taking in spectacular glaciers, gorges and rock pinnacles.

Pontresina & Around

POP 2080 / ELEV 1800M

At the mouth of the Val Bernina and licked by the ice-white tongue of Morteratsch Glacier, Pontresina is a low-key alternative to St Moritz. Check out the pentagonal Moorish tower and the Santa Maria Chapel, with frescos dating from the 13th and 15th centuries.

Detour:
Müstair

Squirreled away in a remote corner of Switzerland, just before the Italian border, Müstair is one of Europe's early Christian treasures and a Unesco World Heritage site. When Charlemagne supposedly founded a monastery and a church here in the 8th century, this was a strategically placed spot below the Ofen Pass, separating northern Europe from Italy and the heart of Christendom.

Vibrant Carolingian (9th century) and Romanesque (12th century) frescos smother the interior of the church of Benedictine **Kloster St Johann** (St John's Convent; www.muestair.ch; guided tour adult/child Sfr10/5; ⊗9am-noon & 1.30-5pm Mon-Sat, 1.30-5pm Sun). Beneath Carolingian representations of Christ in Glory in the apses are Romanesque stories depicting the grisly ends of St Peter (crucified), St Paul (decapitated) and St Steven (stoned). Above all reign images of Christ in Heavenly Majesty. Next door, the **museum** (adult/child Sfr12/6; ⊗9am-noon & 1.30-5pm Mon-Sat, 1.30-5pm Sun) takes you through part of the monastery complex, with Carolingian art and other relics.

Postal buses run along the valley between Zernez and Müstair (Sfr20.80, one hour).

Pontresina's own mountain, **Piz Languard** (3262m), is well suited to families and novice skiers. Use the resort as a base to explore slopes further down the valley at **Piz Lagalb** (2959m) and **Diavolezza** (2973m), with its phenomenal 10km glacier descent. In summer, it's worth taking the cable cars to either for views. The walk from Diavolezza to Morteratsch affords striking glacier close-ups.

ⓘ Information

From the train station, west of the village, cross the two rivers, Rosegg and Bernina, for the centre and the **tourist office** (✆081 838 83 00; www.pontresina.ch; Via Maistra 133; ⊗8.30am-6pm Mon-Fri, 8.30am-noon & 3-6pm Sat, 4-6pm Sun).

THE ENGADINE

The almost-3000km-long Inn River (En in Romansch) springs up from the snowy Graubünden Alps around the Maloja Pass and gives its name to the Engadine. The valley is carved into two: the Oberengadin (Upper Engadine), from Maloja to Zernez, and the Unterengadin (Lower Engadine), stretching from Zernez to Martina, by the Austrian border.

Oberengadin is dominated by the ritzy ski resort of St Moritz, while Unterengadin, home to the country's only national park, is characterised by quaint villages with sgraffito-decorated houses and pristine countryside.

Chalandamarz, a spring and youth festival, is celebrated in the Engadine on 1 March. During **Schlitteda** in St Moritz, Pontresina and Silvaplana in January, lads on flamboyant horse-drawn sleds whisk girls (to their delight or dismay) on rides through the snow.

Zernez

POP 1150 / ELEV 1474M

One of the main gateways to the Swiss National Park, Zernez is an attractive cluster of stone chalets, outlined by the profile of its baroque church and the stout medieval tower of its castle, Schloss Wildenberg.

The village is home to the hands-on Swiss National Park Centre, where an audioguide gives you the low-down on conservation, wildlife and environmental change. The tourist office here can provide details on hikes in the park, including the three-hour trudge from

BERNARD VAN DIERENDONCK / LOOK-FOTO / GETTY IMAGES ©

⭐ Don't Miss
Swiss National Park

The Engadine's pride and joy is the **Swiss National Park** (www.nationalpark.ch) `FREE`, easily accessed from Scuol, Zernez and S-chanf. Spanning 172 sq km, Switzerland's only national park is a nature-gone-wild swathe of dolomitic peaks, shimmering glaciers, larch woodlands, pastures, waterfalls and high moors strung with topaz-blue lakes. Created on 1 August 1914, this was the first national park to be established in the Alps and 100 years later it remains true to its original conservation ethos, with the aims to protect, research and inform.

Given that nature has been left to its own devices for a century, the park is a glimpse of the Alps before the dawn of tourism. Some 80km of well-marked hiking trails lead through the park, where, with a little luck and a decent pair of binoculars, ibex, chamois, marmots and golden eagles can be sighted. The **Swiss National Park Centre** (📞081 851 41 41; www.nationalpark.ch; Zernez; exhibition adult/child Sfr7/3; ⏱8.30am-6pm Jun-Oct, 9am-noon & 2-5pm Nov-May) in Zernez should be your first port of call for information on activities and accommodation. It sells an excellent 1:50,000 park map (Sfr20), which covers 21 different walks through the park.

You can easily head off on your own, but you might get more out of one of the informative guided hikes run by the centre from late June to mid-October. These include wildlife-spotting treks to the Val Trupchun and high-alpine hikes to the Offenpass and Lakes of Macun. Most are in German but many guides speak a little English. Expect to pay around Sfr25 to Sfr35 per person. You should book ahead by calling 📞081 851 41 41.

Entry to the park and its carparks is free. Conservation is paramount here, so stick to footpaths and respect regulations prohibiting camping, littering, lighting fires, cycling, picking flowers and disturbing the animals.

S-chanf to Alp Trupchun (which is particularly popular in autumn, when you might spy rutting deer) and the Naturlehrpfad circuit near Il Fuorn, where bearded vultures can often be sighted.

🛌 Sleeping & Eating

Hotel Bär & Post　　　　Hotel €
(☎ 081 851 55 00; www.baer-post.ch; dm Sfr19-36, s Sfr87-115, d Sfr140-230; P ⃰) Welcoming all-comers since 1905, these central digs have inviting rooms with lots of stone pine and downy duvets, plus basic bunk rooms. There's also a sauna and a rustic restaurant (mains Sfr15 to Sfr43), dishing up good steaks and pasta.

Il Fuorn　　　　　　Hotel €€
(☎ 081 856 12 26; www.ilfuorn.ch; s/d Sfr120/196, without bathroom Sfr95/150; half-board extra Sfr35; ⏰ May-Oct) Bang in the heart of the national park, this guest-house shelters light, comfy rooms with pine furnishings. Fresh trout and game are big on the restaurant menu.

Chasa Veglia　　　　Guesthouse €€
(☎ 081 284 48 68; www.chasa-veglia.ch; Runastch; s Sfr85-90, d Sfr160-180) Step through the heavy arched door and back a few centuries at this lovingly restored 300-year-old house. Warm stone and hunting trophies are in keeping with the history of the place, as are the rooms done out in pine.

ℹ Getting There & Away

Trains run regularly from Zernez to St Moritz (Sfr18.40, 50 minutes), stopping at S-chanf, Zuoz and Celerina. For the latter and St Moritz, change at Samedan.

CHUR

POP 34,087 / ELEV 585M

The Alps rise like an amphitheatre around Chur, Switzerland's oldest city, inhabited since 3000 BC. Linger more than an hour or two and you'll soon warm to the capital of Graubünden. After a stint in the mountains, its gallery showcasing Alberto Giacometti originals, arty boutiques, authentic restaurants and relaxed bars are a refreshing cultural tonic.

⊙ Sights & Activities

Altstadt   Neighbourhood
(Old Town) Near the Plessur River, the **Obertor** marks the entrance to Chur's alley-woven Altstadt. Alongside the stout **Maltesertor** (once the munitions tower), and the **Sennhofturm** (nowadays the city's prison), it's all that remains of the old defensive walls.

Martinskirche   Church
(St Martin's Church; Kirchgasse 12) The city's most iconic landmark is Martinskirche with its distinctive spire and clock face. The 8th-century church was rebuilt in the late-Gothic style in 1491 and is dramatically lit by a trio of Augusto Giaco-metti stained-glass windows. St Martin presides over a burbling stone fountain in front of the church.

Kathedrale St Maria Himmelfahrt   Cathedral
(Hof; ⊙6am-7pm Mon & Wed-Sat, from 8am Tue, from 7am Sun) Chur's 12th-century cathedral conceals a late-1400s Jakob Russ high altar containing a splendid triptych.

Rätisches Museum   Museum
(www.raetischesmuseum.gr.ch; Hofstrasse 1; adult/child Sfr6/free; ⊙10am-5pm Tue-Sun; [🚻]) Housed in a baroque patrician residence, this museum spells out the canton's history in artefacts, with Bronze Age jewellery, Roman statuettes, weapons and agricultural tools, alongside displays on religion and power and politics. Children should ask for the museum key to discover the exhibition from a kid-friendly angle.

If You Like…
Winter Sports

If you like the skiing action you'll find at big names like St Moritz, you might also like these winter sports havens:

1 CELERINA

Sunny Celerina is a 45-minute amble northeast of St Moritz and shares the same ski slopes. It is often mentioned in the same breath as its 1.6km **Olympic bob run** (☎081 830 02 00; www.olympia-bobrun.ch), which is the world's oldest – dating to 1904 – and made from natural ice. A 135km/h run costs Sfr250, but the buzz is priceless.

2 LAAX

(www.laax.com) A snowboarding mecca, Laax boasts both Europe's smallest and largest half-pipe, excellent freestyle parks and many off-piste opportunities. Skiers are equally content to bash 220km of slopes at several interlinked resorts. Slaloming downhill, you'll probably spy the unfortunately named Crap da Flem (*crap* means 'peak' in Romansch). Laax is also a hotspot for mountain-biking. Postal buses make the 20km run from Chur in the east.

3 AROSA & LENZERHEIDE

(www.arosalenzerheide.ch) These neighbouring resorts share 225km of groomed slopes, mostly geared towards beginners and intermediates, as well assome glorious off-piste and backcountry skiing. Snowboarders hit the rails, boxes and kickers at the snowpark. Reach Arosa from Chur by taking the hourly narrow-gauge train (Sfr14.60, one hour). It's a lovely, winding journey.

Brambrüesch
Cable Car

(Kasernenstrasse 15; adult/child return Sfr25/5, bike park Sfr39/20; ⏰8.45am-4.45pm mid-Jun–late Oct & mid-Dec–mid-Mar) This cable car whisks you to Brambrüesch at 1600m, where views reach deep into the surrounding Alps. In summer, the 13km round-trip hike to **Feldis** is superb, leading through wildflower-strewn heights, woods and past glittering lakes. The peak also attracts mountain bikers to the four exhilarating freeride and downhill trails in the **Alpenbikepark** (http://alpenbikepark.ch). The cable car cranks into action again in winter, together with a couple of lifts, with locals warming up for more-serious downhill skiing elsewhere in Graubünden.

🛏 Sleeping

Romantik Hotel Stern
Historic Hotel €€

(☎081 258 57 57; www.stern-chur.ch; Reichsgasse 11; s/d Sfr150/290; P🛜) Part of Switzerland's romantic clan, this centuries-old hotel has kept its flair, with vaulted corridors and low-ceilinged, pine-filled rooms. Call ahead and they'll pick you up from the station in a 1933 Buick.

Zunfthaus zur Rebleuten
Historic Hotel €€

(☎081 255 11 44; www.rebleuten.ch; Pfisterplatz 1; s Sfr74-89, d Sfr128-148, q Sfr216; P🛜) Housed in an imposing frescoed building on a pretty square, the Zunfthaus zur Rebleuten looks proudly back on 500 years of history. The 12 rooms are fresh and inviting. Especially romantic (watch your head) are those in the loft.

Hotel Freieck
Hotel €€

(☎081 255 15 15; www.freieck.ch; Reichsgasse 44; s Sfr100-140, d Sfr150-240, tr Sfr190-270; P🛜) Occupying a beautiful 16th-century building, Freieck is a seamless blend of history and modernity. Exposed stone, beams and vaults lend character, while rooms are bright and contemporary.

🍴 Eating

Da Mamma
Italian €

(☎081 252 14 12; www.damammabistro.com; Obere Gasse 35 ; lunch menu Sfr16.50-17.30; ⏰8am-6.30pm Mon-Wed & Sat, to 8.30pm Thu & Fri) This neat little Italian job has what every bistro needs – people who cook with passion and a serve with a pinch of soul. With its slick surrounds and friendly vibe, this is a terrific choice for an inexpensive lunch of salad followed by homemade pasta. The Sicilian pastries and desserts are divine.

Bündner Stube
Swiss €€

(☎ 081 258 57 57; Reichsgasse 11; mains Sfr25-46; ⏰ 11am-midnight Mon-Sat, to 11pm Sun) Candlelight and wood panelling create a warm atmosphere in Romantik Hotel Stern's highly regarded restaurant. The chef keeps it fresh and seasonal, serving asparagus in spring, game in autumn. Bündner specialities like *Capuns* (egg pasta and sausage wrapped in chard), *Maluns* (like rösti) and *Gerstensuppe* (barley soup) are beautifully cooked and presented.

🔒 Shopping

Keramik Ruth
Handicrafts

(Obere Gasse 31; ⏰ 1.30-5.30pm Thu, 11am-4pm Sat) Ruth displays her sweet-shop-bright pottery at this hobbit-sized shop – from hand-thrown pots to polka-dotty teapots.

Rätische Gerberei
Handicrafts

(Engadinstrasse 30; ⏰ 1.30-6.30pm Mon, 8am-noon & 1.30-6pm Tue-Fri, 9am-noon & 1.30-4pm Sat) Upstairs are mountains of fluffy sheepskins, downstairs are genuine cowbells for a fraction of the price you'd pay elsewhere.

ℹ️ Information

Tourist Office (☎ 081 252 18 18; www.churtourismus.ch; Bahnhofplatz 3; ⏰ 8am-8pm Mon-Fri, 9am-12.15pm & 1.15-6pm Sat, 10am-12.15pm & 1.15-6pm Sun) Has stacks of info and maps on the region and can arrange city tours.

ℹ️ Getting There & Away

There are rail connections to Klosters (Sfr21.80, 1¼ hours) and Davos (Sfr31, 1½ hours), and fast trains

to Sargans (Sfr10.80, 20 minutes), with onward connections to Liechtenstein and Zürich (Sfr39, 1¼ to 1½ hours). Postal buses leave from the terminus above the train station.

Chur is the departure point for one of Switzerland's most memorable rail journeys, the Bernina Express (p256) to Lugano. Climbing high into the glaciated realms of the Alps and skirting Ticino's palm-fringed lakes, the four-hour route takes in 55 tunnels and 196 bridges. The stretch from Thusis to Tirano is a Unesco World Heritage site.

KLOSTERS & DAVOS

Following the N28 road east from Landquart, you enter the broad Prättigau Valley, which stretches east to Klosters. Several valley roads spike off the highway before Klosters, and the one leading to **St Antönien** is the most attractive. This high Alpine country is punctuated by villages and burned-wood Walser houses raised by this rural folk since migrating here from eastern Valais from the 13th century onward.

Chur (p246)
EDER / SHUTTERSTOCK ©

Klosters

POP 3909 / ELEV 1194M

No matter whether you come in summer to hike in the flower-speckled mountains or in winter when the log chalets are veiled in snow and icicle-hung – Klosters is postcard stuff. Indeed, the village has attracted a host of slaloming celebrities and royals with its chocolate-box looks and paparazzi-free slopes. This is where a 14-year-old Prince Charles learned to ski, and where Harry and William whizzed down the slopes as tots.

🏃 Activities

WINTER ACTIVITIES

Davos and Klosters share 320km of ski runs, covered by the Regional Pass (two-/ six day pass Sfr139/332), as well as some glorious off-piste terrain. **Parsenn** beckons confidence-building novices, while experts can tackle black runs like panoramic Schlappin and Gotschnawang. **Madrisa** is a great all-rounder, with long, sunny runs, mostly above the treeline for intermediates, a kids' club, tubing and ski-doo park, and a fun park with kickers and rails. For a back-to-nature experience, 35km of cross-country trails loop through the frozen plains and forest.

SUMMER ACTIVITIES

Hikers hit the trail on one of the region's 700km of well-maintained footpaths, which range from gentle family strolls to high-altitude, multiday treks. Would-be climbers can tackle the rope bridges and climbing trees at Madrisa. Mountain and downhill biking are equally popular. See www.davosklosters.ch for inspiration, GPS downloads and maps.

Bardill Bicycle Rental
(📞081 422 10 40; www.bardill-sport.ch; Landstrasse 185; ⏰8.30am-noon & 2-6.30pm Mon-Fri, 8.30am-12.30pm & 2-5pm Sat) Mountain/ electro/tandem bikes cost Sfr30/49/75 per day.

Gotschna Freeride Mountain Biking
(⏰Jul-Oct) This breathtakingly steep 5.7km trail from Gotschnaboden to Klosters is freeride heaven. Warm up at the skill centre before tackling the banks, jumps and tables.

Snow-covered Klosters

R&M Adventure Adventure Sports

(☎ 079 384 29 36; www.ramadventure.ch; Landstrasse 171) Tailor your own adventure with this reputable company offering white-water rafting and canyoning. Visit the website for prices.

🛏 Sleeping & Eating

R&M Adventure Hostel Hostel €

(☎ 081 422 12 29; www.ramadventure.ch; Landstrasse 171; r per adult Sfr80, child Sfr55-65; P 🛜) Bang in the heart of Klosters, R&M has colourful digs, a lounge where you can prepare tea and snacks, and a TV and playroom in the attic.

Gasthaus Bargis Guesthouse €€

(☎ 081 422 55 77; www.bargis.ch; Kantonsstrasse 8; d Sfr190-220) Erika is your kindly host at this quaint dark-wood chalet on the road into Klosters Dorf, with sunny, immaculate apartments brimming with homely touches, and a pine-clad restaurant (mains Sfr24 to Sfr32.50) serving Bündner specialities like Klosterser hay soup and veal cordon bleu.

Romantik Hotel Chesa Grischuna Historic Hotel €€€

(☎ 081 422 22 22; www.chesagrischuna.ch; Bahnhofstrasse 12; s/d/ste Sfr255/430/540; P 🛜) An archetypal vision of a Swiss chalet, this family-run pad has toasty pine rooms with antique flourishes and ornately carved ceilings. The lantern-lit restaurant (mains Sfr42 to Sfr60) is an Alpine charmer, too. Dirndl-clad waitresses bring fresh, seasonal dishes from local trout to roast beef to the table.

ℹ Information

In the centre of the village is the **tourist office** (☎ 081 410 20 20; www.klosters.ch; Alte Bahnhofstrasse 6; ⏰8.30am-noon & 2-6pm Mon-Fri, 9am-5pm Sat, 9am-1pm Sun).

ℹ Getting There & Away

Klosters is split into two sections. Klosters Platz is the main resort, grouped around the train station. Two kilometres to the left of the station is smaller Klosters Dorf and the Madrisa cable car.

Detour: Bad Ragaz

After days enjoying hikes or downhill runs, take your weary bones to the graceful little spa town of Bad Ragaz, a couple of kilometres west of Maienfeld, which opened in 1840 and has attracted the bath-loving likes of Douglas Fairbanks and Mary Pickford. The fabled waters are said to boost the immune system and improve circulation.

Bad Ragaz' ultra-sleek Tamina Therme, a couple of kilometres south of town, has several pools for wallowing in the 34°C thermal waters, as well as massage jets, whirlpools, saunas and an assortment of treatments and massages.

Bad Ragaz is on the Chur–Zürich train line. Trains from Chur via Maienfeld run hourly (Sfr8.80, 15 minutes).

Klosters is on the same train route as Davos between Landquart and Filisur. Klosters and Davos are linked by free buses for those with Guest Cards or ski passes.

Davos

POP 11,156 / ELEV 1560M

Unlike its little sister Klosters, Davos is more cool than quaint. But what the resort lacks in Alpine prettiness, it makes up for with seductive skiing, including monster runs descending up to 2000m, and après-ski parties. It is also the annual meeting point for the crème de la crème of world capitalism, the World Economic Forum. Global chat fests aside, Davos inspired Sir Arthur Conan Doyle (of Sherlock Holmes fame) to don skis

If You Like…
Villages

If you like the beautiful ancient town of Müstair, you'll love these little Swiss villages with their timeless charms:

1 GUARDA

With its twisting cobbled streets and hobbitlike houses in candy shades, Guarda has storybook appeal. Six kilometres east of Susch, Guarda is a 30-minute uphill hike from its valley-floor train station, or you can take the hourly postal bus (Sfr3).

2 MAIENFELD

Dominated by a colourfully frescoed Rathaus (town hall) and haughty church, it's worth hanging out for the local cuisine and wine from the surrounding vineyards. Catch a train from Chur (Sfr8, 15 minutes).

3 MORCOTE

With its narrow cobbled lanes and endless nooks and crannies, this peaceful former fishing village on Lake Lugano clusters at the foot of Monte Abostora. Narrow steps lead 15 minutes uphill to Chiesa di Santa Maria del Sasso, which commands dazzling lake views. Get here on a postal bus from Lugano (Sfr6.20. 40 minutes).

and Thomas Mann to pen *The Magic Mountain*.

Davos comprises two contiguous areas, each with a train station: Davos Platz and the older Davos Dorf.

SIGHTS

Kirchner Museum   Museum

(www.kirchnermuseum.ch; Ernst-Ludwig-Kirchner-Platz; adult/child Sfr12/5; ⊙10am-6pm Tue-Sun) This giant cube of a museum showcases the world's largest Ernst Ludwig Kirchner (1880–1938) collection. The German expressionist painted extraordinary scenes of the area. When the Nazis classified Kirchner a 'degenerate artist' and emptied galleries of his works, he was overcome with despair and took his own life in 1938.

🏃 Activities

WINTER SPORTS

Naturally blessed with awesome scenery and great powder, Davos has carved out a name for itself as a first-class skiing destination, with varied runs in five different areas. The vast **Parsenn** area reaches as high as Weissfluhjoch (2844m), from where you can ski to Küblis, more than 2000m lower and 12km away. Alternatively, take the demanding run to Wolfgang (1629m) or the scenic slopes to Klosters.

Across the valley, **Jakobshorn** is a favourite playground for snowboarders and freestylers with its half-pipe, terrain park and excellent off-piste opportunities.

Schweizer Schneesportschule   Skiing

(📞081 416 24 54; www.ssd.ch; Promenade 157) One of the best ski and snowboard schools in the country.

SUMMER ACTIVITIES

Together, Davos and Klosters provide 700km of marked hiking paths and 600km of mountain-bike tracks, including some challenging descents and single-track trails; see www.bike-davos.ch for routes, maps and rental outlets.

Summer water sports include windsurfing and sailing on the **Davoser See** (Davos Lake).

Davos Bike Park   Mountain Biking

(Flüelastrasse; ⊙dawn-dusk Jul-Oct) Test your skills on the tables, curves and jumps. Dirt bikes can be hired for Sfr20 per hour.

🛏 Sleeping

Youth Palace   Hostel €

(📞081 410 19 20; www.youthhostel.ch; Horlaubenstrasse 27; dm Sfr39-54, s Sfr98-111, d Sfr122-137; P 🛜) This one-time sanatorium has been transformed into a groovy backpacker palace. Budget-conscious skiers dig the bright, modern dorms with pine bunks (balconies cost a few francs extra), the relaxed lounge and ski storage.

Schraemli's Lengmatta
B&B €€

(☏ 081 413 55 79; www.lengmatta-davos. ch; Lengmattastrasse 19, Davos Frauenkirch; s Sfr120-140, d Sfr220-260 ; P 🛜) Total peace and big mountain views await at this sun-blackened timber chalet, which fits the Alpine idyll bill nicely. You'll feel bug snug in pine-clad rooms with check fabrics and downy bedding. There's a children's playground, a peak-facing terrace and a fine restaurant dishing up Bündner specialities (Sfr17 to Sfr35). Half-board per person is Sfr35. From Davos Platz, it's a three-minute train ride to Davos-Frauenkirch.

Waldhotel Bellevue
Historic Hotel €€€

(☏ 081 415 15 15; www.waldhotel-bellevue. ch; Buolstrasse 3; s Sfr205-275, d Sfr390-460; P 🛜 ⛲) The Magic Mountain in Thomas Mann's eponymous 1924 novel, this sanatorium turned hotel has recently been given a stylish facelift. Even standard rooms come with sunny balconies and luxuries like fruit, mineral water and bathrobes. When you tire of mountain views from your balcony, head down to the spa's saltwater pools and saunas.

The restaurant matches Grisons cuisine with wines drawn from the award-winning cellar.

✗ Eating

Kaffee Klatsch
Cafe €

(Promenade 72; light meals Sfr19-26.50; ⏰7.30am-9pm Mon-Sat, 8am-9pm Sun) 🍴 Warm brick and wood, and mellow music create a relaxed feel in this arty cafe. Try the delicious filled focaccia or organic salad, or stop by for cake with a speciality coffee like vanilla bean or Heidi latte (made with roasted organic oats). Shorter hours in low season.

Strela-Alp
Swiss €

(☏ 081 413 56 83; www.schatzalp.ch; mains Sfr16-30; ⏰9am-6pm Jul–mid-Oct, to 5pm mid-Oct–Jun; 👶) Expansive mountain views, a sunny terrace and Swiss grub like rösti and fondue await at this rustic haunt near Schatzalp funicular top station.

Hänggi's
Italian €€

(☏ 081 416 20 20; www.haenggis.ch; Mattastrasse 11; pizza Sfr16-26, mains Sfr23-48; ⏰11.30am-2pm & 6-9pm; 👶) Wood-fired pizza, crisp and delicious, is what this

En route to the slopes, Davos area

cosy beamed restaurant is known for. Or go for well-executed Italian-inspired dishes such as tagliatelle with fresh chanterelles, market-fresh fish and tangy homemade sorbet.

ℹ Information

The most central branch of the **tourist office** (☎ 081 415 21 21; www.davos.ch; Tourismus-und Sportzentrum, Talstrasse 41; ⏰ 8.30am-6pm Mon-Fri, 1-5pm Sat, 9am-1pm Sun) is in Davos Platz. It's well stocked with maps and brochures and offers a free room-booking service.

ℹ Getting There & Away

For trains to Chur (Sfr29, 1½ hours) or Zürich (Sfr53, 2½ hours), you will change at Landquart. For St Moritz (Sfr28, 1½ hours), take the train at Davos Platz and change at Filisur.

The Guest Card allows free travel on local buses and trains, as does the general ski pass (and the Swiss Pass).

TICINO

The summer air is rich and hot. Vespas scoot along palm-fringed promenades. A baroque campanile chimes. Italian weather. Italian style. And that's not to mention the Italian gelato, Italian pasta, Italian architecture, Italian language. It's Italy Swiss style with the kinds of peaks and valleys commonly associated with the cantons to the north.

Bellinzona

POP 17,744 / ELEV 230M

Placed at the convergence point of several Alpine valleys, Bellinzona is visually striking. Inhabited since Neolithic times, it is dominated by three grey-stone medieval castles that have attracted everyone from Swiss invaders to painters like William Turner. Yet Bellinzona keeps a surprisingly low profile considering that its castle trio is one of only 11 Unesco World Heritage sites in Switzerland.

The main castle, Castelgrande, stands upon a rocky central hill, which was a Roman frontier post and Lombard defensive tower, and was later developed as a heavily fortified town controlled by Milan.

What's Cooking in Ticino?

Switzerland meets Italy in Ticino's kitchen, and some of your most satisfying eating experiences in Ticino will happen in *grotti* – rustic, out-of-the-way restaurants, with granite tables set up under the cool chestnut trees in summer.

Alongside the Ticinese specialities below, perch, whitefish and *salmerino* (a cross between salmon and trout, only smaller) are popular around lakes Lugano and Maggiore. The region's bounty of new wine, chestnuts, game and mushrooms make autumn a tasty season to visit.

Polenta Creamy, savoury maize cornmeal dish.

Brasato Beef braised in red wine.

Capretto in umido alla Mesolcinese Tangy kid meat stew with a touch of cinnamon and cooked in red wine.

Cazzöla A hearty meat casserole served with cabbage and potatoes.

Mazza casalinga A mixed selection of delicatessen cuts.

Cicitt Long, thin sausages made from goat's meat and often grilled.

Robiola Soft and creamy cow's milk cheese that comes in small discs.

KEREN SU / GETTY IMAGES ©

⭐ Don't Miss
Castelgrande

Rising dramatically above the Old Town, the medieval stronghold of **Castelgrande** (www.bellinzonaunesco.ch; Via Salita Castelgrande; ⊙grounds 10am-6pm Mon, 9am-10pm Tue-Sun) **FREE** is Bellinzona's most visible icon. Head up Scalinata San Michele from Piazza della Collegiata, or take the lift, buried deep in the rocky hill in an extraordinary concrete bunker-style construction, from Piazza del Sole.

After wandering the grounds and the **museum** (Castelgrande; adult/child Sfr5/2; ⊙10am-6pm Sep-Jun, 10am-7pm Jul & Aug), stroll west along the **Murata** (⊙10am-7pm), the castle's snaking ramparts, with photogenic views of vine-streaked mountains and castle-studded hills.

◉ Sights & Activities

The city's three imposing castles are the main draw. Read up on them at www.bellinzonaunesco.ch. To visit all three, invest in a Cultura Pass, which also gives access to Villa dei Cedri. It costs Sfr15/7.50/25 for an adult/child/family.

Castello di Montebello   Castle
(www.bellinzonaunesco.ch; Salita al Castello di Montebello; castle admission free, museum adult/child Sfr5/2; ⊙10am-6pm May, Jun, Sep, Oct, 10am-7pm Jul & Aug, closed Nov-Apr) On cloudless days, you can see Lago Maggiore from this 13th-century hilltop fortification. The fortress is one of Bellinzona's most impressive with its drawbridges, ramparts and small museum catapulting you back to medieval times.

Castello di Sasso Corbaro   Castle
(www.bellinzonaunesco.ch; Via Sasso Corbaro; castle admission free, museum & tower adult/child Sfr5/2; ⊙10am-6pm Sep, Oct, May & Jun, 10am-7pm Jul & Aug, closed Nov-Apr) From central Bellinzona it's a 3.5km hike south to the Castello di Sasso Corbaro. Perched high on a wooded hillside, the castle is

Great Rail Journeys

Graubünden's rugged, high-alpine terrain is harnessed by some of Switzerland's greatest railways. The panoramic **Rhätische Bahn** (RhB, Rhaetian Railway; www.rhb.ch) is a staggering feat of early 20th-century engineering, traversing viaducts and tunnels and commanding wide-screen views of forested slopes, jewel-coloured lakes and snowcapped peaks. See the website for advance bookings, seat reservations and special deals. The Half Fare, Swiss Card and Swiss Pass give substantial discounts.

The Rhaetian Railway's two flagship routes are the Glacier Express and the Bernina Express. The **Glacier Express** (www.glacierexpress.ch; 2nd/1st class Sfr145/254, obligatory seat reservation summer/winter Sfr33/13; ⊙7½hr, daily) from St Moritz to Zermatt is a once-in-a-lifetime journey, scaling the Furka, Oberalp and Bernina passes, and taking in highlights such as the canyon-like Rhine Gorge and the six-arched, 65m-high Landwasser Viaduct. The **Bernina Express** (www. berninaexpress.ch; one way Sfr84, seat reservation summer/winter Sfr14/10; ⊙mid-May–early Dec) from Chur to Lugano climbs high into the glaciated realms of the Alps and skirts Ticino's palm-fringed lakes. The stretch from Thusis to Tirano is a Unesco World Heritage site.

an austere beauty with its impenetrable walls and sturdy towers.

🛏 Sleeping

Charming digs are few and far between. Many functional hotels are strung out along Viale della Stazione.

Hotel Internazionale   Hotel €€
(☑ 091 825 43 33; www.hotel-internazionale.ch; Viale della Stazione 35; s Sfr139-185, d Sfr200-240, tr Sfr285-315; P ❄ 🛜) Sitting opposite the train station, this candyfloss-pink hotel seamlessly blends turn-of-the-20th-century features like wrought iron and stained glass with streamlined 21st-century design. A slick makeover in 2014 has brought the light, contemporary rooms bang up to date, and the new spa invites relaxation with its sauna, steam room, hydro-massage and salt inhalation room.

Croce Federale   Hotel €€
(☑ 091 825 16 67; www.hotelcrocefederale.ch; Viale della Stazione 12; s/d/tr/q Sfr110/160/190/220; 🛜) Just inside the Old Town, this is a petite and friendly mid-range pick. Rooms are straightforward

but light; the best have balconies with knockout views of Castelgrande. Breakfast can be taken on the street-facing terrace downstairs.

🍴 Eating

Ristorante Castelgrande   Italian €€
(☑ 091 814 87 87; www.ristorantecastelgrande. ch; Castelgrande; mains Sfr29-39, menus Sfr68-80; ⊙7-10pm Tue-Sun Sep-Jun) It's not often you get the chance to eat inside a Unesco World Heritage site. The medieval castle setting alone is enough to bewitch. Seasonal specialities like pike perch filets with vanilla-cauliflower puree are married with top-notch wines.

Grotto Castelgrande   Italian €€
(☑ 091 814 87 87; www.castelgrande.ch; Via Salita Castelgrande; mains Sfr29-39, 2-/3-course menu Sfr25/31; ⊙11am-11pm Tue-Sat, 11.30am-2pm Sun) For the best view of Bellinzona's illuminated castles, book a table on the vine-strewn terrace of this atmospheric vaulted cellar for dishes such as filet of beef served with porcini mushrooms and Grana cheese.

Locanda Orico
Gourmet €€€

(091 825 15 18; www.locandaorico.ch; Via Orico 13; menus Sfr48-120; 11.45am-2pm & 6.45pm-midnight Tue-Sat) Seasonality is the name of the game at this Michelin-starred temple to good food, housed in a slickly converted palazzo in the old town. Creations such as pumpkin gnocchi in jugged chamois meat, and wild turbot with fettuccine and basil butter are served with finesse.

ℹ Getting There & Away

Bellinzona has frequent train connections to Locarno (Sfr8.20, 29 minutes) and Lugano (Sfr10.20, 30 minutes). It is also on the Zürich–Milan route. Bus 171 runs roughly hourly northeast to Chur (Sfr51, 2¼ hours), departing from beside the train station.

Lugano

POP 61,837 / ELEV 270M

Ticino's lush, mountain-rimmed lake isn't its only liquid asset. The largest city in the canton is also the country's third most important banking centre. Suits aside, Lugano is a vivacious city, with chic boutiques, bars and pavement cafes huddling in the spaghetti maze of steep cobblestone streets that untangle at the edge of the lake and along the flowery promenade.

◎ Sights

Take the stairs or the **funicular** (one way Sfr1.10; 5.20am-11.50pm) down to the centre, a patchwork of interlocking *piazze*. Porticoed lanes weave around the busy main square, Piazza della Riforma, which is presided over by the 1844 neoclassical Municipio (town hall) and even more lively when the Tuesday and Friday morning markets are held.

Cattedrale di San Lorenzo
Cathedral

(St Lawrence Cathedral; Via San Lorenzo; 6.30am-6pm) Lugano's early 16th-century cathedral conceals some fine frescos and ornate baroque statues behind its Renaissance facade. Out front are far-reaching views over the Old Town's jumble of terracotta rooftops to the lake and mountains.

Lugano city centre

TRAVELSTOCK44 / GETTY IMAGES ©

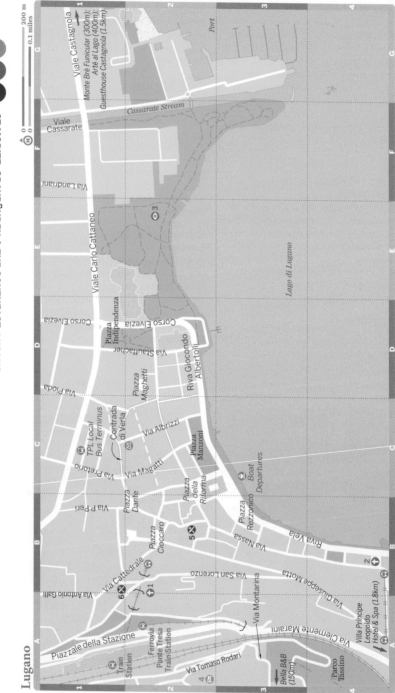

Lugano

Chiesa di Santa Maria degli Angioli
Church

(St Mary of the Angel; Piazza Luini; ⊙7am-6pm) This simple Romanesque church contains two frescos by Bernardino Luini dating from 1529. Covering the entire wall that divides the church in two is a grand didactic illustration of the crucifixion of Christ. The power and vivacity of the colours are astounding.

Lungolago
Gardens

(⊙Parco Civico 6am-11pm) **FREE** This lakefront promenade necklaces the shore of glassy Lago di Lugano, set against a backdrop of rugged mountains. Linden and chestnut trees provide welcome shade in summer, while tulips, camellias and magnolias bloom in spring. The flower-strewn centrepiece is **Parco Civico.**

Museo del Cioccolato Alprose
Museum

(www.alprose.ch; Via Rompada 36, Caslano; adult/child Sfr3/1; ⊙9am-5.30pm Mon-Fri, to 4.30pm Sat & Sun) Chomp into some cocoa culture at this choc-crazy museum – a sure-fire hit with kids. Whiz through chocolate history, watch the sugary substance being made and enjoy a free tasting. The shop, cunningly, stays open half an hour longer. Take the train to Caslano (Sfr6.20, 26 minutes).

🏃 Activities

Swimming, sailing, wakeboarding and rowing on the lake, as well as hiking in the surrounding mountains and valleys, are popular summer pursuits – the tourist office has details.

Lugano Tours
Guided Tour

Departing from the tourist office, Lugano's brilliant free guided tours include a spin of the city centre on Mondays (9.30am to noon), of the city's parks and gardens on Sundays (10am to noon) and, best of all, to the peak of Monte Brè on Fridays (2.20pm to 6.30pm) – even the funicular ride up there is free!

🛏 Sleeping

Many hotels close for at least part of the winter.

Hotel & Hostel Montarina
Hotel, Hostel €

(🕿091 966 72 72; www.montarina.ch; Via Montarina 1; dm Sfr29, s Sfr82-92, d Sfr112-132; [P][🛜][♿]) Occupying a pastel-pink villa dating to 1860, this hotel/hostel duo extends a heartfelt welcome. Mosaic floors, high ceilings and wrought-iron balustrades are lingering traces of old-world grandeur. There's a shared kitchen-lounge, toys to amuse the kids, a swimming pool set in palm-dotted gardens and even a tiny vineyard. Breakfast costs an extra Sfr15.

SYHA Hostel
Hostel €

(🕿091 966 27 28; www.luganoyouthhostel.ch; Via Cantonale 13, Savosa; dm/s/d/q Sfr37/57/118/172; ⊙mid-Mar–Oct; [♿]) Housed in the Villa Savosa, this is one of the more enticing youth hostels in the country, with bright well-kept dorms, a barbecue area, a swimming pool and lush gardens. Take bus 5 from the train station to Crocifisso.

Guesthouse Castagnola
Guesthouse €€

(🕿078 632 67 47; www.gh-castagnola.com; Salita degli Olivi 2; apt Sfr120-180; [P][🛜]) Kristina and Mauro bend over backwards to please at their B&B, lodged in a beautifully restored 16th-century townhouse. Exposed stone, natural fabrics and earthy colours dominate in apartments kitted out with Nespresso coffee machines and flat-screen TVs. A generous breakfast (Sfr10 extra) is served in the courtyard.

Take bus 2 to Castagnola, 2km east of the centre.

Bella B&B
B&B €€

(📞 079 198 07 65; www.luganobella.ch; Via Montarina 12; s Sfr100-125, d Sfr130-180; 🅿️ 🛜)
🌱 'Bella' is indeed the word that springs to mind when you clap eyes on this charming B&B atop Montarina hill, 500m west of the train station. Surrounded by mature gardens and orchards, the beautifully restored stone house sits at the location where Hungarian pianist Franz List once lived. Come here for peace, Monte San Salvatore views and organic breakfasts.

Villa Principe Leopoldo Hotel & Spa
Luxury Hotel €€€

(📞 091 985 88 55; www.leopoldohotel.com; Via Montalbano 5; s Sfr300-2000, d Sfr360-2500; 🅿️ ❄️ 🛜 🏊) This red-tiled residence set in sculptured gardens was built in 1926 for Prince Leopold von Hohenzollern, of the exiled German royal family. It oozes a regal, nostalgic atmosphere. The gardens and many of the splendid rooms offer lake views. Prices reach for the stars but so does the luxury – gourmet restaurants, tennis courts, a spa, heated pools, personal trainers, you name it.

Eating

Pasta e Pesto
Italian €

(📞 091 922 66 11; Via Cattedrale 16; pasta Sfr9.80-12.80; ⏰ 9.30am-7pm Mon-Tue, 9.30am-9.30pm Wed-Sat) Doing pretty much what it says on the tin, this newcomer near the cathedral has a pocket-size terrace for digging into fresh homemade pasta with a variety of toppings.

Grand Café Al Porto
International €€

(📞 091 910 51 30; www.grand-cafe-lugano.ch; Via Pessina 3; meals Sfr27-38; ⏰ 8am-6.30pm Mon-Sat) Going strong since 1803, this cafe is the vision of old-world grandeur with its polished wood panelling and pineapple-shaped chandeliers. The tortes, pastries and fruit cakes are irresistible.

Arté al Lago
Gourmet €€€

(📞 091 973 48 00; www.villacastagnola.com; Piazza Emilio Bossi 7; mains Sfr49-54, menus Sfr105-115; ⏰ noon-2pm & 7-9.30pm Tue-Sat) This Michelin-starred restaurant at the exclusive lakefront Villa Castagnola is Lugano's culinary star. Chef Frank Oerthle does remarkable things with fish and seafood, with ingredient-focused specialities such as lobster tail on lemon-thyme emulsion and black cod with squid, chanterelles and carrot-ginger puree. Gaze out across the lake through the picture windows or up to the contemporary artworks gracing the walls.

itorante

Gandria, on the shores of Lake Lugano

🔒 Shopping

Pedestrian-friendly Via Nassa is a catwalk for designers like Bulgari, Louis Vuitton and Versace. Its graceful arcades also harbour jewellery stores, cafes and gelaterias. For one-off gifts, explore steep, curving Via Cattedrale, where boutiques and galleries sell antiques, vintage clothing, crafts and handcrafted jewellery.

ⓘ Getting There & Away

To St Moritz, postal buses runs direct via Italy (Sfr73, 3¾ hours, daily late June to mid-October and late December to early January). All postal buses leave from the main bus depot at Via Serafino Balestra, but you can pick up the St Moritz and some other buses outside the train station 15 minutes later.

Lago di Lugano

Much can be seen in one day if you don't fancy a longer excursion. Boats are operated by the **Società Navigazione del Lago di Lugano** (☎ 091 971 52 23; www.lakelugano.ch). Examples of return fares from Lugano are Melide (Sfr27.40), Morcote (Sfr38) and Ponte Tresa (Sfr45.60). If you want to visit several places, buy a pass: one, three or seven days cost Sfr49, Sfr59 or Sfr76 respectively. There are reduced fares for children.

The departure point from Lugano is by Piazza della Riforma. Boats sail year-round, but the service is more frequent from late March to late October.

Lago Maggiore

Only the northeast corner of Lago Maggiore is in Switzerland; the rest slices into Italy's Lombardy region. Navigazione Lago Maggiore operates boats across the entire lake. Limited day passes cost Sfr20.70, but the Sfr36.60 version is valid for the entire Swiss basin. There are various options for visiting the Italian side.

Lugano Region Don't Miss List

PATRICIA CARMINATI, GUIDE

1 **MARKET FOOD & PARKS**
Visit Lugano's **street market** (🕐 Tue, Fri & Sat) and at lunch time, do as local people do – buy some polenta with gorgonzola cheese sold by one local farmer who cooks it on Piazza della Riforma. Take it away and go to **Ciani Park** where you can eat under the trees with a wonderful view of the lake. After lunch, relax at the 'park and read' open-air library where you can borrow a book and a comfortable chair.

2 **BOAT & SWIM LAKE LUGANO**
Take a boat to **Cantine di Gandria**; after 20 minutes you will be on the opposite shore of the lake. You can swim in Lake Lugano and then enjoy a typical lunch in one of the *grottos* there.

3 **TREKKING**
Take the cable car to **Monte Brè** and then walk to **Monte Boglia** (this is only one of the many trekking paths in the Lugano area). Don't miss the lakeside Gandria walking path, which takes about one hour and is nice and easy.

4 **BELLINZONA'S CASTLES**
After 30 minutes by train from Lugano, you get to **Bellinzona** (p254) with its three medieval castles. If possible, travel here on Saturday morning when the colourful **food market** takes place, people speak dialect and farmers sell their products from the valleys.

5 **TRAIN TO CASLANO**
Take the little orange train in front of Lugano's train station to the nearby village of Caslano. Here you'll find local handicrafts. Afterwards, you can go trekking around **Monte Caslano** or swim in the lake.

Locarno

POP 15,483 / ELEV 205M

With its palm trees and much-vaunted 2300 hours of sunshine a year, Locarno has attracted pasty northerners to its warm, Mediterranean-style setting since the late 19th century.

◉ Sights

Santuario della Madonna del Sasso

Church

(⏱6.30am-6.30pm) **FREE** Overlooking the town, this sanctuary was built after the Virgin Mary supposedly appeared in a vision to a monk, Bartolomeo d'Ivrea, in 1480. There's a highly adorned church and several rather rough, near-life-size statue groups (including one of the Last Supper) in niches on the stairway. The best-known painting in the church is *La Fuga in Egitto* (Flight to Egypt), painted in 1522 by Bramantino.

A **funicular** (adult one way/return Sfr4.80/7.20, child Sfr2.20/3.60; ⏱8am-10pm) runs every 15 minutes from the town centre past the sanctuary to Orselina, but a more scenic, pilgrim-style approach is the 20-minute walk up the chapel-lined Via Crucis (take Via al Sasso off Via Cappuccini).

Città Vecchia

Neighbourhood

Locarno's Italianate Old Town fans out from **Piazza Grande**, a photogenic ensemble of arcades and Lombard-style houses. A craft and fresh-produce market takes over the square every Thursday.

Castello Visconteo

Museum, Castle

(Piazza Castello; adult/student Sfr7/5; ⏱10am-noon & 2-5pm Tue-Sun Apr–mid-Nov) Named after the Visconti clan that long ruled Milan, this stout 15th-century castle's nucleus was raised around the 10th century. It now houses a museum with Roman and Bronze Age exhibits and also hosts a small display (in Italian) on the Locarno Treaty.

Giardini Pubblici

Gardens

(Lungolago Motta) Locarno's climate is perfect for lolling about the lake. Bristling with palms and banana trees, these botanic gardens are a scenic spot for a picnic or swim, and tots can let off steam in the adventure playground.

Ticino (p254)

WALTER BIBIKOW / GETTY IMAGES ©

🤸 Activities

The lakefront is made for aimless ambles, or rent an e-bike (Sfr33 per day) from the tourist office to explore further.

🛏 Sleeping

Pensione Olanda   B&B €
(📞 091 751 47 27; www.pensione-olanda.ch; Via ai Monti 139a; s Sfr65, d Sfr130-140; P 🛜) Set in pretty gardens above Locarno, Pensione Olanda keeps it sweet and simple – though the views reaching across the lake to the mountains beyond are priceless. It's a 15-minute uphill walk from the centre, or take bus 32 from the station to 'Olanda' stop.

Villa Sempreverde   B&B €€
(📞 079 322 78 65; www.sempreverde.ch; Via alla Basilica 1; d Sfr130-180, tr Sfr195-270, q Sfr260-360; P 🛜) With lake and mountain views to swoon over, this 18th-century house turned B&B reclines in flower-draped gardens on a hill above Locarno. The bright, wood-floored rooms are full of homey touches. Fiorenza's homemade jams and cakes feature at breakfast. It's a 15-minute walk west of the centre or a minute's stroll from Monti della Trinità funicular stop.

Caffè dell'Arte   Boutique Hotel €€
(📞 091 751 93 33; www.caffedellarte.ch; Via Cittadella 9; d Sfr269-289; 🛜) Styling itself as a B&B, this charming place above a cafe and art gallery weds personal attention to a designer aesthetic. Some rooms have mock frescoes, others sport leopard-print sofas and all have Nespresso coffee machines.

🍴 Eating

Locanda Locarnese   Ticinese €€
(📞 091 756 8 756; www.locandalocarnese.ch; Via Bossi 1; mains Sfr36.50-45.50; ⏰11.30am-2.30pm & 6.30-11.30pm Mon-Sat) Elegant rusticity sums up this smart restaurant, with a beamed ceiling, crisp white tablecloths and an open fire, as well as a smattering of pavement seating. It's a romantic and intimate choice for season-driven dishes such as bresaola with artichokes and wild sea bass with chanterelle sauce and peaches.

Osteria Chiara   Italian €€
(📞 091 743 32 96; www.osteriachiara.ch; Vicolo dei Chiara 1; mains Sfr34-45; ⏰9am-2pm & 7pm-midnight Tue-Sat) Tucked away on a cobbled lane, this has all the cosy feel of a *grotto*. Sit at granite tables beneath the pergola or at timber tables by the fireplace for homemade ravioli and hearty meat dishes such as veal with chanterelles. From the lake follow the signs up Vicolo dei Nessi.

ℹ Information

The tourist office (📞091 791 00 91; www.ascona-locarno.com; Largo Zorzi 1; ⏰9am-6pm Mon-Fri, 10am-6pm Sat, 10am-1.30pm & 2.30-5pm Sun) is nearby.

ℹ Getting There & Away

Trains run roughly hourly from Brig (Sfr52, 2¾ hours), passing through Italy (bring your passport). Change trains at Domodossola. There are also at least hourly connections to L ucerne (Sfr56, 2¾ to three hours). Most trains to Zürich (Sfr60, 2¾ to 3¼ hours) go via Bellinzona.

Switzerland
In Focus

The hypnotic Matterhorn (p178), near Zermatt
LU HENG / GETTY IMAGES ©

Switzerland Today

Sunset in Zürich (p198)

> *The country remains happy to cultivate its independent streak and unique reputation.*

belief systems
(% of population)

38	33	24	5
Roman Catholic	Protestant	Other	Muslim

if Switzerland were 100 people

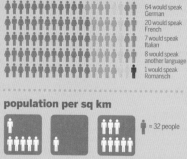

64 would speak German
20 would speak French
7 would speak Italian
8 would speak another language
1 would speak Romansch

population per sq km

👤 ≈ 32 people

SWITZERLAND   USA   UK

They don't call it 'Fortress Switzerland' for nothing. Seemingly immune to the troubles and travails of the countries that surround it, Switzerland appears intent on reinforcing its 'otherness' and its 'not in my backyard' mentality. With a strong economy, social stability and an emphasis on sustainability, the country remains happy to cultivate its independent streak and unique reputation.

Popular Initiatives?

Most Swiss popular initiatives come and go with scant attention paid by those beyond Switzerland's borders. Not so the initiative against mass immigration, which aims to put the brake on immigration through the use of quotas, launched by the Swiss People's Party (SVP; the same party that in 2009 formulated the successful initiative against the construction of minarets in Switzerland).

In February 2014 the initiative, with a voter turn-out of 55.8%, passed with the slimmest of majorities (50.3%, with most support in the German- and Italian-speaking cantons),

SANDRO BISARO / GETTY IMAGES ©

franc, long acknowledged as one of the world's most stable currencies, had become so overvalued it was threatening the traditionally robust Swiss economy.

So strong was the franc that Swiss exports were falling, along with the number of incoming tourists, as price-conscious visitors calculated just what a cup of coffee would cost them. In an unprecedented move, the Swiss National Bank made the value of the Swiss franc tumble in an instant (by 9% in 15 minutes!) by pegging it at 1.20 to the euro. Two years later, the SNB's chairman, Thomas Jordan, declared that the peg was still necessary in order to ward off the threat of deflation.

The drama is not yet over. In early 2015 the SNB ditched the €1.20 cap in a shock move that left economists reeling in disbelief. The Swiss franc soared in value, increasing by 30% in value against the euro in an instant and reaching parity a few days later. Markets worldwide were temporarily flung into chaos, while travellers bound for Switzerland found their Swiss holiday (not to mention the chocolate) had become unexpectedly more expensive overnight.

leaving the country (and the parliament, which has three years to turn the result into law) to deal with the fall-out from what has been regarded as a 'stunt gone wrong'. Given that over 20% of the Swiss population are foreigners, and that many industries depend on foreign workers, the ramifications could be severe. In the immediate aftermath of the vote, the European Commission expressed its disappointment with the result and questions have been raised about Switzerland's bilateral agreements with the EU, in particular the Agreement on the Free Movement of Persons.

The result has left pundits and voters wondering whether the initiative will have an effect on the federal elections in 2015.

Victim of its own Success: Franc Matters

This privileged land of quality living and global finance found itself the victim of its own success in 2011, when the Swiss

Mad about their Land

Given the overwhelming beauty of their country, it's natural that the Swiss are mad about their land. 'Go green' is the dominant vibe and 'sustainable technology' the buzzword for both the average citizen on the street and for pioneering scientists striving to go around the world Jules Verne–style in solar-powered transport. In September 2011, the Swiss parliament banned the construction of new nuclear power plants and called for a nuclear phase-out (in favour of hydro-electric power). There are five nuclear power plants in Switzerland; the first closure will take place in 2019, with the other four to follow by 2034.

Schloss Thun (p147)

IMAGEBROKER / ALA

Switzerland is unique, and nowhere is this more startlingly explicit than in its history. Commonly regarded as Sonderfall Schweiz (literally 'special case Switzerland'), this small landlocked country in Europe is a privileged and neutral country, with a long history of independence to support this. Despite the presence of global institutions (the UN, Red Cross etc) and moves towards greater international cooperation, modern-day Switzerland remains idiosyncratic, insular and one-of-a-kind.

Clans & Castles: Swiss Roots

Modern Swiss history might start in 1291 but that is not to say that the thousands of years leading up to Switzerland's birth are not significant – this was the period that gave Switzerland the best of its fairytale châteaux and *schlösser* (castles).

The earliest inhabitants were Celtic tribes, including the Helvetii of the Jura and the Mittelland Plain, and

58 BC

Julius Caesar establishes the Celtic tribe, Helvetii, between the Alps and the Jura.

the Rhaetians near Graubünden. Their homelands were first invaded by the Romans, who had gained a foothold under Julius Caesar by 58 BC and established Aventicum (now Avenches) as the capital of Helvetia (Roman Switzerland). Switzerland's largest Roman ruins are at Augusta Raurica. By AD 400, Germanic Alemanni tribes arrived to drive out the Romans.

The Alemanni groups settled in eastern Switzerland and were later joined by another Germanic tribe, the Burgundians, in the western part of the country. The latter adopted Christianity and the Latin language, laying the seeds for the division between French- and German-speaking Switzerland. The Franks conquered both tribes in the 6th century, but the two areas were torn apart again when Charlemagne's empire was partitioned in 870.

When it was reunited under the pan-European Holy Roman Empire in 1032, Switzerland was initially left to its own devices. Local nobles wielded the most influence: the Zähringen family, who founded Fribourg, Bern and Murten, and built a fairytale castle with soaring towers and red turrets in Thun in the Bernese Oberland; and the Savoy clan, who established a ring of castles around Lake Geneva, most notably Château de Morges and magnificent Château de Chillon, right on the water's edge near Montreux.

When the Habsburg ruler Rudolph I became Holy Roman Emperor in 1273, he sent in heavy-handed bailiffs to collect more taxes and tighten the administrative screws. Swiss resentment grew quickly.

The Best...
Castles

1 Château de Morges, Morges

2 Schloss Thun, Thun

3 Medieval castles, Bellinzona

4 Burg Hohenklingen, Stein am Rhein

5 Château de Gruyères, Gruyères

Confoederatio Helvetica: Modern Switzerland

Rudolph died in 1291, prompting local leaders to make an immediate grab for independence. On 1 August that year, the forest communities of Uri, Schwyz and Nidwalden – so the tale goes – gathered on Rütli Meadow in the Schwyz canton in central Switzerland to sign an alliance vowing not to recognise any external judge or law. Historians believe this to be a slightly distorted version of events but, whatever the scenario, a pact does exist, preserved in the town of Schwyz. Displayed at the Bundesbriefmuseum in Schwyz, the pact is seen as the founding act of the Swiss Confederation whose Latin name, Confoederatio Helvetica, survives in the 'CH' abbreviation for Switzerland (used, for example, on car number plates and in internet addresses).

AD 1032
Clans in western Switzerland are swallowed up by the Holy Roman Empire.

1273
Habsburg ruler Rudolph I becomes Holy Roman Emperor and takes control of much Swiss territory.

1291
Modern Switzerland officially 'begins' with the independence pact at Rütli Meadow (some claim it was 1307).

William Tell: Man or Myth?

Regardless of whether or not the patriotic William Tell existed or was responsible for even half the deeds attributed to him, the 14th-century crossbow maker from the Uri canton is a key figure in the Swiss identity. A national legend, the man who helped drive out Switzerland's foreign rulers by shooting an apple off his son's head has perfectly embodied the country's rather singular approach to independence throughout the ages.

In 1315, Duke Leopold I of Austria dispatched a powerful army to quash the growing Swiss nationalism. Instead, however, the Swiss inflicted an epic defeat on his troops at Morgarten, which prompted other communities to join the Swiss union. The next 200 years of Swiss history was a time of successive military wins, land grabs and new memberships. The following cantons came on board: Lucerne (1332), Zürich (1351), Glarus and Zug (1352), Bern (1353), Fribourg and Solothurn (1481), Basel and Schaffhausen (1501), and Appenzell (1513). In the middle of all this, the Swiss Confederation gained independence from Holy Roman Emperor Maximilian I after a victory at Dornach in 1499.

No More Stinging Defeats: Swiss Neutrality

Swiss neutrality was essentially born out of the stinging defeat the rampaging Swiss, having made it as far as Milan, suffered against a combined French and Venetian force at Marignano, 16km southeast of Milan, in 1515. After the bloody battle, the Swiss gave up their expansionist dream, withdrew from the international scene and declared neutrality for the first time. For centuries since, the country's warrior spirit has been channelled solely into mercenary activity – a tradition still echoed in the Swiss Guard that protects today's pope at the Vatican.

When the religious Thirty Years War (1618–48) broke out in Europe, Switzerland's neutrality and diversity combined to give it some protection. The Protestant Reformation, led by preachers Huldrych Zwingli and Jean Calvin, made some inroads in Zürich and Geneva, while Central Switzerland (Zentralschweiz) remained Catholic. Such was the internal division that the Swiss, unable to agree even among themselves which side to take in the Thirty Years War, stuck to neutrality.

The French invaded Switzerland in 1798 and established the brief Helvetic Republic, but they were no more welcome than the Austrians before them and internal fighting prompted Napoleon (then in power in France) to restore the former Confederation

1315

Swiss militias win a surprise victory over Habsburg Austrian forces at the Battle of Morgarten.

1476

Charles the Bold, Duke of Burgundy, is crushed at the Battle of Murten.

1499

The Swiss Confederation wins virtual independence from the Habsburg-led Holy Roman Empire.

of Cantons in 1803 – the cantons of Aargau, St Gallen, Graubünden, Ticino, Thurgau and Vaud joined the Confederation at this time.

Swiss neutrality as we know it today was formally established by the Congress of Vienna peace treaty in 1815 that, following Napoleon's defeat by the British and Prussians at Waterloo, formally guaranteed Switzerland's independence and neutrality for the first time. (The same treaty also added the cantons of Valais, Geneva and Neuchâtel to the Swiss confederation.)

Despite some citizens' pro-German sympathies, Switzerland's only involvement in WWI lay in organising Red Cross units. After the war, Switzerland joined the League of Nations, but on a strictly financial and economic basis (which included providing its headquarters in Geneva) – no military involvement.

WWII likewise saw Switzerland remain neutral, the country being largely unscathed bar some accidental bombings on Schaffhausen when Allied pilots mistook the town in northeastern Switzerland for Germany, twice dropping bombs on its outskirts in April 1944. Indeed, the most momentous event of WWII for the Swiss was when Henri Guisan, general of the civilian army, invited all top military personnel to Rütli Meadow (site of the 1291 Oath of Allegiance) to show the world how determined the Swiss were to defend their own soil.

Give Cantons a Voice: The Constitution

In 1847, civil war broke out. The Protestant army, led by General Dufour, quickly crushed the Sonderbund (Special League) of Catholic cantons, including Lucerne. The war only lasted 26 days, prompting the German chancellor Otto von Bismarck to subsequently dismiss it as 'a hare shoot'. But for the peace-loving Swiss, the disruption and disorder

Switzerland's Würste Affair

Protestant Swiss first openly disobeyed the Catholic Church during 1522's 'affair of the sausages', when a printer and several priests in Zürich were caught gobbling *Würste* on Ash Wednesday when they should have been fasting.

The Best...
Old Towns

1 St Gallen

2 Appenzell

3 Vevey

4 Mürten

5 Schaffhausen

1515

After Swiss forces take Milan and Pavia in Italy in 1512, the Swiss are defeated.

1519

Protestant Huldrych Zwingli preaches 'pray and work' in Zürich; the city adopts his reform proposals.

1590–1600

Some 300 women in Vaud are captured, tortured and burned alive on charges of witchcraft.

were sufficient to ensure they rapidly consolidated the victory by Dufour's forces with the creation of a new federal constitution. Bern was named the capital.

The 1848 constitution, largely still in place today, was a compromise between advocates of central control and conservative forces wanting to retain cantonal authority. The cantons eventually relinquished their right to print money, run postal services and levy customs duties, giving these to the federal government. However, they retained legislative and executive control over local matters. Furthermore, the new Federal Assembly was established in a way that gave cantons a voice. The lower national chamber, the *Nationalrat,* has 200 members, allocated from the 26 cantons in proportion to population size. The upper states chamber, the *Ständerat,* comprises 46 members, two per canton.

Opposition to political corruption sparked a movement for greater democracy. The constitution was revised in 1874 so that many federal laws had to be approved by national referendum – a phenomenon for which Switzerland remains famous today. A petition with 50,000 signatures can challenge a proposed law; 100,000 signatures can force a public vote on any new issue.

Famously Secret: Swiss Banking

Banking confidentiality, dating back to the Middle Ages, was enshrined in Swiss law in 1934 when numbered (rather than named) bank accounts were introduced. The Swiss banking industry has thrived ever since, thanks mainly to the enviable stability that guaranteed neutrality brings. When the Bank for International Settlements (BIS; the

The Magic Formula: Swiss Government

The make-up of Switzerland's Federal Council, the executive government, is determined not by who wins the most parliamentary seats (ie the winning party rules), but by the 'magic formula' – a cosy power-sharing agreement made between the four main parties in 1959.

○ The Federal Council consists of seven ministers.

○ The four largest parties in parliament are guaranteed seats in the Federal Council in accordance with their shares of the popular vote.

○ The president is drawn on a rotating basis from the seven federal ministers, so there's a new head of state each year.

○ Many federal laws must first be approved by public referendum; several are held every year.

1847
Civil war between Protestants and Catholics lasts 26 days, leaving 86 dead and 500 wounded.

1863
Horrified by wartime slaughter, Henri Dunant co-founds the International Red Cross in Geneva.

1918
With a sixth of the population in poverty and 20,000 dead from flu, workers strike.

organisation that facilitates cooperation between central banks) chose Basel as base in 1930 it was for one good reason – Switzerland was a neutral player.

In the late 1990s a series of scandals erupted, forcing Switzerland to start reforming its famously secretive banking industry, born when a clutch of commercial banks were created in the mid-19th century. In 1995, after pressure from Jewish groups, Swiss banks announced that they had discovered millions of dollars lying in dormant pre-1945 accounts and belonging to Holocaust victims and survivors. Three years later, amid allegations they'd been sitting on the money without seriously trying to trace its owners, Switzerland's two largest banks, UBS and Crédit Suisse, agreed to pay US$1.25 billion in compensation to Holocaust survivors and their families.

Switzerland has long been a favourite spot for the wealthy to deposit their fortunes in private banks. Almost one-third of the world's US$7 trillion offshore deposits are said to be in Switzerland – hence the immense pressure on Switzerland in 2009 from the US, Britain, Germany and other high-tax countries to change its 1934 banking law protecting depositors accused of tax evasion by their home countries. The Swiss conceded, prompting critics to triumphantly ring the death knell for Swiss banking

UBS, one of Switzerland's largest banks
ADRIAN MOSER / GETTY IMAGES ©

1940
More than 430,000 troops are mobilised in case of German invasion.

1949
Orson Welles delivers line about the Swiss inventing the cuckoo clock in *The Third Man*.

1979
Jura (majority French-speaking Catholics) leaves Bern (German-speaking Protestants) to become an independent canton.

secrecy. This followed hot on the heels of the Swiss decision in 2004 to tax accounts held in Switzerland by EU citizens – again in reaction to external pressure.

Forever Neutral: A Nation Apart

Since the end of WWII, Switzerland has enjoyed an uninterrupted period of economic, social and political stability – thanks, in predictable Swiss fashion, to the neutrality which saw it forge ahead from an already powerful commercial, financial and industrial base while the rest of Europe was still picking up and rebuilding the broken pieces from the war. Zürich developed as an international banking and insurance centre, and the World Health Organization and a stash of other international bodies set up headquarters in Geneva. To preserve its much-vaunted neutrality, however, Switzerland opted to remain outside the UN (although Geneva has hosted its second-largest seat after the main New York headquarters from the outset) and, more recently, the European Union.

A hefty swing to the conservative right in the 2003 parliamentary elections served to further enhance Switzerland's standing as a nation staunchly apart. In 2006, the anti-EU, anti-immigration Swiss People's Party (SVP) called for the toughening up

CERN's Globe of Science & Innovation (p65), designed by architects T Büchi and H Dessimoz

1988
Switzerland wins Eurovision. French-Canadian Céline Dion performs the winning song, *Ne Partez Pas Sans Moi*.

1990
The internet is 'born' at Geneva's CERN, which develops the language essential to the web.

2001
Swissair collapses, Zug parliament massacre, canyoning accident and St Gotthard Tunnel fire cause many deaths.

of immigration and political asylum laws; the policies were passed with an overwhelming majority at national referendum. Then there was the rumpus over its bid to ban building new minarets for Muslim calls to prayer – an idea that aroused much anger internationally, but was approved by the constitution after 57.7% of voters said yes to the ban in a national referendum. During the campaign, the SVP published anti-immigrant posters featuring three white sheep kicking one black sheep off the striking white cross of the Swiss flag.

In spite of the SVP's tough conservative line, there have been concrete signs that Switzerland is opening up to the wider world. The country became the 190th member of the UN in 2002 (a referendum on the issue had last been defeated in 1986) and three years later it voted to join Europe's passport-free travel zone, Schengen (finally completing the process at the end of 2008). In another referendum the same year, the Swiss narrowly voted in favour of legalising civil unions for same-sex couples (but not marriage), one more defeat for the SVP.

Yet few expect Switzerland to even consider joining either the EU or the Euro single-currency zone any time soon (if ever). Traditionally, the French-speaking western cantons have long desired both, while the German-speaking cantons (and Ticino) have generally been opposed.

The Best...
History Museums

1 Stiftsbibliothek, St Gallen

2 Schweizerisches Landesmuseum, Zürich

3 Historisches Museum, Arbon

4 Château de Chillon, Montreux

5 Augusta Raurica, Kaiseraugst

IN FOCUS HISTORY

2008
The world financial crisis endangers Switzerland's two biggest banks, UBS and Crédit Suisse.

2012
CERN scientists possibly discover the Higgs boson subatomic particle, a key to understanding the universe.

2014
A popular initiative to set immigration quotas is successful at the Swiss polls.

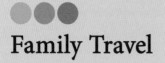

Family Travel

Ski school, Bernese Oberland

BERNARD VAN DIERENDONCK / GETTY IMAGE

Orderly, clean and not overly commercial, Switzerland is a dream for family travel and promotes itself heavily as such. Every ski resort works hard at being family-friendly, with good summertime activities on offer, and hotels and B&Bs cater well for families. Check out Swiss Tourism's Families brochure (order or download it online at www.myswitzerland.com). It's jam-packed with ideas, as is the website, which lists child-friendly accommodation, family offers and so on.

Activities

Winter resorts go to great trouble to provide family-friendly plans and activities. Everything from lessons to special non-adult areas are near-universal and programs are varied by ages, so the rebellious young teen need be nowhere near their seven-year-old sibling. A trip to one of the best snowboarding destinations on the planet is rarely going to disappoint.

In summer, adventure-sports companies often have programs just for kids and most have programs designed for the entire family. You can go hike with goats, walk a St Bernard, go on a GPS hiking treasure hunt, spot a marmot, swing like mad on ropes and much, much more.

Transport

Family train travel is good value. Kids under six years old travel for free with **Swiss Railways (www.sbb.ch)** and those aged six to 16 years revel in free unlimited rail travel with its annual Junior Card (Sfr30) or – should it be grandparents travelling with the kids – the grandchild travel card (Sfr30). Childen not travelling with a relative can get unlimited travel for one day with a one-day children's travel pass (Sfr16). Switzerland's mountain of scenic journeys by train and boat enchant children of all ages. Upon arrival at point B, dozens of segments of the perfectly signposted hiking, biking, rollerblading and canoeing trails are flagged as suitable for younger children. These are designed strictly for non-motorised traffic by Switzerland Mobility.

It's worth mentioning the travel itself: from railways in every shape and size to lake boats to cable cars and gondolas seemingly out of an adventure flick, just getting around Switzerland is a thrilling adventure.

Hotels

All types of accommodation will have family rooms, and deals geared for families are common at larger places. Resorts will often have childcare facilities or programs designed to allow parents to enjoy their own holiday within the holiday.

Staying in a B&B is family fabulous: little kids can sweetly slumber upstairs while weary parents wine and dine in peace downstairs. Pick a B&B on a farm or kip on straw in the hay barn for adventurous kids.

Additionally, many hotels in resort areas have outdoor playgrounds and a new increasingly popular trend is rooms geared for kids. Bright colours, games on the TV, every channel a child could hope for, pint-sized beds, rubber ducks in the tub and much more. In resort areas, teens will occasionally find night-time social clubs where they can meet other under 16s from around the world.

Restaurants & Food

Children are generally welcome in most restaurants. Some even offer smaller, kid-sized menus and servings. Toddlers are usually fed straight from their parents' plates and if high-chairs aren't available, staff will improvise.

Need to Know

Car seats Switzerland has the toughest child car-seat rules in the world: children age 12 years or under 150cm in height must use car seats or booster seats. Car hire/rental firms charge around Sfr50 for these.

Changing facilities Uncommon in traditional establishments; only really found in modern, major facilities.

Cots Usually available at all accommodation, except perhaps a remote mountain hut.

Health As you would do at home.

Highchairs Usually available.

Kids' menus At many restaurants.

Nappies (diapers) Readily available.

Strollers Larger resorts may have them.

Transport Myriad family passes and kids' discounts available.

The Best...
Places to Delight Kids

1 Verkehrhaus, Lucerne

2 Alimentarium, Vevey

3 Gstaad Ski Resort

4 Interlaken & Grindelwald adventure outfitters

5 Cailler Chocolate Factory

As far as the menu goes, any country with a fondness for cheese and potatoes like Switzerland is bound to be popular with kids of *all* ages (including large ones called 'adults'). And there's also the Swiss mania for ice cream in virtually all weather conditions.

Then there's the big elephant in the room, the big cocoa elephant: chocolate. From iconic Alpine-shaped Toblerone to a plethora of bars sold in all sizes and flavours, the country is awash in treats. One final item that should seal the deal for most kids: one of life's great pleasures is sitting outside at a ski resort and drinking the richest, creamiest hot chocolate imaginable.

Towns & Cities

Swiss cities are also child-friendly. There's lots to do in both Zürich and Geneva and at every other city and town in between. None are huge and intimidating – even in Zürich you can take the time to admire a white swan gliding past the busiest part of town. Castles abound and you've got ancient and thrilling features like the old wooden bridges in Lucerne.

Up in the Alps, kids can run free in a town like Wengen, where trails set off across the gorgeous countryside but there are few opportunities to get in trouble.

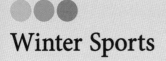

Winter Sports

Skiing at Davos (p252)

BERNARD VAN DIERENDONCK / GETTY IMAGES ©

In a land where every 10-man, 50-cow hamlet has a ski lift, the question is not where you can ski but how. Ritzy or remote, party-mad or picture-perfect, virgin or veteran, black run or blue – whatever your taste and ability, Switzerland has a resort to suit.

Regions

The following winter sports regions are just a glimpse of what's available in the Alps. Switzerland has scores of fantastic resorts and we are unable to cover them exhaustively here. See regional chapters for more.

Bernese Oberland & Central Switzerland

If only all ski resorts were like those in the Bernese Oberland. At its winter wonderland heart is the Jungfrau, an unspoilt Alpine region with dark timber villages and scenery lovely enough to distract anyone from mastering parallel turns.

The region is criss-crossed with 214km of well-maintained slopes, ranging from easy-peasy to hair-raising, which afford fleeting views of the 'Big Three': the Eiger, Mönch and Jungfrau. Grindelwald, Wengen and Mürren all offer varied skiing and have a

Online Ski Deals

For last-minute ski deals and packages, check out websites like www.igluski.com and www.j2ski.com. Local tourist offices, **Snowfinders** (www.snowfinders.co.uk) and **My Switzerland** (www.myswitzerland.com) might also have good-value offers.

Speed to the slopes by prebooking your ski and snowboard hire at **Ski Set** (www.skiset.co.uk) or **Snowbrainer** (www.snowbrainer.com), both of which offer discounts of up to 40% on shop rental prices. If you want to skip to the front of the queue, consider ordering your lift pass online, too. Swiss Passes (www.swisspasses.com) gets you a reduction of up to 30% on standard lift pass prices.

relaxed, family-friendly vibe. For more glitz and Gucci, swing west to Gstaad, which has fine downhill on 220km of slopes and pre- and post-season glacier skiing at nearby Glacier 3000, framed by 4000m peaks.

Surprisingly little-known given its snow-sure slopes and staggering mountain backdrop, Engelberg is dominated by the savage rock and ice walls of glacier-capped Mt Titlis. The real treasures here are off-piste, including Galtiberg, a 2000m vertical descent from the glacier to the valley.

Valais & Zermatt

One of Switzerland's most-enduring images is the perfect pyramid-shaped peak of the Matterhorn, soaring 4478m above Zermatt. Snowboarders, intermediates and off-pisters are all catered for in this car-free resort with 360km of eye-poppingly scenic runs. You can even ski over to Cervinia in Italy. Verbier has some terrifically challenging off-piste for experts. Hard-core boarders favour snow-sure, glacier-licked Saas Fee. Snuggling up to France's mammoth Portes du Soleil ski arena, Champéry has access to 650km of slopes. Queues are few and families are welcome in lesser-known beauties such as Bettmeralp.

St Moritz & Graubünden

Rugged Graubünden has some truly legendary slopes. First up is super-chic St Moritz, with 350km of groomed slopes (intermediates are in heaven), fine glacier descents and freeride opportunities. The twin resorts of (pretty) Klosters and (popular) Davos share 320km of runs; the latter is superb for cross-country and has excellent parks and half-pipes. Boarders also rave about the terrain parks, freeriding and après-ski scene in Laax. Family-oriented Arosa and Lenzerheide in the next valley are scenic picks for beginners, intermediates and crosscountry fans. Want to give the crowds the slip? Celerina shares many of the slopes with St Moritz but is low-key and has a famous bob run.

When?

The slopes buzz with skiers and boarders from mid-December until Easter. Unless you're tied by school holidays (Christmas, February half-term and Easter), avoid them to get better deals and avoid crowds.

Passes, Hire & Tuition

Yes, Switzerland is expensive and no, skiing is not an exception. That said, costs can be cut by avoiding school-holiday times and choosing low-key villages over upscale resorts. Ski passes are a hefty chunk out of your budget and will set you back around Sfr70 per day or Sfr350 per week. Factor in around Sfr40 to Sfr70 per day for ski hire and Sfr20 for boot hire, which can be reserved online at www.intersportrent.com. Kids' equipment is roughly half-price.

All major resorts have ski schools, with half-day group lessons typically costing Sfr50 to Sfr80 and a full-day off-piste around Sfr100. **Swiss Snowsports** (www. snowsports.ch) has a clickable map of 158 ski schools across the country.

Ski Run Classifications

Piste maps are available on most tourist-office websites and at the valley stations of ski lifts; runs are colour-coded according to difficulty as follows:

Blue Indicates easy, well-groomed runs that are suitable for beginners.

Red Indicates intermediate runs that are groomed but often steeper and narrower than blue runs. Skiers should have a medium level of ability.

Black For expert skiers with polished technique and skills. They are mostly steep and not always groomed, and may have moguls and steep vertical drops.

Safety on the Slopes

○ Avalanche warnings should be heeded and local advice sought before detouring from prepared runs.

Top Slopes for...

Snowboarding Freeriders seeking deep powder, big air and, like, totally *awesome* terrain parks, head to Saas Fee, Laax and Davos.

Families Picture-book pretty Arosa, Lenzerheide, Bettmeralp and Klosters for their fine nursery slopes, kids' clubs and slope-side activities ranging from sledding to skidooing.

Off-piste Explore the virgin powder in the glorious backcountry of Engelberg, Andermatt, Verbier and Davos.

Glacier skiing For pre- and post-season skiing, schuss across to Glacier 3000 near Gstaad, glacier-encrusted Mt Titlis in Engelberg and the snow-sure slopes of Saas Fee.

Scenic skiing Zermatt for its legendary Matterhorn views and the Jungfrau region to slalom in the shadow of the Eiger, Mönch and Jungfrau.

Scary-as-hell descents Dare to ski the near-vertical Swiss Wall, the mogul-riddled Mont-Fort in Verbier and the Inferno, a 16km black-run marathon from Schilthorn to Lauterbrunnen.

Cross-country skiing Master your classic or skating technique on the twinkling *Loipen* in Davos, Arosa and Kandersteg.

Non-skiers Still ski-shy? Try Gstaad or Grindelwald, where off-piste fun like ice skating, curling, airboarding, horse-drawn sleigh rides, winter hiking and husky sledding keeps non-skiers amused.

The Best...
Famous Ski Resorts

1 Verbier

2 Zermatt

3 St Moritz

4 Davos

5 Klosters

○ If you're going off-piste or hiking in snowy areas, never go alone and take an avalanche pole, a transceiver or a shovel and, most importantly, a professional guide.

○ Before setting foot in the mountains check the day's avalanche bulletin by calling ☎187 or checking online at www.slf.ch.

○ The sun is powerful in the Alps and is intensified by snow glare. Wear ski goggles and high-factor sunscreen.

○ Layers help you to adapt to the constant change in body temperature. Your head, wrists and knees should be protected.

○ Black run look tempting? Make sure you're properly insured first; sky-high mountain rescue and medical costs can add insult to injury.

Resources

Bergfex (www.bergfex.com) Comprehensive website with piste maps, snow forecasts of the Alps and details of 111 ski resorts in Switzerland.

On the Snow (www.onthesnow.co.uk) Handy website with reviews of Switzerland's ski resorts, plus snow reports, webcams and lift pass details.

If You Ski (www.ifyouski.com) Resort guides, ski deals and info on ski hire and schools.

MadDogSki (www.maddogski.com) Entertaining ski guides and insider tips on everything from accommodation to après ski.

World Snowboard Guide (www.worldsnowboardguide.com) Snowboarder central. Has the lowdown on most Swiss resorts.

Where to Ski and Snowboard (www.wheretoskiandsnowboard.com) Resort overviews and reviews, news and weather.

Summer Sports

Climb every mountain: hikers near Grindelwald, Jungfrau Region (p134)

GUENTER FISCHER / GETTY IMAGES ©

Switzerland is a sporty nation and it's easy to see why: glacial brooks and thundering waterfalls, colossal peaks and beckoning valleys. The water is mineral pure, the sky a brighter shade of blue, the air piney fresh. No wonder the Swiss can't keep still with that phenomenal backyard. And what's good for the locals is fabulous for visitors. Long summer nights let you pack in as much as possible.

When to Go

Except for the depths of winter – which offers its own options for fun – you can revel in the Swiss outdoors free of winter gear for much of the year.

- **May–June** The crowds are thin and the weather is often fine. Snow patches still linger above 2000m. June is great for hiking with long, warm days and wildflowers carpeting the slopes. Many huts are still closed and mountain transport is limited.

- **July–August** A conga line of high-altitude hikers and cyclists makes its way through the Swiss Alps. All lifts and mountain huts are open (book ahead). The lakes beckon all water-sports fans.

- **September–early October** Pot luck: can be delightful or drab. The larch forests look beautiful in their autumn mantle of gold, and temperatures at lower altitudes are still mild.

Weather Reports

The weather is notoriously fickle in the Alps. Even in August, conditions can skip from foggy to sunny, stormy to snowy in the course of a day, so check the forecast on www.meteoschweiz.ch before embarking on long hikes at high altitudes.

Accommodation prices drop, as do the crowds, but many hotels and lifts close.

○ **Mid-October–November** Days get shorter and the weather is unpredictable. Expect rain, fog and snow above 1500m. Most resorts go into hibernation.

Walking & Hiking

Mighty glaciers and 4000m mountains, remote moors and flower-flecked meadows, limestone ravines and sparkling rivers – Switzerland has an almost indecent amount of natural splendour for its size. More than 60,000km of marked trails criss-cross the country and only by slinging on a backpack and hitting the trail can you begin to appreciate just how *big* this tiny country really is.

Walk Designations

As locals delight in telling you, Switzerland's 62,500km of trails would be enough to stretch around the globe 1.5 times. And with (stereo)typical Swiss precision, the footpaths that criss-cross the country are remarkably well signposted and maintained. That said, a decent topographical map and compass is still recommended for Alpine hikes. Like ski runs, trails are colour-coded according to difficulty:

Yellow Easy. No previous experience necessary.

White-red-white Mountain trails. You should be sure-footed as routes may involve some exposure.

White-blue-white High Alpine routes. Only for the physically fit; some climbing and/or glacier travel may be required.

Pink Prepared winter walking trails.

Regions

Alpine hikers invariably have their sights set high on the trails in the Bernese Oberland, Valais and Graubünden, which offer challenging walking and magnificent scenery. That said, lowland areas such as the vine-strewn Lavaux wine region and the bucolic dairy country around Appenzell can be just as atmospheric and are accessible virtually year-round.

In summer, many tourist offices run guided hikes – free with a local guest card – including Lugano. Other resorts such as Davos-Klosters and Arosa give you a head start with free mountain transport when you stay overnight in summer.

Accommodation

Want to overnight on your walk? **Wanderland** (www.wanderland.ch) should be your first port of call for hiker-friendly accommodation, with farmstays, hotels, campsites and Swiss Alpine Club (SAC) huts searchable by route and region.

Resources

Local tourist offices are excellent sources of recommendations and info for walking and hiking. Tell them what you want to do and they can set you up. They also have all types of maps for sale.

Get planning with the routes, maps and GPS downloads on the following websites:

My Switzerland (www.myswitzerland.com) Excellent information on walking in Switzerland, from themed day hikes to guided treks and family-friendly walks. An iPhone app covering 32 walks is available for download.

Wanderland (www.wanderland.ch) The definitive website on hiking in Switzerland, with walks and accommodation searchable by region and theme, plus information on events, guides, maps and packages.

Cycling & Mountain Biking

Routes

Switzerland is an efficiently run paradise for the ardent cyclist, laced with 9000km of cycling trails and 4500km of mountain-biking routes.

Mountain and downhill bikers whizz across to Alpine resorts like Arosa in summer, where cable cars often allow you to take your wheels for free or for a nominal fee. To hone your skills on obstacles, check out the terrain parks in Davos and Verbier.

Bike Hire

Reliable wheels are available in all major towns and many now offer free bike hire from April to October as part of the eco-friendly initiative **Suisse Roule** (www.suisse roule.ch), including Bern, Zürich, Geneva, Martigny, Sion and Neuchâtel.

Available at all major train stations, **Rent a Bike** (www.rent-a-bike.ch) has city bikes, mountain bikes, e-bikes and tandems for Sfr35, Sfr35, Sfr54 and Sfr80 per day respectively. For a small additional charge, you can pick your bike up at one station and drop it off at another. Bikes can be reserved online. A one-day bike pass for SBB trains costs Sfr18.

Mountain biking, Martigny area (p170)
MIKE KEMP IMAGES / GETTY IMAGES ©

The Best...
Summer Sports Towns

Resources

Veloland (www.veloland.ch) For maps, route descriptions and the lowdown on Switzerland's nine national routes, plus details on bike rental and e-bike stations.

Mountainbikeland (www.mountainbikeland.ch) Useful website for mountain bikers, with details on Switzerland's single-trail and fun tours, and three national routes.

Adventure & Water Sports

Rock Climbing & Mountaineering

Switzerland has been the fabled land for mountaineers ever since Edward Whymper made the first successful ascent of the Matterhorn in 1865, albeit a triumph marred with rope-breaking tragedy. Today, Zermatt's Alpin Center arranges some first-class climbs to surrounding 4000-ers.

The climbing halls in Chur and Interlaken are perfect for limbering up.

Swiss Alpine Club (SAC; www.sac-cas.ch) Browse for information on countrywide climbing halls, tours and courses.

Schweizer Bergführerverband (Swiss Mountain Guide Association; www.4000plus.ch) Search for a qualified mountain guide or climbing instructor.

Vie Ferrate

For the buzz of mountaineering but with the security of being attached to the rock face, clip onto a *via ferrata* (*Klettersteig* in German). These head-spinning fixed-rope routes are currently all the rage in Switzerland. Some of our favourites include those in Mürren for scenery and Kandersteg for more of a challenge.

Via Ferrata (www.viaferrata.org) provides maps and routes graded according to difficulty.

Rafting & Hydrospeeding

In summer, the raging Saane, Rhine, Inn and Rhône rivers create a dramatic backdrop for rafting and hydrospeeding (surfing rapids solo on a glorified bodyboard). Memorable splashes include the thundering Vorderrhein through the limestone Ruinaulta gorge and rivers near Interlaken.

Swissraft (www.swissraft.ch) has bases all over the country. Expect to pay around Sfr110 for a half-day rafting tour and Sfr150 for hydrospeeding, including transport and equipment.

Kayaking & Canoeing

Lazy summer afternoons are best spent absorbing the slow, natural rhythm of Switzerland's crystal-clear lakes and rivers (for instance, Lake Constance and fjord-like Lake Uri).

See http://kanuland.myswitzerland.com for routes and paddle-friendly accommodation tips. A half-day canoeing tour will set you back between Sfr85 and Sfr120. Tourist offices can provide details on local outfits.

Scenic Transport

The Glacier Express (p256) passes along the Landwasser Viaduct

MARTIN MOOS / GETTY IMAGES ©

Never does the expression 'the journey is the destination' ring truer than in Switzerland, little land of big journeys and once-in-a-lifetime train rides. Prepare to have your mind blown by Alpine scenery on dinky red trains that unzip valleys and glide below glacier-capped peaks. Play spot the marmot as you creak up to giddy peaks in vintage funiculars, or listen to legends of mighty mountains as you cruise the waterways in glorious slow motion.

Moving Moments

No matter how you travel, you'll never look at public transport in the same way again. Switzerland has it down to a fine art, with even bog-standard buses taking you up to remote mountain passes for eye-to-eye peak and wildlife encounters. The Swiss Travel System is an interconnected web of trains, boats, cable cars and postal buses that puts almost the entire country within easy car-free reach – and naturally, with stereotypical precision, you can set your watch by it.

Boats

Gliding along the clear waters of a Swiss lake aboard a boat is one of the nation's restful pleasures. Scenic rides abound. Many of these are circular journeys aimed at visitors, but in other places they are a great means of transport from A to B. And

in summer, you might find that your boat is a historic steam-driven classic, complete with tooting horn.

The following are some of the best places to try out lake travel:

● **Lake Geneva** (☎ 0848 811 848; www.cgn.ch) There's almost no place on this huge lake without a boat dock. You can mix and match boat and train travel while enjoying soul-stirring mountain and vineyard views.

● **Lake Lucerne** Boats fan out from the heart of Lucerne and you can enjoy views of Alps near and far while you glide along. A classic trip is a circular visit to Mt Pilatus, which includes a beautiful stretch aboard a lake boat.

● **Lake Lugano** One of the mildest Swiss places climate-wise, you get views of the lush mountains along the lake and there are little chapel-topped, Italian-speaking villages to explore during a day of boat-hopping.

By Boat & Rail

Named after Switzerland's apple-shooting legend, the **Wilhelm Tell Express** (www.williamtellexpress.ch; ⏱ May-Oct) starts with a wonderful 2½-hour cruise across Lake Lucerne to Flüelen, from where a train winds its way through ravines and past mountains to Locarno on the palm-fringed shores of Lago Maggiore.

Cable Cars

It's the stuff of movies: dangling cable cars, century-old funiculars and tiny gondolas zipping up the sides of impossibly sheer mountainsides to summits with views that literally leave you speechless. Getting there is truly half the fun.

Here are a few rides to whet your appetite, but they are just a taste of what's out there:

● **Schynige Platte** (p134) Hop aboard a 19th-century cog-wheel train in Wilderswil

Mt Titlis cable car (p156)
HANS GEORG EIBEN / LOOK-FOTO / GETTY IMAGES ©

to reach this high plateau, with an Alpine garden and hiking trails that grant ringside views of Eiger, Mönch and Jungfrau.

○ **Mt Titlis** (www.titlis.ch/en/tickets/cable-car-ride; adult/child return Sfr89/44.50; ⊙8.30am-5pm) Feel your heart do somersaults as you spin above the dazzling Titlis Glacier in the world's first revolving cable car. A sea of Alpine peaks spreads out before you at the 3020m summit.

○ **Säntisbahn** (p226) Rise to the Säntis peak (2503m) in a panoramic cable car. The view of Lake Constance, Zürichsee, the Alps and the Vorarlberg Mountains at the top is out of this world.

Trains

Try as they might, few countries can rival Switzerland when it comes to silky smooth railways. The trains look like the life-sized models of a fastidious Hornby collector, the views keep you glued to the windows, ever so often eliciting gasps of wonder as you traverse a viaduct or edge close to a mighty glacier. Trains are bound to be a huge part of your travel experience here, leaving with memories that linger long after you chug into the station.

The Glacier Express, Golden Pass Route and Bernina Express have panoramic coaches with extra-large windows.

In addition to the journeys listed below, almost any train in the Jungfrau region provides beautiful views:

Bernina Express (www.rhb.ch)

Chocolate Train (www.mob.ch)

Glacier Express (www.glacierexpress.ch)

Golden Pass Route (www.goldenpass.ch)

Mont Blanc/St Bernard Expresses (www.tmrsa.ch)

The Best...
Great Journeys

1 Jungfraujoch

2 Mt Titlis

3 Schilthorn

4 Mt Pilatus

5 Aletsch Glacier

The Swiss Table

Cheesemaking, Graubünden region

GEORG KNOLL / GETTY IMAGE

There is far more to Swiss cuisine than chocolate, cheese and Swiss-German rösti, and the very best dining in this essentially rural country is all about the nation's own foods. While the chic city crowd feasts on international fare, the Swiss kitchen is extraordinarily rich thanks to French, German and Italian influences on the local dishes.

Cheese

First things first: not all Swiss cheese has holes. Emmental, the hard cheese from the Emme Valley east of Bern, does – as does the not dissimilar Tilsiter from the same valley. But, contrary to common perception, most of Switzerland's 450 different types of cheese (*käse* in German, *fromage* in French, *formaggio* in Italian) are hole-less. Take the well-known hard cheese Gruyère, made in the town of Gruyères near Fribourg; or the overwhelmingly stinky Appenzeller, used in a rash of tasty, equally strong-smelling dishes in the same-name town in northeastern Switzerland. Or there's Sbrinz, Switzerland's oldest hard cheese and transalpine ancestor to Italian parmesan, ripened for 24 months to create its distinct taste – eat it straight and thinly sliced like carpaccio or grated on top of springtime asparagus.

Another distinctive Swiss cheese with not a hole in sight is hard, nutty-flavoured Tête de Moine (literally 'monks's head') from the Jura, which comes in a small round and is cut with a flourish in a flowery curl using a special handled cutting device known as a *girolle* (great present to take back home – supermarkets sell them).

As unique is L'Etivaz, which, in the finest of timeless alpine tradition, is only made up high on lush summer pastures in the Alpes Vaudoises (Vaud Alps). As cows graze outside, shepherds inside their century-old *chalets d'alpage* (mountain huts) heat up the morning's milk in a traditional copper cauldron over a wood fire. Strictly seasonal, the Appellation d'Origine Contrôllée (AOC) cheese can only be made from May to early October using milk from cows that have grazed on mountains between 1000m and 2000m high.

The Best...
Swiss Foods

1 Fondue

2 Raclette

3 Rösti

4 *Bündnerfleisch*

5 Chocolate

Fondue & Raclette

It is hard to leave Switzerland without dipping into a fondue (from the French verb *fondre,* meaning 'to melt'). And you shouldn't! The main French contribution to the Swiss table, a pot of gooey melted cheese is placed in the centre of the table and kept on a slow burn while diners dip in cubes of crusty bread using slender two-pronged fondue forks. Just the sight of the creamy cheese languidly glistening on the bread is enough to make some diners swoon.

The classic fondue mix in Switzerland is equal amounts of Emmental and Gruyère cheese, grated and melted with white wine and a shot of kirsch (cherry-flavoured liquor); order a side platter of cold meats and tiny gherkins to accompany it.

Switzerland's other signature alpine cheese dish is raclette. Unlike fondue, raclette – both the name of the dish and the cheese at its gooey heart – is eaten year-round. A half-crescent slab of the cheese is screwed onto a specially designed 'rack oven' that melts the top flat side. As it melts, cheese is scraped onto plates for immediate consumption with boiled potatoes, cold meats and pickled onions or gherkins.

Rösti

Be sure not to miss rösti (a shredded, oven-crisped potato bake). Baked to a perfect crisp, the shredded potato is mixed with seasonal mushrooms and bacon bits to create a perfect lunch, paired with nothing more than a simple green salad. This is Swiss Alpine heaven.

Meats

For a quintessential Swiss lunch, nothing beats an alfresco platter of air-dried beef, a truly sweet and exquisitely tender delicacy from Graubünden that is smoked, thinly sliced and served as *Bündnerfleisch*.

Travel east and *Würste* (sausages) become the local lunch feast, typically served with German-speaking Switzerland's star dish: rösti. Veal is highly rated and is tasty thinly sliced and smothered in a cream sauce as *geschnetzeltes Kalbsfleisch* in Zürich.

For true blue-blooded meat lovers there is no better season to let tastebuds rip in this heavily forested country than autumn, when restaurants up and down the country

cook up *Wildspezialitäten/specialités de gibier,* or *chasse/cacciagione* (fresh game). Venison and wild boar are also popular.

Pork

With its fresh game, abundance of wild mushrooms, chestnuts and grape harvests, autumn is exquisitely gourmet in Switzerland and as the days shorten this season only gets better. Fattened over summer, the family pig – traditionally slaughtered on the feast of St Martin (11 November) marking the end of agricultural work in the fields and the start of winter – is ready for the butcher. On farms and in villages for centuries, the slaughter would be followed by the salting of meat and sausage-making. Work done, folk would then pass over to feasting to celebrate the day's toil. The main dish for the feast: pork.

In the French-speaking Jura, in particular, the feasting tradition around Fête de la St-Martin lives on with particular energy and enthusiasm in Porrentruy. Local bars and restaurants organise feasts for several weekends on the trot in October and November. A typical pork feast consists of gorging on seven copious courses.

Pork dishes to look out for year-round include *Rippli* (a bubbling pot of pork rib meat cooked up with bacon, potatoes and beans) in and around Bern, and in the canton of Vaud, *papet vaudois* (a potato, leek, cabbage and sausage stew) and *taillé aux greubons* (a crispy savoury pastry, soft and dotted inside with pork-lard cubes). In the Engadine, sausage is baked with onions and potato to make *pian di pigna*.

Fish

Fish is the speciality in lakeside towns. Perch (*perche,* in French) and whitefish fillets (*féra*) are common, but don't be fooled into thinking the *filets de perche* chalked on the blackboard in practically every Lake Geneva restaurant are from the lake; much comes frozen from Eastern Europe.

Potato rösti
WESTEND61 / GETTY IMAGES ©

Fruit, Sweets & Chocolate

Plump Valais apricots, plums, pears and sweet black cherries fill orchards with a profusion of pretty white blossoms in April and May. For year-round pleasure, the Swiss dry, preserve and distil their abundance of fruit to create fiery liqueurs, winter compotes and thick-as-honey syrups for baking or spreading on bread.

The Botzi pear cultivated around Gruyères is deemed precious enough to have its own AOC. Bite into it as nature intended or try it with local *crème de Gruyères*, the thickest cream ever. *Cuisses de dame* (lady's thighs) are sugary deep-fried thigh-shaped pastries, found in French-speaking cantons next to *amandines* (almond tarts). Apart from the ubiquitous *Apfelstrudel* (apple pie), typically served with runny vanilla sauce, German cantons cook up *Vermicelles,* a chestnut-cream creation resembling something like spaghetti.

Then, of course, there is chocolate...

Swiss Wine

Savouring local wine in Switzerland is an exquisite, increasingly rare gastronomic joy in this globalised world. Switzerland exports little of its wine, meaning that most of its quality reds, whites and rosé vintages, including dozens by small vignerons, can only be tasted and enjoyed in situ.

Lake Geneva & Vaud

The bulk of Swiss wine production takes place in the French-speaking part of the country, where vineyards line the shore of Lake Geneva and stagger sharply up hillsides in tightly-packed terraces knitted together by ancient dry-stone walls.

Most of Lake Geneva's winemaking estates are found on either side of Lausanne in the canton of Vaud. Whites from the pea-green terraced vineyards of the Lavaux wine region between Lausanne and Montreux are so outstanding that the area has been designated a Unesco World Heritage site. Lavaux's two grands crus are Calamin and Dézaley.

Swiss Chocolate

In the early centuries after Christ's death, as the Roman Empire headed towards slow collapse on a diet of rough wine and olives, the Mayans in Central America were pounding cocoa beans, consuming the result and even using the beans as a system of payment.

A millennium later, the Spanish conquistador Hernando Cortez brought the first load of cocoa to Europe in 1528. He could not have anticipated the subsequent demand for his cargo. The Spaniards, and soon other Europeans, developed an insatiable thirst for the sweetened beverage produced from it. The solid stuff came later.

Swiss chocolate (www.chocolat.ch) built its reputation in the 19th century, thanks to familiar names such as François-Louis Cailler (1796–1852), Philippe Suchard (1797–1884), Henri Nestlé (1814–90), Jean Tobler (1830–1905), Daniel Peter (1836–1919) and Rodolphe Lindt (1855–1909). For factory visits, see p117.

Valais

Drenched in an extra bonanza of sunshine and light from above the southern Alps, much of the land north of the Rhône River in western Valais is planted with vines – and this is where some of Switzerland's best wines are produced.

Dryish white Fendant, the perfect accompaniment to fondue and raclette, and best served crisp cold, is the region's best-known wine, accounting for two-thirds of Valais wine production. Johannisberg is another excellent white and comes from the Sylvaner grape; while Petite Arvine and Amigne are sweet whites.

Dôle, made from Pinot noir and Gamay grapes, is the principal red blend and is as full bodied as an opera singer with its firm fruit flavour.

Ticino

The favourite liquid for lunch in Switzerland's Italianate climes is Merlot, which accounts for almost 90% of Ticino's wine production. The main winemaking areas are between Bellinzona and Ascona, around Biasca and between Lugano and Mendrisio.

Swiss chocolates
CCLICKCLICK / GETTY IMAGES ©

Spa Resorts & Treatments

Spa time, Leukerbad (p178)

STEVEN ALLAN / GETTY IMAGES ©

The healthy action in Switzerland isn't all in the great outdoors. There's a lot of good stuff – steamy stuff even – going on in the country's renowned spas, saunas and health centres. Many feature mineral baths with natural springs bubbling with water heated deep in the earth. You can go lavish or simple, choose a simple massage or a full-on beauty and health regimen.

Spa Treatments

Here are some of the activities, treatments and blissful interludes you can enjoy at various Swiss spas.

o Beauty treatments Many spas have their own branded lines of products and treatments geared towards making you a more beautiful you.

o Facials A standard offering at almost every spa but with myriad variations.

o Hay baths How to get the Swiss cows jealous: you're covered in freshly cut hay, which releases oils through heat and makes you all supple.

o Massage If you're expecting some Asian experience with lots of little candles and bells, think again. Swiss masseuses are incredibly skilled and the focus is on getting that kink out, not creating a mood.

The Best...
Spa Therapies

1 Facials

2 Massage

3 Roman-Irish bath

4 Sauna

5 Whirlpool

○ **Physiotherapy** Popular with visitors from dark northern climes. Light, massage and physical activity are combined.

○ **Roman-Irish bath** A staple of the traditional thermal baths that draw heated water from deep inside the earth. Get naked and enjoy a series of steamy baths from 40°C to 70°C and then nap it all off.

○ **Sauna** Even small hotels often have saunas. Let that 60°C or more heat open your pores and the poisons run right out. Whack yourself with a birch branch if they have one.

○ **Thalasso therapy** Saltwater baths and algae packs combine to nourish the body.

○ **Whirlpool** A fixture at virtually every spa and plenty of resort hotels. After a long day on the slopes, what's better than a bubble in hot water with friends.

○ **Yoga** As popular in Switzerland as elsewhere, common at resorts, large hotels and spas.

Top Spas

The following list includes some of the top spas you'll find in this book. For more spas, **Switzerland Tourism** (www.myswitzerland.com) has comprehensive listings.

○ **Romantik Hotel Schweizerhof** In Alps-happy Grindelwald, the spa has massage jets, treatment rooms, a teeth-chattering ice grotto and a pool with wide-screen mountain vistas.

○ **Leukerbad** Europe's largest thermal spa resort is in the heart of Valais. Lindner Alpentherme offers a twinset of pools – one in, one out, both 36°C – with whirlpools, jets, Jacuzzi and mountain views.

○ **Medizinisches Therapiezentrum Heilbad** After a hard session on the slopes of St Moritz, rest in a mineral bath or with an Alpine herb pack.

○ **Bad Ragaz** An entire little spa town near Chur, the main event is the chic Tamina Therme, which is renowned for its 34°C thermal waters.

Survival Guide

CAPTURED WITH LOVE / GETTY IMAGES ©

A-Z

Directory

●●●●

Accommodation

Switzerland sports accommodation in every price range, from budget to midrange and top end. Listed prices are for high season, include breakfast (unless otherwise noted), and are categorised as follows:

○ **Budget** (€) Includes campsites, farmstays, hostels and simple hotels, a handful of which offer rooms with shared bathroom facilities. Budget hotels cost up to Sfr170 for a double.

○ **Midrange** (€€) With all the comforts of a private bathroom, TV, telephone and more; double-room rates peak at Sfr350.

○ **Top end** (€€€) Pure unadulterated, time-honoured Swiss luxury costs you anything from Sfr350 for a double to the sky's the limit.

Rates in cities and towns remain constant year-round, bar Christmas and New Year when rates rise; in 'business' cities like Geneva and Zürich, pricier weekday rates drop slightly at weekends. In mountain resorts prices are seasonal: low season (mid-September to mid-December and mid-April to mid-June) is the cheapest time to visit, mid-season (January to mid-February and mid-June to early July and September) begins to get pricey, and high season (July, August, Christmas, and mid-February to Easter) is the busy period.

Tourist offices have accommodation listings and often make reservations.

B&Bs

Some of Switzerland's most charming accommodation comes in the form of bed and breakfast – a room in a private home (anything from castle to farm), which includes breakfast, often made from home-made produce. Some hosts will also, if you order in advance, cook up an evening meal served for an additional Sfr30 to Sfr40 per person including wine.

Tourist offices have lists of B&Bs in their area – urban rarities but plentiful in the countryside areas – and hundreds can be tracked through **BnB** (www.bnb.ch).

In rural areas, private houses frequently offer inexpensive 'room(s) vacant' (*Zimmer frei* in German, *chambres libres* in French, *camere libere* in Italian), with or without breakfast.

Hotels & Pensions

○ The cheapest hotel rooms have a sink, but share a toilet and shower in the corridor, costing around Sfr70 for a single and Sfr100 for a double in a small town, and around Sfr90 for a single and Sfr140 for a double in cities or mountain resorts. Pop in a private shower and the nightly rate rises by at least Sfr20. Rates usually include breakfast.

○ A *Frühstückspension* or *Hotel-Garni* serves only breakfast. Small pensions with a restaurant often have a 'rest day' when check-in may not be possible except by prior arrangement (telephone ahead).

○ Hotels carrying an Ibex Fairplay label (formerly the Steinbock Label) are eco-hotels, labelled with one to five *Steinböcke* (ibexes) to reflect their sustainability.

Rental Accommodation

Self-caterers can opt for a chalet or apartment, both of which need booking in advance; for peak periods, reserve six to 12 months ahead. A minimum stay of one week (usually Saturday to Saturday) in season is common.

Useful online resources include **REKA** (www.reka.ch), **Interhome** (www.interhome.

Book Your Stay Online

For more accommodation reviews by Lonely Planet authors, check out http://hotels. lonelyplanet.com. You'll find independent reviews, as well as recommendations on the best places to stay. Best of all, you can book online.

ch) and **Switzerland Tourism** (www.myswitzerland.com). For self-catering chalets and apartments in ski resorts – summer and winter – surf **Ski Suisse** (http://en.ski-suisse.com).

●●●
Customs Regulations

Visitors may import 200 cigarettes, 50 cigars or 250g of pipe tobacco. The allowance for alcoholic beverages is 1L for beverages containing more than 15% alcohol by volume, and 2L for beverages containing less than 15%. Alcohol and tobacco may only be brought in by people aged 17 or over.

Gifts up to the value of Sfr100 may also be imported, as well as food provisions for one day.

●●●
Discount Cards

Senior Cards

Senior citizens are not entitled to discounts on Swiss railways, but discounts are available on museum admission, ski passes and some cable cars. Discounts often start for those as young as 62 (proof of age necessary), although sometimes a higher limit is observed. The abbreviation for senior citizens is AHV in German and AVS in French.

Student & Youth Cards

An International Student Identity Card (ISIC) yields discounts on admission prices, air and international train tickets, and even some ski passes. If you're under 26 but not a student, apply for the IYTC (International Youth Travel Card). Cards are issued by student unions and youth-oriented travel agencies in your home country.

Swiss Museum Pass

Regular or long-term visitors to Switzerland may want to buy the **Swiss Museum Pass** (www.museumspass.ch; adult/family Sfr155/277), which covers entry to 480 museums countrywide.

Visitors' Cards

In many resorts and cities there's a visitors' card (*Gästekarte*), which provides various benefits such as reduced prices for museums, swimming pools or cable cars, as well as free use of public transport within the resort. Cards are issued by your accommodation.

●●●
Electricity

The electricity current is 230V, 50Hz, Swiss sockets are recessed, three-holed, hexagonally shaped and incompatible with many plugs

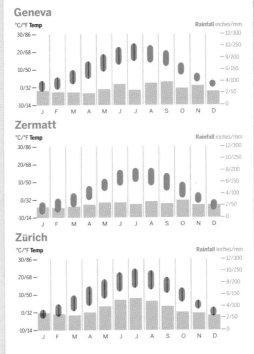

Climate

Geneva

Zermatt

Zürich

from abroad. They usually, however, take the standard European two-pronged plug.

230V/50Hz

230V/50Hz

admin.ch. Embassies are in Bern, but Zürich and Geneva have several consulates.

●●● Food

Price indicators in this guide refer to the average cost of a main meal, on top of which you need to add any other courses you might fancy plus drinks; two- or three-course menus (pre-set meals at a fixed price) yield best-value, with lunch menus usually being the best deal out.

- € budget < Sfr25
- €€ midrange Sfr25–50
- €€€ top end > Sfr50

●●● Gay & Lesbian Travellers

Attitudes to homosexuality are progressive. Same-sex partnerships are recognised (although gay couples are not permitted to adopt children or have fertility treatment). The age of consent for gay sex is the same as for heterosexuals, 16 years.

Major cities have gay and lesbian bars, and pride marches are held in Geneva (early July) and Zürich (mid-July). Useful websites:

www.gay.ch (in German)

www.lesbian.ch (in German)

www.myswitzerland.com
Information on gay-friendly accommodation and events if you type 'Gay & Lesbian' into the search function.

●●● Embassies & Consulates

For a list of Swiss embassies abroad and embassies in Switzerland, see www.eda.

www.pinkcross.ch (in German and French)

●●● Health

An embassy, consulate or hotel can usually recommend a local doctor or clinic. The quality of health care in Switzerland is generally very high.

Altitude Sickness

This disorder can occur above 3000m, but very few treks or ski runs in the Swiss Alps reach such heights. Headaches, vomiting, dizziness, extreme faintness, and difficulty in breathing and sleeping are signs to heed. Treat mild symptoms with rest and simple painkillers. If mild symptoms persist or get worse, descend to a lower altitude and seek medical advice.

Hypothermia

Hypothermia occurs when the body loses heat faster than it can produce it and the core temperature of the body falls. It is surprisingly easy to progress from very cold to dangerously cold due to a combination of wind, wet clothing, fatigue and hunger, even if the air temperature is above freezing. It is best to dress in layers of good insulating material and to wear a hat and a strong, waterproof outer layer when hiking or skiing. A 'space' blanket for emergencies is essential. Carry basic supplies, including food containing simple sugars and fluid to drink.

Symptoms of hypothermia are exhaustion, numb skin (particularly toes and fingers), shivering, slurred speech, irrational or violent behaviour, lethargy, stumbling, dizzy spells, muscle cramps and violent bursts of energy.

To treat mild hypothermia, get the person out of the wind and/or rain, remove their clothing if wet and replace it with dry, warm clothing. Give them hot liquids – not alcohol – and high-kilojoule, easily digestible food. Do not rub victims; allow them to slowly warm themselves. The early recognition and treatment of mild hypothermia is the only way to prevent severe hypothermia (a critical condition).

Ticks

These small creatures can be found throughout Switzerland up to an altitude of 1200m, and typically live in underbrush at the forest edge or beside walking tracks.

Always check your whole body if you've been walking through a potentially tick-infested area. If a tick is found attached, press down around the tick's head with tweezers, grab the head and gently pull upwards. Avoid pulling the rear of the body as this may squeeze the tick's gut contents through the attached mouth-parts into the skin, increasing the risk of infection and disease. Smearing chemicals on the tick is not recommended.

Lyme Disease

This is an infection transmitted by ticks that may be acquired in Europe. The illness usually begins with a spreading rash at the site of the tick bite and is accompanied by fever, headache, extreme fatigue, aching

Practicalities

o **Newspapers** German readers can gen up with Zürich's *Neue Zürcher Zeitung* (www.nzz.ch) and *Tages Anzeiger* (www.tagesanzeiger.ch); Geneva's *Le Temps* (www.letemps.ch) and *La Tribune de Genève* (www.tdg.ch) are sold in Suisse Romande; Lugano-based *Corriere del Ticino* (www.cdt.ch, in Italian) is in Italian.

o **Radio** WRS (World Radio Switzerland; FM 101.7; www.worldradio.ch) is a Geneva-based English-language station broadcasting music and news countrywide.

o **Smoking** Smoking is illegal in all enclosed indoor public spaces, including restaurants, pubs, offices and public transport. It is allowed in separate smoking rooms and outside on pavement terraces.

o **Twitter** Follow a dose of daily news and insights into Swiss cultural affairs 'n' happenings, follow @Switzerland, @TheLocalSwitzer, @swissinfo_en, @MySwitzerland_e.

o **Websites** Swissinfo (www.swissinfo.org) is the national news website.

o **Weights & Measures** The metric system is used. Like other continental Europeans, the Swiss indicate decimals with commas and thousands with full points.

joints and muscles, and mild neck stiffness. If untreated, these symptoms usually resolve over several weeks, but over subsequent weeks or months, disorders of the nervous system, heart and joints may develop. Seek medical help.

Tick-borne Encephalitis

This disease is a cerebral inflammation carried by a virus. Tick-borne encephalitis can occur in most forest and rural areas of Switzerland. If you have been bitten, even having removed the tick, you should keep an eye out for symptoms, including blotches around the bite, which are sometimes pale in the middle. Headache, stiffness and other flu-like symptoms, as well as extreme tiredness, appearing a week or two after the bite, can progress to more serious problems. Medical help must be sought. A vaccination is available.

Insurance

Free health treatment in Switzerland is very limited; health care generally is very expensive.

If you're skiing, snowboarding or trekking, check whether your policy covers helicopter rescue and emergency repatriation. Mountain rescue is shockingly expensive and most normal policies don't cover many outdoor activities; you'll need to pay a premium for winter-sports cover and further premiums for adventure sports like bungee jumping and skydiving.

Worldwide travel insurance is available at www.lonelyplanet.com/bookings. You can buy, extend and claim online any time – even if you're already on the road.

Internet Access

○ Public wireless access points can be found at major airports, at dozens of Swiss train stations and airports, and in business seats of 1st-class train carriages on many routes.

○ Most hotels have wi-fi (free), as do an increasing number of cafes and public spaces.

○ Public hotspots, like those provided by **Swisscom** (www.swisscom-mobile.ch), levy a charge – usually around Sfr5 for 30 minutes' access over seven days to Sfr125 for 150 hours' access over 31 days, payable by credit card or prepaid card sold at Swisscom's 2200 hotspots; locate them at http://hotspotlocator.swisscom.ch.

○ The odd Internet cafe can be found in larger towns and cities. Prices range from Sfr5 to Sfr15 per hour.

Legal Matters

Swiss police have wide-ranging powers of detention, allowing them to hold a per-son without charges or a trial. If approached by them, you will be required to show your passport, so always carry it.

There are some minor legal variations between the 26 cantons: busking (playing music in the streets) is allowed in some places but not in others. If in doubt, ask.

Money

ATMs

Automated teller machines (ATMs) – called *Bancomats* in banks and *Postomats* in post offices – are widespread and accessible 24 hours. They accept most international bank or credit cards and have multi-lingual instructions. Your bank or credit-card company will usually charge a 1% to 2.5% fee, and there may also be a small charge at the ATM end.

Cash

Swiss francs are divided into 100 centimes (*Rappen* in German-speaking Switzer-land). There are notes for 10, 20, 50, 100, 200 and 1000 francs, and coins for 5, 10, 20 and 50 centimes, as well as for one, two and five francs.

Businesses throughout Switzerland, including most hotels and some restaurants and souvenir shops, will accept payment in euros. Change will be given in Swiss francs at the rate of exchange calculated on the day.

Credit Cards

The use of credit cards is less widespread than in the UK or USA and not all shops, hotels or restaurants accept them. EuroCard/MasterCard and Visa are the most popular.

Moneychangers

You can change money at banks, airports and nearly every train station until late into the evening. Banks tend to charge about 5% commis-sion; some money-exchange bureaus don't charge com-mission at all. Exchange rates are *slightly* better for travel-lers cheques than for cash.

Tipping

○ Tipping is not necessary, given that hotels, restaurants, bars and even some taxis are legally required to include a 15% service charge in bills.

○ You can round up the bill after a meal for good service, as locals do.

○ Hotel and railway porters expect a franc or two per bag.

○ Bargaining is non-existent.

Opening Hours

Each Swiss canton currently decides how long shops and businesses can stay open for, although there is talk of a federal law being passed to set uniform opening hours for shops countrywide. Shops in Lucerne, for example, must close by 4pm on Saturdays while those in Zürich are al-lowed to stay open until 8pm.

○ With the exception of souvenir shops and supermarkets at some train stations, shops are shut on Sunday. Many close Monday too.

○ Many service stations open 24 hours a day and stock basic groceries.

- Restaurants generally close one or two days of the week, chosen according to the owner's whim.

- Many museums are closed on Monday or Tuesday, though in summer some open daily. Many have a late-night opening one day a week (often Thursday).

- Listed hours are high-season opening hours for sights and attractions; hours are almost always shorter during low season.

Standard opening hours are as follows:

Banks 8.30am-4.30pm Mon-Fri

Offices 8am-noon & 2-5pm Mon-Fri

Restaurants Lunch noon-2pm, dinner 6-10pm five or six days a week

Shops 9am-7pm Mon-Fri (with a one- to two-hour break for lunch at noon in small towns), 9am-6pm Sat

Public Holidays

New Year's Day 1 January

Good Friday March/April

Easter Sunday & Monday March/April

Ascension Day 40th day after Easter

Whit Sunday & Monday 7th week after Easter

National Day 1 August

Christmas Day 25 December

St Stephen's Day 26 December

Some cantons observe their own special holidays and religious days, such as 2 January, Labour Day (1 May), Corpus Christi, Assumption (15 August) and All Saints' Day (1 November).

Safe Travel

- Street crime is relatively uncommon in Switzerland. As in any urban situation, though, watch your belongings; pickpockets thrive in city crowds.

- Swiss police aren't very visible but have a reputation for performing random street searches of questionable necessity on people of non-European background or appearance.

Telephone

National telecom provider **Swisscom** (www.swisscom. ch) operates one of the world's densest networks of public phone booths. Phones take coins (Swiss francs or euros) or 'taxcards' (phone-cards) sold in values of Sfr5, Sfr10 and Sfr20 at post of-fices, newsagents and so on. Some booths accept major credit cards and can be used to send SMS worldwide.

Search for phone numbers online at http://tel.local. ch/en.

Warning: Dial All Numbers

Area codes do not exist in Switzerland. Although the numbers for a particular city or town share the same three-digit prefix (for example Bern 031, Geneva 022), numbers must always be dialled in full, even when calling from next door.

Mobile Phones

Most phones on European GSM networks function in Switzerland; check with your provider about costs.

Prepaid local SIM cards are available from network operators **Orange** (www.orange.ch), **Sunrise** (www.sunrise.ch) and **Swisscom Mobile** (www.swisscom.ch). Buy these via the nationwide **Mobile Zone** (www.mobilezone.ch) chain of shops. Prepaid cards must be officially registered, so bring your passport.

Phone Codes

- The country code for Switzerland is ☎41. When calling Switzerland from abroad drop the initial zero from the number; hence to call Bern, dial ☎41 31 (preceded by the overseas access code of the country you're dialling from).

- The international access code from Switzerland is ☎00.

- Telephone numbers with the code ☎0800 are toll-free; those with ⌨0848 are charged at the local rate. Numbers beginning with 156 or 157 are premium rate.

● Mobile phone numbers start with ⌨076, ⌨078 or ⌨079.

Phonecards

Save money on the normal international tariff by buying a prepaid Swisscom card worth Sfr10, Sfr20, Sfr50 or Sfr100.

Time

Swiss time is GMT/UTC plus one hour. Daylight-saving time comes into effect at midnight on the last Saturday in March, when the clocks are moved forward one hour, making Switzerland two hours ahead of GMT/UTC; clocks go back again on the last Saturday in October.

Note that in German *halb* is used to indicate the half-hour before the hour, hence *halb acht* (half eight) means 7.30, not 8.30.

The following table shows the time difference between Switzerland and major cities around the world; times do not take daylight saving into account.

CITY	LOCAL TIME
Auckland	11pm
Bern	Noon
London	11am
New York	6am
San Francisco	3am
Sydney	9pm
Tokyo	8pm
Toronto	6am

Tourist Information

Make the Swiss tourist board, **Switzerland Tourism** (www.myswitzerland.com) your first port of call. For detailed information, contact local tourist offices. Information and maps are available for free and somebody invariably speaks English; many offices book hotel rooms, tours and excursions for you. In German-speaking Switzerland, tourist offices are known as *Verkehrsbüro,* or *Kurverein* in some resorts. In French these offices are called *office du tourisme* and in Italian *ufficio turistico.*

Travellers with Disabilities

Switzerland ranks among the world's most easily navigable countries for travellers with physical disabilities. Most train stations have a mobile lift for boarding trains, city buses are equipped with ramps, and many hotels have disabled access (although budget pensions tend not to have lifts).

....

Switzerland Tourism (www.myswitzerland.com) has excellent travel tips for people who have physical disabilities. Or get in touch with **Mobility International Switzerland** (⌨ 062 212 67 40; www.mis-ch.ch).

Visas

For up-to-date details on Switzerland's visa requirements, head to the **Swiss Federal Office for Migration** (www.bfm.admin.ch).

Visas are not required if you hold a passport from the United Kingdom, Republic of Ireland, the United States, Canada, Australia or New Zealand, whether you're visiting the country as a tourist or are on business. Citizens of the EU, Norwegians and Icelanders may also enter Switzerland without a visa. A maximum 90-day stay in a 180-day period applies, but passports are rarely stamped.

Other people wishing to come to Switzerland will need to apply for a Schengen Visa, which is named after the agreements that abolished passport controls between 15 European countries: Austria, Belgium, Denmark, Finland, France, Germany, Greece, Iceland, Italy, Luxembourg, the Netherlands, Norway, Portugal, Spain and Sweden. The visa allows for unlimited travel throughout the entire Schengen zone for a 90-day period. Apply to the consulate of the country you are entering first, or your main destination.

While you're visiting Switzerland, be sure to carry your passport at all times. Swiss citizens are required to always carry ID, so you will also need to be able to identify yourself at any time.

Transport

●●●

Getting There & Away

Flights, tours and rail tickets can be booked online at www.lonelyplanet.com/bookings.

Entering the Country

Formalities are minimal when entering Switzerland by air, rail or road thanks to the Schengen Agreement which means those arriving from the EU don't need to show a passport. When arriving from a non-EU country, you'll need your passport or EU identity card – and visa if you need one – to clear customs.

✈ Air

Airports

Bern Airport (Flughafen Bern; www.flughafenbern.ch) Base to Bernese carrier, SkyWork Airlines (www.flyskywork.com), with flights to many European destinations including London City and 'London' Southend.

EuroAirport (MLH or BSL; ☎ +33 3 89 90 31 11; www.euroairport.com) EuroAirport serves Basel (as well as Mulhouse in France and Freiburg in Germany). Located 5km north in France, it has flights to and from a host of European cities.

Geneva Airport (Aéroport International de Genève; www.gva.ch)

Lugano Airport (www.lugano-airport.ch) Direct fights to Geneva and Zürich, plus seasonal hops to a couple of Spanish cities and the Tuscan island of Elba in Italy.

Zürich Airport (Flughafen Zürich; www.zurich-airport.com)

Land

Bus

Eurolines (www.eurolines.com), a grouping of 32 long-haul coach operators, runs buses all over Europe from most large towns and cities in Switzerland, including Basel, Bern, Bellinzona, Fribourg, Geneva, Lausanne, Lucerne, Lugano, Martigny, Sion and Zürich. Discounts are available to people under 26 and over 60. Make advance reservations, especially in July and August.

Car & Motorcycle

Fast, well-maintained roads run from Switzerland through to all bordering countries; the Alps present a natural barrier meaning main roads generally head through tunnels to enter Switzerland. A foreign motor vehicle entering the country must display a sticker or licence plate identifying its country of registration.

Climate Change & Travel

Every form of transport that relies on carbon-based fuel generates CO_2, the main cause of human-induced climate change. Modern travel is dependent on aeroplanes, which might use less fuel per kilometre per person than most cars but travel much greater distances. The altitude at which aircraft emit gases (including CO_2) and particles also contributes to their climate change impact. Many websites offer 'carbon calculators' that allow people to estimate the carbon emissions generated by their journey and, for those who wish to do so, to offset the impact of the greenhouse gases emitted with contributions to portfolios of climate-friendly initiatives throughout the world. Lonely Planet offsets the carbon footprint of all staff and author travel.

○ An EU driving licence is acceptable throughout Europe.

○ Third-party motor insurance is a minimum requirement; get proof of this in the form of a Green Card issued by your insurers. Also ask for a 'European Accident Statement' form. Taking out a European breakdown assistance policy is a good investment.

○ A warning triangle, to be displayed in the event of a breakdown, is compulsory.

○ Recommended accessories include first-aid kit, spare bulb kit and fire extinguisher.

Fly-Rail Baggage Service

Travellers bound for Geneva, Zürich or Bern airports can send their luggage directly to any one of 50-odd Swiss train stations, without waiting for their bags at the airport. Upon departure, they can also check their luggage in at any of these train stations up to 24 hours before their flight and collect it upon arrival at their destination airport. The cost is Sfr22 per item of luggage; maximum weight per item is 32kg and bulky stuff like bicycles and surfboards are no go. Similar luggage forwarding is likewise possible within Switzerland; see www.sbb.ch.

Train

Ecofriendly Switzerland makes rail travel a joy.

○ Book tickets and get train information from **Rail Europe** (www.raileurope.com). In the UK contact **Railteam** (www.railteam.co.uk), an alliance of several high-speed train operators in Europe including Switzerland's very own train operator, **Swiss Federal Railways** (www.sbb.ch), commonly abbreviated to SBB in German, CFF in French and FFS in Italian. The latter accepts internet bookings but does not post tickets outside of Switzerland.

○ For details on Europe's 200,000km rail network, surf **RailPassenger Info** (www.railpassenger.info).

○ A very useful train-travel resource is the information-packed website **The Man in Seat 61** (www.seat61.com).

○ From the UK, hourly **Eurostar** (www.eurostar.com) trains scoot from London (St Pancras International) to Paris (Gare du Nord) in 2¼ hours, then onwards by French TGV from Paris (Gare de Lyon) to Geneva, Lausanne, Bern, Basel, Biel-Bienne and Zug, Zürich and more; passengers aged under 26 and over 60 get slight discounts.

○ Zürich is Switzerland's busiest international terminus, with trains to Munich and Vienna, from where there are extensive onward connections to cities in Eastern Europe.

○ Most connections from Germany pass through Zürich or Basel.

○ Nearly all connections from Italy pass through Milan before branching off to the Swiss cities of Zürich, Lucerne, Bern or Lausanne.

Sea & River

Switzerland can be reached by steamer from several lakes, but it's a slightly more unusual option. From Germany, arrive via Lake Constance and from France via Lake Geneva. You can also cruise down the Rhine to Basel.

●●● Getting Around

Switzerland's fully integrated public transport system is among the world's most efficient. However, travel within Switzerland is expensive and visitors planning to use public transport on inter-city routes should consider investing in a Swiss travel pass.

Timetables often refer to *Werktags* (work days), which means Monday to Saturday, unless there is the qualification '*ausser Samstag*' (except Saturday).

✈ Air

Switzerland's compact size and excellent rail transport render internal flights almost unnecessary.

Swiss (www.swiss.com) serves the major hubs of EuroAirport (Basel), Geneva and Zürich airports, with return fares fluctuating wildly. Swiss no-frills carrier **Etihad Regional** (www.etihadregional.com) flies between Geneva and Lugano.

ᖍᖋ Bicycle

Hire

SBB Rent-a-Bike (☎ 041 925 11 70; www.rentabike.ch; half/full day Sfr27/35) This super-efficient bike-rental service run by Swiss railways allows you to rent two wheels at 80 train stations in Switzerland. Bikes can be reserved in advance online or by telephone, and – for an Sfr8 surcharge – can be collected from one station and returned to another.

Suisseroule (Schweizrollt; www.schweizrollt.ch) Under this fabulous initiative, you can borrow a bike for free or dirt-cheap rates in large towns and cities, including Geneva, Sion, Bern, Zürich and Neuchâtel. Bike stations are usually strategically placed next to the train station or central square.

Transport

Bikes can be taken on slower trains (buy a 'bike ticket' for the price of a standard half-fare, 2nd-class ticket), and sometimes even on InterCity (IC) or EuroCity (EC) trains, when there's room in the luggage carriage (one-day bike ticket with/without Swiss Travel Pass Sfr12/18). Between 21 March and 31 October, you must book (Sfr5) to take your bike on ICN (inter-city tilting) trains.

Trains that don't permit accompanied bikes are marked with a crossed-out pictogram in the timetable. Sending a standard bike unaccompanied costs Sfr18. Taking your bike as hand luggage in a transport bag is free.

🚢 Boat

All the larger lakes are serviced by steamers operated by **Swiss Federal Railways** (www.sbb.ch), or allied private companies for which national travel passes are valid. These include Geneva, Constance, Lucerne, Lugano, Neuchâtel, Biel, Murten, Thun, Brienz and Zug, but not Lago Maggiore.

Rail passes are not valid for cruises offered by smaller boat companies.

🚌 Bus

Canary-yellow postal buses supplement the rail network, following postal routes and linking towns to the less accessible mountain regions. They are regular, and departures tie in with train arrivals, invariably from next to train stations. Travel is one class only and fares are comparable to train fares.

◦ Swiss national travel passes are valid on postal buses, but a few tourist-oriented Alpine routes levy a surcharge.

◦ Tickets are purchased from the bus driver, though on some scenic routes over the Alps (eg the Lugano–St Moritz run) advance reservations are necessary. See www.postbus.ch for details.

🚗 Car & Motorcycle

Public transport is excellent in city centres – unlike parking cars which is usually hard work. The **Swiss Touring Club** (Touring Club der Schweiz; www.tcs.ch) and **Swiss Automobile Club** (Automobil-Club der Schweiz, ACS; www.acs.ch; Wasserwerkgasse 39, CH-3000, Bern 13) provide details on driving in Switzerland.

Car Sharing

Mobility (☎ 0848 824 821; www.mobility.ch) has some 2650 cars at 1380 points throughout Switzerland and you can use the cars from one hour to up to 16 days, although one-way travel is not permitted. Reserve a car online or by phone, collect it at the reserved time, and drive off. If you don't want to take out an annual subscrip-

tion (Sfr290), you can pay a single-use subscription (Sfr25) plus Sfr1 per hour on top of the standard hourly rates (from Sfr2.80 per hour, plus Sfr0.52 per kilometre).

Fuel

Unleaded (*bleifrei, sans plomb, senza piombo*) petrol is standard, found at green pumps, and diesel is also widely available. Expect to pay around Sfr1.71 per litre for unleaded and Sfr1.75 for diesel.

Hire

◦ Major car-rental companies have offices at airports and in major cities and towns.

◦ Reserve cars in advance online. If you're flying into Geneva Airport, note it's cheaper to rent a car on the French side.

◦ The minimum rental age is usually 25, but falls to 20 at some local firms; you always need a credit card.

◦ Rental cars are usually equipped with winter tyres in winter.

Road Conditions

◦ Swiss roads are well built, well signposted and well maintained.

◦ Phone ☎163 for up-to-the-hour traffic conditions (information in French, German, Italian and English).

◦ Most major Alpine passes are negotiable year-round, depending on the weather. However, you will often have to use a tunnel instead at the Great St Bernard, St Gotthard and San Bernardino passes.

◦ Passes that are open only from June to October: Albula,

Child Seat Rules

Car-seat rules for children in Switzerland are among the most stringent in Europe:

○ Children under 12 years and measuring less than 150cm tall must use a size-appropriate type of front-facing child seat or booster car seat.

○ Providing they are strapped in the appropriate seat or booster for their weight, children of any age are permitted to ride in the front seat.

○ Many taxis carry booster seats appropriate for children weighing 15kg or more; taxis that don't have a booster and/or the appropriate car seat for your child are highly likely to refuse to take you.

Furka, Grimsel, Klausen, Oberalp, Susten and Umbrail. Other passes are Lukmanier (open May to November), Nufenen (June to September), and Splügen (May to October).

Take your car on trains through these tunnels and passes, open year-round:

Furka Pass (☎ 027 927 70 00; www.mgbahn.ch; car & passengers high/low season Sfr33/27) From Oberwald to Realp in just 15 minutes through this 15.4km-long tunnel.

Lötschberg Tunnel (☎ 0900 553 333; www.bls.ch) From Kandersteg to Goppenstein (car and passengers Monday to Thursday/Friday to Sunday Sfr22/27, 15 minutes) or Iselle in Italy (car and passengers Sfr91, one hour, April to October) which must be booked in advance.

Vereina Tunnel (☎ 081 288 65 65; www.rhb.ch; car & passengers low/mid/high season Sfr33/38/43) Alternative to the Flüela Pass, which is closed in winter; from Selfranga outside Klosters to Sagliains in the Engadine. Frequency and journey time are both 30 minutes.

Road Rules

○ Headlights must be on at all times, day and night; the fine for not doing so is Sfr40.

○ The minimum driving age for cars and motorcycles is 18 and for mopeds it's 14.

○ The Swiss drive on the right-hand side of the road.

○ Give priority to traffic approaching from the right. On mountain roads, the ascending vehicle has priority, unless a postal bus is involved, as it always has right of way.

○ The speed limit is 50km/h in towns, 80km/h on main roads outside towns, 100km/h on single-lane freeways and 120km/h on dual-lane freeways.

○ Car occupants must wear a seatbelt at all times and vehicles must carry a breakdown-warning triangle.

○ Headlights must be dipped in all tunnels.

○ Motorcyclists and their passengers must wear crash helmets.

○ The blood alcohol content (BAC) limit is 0.05%.

○ If you're involved in a car accident, the police must be called if anyone receives more than superficial injuries.

○ Proof of ownership of a private vehicle should always be carried.

Road Signs

Signs you may not have seen before include these:
○ Criss-crossed white tyre on a blue circular background, which means that snow chains are compulsory.

○ Yellow bugle on a square blue background, which means that you should obey instructions given by postal bus drivers.

Road Tolls

There's an annual one-off charge of Sfr40 to use Swiss freeways and semi-freeways, identified by green signs. The charge is payable at the border (in cash, including euros), at petrol stations and at Swiss tourist offices abroad. The sticker (*vignette* in French and German, *contrassegno* in Italian) you receive upon paying the tax can also be bought at post offices and petrol stations. It must be displayed on the windscreen and is valid for one year, from 1 December to 31 January of the following year. If you're caught without it, you'll be fined Sfr100. A separate *vignette* is required for trailers and caravans. Motorcyclists are also charged the Sfr40. For more details, see www.vignette.ch.

On the Swiss–Italian border you'll need to pay an additional toll if using the Great St Bernard Tunnel between Aosta, Italy and Valais (car and passengers single/return Sfr30.90/49.40).

Public Transport

All local city transport is linked via the same ticketing system, so you can change lines on one ticket. Buy tickets from dispensers (coins only), at stops or on board. Single tickets may give a time limit (eg one hour) for travel within a particular zone, and you can only break the journey within that time.

Mountain Transport

The Swiss have many words to describe mountain transport: funicular (*Standseilbahn* in German, *funiculaire* in French, *funicolare* in Italian), cable car (*Luftseilbahn*, *téléphérique*, *funivia*), gondola (*Gondelbahn*, *télécabine*, *telecabinoia*) and chair lift (*Sesselbahn*, *télésiège*, *seggiovia*). All are subject to regular safety inspections.

Always check what time the last cable car goes down the mountain – in winter it is as early as 4pm in mountain resorts.

🚌 Train

The Swiss rail network combines state-run and private operations. The **Swiss Federal Railway** (www.sbb. ch) is abbreviated to SBB in German, CFF in French and FFS in Italian.

◦ Second-class compartments are perfectly acceptable, but are often close to full; 1st-class carriages are more spacious and have fewer passengers.

Power points for laptops let you work aboard and some seats are in wi-fi hotspots.

◦ Standard 2nd-class fares cost about Sfr40 per 100km; 1st-class fares average 50% to 65% more. Return fares are only cheaper than two singles for longer trips.

◦ Train schedules, revised every December, are available online and at train stations. For information see www.sbb.ch or call **train information & reservations** (📞0900 300 300; calls per min Sfr1.19).

◦ Larger train stations have 24-hour left-luggage lockers, usually accessible 6am to midnight.

◦ Seat reservations (Sfr5) are advisable for longer journeys, particularly in high season.

◦ European rail passes such as Eurail and Interrail passes are valid on Swiss national railways. However, you cannot use them on postal buses, city transport, cable cars or private train lines (eg the Zermatt route and the Jungfraubahn routes at the heart of the Bernese Oberland) – making Swiss travel passes more interesting for those exploring scenic Switzerland.

Swiss Travel Passes

The following national travel passes offer fabulous savings on extensive travel within Switzerland. Passes can be purchased in the UK from the **Switzerland Travel Centre** (📞0207 420 49 34; www.stc. co.uk), online from its hugely informative website and at train stations in Switzerland. For comprehensive information see www.swisstravel system.ch and http://train-tickets.myswitzerland.com.

Swiss Pass This entitles the holder to unlimited travel on almost every train, boat and bus service in the country, and on trams and buses in 41 towns, plus free entry to 400-odd museums. Reductions of 50% apply on funiculars, cable cars and private railways. Different passes are available, valid between four days (Sfr272) and one month (Sfr607).

Swiss Flexi Pass This pass allows you to nominate a certain number of days – from three (Sfr260) to six (Sfr414) days – during one month when you can enjoy unlimited travel.

Swiss Half-Fare Card As the name suggests, you pay only half the fare on trains with this card (Sfr120 for one month), plus you get some discounts on local-network buses, trams and cable cars.

Junior Travelcard This card (Sfr30), valid for one year, gets a child aged 6 to 16 years free travel on trains, boats and some cable cars when travelling with at least one of their parents. Children travelling with a grandparent can buy an equivalent Grandchild travelcard. Childen not travelling with a relative can get unlimited travel for one day with a one-day children's travel pass (Sfr16).

Regional Passes Network passes valid only within a particular region are available in several parts of the country. Such passes are available from train stations in the region.

a b c

Language

Switzerland has three official federal languages: French, German and Italian. A fourth language, Romansch (semi-official since 1996), is spoken by less than 1% of the population, mainly in the canton of Graubünden.

Read our pronunciation guides as if they were English, and you'll be understood just fine. The stressed syllables are in italics.

To enhance your trip with a phrasebook, visit **lonelyplanet.com**. Lonely Planet iPhone phrasebooks are available through the Apple App store.

FRENCH

Hello.	Bonjour.	bon·zhoor
Goodbye.	Au revoir.	o·rer·vwa
Yes.	Oui.	wee
No.	Non.	non
Please.	S'il vous plaît.	seel voo play
Thank you.	Merci.	mair·see
Excuse me.	Excusez-moi.	ek·skew·zay·mwa
Sorry.	Pardon.	par·don
Help!	Au secours!	o skoor
Cheers!	Santé!	son·tay

Do you speak English?
Parlez-vous anglais?   par·lay·voo ong·glay
I don't understand.
Je ne comprends pas.   zher ner kom·pron pa
How much is this?
C'est combien?   say kom·byun
I'd like ..., please.
Je voudrais ...,   zher voo·dray ...
s'il vous plaît.   seel voo play
Where are (the toilets)?
Où sont (les toilettes)?   oo son (lay twa·let)
I'm lost.
Je suis perdu(e). (m/f)   zhe swee·pair·dew

GERMAN

Hello.	Guten Tag.	goo·ten taak
Goodbye.	Auf Wiedersehen.	owf vee·der·zey·en
Yes.	Ja.	yaa
No.	Nein.	nain
Please.	Bitte.	bi·te
Thank you.	Danke.	dang·ke
Excuse me.	Entschuldigung.	ent·shul·di·gung
Sorry.	Entschuldigung.	ent·shul·di·gung
Help!	Hilfe!	hil·fe
Cheers!	Prost!	prawst

Do you speak English?
Sprechen Sie Englisch?   shpre·khen zee eng·lish
I don't understand.
Ich verstehe nicht.   ikh fer·shtey·e nikht
How much is this?
Was kostet das?   vas kos·tet das
I'd like ..., please.
Ich hätte gern ..., bitte.   ikh he·te gern ... bi·te
Where are (the toilets)?
Wo sind   vaw zind
(die Toilette)?   (dee to·a·le·te)
I'm lost.
Ich habe mich verirrt.   ikh haa·be mikh fer·irt

ITALIAN

Hello.	Buongiorno.	bwon·jor·no
Goodbye.	Arrivederci.	a·ree·ve·der·chee
Yes.	Sì.	see
No.	No.	no
Please.	Per favore.	per fa·vo·re
Thank you.	Grazie.	gra·tsye
Excuse me.	Mi scusi.	mee skoo·zee
Sorry.	Mi dispiace.	mee dees·pya·che
Help!	Aiuto!	a·yoo·to
Cheers!	Salute!	sa·loo·te

Do you speak English?
Parla inglese?   par·la een·gle·ze
I don't understand.
Non capisco.   non ka·pee·sko
How much is this?
Quanto costa?   kwan·to ko·sta
I'd like ..., please.
Vorrei ..., per favore.   vo·ray ... per fa·vo·re
Where are (the toilets)?
Dove sono   do·ve so·no
(i gabinetti)?   (ee ga·bee·ne·ti)
I'm lost.
Mi sono perso/a. (m/f)   mee so·no per·so/a

Behind the Scenes

Author Thanks

Nicola Williams

Huge thanks as always to the many friends/strangers/acquaintances/colleagues who aided and abetted in tracking down the very best, including Christian Keel, Christine Schröder and Pascal Gebert in Zermatt; born-and-bred Sion girl Sabin Van Vliet; Sami Lamaa from fave piste-side pad Chetzeron; and, for top Glacier Express tips, Lonely Planet destination editor Kate Morgan. Extra-special kudos to my very own, super-powered, trilingual 'Switzerland-with-kids' research team: Niko, Mischa and Kaya Luefkens (kept in check on the road by super-husband Matthias).

Kerry Christiani

I would like to thank all the super-efficient tourism professionals up and down the country who made research run like (Swiss) clockwork, especially those in the Jungfrau Region and the SBB team. A big *grazia* to Hans Lozza and Roman Gross for their insight into the Swiss National Park. As always, thanks to my husband, Andy Christiani, for his ongoing support.

Acknowledgments

Climate map data adapted from Peel MC, Finlayson BL & McMahon TA (2007) 'Updated World Map of the Köppen-Geiger Climate Classification', *Hydrology and Earth System Sciences*, 11, 1633-44.

Cover photographs: Front: The Matterhorn, Gareth McCormack/Alamy ©; Back: Tarasp, Graubünden, nagelstock.com/Alamy ©

This Book

This 2nd edition of Lo...
Switzerland guidebook...
Williams and Kerry Ch...
searched by Nicola an...
Sally O'Brien. This gui...
following:

Destination Editor Ka...
Product Editors Samantha Forge, Katie O...
Senior Cartographer Corey Hutchinson
Book Designer Katherine Marsh
Assisting Editors Melanie Dankel, Kate Mathews, Martine Power, Amanda Williamson
Assisting Book Designer Mazzy Prinsep
Cover Researcher Naomi Parker
Thanks to Ellie Simpson, Tony Wheeler

Our Readers

Many thanks to the travellers who used the previous edition of *Discover Switzerland* and wrote to us with helpful hints, useful advice and interesting anecdotes: Juerg Balsiger, Michael Duxfield and Mariana Villas-Boas.

Index

Y

Z

NOTES